W0205050

Dein Englischbuch enthält folgende Teile:

Introduction	Hier lernst du die jungen Leute von Band 3 kennen.
Units	die fünf Kapitel des Buches
Getting ready for a test	Hier kannst du dich gezielt auf einen Test vorbereiten.
EXTRA: Text File	viele interessante Texte zum Lesen (passend zu den Units)
Skills File (SF)	Beschreibung wichtiger Lern- und Arbeitstechniken
Grammar File (GF)	Zusammenfassung der Grammatik jeder Unit
Vocabulary	Wörterverzeichnis zum Lernen der neuen Wörter jeder Unit
Dictionary	alphabetische Wörterverzeichnisse zum Nachschlagen

Die Units bestehen aus diesen Teilen:

Lead-in	Einstieg in das neue Thema
A-Section	neuer Lernstoff mit vielen Aktivitäten und **Background File**
Practice	Übungen
Text	eine spannende oder lustige Geschichte
How am I doing?	Hier kannst du dein Wissen und Können überprüfen.

In den Units findest du diese Überschriften und Symbole:

Looking at language	Hier sammelst du Beispiele und entdeckst Regeln.
STUDY SKILLS	Einführung in Lern- und Arbeitstechniken
Dossier	Schöne und wichtige Arbeiten kannst du in einer Mappe sammeln.
All about ...	Hier übst du Wortschatz zum Thema der Unit.
WRITING COURSE	Schreibkurs in fünf Kapiteln mit Hilfen zum Schreiben von Texten
EVERYDAY ENGLISH	Übungen zum Bewältigen wichtiger Alltagssituationen
MEDIATION	Hier vermittelst du zwischen zwei Sprachen.
LISTENING	Aufgaben zu Hörtexten auf der CD
Now you	Hier sprichst und schreibst du über dich selbst.
PRONUNCIATION	Ausspracheübungen
REVISION	Übungen zur Wiederholung
WORDS	Übungen zu Wortfamilien, Wortfeldern und Wortverbindungen
Extra	zusätzliche Aktivitäten und Übungen
	Partnerarbeit/Gruppenarbeit
	nur auf CD / auf CD und im Schülerbuch
>	Textaufgaben

Contents

Die folgenden Angebote sind nicht obligatorisch abzuarbeiten. Die Auswahl der Übungen und Übungsteile richtet sich nach den Schwerpunkten des schulinternen Curriculums.

Contents

For six days every year, over 10,000 young musicians, singers and dancers take part in the 'Music for Youth' festival. They come from all over the United Kingdom to play, sing, listen to and learn about all kinds of music.

1 The UK

a) *'Music for Youth' is a festival for young people from all over the United Kingdom. Look at the map at the front of the book. What countries are there in the United Kingdom? Find the city of Birmingham on the map too.*

b) *What do you know about each of the countries in the UK? Tell your partner.*

2 The festival

Look at the poster. Match as many music words as you can to each photo. There's some help in the box.

choir • classical music • drum • jazz • musical • pop • rock • sing • soul • violin • world music ...

A day at the festival

6
Hi. Are you in the girls' hostel too?
Aye, I am.
Do you know where it is?
No, I don't.
7
Well, maybe we can find it together. I'm Latisha.
I'm Katrina. Er, Latisha, what's that?
8
'That' is my instrument – it's a steel drum.
A steel drum. I've never heard one of those.
Well, let's find our rooms and I can play you a tune.
And I'll play you one too.
9
Asian Fusion concert tonight!
Hey, Katrina!
Oh, hi, Asif. Latisha, this is Asif. He's a roadie.
Hi, Latisha. What have you got in there?
Hi, Asif!
Asif!
Sorry, the boss is calling. Come to the gig tonight – 8 o'clock, OK?

10
Asian Fusion concert tonight!
National Festival of Music for Youth
11
Want to be a DJ?
Come to the DJ
Workshop!
Saturday 10-12 - (Hall 3A)
Asian Fusion concert tonight!
12
Er, excuse me, do you know where I can get tickets?
13
At the box office, I suppose. There's a good concert tonight.
Yes, I saw that. What's Asian Fusion?
14
A mixture of Asian and western music. It's my brother's band. – I'm Asif. Hi.
Hi, Asif. I'm Robert. I'm in Birmingham with my parents – we're visiting family. It's really boring!

I know what you mean: we do a lot of that! You're from the US, aren't you?
No, from Canada – Toronto.
Asian Fusion concert
Hey, what about a snack?
Great idea: I'm pretty hungry.
15

Do you play an instrument?
No, I don't. But I'm a DJ.
I'd like to DJ. Did you see? There's a workshop tomorrow.
16

Yes. Do you think we can go to it?
We'll probably have to pay.
17

That's OK.
Well, I hope it's not too much. Oh look, there are Katrina and Latisha.
Who?
18

19
Hi, come and sit down. This is Robert, from Toronto. This is Katrina, from the Orkney Islands ...
Hi, nice to meet you.
... and Latisha from ...
... Manchester. Hi, Robert!
Hi!

1 The people

a) *Look through the book. Can you find the four kids from the photo story? What are their full names? What do the pictures in the other units tell you about them?*

b) **Extra** *On four cards start a file (name, from, ...) on each of the characters in the story. Add as much information as you can.*

2 The music

Write down the names Asif, Katrina, Latisha and Robert. Listen to four recordings from the festival. Which recording goes with which person? Why do you think that? You can find useful words and phrases in the box.

> I think the first/... recording goes with ...
> because she plays ...
> I know ... likes/wants to do ..., so the first/ ...

► *WB 1–3 (pp. 1–3) • WB Revision 1–9 (pp. 4–7) • SF Learning words (Revision) (pp. 133–134)*

3 Now you

a) *Look at these questions. Make notes of your answers. For help look again at 2 on page 6 or at the box below or use a dictionary.*

- What kinds of music do you like?
- When and where do you listen to music?
- Do you sing? When? Where?
- Do you like German/English/Italian/... songs best?
- Do you play any instruments? What? Where?

> band • bass • cello • clarinet • drums • flute • (electric) guitar • keyboards • piano • recorder • saxophone • trombone • trumpet • ...

b) *Now stand (or sit) in a double circle. Ask three different partners questions about music from a).*

c) **Extra** *Make notes and report to the class on one of your partners.*

My London

> *Have you ever been to London? What do you know about this city? What would you like to see or do there?*

To: Katrina; Latisha; Robert

Subject: Meet on Messenger and visit London

Hi everybody,

Fantastic festival! It was great to meet you all. :-)) Let's all meet again on Messenger this Saturday at 6 pm, OK? But before that why don't you visit my website at www.asifspage.co.uk? You'll find five good reasons with photos to come and visit me in the capital. I'd love to show you around! :-)

Asif

PS Robert: Great that you and your parents are coming.
CU soon.

1 The London Eye

This is the famous big wheel on the River Thames. You get the best views of London from the Eye. I've always wanted to go on it. They say you can see all the sights from up there, but it's very expensive, so I'm waiting for a good excuse – like a visitor :-) So, join me! (No sound file yet.)

2 Funland, London Trocadero

This is one of my favourite places in London, although I've only been here three times with Hassan! It's at Piccadilly Circus, right in the centre of town and it's got hundreds of video and virtual reality games. Come and play with me! Click here for my sound file.

3 Hyde Park

Hyde Park is one of the royal parks – yes, it belongs to the Queen! In the summer it's a great place for open-air concerts. Hassan hopes to play there one day – dream on, big brother!
Click here for my sound file.

4 The Science Museum

The greatest museum in the world – and it's free! Join me and find out all about the history and future of science. There are lots of famous things to see, like Stephenson's *Rocket*, the first modern locomotive.
Click here for my sound file.

5 Brick Lane

This is 'my' market. There are lots of great markets in London, but Brick Lane is my favourite. It's quite near where I live, in the borough of Tower Hamlets. It's a Sunday flea market where you can find everything – from second-hand DVDs to computers and sweets. There's lots of great Bangladeshi food too.
Click here for my sound file.

STUDY SKILLS Listening

Listening for gist: When you listen to something for the first time, just try to understand what it is about generally.
Listening for detail: The second time, just listen for the exact information that you need. Don't worry about other details and don't panic!

1 Asif's sound files

a) *What do you think you will hear in Asif's sound files? Make notes, then listen to the sound files and match them to the photos.*

b) *Listen again and answer the questions.*

1 What does the family see at the museum?
2 What's the video game called? Who wins?
3 What is the man in the market selling?
4 How many times has the band played in Hyde Park?

2 Asif's tips

a) *What would you most like to do in London? Rank Asif's tips from 1 to 5. Find reasons for your choices.*

b) *Compare lists with a partner. You can use phrases from the box.*

+ It's fun/cool/fantastic/cheap/...
  You can only do/see/... this in London.
  I like video games/shopping/...
  ...

– It's very expensive. / You probably have to wait a long time. / ...
  You can do that in other places too.
  ...

▸ *SF Listening (p. 139)* • *WB 1 (p. 8)*

All about ... the London Underground

1 At Queensway underground station

Mr Smith Well, we've got our tickets. We can see everything in London with these!

Robert In Zones 1 and 2, Dad. And it's only a one-day Travelcard. We can't see all of London in a day!

Mrs Smith That's enough, you two. Now let's try and find where we are on this map ...

▶ *Find Queensway on the Tube map below.*

Robert Our London Eye tickets are for 11. Asif is going to meet us there.

Mrs Smith The London Eye is near Waterloo station, isn't it?

Mr Smith Yes. So what's the best way to get there?

Robert That's easy, Dad. Look, there's Waterloo. So we take the red line ...

Mr Smith That's the Central Line.

Robert Right. We take the Central Line eastbound to Bond Street.

Mrs Smith And then we change to the Jubilee Line. We take that southbound to Waterloo.

▶ *Find Waterloo on the Tube map. Follow the Smiths' route from Queensway to Waterloo.*

London sights	Tube stations
Brick Lane	Aldgate East
British Museum	Russell Square
Trocadero	Piccadilly Circus
Hyde Park	Marble Arch
Natural History Museum	South Kensington
Tower of London	Tower Hill

2 Excuse me please, how do I get to ...?

a) *Partner A: Imagine you're at Victoria Station. Ask your partner how to get to the first three sights on the list.*

b) *Partner B: Imagine you're at Baker Street. Ask your partner how to get to the last three sights on the list.*

▶ P 1–3 (pp. 20–21) • WB 2–4 (pp. 9–10)

3 On the London Eye

a) Look at the photos. Then listen to the CD and find out:
- *Who is on the London Eye?*
- *In what order do they take the photos?*
- *Which building in the photos can't they see?*

b) Listen again. What do you learn about each of the buildings? Take notes under these headings:
- How high?
- How old?
- Who lives/works there?
- Other facts
- What can you do there?

A 'The Gherkin'

B St Paul's Cathedral

C Buckingham Palace

D Tower Bridge

E Hi, from the London Eye!

Extra **Background File**

The **London Eye** is one of the tallest big wheels in the world – it's 135 m high. It stands on the south bank of the River Thames and has the best views over London. About 10,000 visitors ride on the London Eye every day.
Husband and wife architects David Marks and Julia Barfield first had the idea for the London Eye in 1993. Their dream came true when the London Eye opened to the public in March 2000 and passengers could travel in one of the 32 capsules on their 30-minute ride above London.

c) **Extra** *Read the information about the London Eye. Then choose one of the other London sights on this page. Use your notes from b), find more information (library, travel guides, internet), and write about it. Put it in your DOSSIER.*

▸ P 4 (p. 21) • WB 5–6 (pp. 10–11)

4 Time for lunch

After the Eye, the four walked along the river.

'Dad, Mom,' Robert said. 'I haven't seen where Asif lives yet. He wants to take me there.'

'Well, I don't know,' said Mrs Smith.

'Come on, dear,' her husband said. 'Robert's got his cellphone. They'll be OK. But you have to be back at our hotel at six, Robert.'

'Thanks, Dad,' said Robert, and the two boys went back to the Tube station.

The borough of Tower Hamlets was a surprise to Robert. 'There are more Bangladeshis than British people,' he said.

'Most of us *are* British,' Asif answered.

'Right. Sorry.'

'That's OK,' Asif said. Then he pointed to a building. 'That's my mosque, by the way.'

'It doesn't look like a mosque,' Robert said.

'A mosque doesn't have to be in a special building,' Asif explained. 'And it hasn't always been a mosque. It was a church and a synagogue before that.'

'Wow, is that right?' said Robert.

'Hey, what do you want to have for lunch?' Asif asked. 'We could have a Bangladeshi meal.'

'Good idea.'

'OK,' said Asif. 'There are lots of cheap restaurants and takeaways here in Brick Lane.'

▸ *GF 1: Present perfect and simple past in contrast (p. 149) • P 5 (p. 21) • WB 7, 9–10 (pp. 11–13)*

STUDY SKILLS English–German dictionary

If you don't know an English word try to guess it first. Which of these food words from **5** and the menu on the right can you understand?
spicy • allergic • nut • dry • yogurt • sauce • fry • spice • herb • onion • vegetable • sour
Look the others up in an English–German dictionary. Read the whole dictionary entry and find the right meaning. Don't just use the first one.

5 Lunch in Brick Lane

Read the dialogue. Then scan the menu on the right. What can Robert and Asif eat?

Robert I'd like a mild or medium spicy dish. But I'm allergic to nuts. Hmmm, maybe something with vegetables?

Asif I always eat something spicy or very spicy. But I don't like lentils. And nothing dry for me. I love sauces.

Robert	*can try ... or ...*
Asif	*would like the ..., ... or the ...*
	can't have the ...
	won't like the ...

▸ *SF Scanning (Revision) (p. 140) • SF English–German dictionary (p. 135) • P 6 (p. 22) • WB 8 (p. 12)*

BANGLA SPICE

TIKKA DISHES
We marinate meat in a yogurt sauce, fry it with spices and herbs, then serve it dry with onion and a salad. Spicy.

Chicken Tikka	£3.75
Lamb Tikka	£3.95

BIRYANI DISHES (MILD)
Basmati rice with spices, nuts and sultanas and ...

Chicken Biryani	£4.25
Prawn Biryani	£4.75
Vegetable Biryani	£3.95

DANSAK DISHES
We cook lentils in a medium spicy sauce, for a sweet and sour taste; with ...

Chicken/Lamb Dansak	£4.50
Prawn Dansak	£5.00
Vegetable Dansak	£4.25

JALFREZI DISHES
We cook meat with fresh green chillies, green pepper and onion. Very spicy.

Chicken Jalfrezi	£4.50
Lamb Jalfrezi	£4.75
Prawn Jalfrezi	£5.00

6 Time for a break

After lunch Asif and Robert took the Tube back to the West End and walked around town.

At Covent Garden, they watched the street performers and then Robert went into an internet café and e-mailed a friend.

> Hey Ryan!
>
> We've been in the UK since Sept. 1st. That's only 10 days but it seems much longer. I'm in London with a British-Bangladeshi guy, Asif.
>
> I met him at a music festival in Birmingham. He's cool. I feel like I've known him for years.
>
> We went to his part of town, the East End, and had lunch. He's lived there for 10 years – in one house. It's a really interesting area. Banglatown, they call it. There are lots of places to eat Bangladeshi food and we had a yummy lunch in Brick Lane. Then we got lost back in the West End, but an old Londoner helped us. Asif wants to show me this neat video game place next.
>
> I haven't seen Mom and Dad since 12 o'clock but I have to meet them at our hotel at six. Our flight back to Toronto is this evening.
>
> We've been very busy since we got here. See you in a couple of days.
>
> Robert

7 Where's Asif?

Robert went back to Covent Garden. Asif was in the middle of the crowd, so Robert stood and watched one of the performers. A few minutes later someone shouted: 'Hey, Robert!'

He turned and saw his parents.

'Where's Asif?' his mother asked.

'Hi, Mom, hi, Dad. He's in the crowd somewhere. I've been watching this acrobat for a few minutes. He's fantastic. What have you two been doing since our trip on the Eye?'

'Oh, we've just been walking around since lunchtime,' his dad said. 'Look, here's Asif.'

'Hi, Mr Smith, Mrs Smith. Right, let's all go to Funland together. Great video games.'

'No, I don't think so,' said Mrs Smith. 'Six o'clock back at the hotel, Robert. OK?'

Looking at language

a) *Find the sentences with **since** and **for** in the e-mail in **6**. Make a table like this:*

Sentences with 'since'	Sentences with 'for'
...	...

b) *What German word do you use for **since** and **for**? When do you use **since**, when **for**? What do you call the tense in these sentences?*

c) *Now find the sentences with **since** and **for** in **7**. Look at the verb forms (I've been watching, ...) – what do you think this tense is called?*

8 Now you

Interview a partner with these questions. Report back on your partner to the class.

1. How long have you been a student at your school?
2. How long have you lived in your house or flat?
3. Who's your best friend? How long have you known him/her?
4. Who's your favourite star? How long have you been a fan?

► *GF 2–3: Present perfect simple/progressive with since/for (pp. 150–151) • P 7–13 (pp. 22–25) • WB 11–14 (pp. 13–15) •* **Text File 1** *(p. 115)*

Extra | Background File | **LONDON**

A day in London for kids on a budget

London is huge: 1572 square kilometres. That's almost twice as big as Berlin. So, if you've only got one day and not much money, you need to plan carefully.

Step 1 Get a Travelcard. You can hop on and off buses (you see more) or Tubes (quicker) all day. Just check that you get it for the right zones. Oh, and Monday to Friday, wait till 9.30 before you start your day in town – you can only use your Travelcard after the rush hour!

7.5 million people live in London (Berlin: 3.4 million) and another million come into the city to work every morning – so the rush hour is pretty busy.

Step 2 You're on a budget, remember? No problem! Lots of London's famous sights won't cost you a penny. You can look at them from the outside.

Mix with the crowds at Leicester Square. Then it's only five minutes' walk to Trafalgar Square and Nelson's Column. And if you like art, some of the most famous paintings in the world are in the National Gallery. And it's free!

Step 3 What about some shopping? Remember, London is the capital of cool! What the young and trendy people are wearing in London today, you'll find in your shops tomorrow. You can look at designer clothes in hundreds of shops all over town, but – all too expensive for you. So try the markets at Covent Garden, Camden Lock or Brick Lane. You'll find young designers – maybe tomorrow's fashion stars – with interesting new ideas. And you'll find lots of second-hand clothes too!

Step 4 Hungry? The Londoners' favourite lunch is a sandwich. They say the 4th Earl of Sandwich invented the sandwich in 1762, and it comes in every size and flavour. In good weather, enjoy one in a park with free lunchtime music.

Step 5 Now it's time for a bit of culture. Don't worry, it won't hurt! Try the Natural History Museum or the British Museum – both are FREE! Learn about the natural world at the NHM and don't miss their dinosaurs. At the BM, find out about the world's cultures and you must see the mummies. The museum shops are great for interesting souvenirs or a present for the family.

Step 6 Need to rest your feet now? Well, if you didn't have lunch in a park, why not sit by the water and watch the birds in Hyde Park? But don't stay too long because there is still so much of London to see. Stay near the park to watch the Changing of the Guard at Buckingham Palace. Or walk along the South Bank of the Thames from Westminster Bridge to the Tate Modern, another great free art gallery. Then go across the Millennium Bridge to see Christopher Wren's famous St Paul's Cathedral.

Step 7 What about a trip on the DLR (Docklands Light Railway) to end your day? It goes past the shiny skyscrapers of the City of London, one of the world's most important financial centres. But because London is such an expensive city, it has thousands of homeless people too. When you get off the DLR, maybe you can spend your last two pounds on 'The Big Issue'. Homeless people sell this magazine on the street. Buy it and help a homeless person.

1 A day in London

a) *Work in groups (A, B, ...). Each person in the group has a number (A1, A2, ... / B1, B2, ...). Each group chooses a different sight/activity/place in London and collects information (pp. 12–19, guide books, internet, tourist brochures, etc.) and material about it.*

b) *Discuss your information in your group. Then join students from other groups (A1, B1, C1, .../A2, B2, ...) to make a new group. Share your information.*

c) *Go back to your first group. Together, plan a sightseeing tour of London for a day.*

d) *Now your group is the guide. Take your class (the tourists) on your sightseeing tour.*

► **Text File 2** *(p. 116)* • *WB 15–17 (pp. 16–17)*

1 WORDS A transport wheel

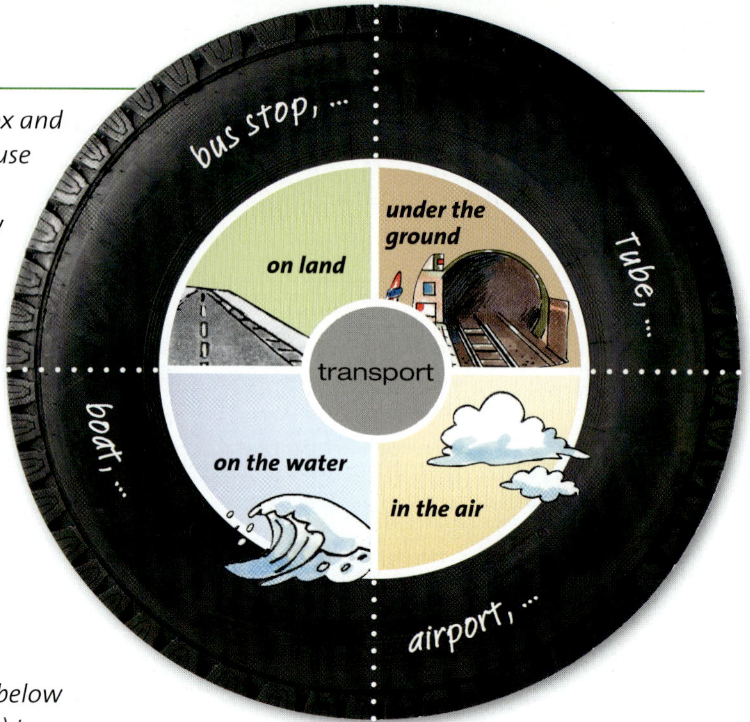

a) Choose words and phrases from the box and put them in a copy of the wheel. You can use some words more than once. The words with +are new. Only look in the Dictionary (pp. 195–222) if you have to.

+airport • bike • boat • bridge • bus • +bus pass • +bus stop • car • +ferry • +harbour • helicopter • line • northbound • +on foot • plane • +platform • road/street • river • sea • ship • southbound • station • +taxi • ticket • +ticket machine • train • +tram • Travelcard • Tube • Tube map • tunnel • underground

b) Write the verbs and prepositions from below into your exercise book. Find words from a) to go with each pair, like this:
arrive at the station
change to the underground
...

arrive at • change to • drive over • drive through • get off • get on • go by • take ... to • wait at

c) **Extra** *Imagine Asif and Robert are coming from London to visit you. How can they get from London to your town? Where will they arrive (station, airport, ...)? How – by plane, by car, by train, by bus, by boat, on foot? And how can they then get to your house?*
Asif and Robert will arrive at ... by ... Then they can take ... to ... They change to ...

2 LISTENING Travel announcements

a) Look at the pictures. Then write down the numbers 1–5. Listen to the announcements and match a picture to each number. The sounds that you hear may help you.

b) Now listen again, take notes, and answer these questions. Remember: you don't need to understand every word.

1 Which platform do you need if you want the Bristol train?
2 Where must you change if you want to get to Waterloo?
3 What must you always watch at the airport?
4 Where must you change if you want to go to Wimbledon?
5 Which gate do you need if you want to fly to Berlin?

A

B

C

3 MEDIATION The right ticket

a) Vanessa Beck is visiting London with her grandparents, who don't speak English very well. At the Tube station she asks about tickets for a day's sightseeing. What does she say?

Grandfather	Ich glaube, es gibt Tageskarten. Wir brauchen drei.
Vanessa	Er, hello. We need three ..., please.
Assistant	Three one-day Travelcards? Now, are you travelling together?
Grandfather	Was fragt er?
Vanessa	...
Grandfather	Natürlich fahren wir zusammen.
Vanessa	...
Assistant	And how old are you?
Vanessa	Dreizehn. Sorry, ...
Assistant	Well, a Travelcard for you is only £1 then.
Vanessa	...
Grandfather	Schön, und für uns, was kosten die Karten?
Vanessa	...

b) *Now you're Vanessa. Listen to the CD. What could you say?*

4 PRONUNCIATION now [aʊ] – no [əʊ]

a) *Listen to the poems. Say them out loud. Write them down and mark the [aʊ] and [əʊ] sounds.*

All around the underground,
All around London town,
The loud sounds of brown cows
That never sit down.

Ten cold poltergeists
Were riding up the coast.
They weren't wearing trousers
But they were eating toast.

b) *Now say the words below. Which is the odd one out? Listen and check.*

1	shout	snow	phone
2	nose	down	photo
3	brown	slow	underground
4	open	cloudy	town
5	hope	window	trousers
6	about	cold	outside
7	pound	throat	rode
8	down	joke	suppose

5 REVISION A week in London (Present perfect)

a) *Janina and Katrin are in London. Look at their list. Say what they have already done and what they haven't done yet.*

1 Janina and Katrin have already visited the Tower of London.

2 Janina hasn't taken a ... yet.

b) **Extra** *Write down two things you have and two things you haven't done this week.*

What we want to do in London:

J + K	visit the Tower of London ✓
J	go on a boat trip on the River Thames
K	go shopping in Oxford Street ✓
J	see a musical ✓
J + K	travel all around the Circle Line on the Underground
K	take photos of Buckingham Palace
J + K	go for a ride on the London Eye ✓

6 STUDY SKILLS English–German dictionary

a) *Read 'Gary's Greens' and 'Brick Lane'. Try to understand the underlined words first. Then look them up in an English–German dictionary. Find the right German meaning.*

b) *Check your translations with your partner. Agree on the right one for each word.*

c) *Together, look at the other information which the dictionary gives you about the words (noun, verb, adjective; pronunciation; ...). Agree on the right pronunciation of the words. Then check with your teacher.*

GARY'S GREENS

Your local, friendly greengrocer for all your fresh fruit and vegetables. We supply many of the best restaurants in the area and specialize in organic produce.

Brick Lane got its name because in the Middle Ages it was a centre of brick making. From about 1680 many Huguenots, Protestants who had to leave Catholic France, came to live there. Later Brick Lane became the centre of the Jewish community. In the 19th century the area was overcrowded and very poor. From the 1960s Bangladeshi immigrants made it their home. They brought their food with them and the first curry shops hit the UK.

7 The Smiths and the Azads (Present perfect simple with since/for)

a) *Use the table and talk or write about Robert and Asif's families. Be careful: do you need* **since** *or* **for**?

1 *Robert has lived in Toronto for ...*
2 *Mr Smith has known his wife since ...*

b) *Look at these questions. Write down how you think your partner will answer them. Then ask him/her the questions. Were you right?*

1 How long have you known your best friend?
2 How long have you lived in this town?

Who	What	How long?
Robert	live in Toronto	ten years
Mr Smith	know his wife	1992
Mrs Smith	be married	fourteen years
The Smiths	have a cat	last winter
Asif	live in London	all his life
Mr Azad	speak English	1981
Hassan	be in a band	a few years
Mrs Azad	live in England	1980

8 How long? (Present perfect simple with since/for)

Partner B: Go to page 110.
Partner A: Ask questions about the people in the blue box. Then use the notes and answer your partner's questions about the people in the yellow box. Be careful: do you need **since** *or* **for** *in your answers?*

A: How long has Lisa had piano lessons?
B: Since/For ...

Lisa: have piano lessons – ??
Maggie: live with her sister – ??
Phil: be a fireman – ??
Asif: know Robert – ??

Johnny: be a footballer – five years
Alicia: live in New Zealand – June
Pia: know Alicia – yesterday
Chris: have his new car – three months

9 On the Circle Line (Present perfect progressive with since/for)

*You're watching the other people on a Circle Line train. Who do you think they are? What have they been doing on the train? Use the present perfect progressive with **since** or **for**.*

1 Man: tired – sit on this train –15 minutes
That man is tired. He's been sitting on this train for 15 minutes.
2 Woman: a teacher – read the newspaper – last station
3 Two young men: students – listen to their MP3 players – a long time
4 Man with the hat: detective – watch a thief – 4.02 pm
5 Girl: student – dream about a boy in her class – she sat down
6 Boy: twelve – play a game on his mobile – the last half hour
7 Young people: tourists – travel in circles – more than a day. They don't know where to get off!

10 Hanson's of London (Present perfect simple/progressive with since/for)

***a)** Look at the picture. Complete the sentences, once with **since** and once with **for**. Use the present perfect progressive.*

1 Hanson's of London (sell tea) *Hanson's of London have been selling tea for 200 ... / since ...*
2 The girl (drink her tea) – a few minutes/ten to five
3 The boy (wait for his girlfriend) – half an hour/four-thirty
4 The three women (wait for the bus) – 15 minutes/they finished work
5 The man (eat his sandwich) – five minutes/five to five
6 The bird (sit next to him) – a couple of minutes/it saw the man

***b)** **Extra** Complete the following sentences with the right form, present perfect simple or progressive.*

1 I (know) my best friend since/for ...
2 I (learn) English since/for ...

WRITING COURSE Part 1

11 WRITING Writing better sentences (An e-mail)

This is the beginning of a five-part writing course. In this first part you will learn to improve the style of your sentences and then use these skills to write an e-mail.

a) *Read the two e-mails. Which one has the better style? Can you say why?*

Dear James,

I'm in Majorca. I'm on holiday. It's nice. There are lots of people here.
The weather is nice. I've got a suntan. I go swimming in the sea. The hotel has got a pool. I haven't been in it.
We went to Palma yesterday. We went on a tour of the old town. It was nice. We made some new friends. We're having a good time. I want to stay.

Love, Lena

Dear James,

I'm on holiday in Majorca. It's a really great place. It's very beautiful but very crowded too.The weather is fantastic and I've already got a suntan. I go swimming in the sea every day. Our hotel has got a pool but I haven't been in it yet.
We went to Palma yesterday, where we went on an interesting tour of the old town. It was a lot of fun and we made some new friends. We're having a great time so I wish I could stay longer!

Love, Lena

You can improve the style of your sentences in lots of different ways. For example:
Use ***adjectives*** *(e.g. great, beautiful, ...),* ***adverbs*** *(e.g. really, ...),* ***time phrases*** *(e.g. every day, since, ...) and* ***linking words*** *(e.g. and, but, ...) to link short sentences.*
Look for more examples of adjectives, adverbs, time phrases and linking words in the e-mails.

b) *Improve the style of the sentences: add the words from the brackets to them.*

1. I'm having fun here. (really • lots of)
   I'm really having lots of fun here.
2. We've got a pool. (fantastic)
3. I go there. (usually • in the mornings)
4. We have lunch in a restaurant. (a big • different • every day)
5. My parents have been taking me to churches and museums. (in the afternoons • lots of)
6. I don't like the churches, but the museums are interesting. (very much • often)
7. We went to an animal show. (yesterday • really great)

c) *Use words from the box to link the sentences. Make changes if necessary.*

after • although • because • but • so • when

1. The weather is terrible. We can't go swimming. *The weather is terrible, so we ...*
2. The hotel isn't very good. Our room is quite nice.
3. The other guests are friendly. Nobody speaks English.
4. We have to stay another day. There's a problem with our plane tickets.
5. I try to sleep. I can't. There's always a party in the next room.
6. We get back home on Sunday. I'm going to send an angry letter to the hotel.

d) *Imagine you are on holiday and are having a fantastic time. Write an interesting e-mail to tell a friend all about your holiday. Then swap e-mails with your partner.*
Remember what you have learned on this page and improve the style of his/her e-mail. Swap again and read your new e-mail.
Do you agree with the changes?
You could say where you are, what you have been doing, what's special, how long you plan to stay.
Remember to start with a greeting and finish with a closing phrase and your name.
Print out your e-mail and put it in your DOSSIER.

12 REVISION Lost in London (Directions)

a) Asif and Robert got lost in London when they were looking for Covent Garden. An old Londoner helped them. Look at the map and listen to the CD. Are the boys at point 1, 2, 3 or 4 when they ask the old man for help?

b) Think of a place near your school. Ask your partner how to get there. (Look at the phrases in the boxes first.) If you don't understand your partner, ask him or her to explain again.

c) Swap roles.

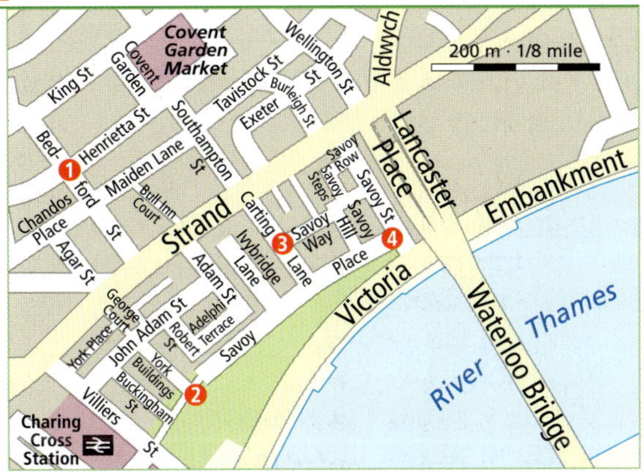

- Excuse me. Can you tell me how to get to ...?
- I'm looking for ... Can you help me?
- I'm sorry, I didn't get that. Can you say that again?

Yes, of course.
You go up/down/along/straight on/past ...
You turn right/left ...

13 EVERYDAY ENGLISH Asking for and giving information

a) What should you say to these people in these situations?

1 To somebody on the street: Du willst wissen, wie du zum Leicester Square kommst.
Excuse me, please ...
2 To your mum or dad in the late morning: Du willst wissen, was es zum Mittagessen gibt.
3 To a new friend: Du willst wissen, ob er/sie Asian Fusion mag.
4 To a shop assistant: Du hast ihn/sie nicht verstanden und willst wissen, ob er/sie £ 2.50 oder £ 2.15 gesagt hat.
5 To a bus driver in London: Du willst wissen, ob der Bus an der Victoria Station hält.
6 To your English teacher or another student: Du willst wissen, wie man „umsteigen“ auf Englisch sagt.

b) Listen to the CD and check your answers.

c) Complete the dialogue.

A: *Excuse me*, are you from around here?
B: Yes, ... Can I ...?
A: Yes, we're looking for the Volksfest. Can you ..., please?
B: Yes, of ... It's quite easy really. You get a tram, number 9, from over there.
A: I'm ..., I didn't ... Which number was that?
B: The number 9.
A: OK, ... very much.

d) **Extra** *Choose one of these situations and prepare a dialogue. Act it out in class.*

1 You are on holiday and have just met a girl from Sweden. Find out about her and tell her about yourself.
2 An American student is visiting your house. Explain to him what your mum has cooked.
3 A visitor from Italy is in your town. She wants to know how to use public transport (how much it costs, where to pay, how she can find out where the buses go, ...).

Only a game

Do you play video games? And if you do, how often do you play them? Which ones do you find the most exciting? Or the most realistic? Some of the new words in the text aren't in the Dictionary in this book. You can use your English–German dictionary if you need help.

When they arrived at the Trocadero, Asif and Robert went to Funland.

'Wow!' Robert said.

'They've got over 250 video games,' Asif said. 'The virtual reality games are the best.'

'How do they work?' asked Robert.

'Well,' Asif explained, 'you wear this helmet. Then you can see places all around you. It's like you're really there.'

'Sounds cool,' Robert said. 'Let's try one.'

The two boys looked around. There were so many games! Then Asif saw something. 'Robert, over here!'

Asif was in a corner, away from all the action.

'I don't think we can play here,' Robert said. 'It's not open, is it?'

'Oh come on,' Asif said. 'If they don't want us here, they'll come and tell us. Look at this.'

Asif pointed to a sign next to the two VR helmets. Robert read it, 'Experimental game.'

'You didn't read the best part,' Asif said.

'What do you mean?' Robert asked. Then he saw it. Under the big black letters there was another sentence. He looked at the sign more closely. 'Play at your own risk,' he read. 'This is a joke, right?'

'Of course it's a joke,' Asif laughed.

'But maybe it really is dangerous,' said Robert. 'I mean, ...'

But Asif was already putting on one of the helmets. Robert didn't like the idea, but he took the other helmet and put it on.

'There's a menu,' Robert said. 'Can you see it too?'

'Yes, I can,' Asif answered. 'Look, we can choose a virtual world. They're all from the past here in London.'

'Elizabethan London?' Robert said. 'What's that?'

'The time of the first Queen Elizabeth ...' Asif said.

'No, I don't want that,' Robert said. 'What's the next one? Oh look, Roman London.'

'Everybody in togas?' Asif laughed. 'I don't think so.'

'The next one's Victorian London,' said Robert.

'That was part of my London project for school,' Asif told his friend. 'Let's do that.'

'OK,' said Robert. 'But how do we start it?'

'Push the button,' Asif told him.

Robert pushed it. 'Hey, I can see my hand in the game!'

'That's virtual reality,' Asif explained.

A few moments later, London in the year 1888 appeared in front of their eyes.

'Wow! Where are we?' Robert asked.

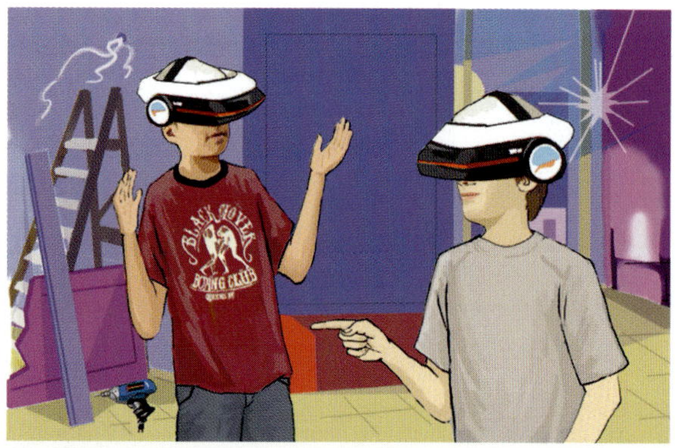

'This looks like Whitechapel,' said Asif.

'Whitechapel?' Robert asked.

'It's in the East End,' Asif said, 'not far from my house. – Come on, let's look around.'

The two boys walked through the narrow streets. 'It's getting dark,' Asif said.

'Yeah, kind of scary,' said Robert.

'You know,' said Asif slowly, 'Whitechapel is where Jack the Ripper killed all those people.'

'Ooh,' laughed Robert, 'Jack the Ripper is coming to get you.'

'Don't make jokes about the murders,' said a woman's voice from a dark doorway.

The boys turned to look. An old woman moved towards them. 'They found the last victim right there,' she said.

The boys looked where the woman was

pointing. There was dry blood on the road and the walls. And a flower – lavender, Asif knew. Then he felt something on his foot. A rat! 'A good thing this is only a game,' he thought.

As they walked on, a fog came down on the street. They heard a fog horn.

'We must be near the river,' Asif said.

'Yeah,' said Robert. 'I can smell it.'

With the fog came a terrible smell of dead fish and rubbish.

'You know what?' Robert said. 'This is getting too realistic for me.'

'Yeah, me too,' Asif answered. 'Let's take these helmets off and try a different game.'

Both boys took off their helmets at the same time.

Asif looked around. 'Robert!' Asif called.

But Robert already knew what his friend wanted to say. 'Nothing happened.'

'We're still here!' Asif was scared. 'How can that be?'

'I don't know! This was your idea,' Robert shouted. 'Do something!'

'I know,' said Asif. 'We can just pull the plug. Without electricity, the game will stop.'

'I don't see any plugs, Asif,' said Robert.

All the boys could see were fog, dirty brick walls, blood – and the lavender.

'It has to be here somewhere,' Asif said. 'Check the walls!'

'There's blood on them!' Robert grumbled.

'So go over there and look,' said Asif. He was getting angry. 'It's only a game, Robert.'

Suddenly there was a flash.

'What was that?' Robert asked.

'What do you mean?'

'That flash.'

'I didn't see anything,' said Asif. 'Now just feel the walls for a plug.'

The boys felt along the walls. All they could feel was cold brick.

'You know what's strange?' Asif said. 'I can really feel these bricks.'

'So?' asked Robert.

'The thing is: you can see and hear VR ...'

'And you can smell it!' said Robert.

'But you can't *feel* VR. It's impossible.'

'Are you saying ...?'

'Yeah,' said Asif. 'I think we're really here.'

'But how?'

Asif didn't answer. Out of the fog, they suddenly heard footsteps. They weren't far away, and they were getting closer.

'Asif, I'm scared,' said Robert.

Just then a lamp went on at the other end of the little street. A long shadow appeared on the road, the shadow of a man.

'It's him,' whispered Robert. 'It's Jack the Ripper.'

The shadow was moving closer, and it had something in its hand. A knife?

Then they heard a voice, the voice of a little girl. 'Flowers? Won't you buy my flowers?'

'A flower girl,' Robert said.

'She's selling lavender, Robert,' Asif said. 'Like the flower where the last victim died.'

The girl came closer. 'Won't you buy my flowers?' She looked into Asif's eyes. Her face was so sad. Suddenly Asif realized that the last victim was the girl's mother.

Asif put his arms around her. 'Everything will be fine.'

Suddenly there was a light from an open door. 'What are you doing with that girl?' a man shouted angrily. 'We've seen enough murders here, you!'

Another light, another voice: 'It's him. It's the Ripper!'

'There's two of them!' a third voice shouted.

People started to come out of the houses. 'Get the police!' called one woman.

'We don't need the police,' said another. 'We can take care of them.'

'Get away from the girl!' said the first man.

Asif took his arms from the little flower girl. 'We haven't done anything!' he shouted.

From far away the boys could hear police whistles. 'Quick, let's do it before the police get here!' said a woman.

'Oh no!' Asif said. 'They're going to kill us.'

'I don't want to die, Asif!' cried Robert.

Working with the text

1 What happened when ...

1 ... Asif and Robert arrived at the Trocadero?
2 ... they found an experimental game in a quiet corner?
3 ... Robert pushed the button for the virtual world of Victorian London?
4 ... Asif said, 'It's only a game, Robert'?
5 ... Asif put his arms around the little girl?
6 ... they heard police whistles?

2 Extra New words

Look at these words from the story again. Which ones could you understand without a dictionary? How?

work (l. 6) • helmet (l. 7) • risk (l. 26) • narrow (l. 63) • murder (l. 70) • victim (l. 74) • flash (l. 116) • shadow (l. 139) • take care of (l. 170)

3 The ending

Listen to the CD and find out how the story ends.

4 Only a game?

How do Robert and Asif feel about the game in the end? Will they play an experimental game again? What would you do if you were them?

5 Video games – your view

a) *What makes a video game a good game? Think of reasons.*

b) *Read the statements below. Do you agree with them? Why or why not?*

1 Kids play games all the time and can't talk to real people any more.
2 If you kill people in games, you'll hurt people in real life too.

c) *How dangerous are video games in your view – very dangerous, quite dangerous or not dangerous? Why?*

► *WB 18 (p. 18)* • **Checkpoint 1** *WB (p. 19)*

How am I doing? ► SF Multiple-choice exercises (p. 139)

a) *Fill in or choose the correct answers.*

London

1 London is on the River ...
2 Another word for the London Underground is 'the ...'.
3 Tower Hamlets is one of the many ... of London.
4 A market in London with lots of street performers. It's called ...
5 The Queen's home in London is ...
6 In one of London's great museums, the ..., you can see the first modern locomotive.

Words

7 Which word doesn't fit?
A ticket B bus C boat D underground
8 'Excuse me, how can I ... to Victoria Station?'
A come B go C get D move
9 'Does this line go to Leicester Square, or do I have to ...?'
A change B get off C get on D get around
10 Which word is the group word?
A chicken B food C lamb D fish
11 Which of these words is like 'danger'?
A victim B murder C shadow D risk
12 To stop a video game you pull the:
A electricity B flash C fog D plug

Writing

13 It's been rainy, ... we've spent most of the holidays inside.
A because B so C when
14 Where can you add 'after' to this sentence?
A ... I spoke to the teacher, B ... I tried to work C ... harder.
15 Where can you add 'usually' to this sentence?
I don't A ... like trying food from B ... different countries, but I C ... liked the food at the Bangladeshi café.
16 Which is the right way to start an e-mail to somebody that you don't know?
A Hey ... B Hi ... C Dear ...

Grammar

17 Have you ever tried Indian food?
A Yes, I did. B No, I didn't. C Yes, I have.
18 I'm sorry, Mrs Frisch, but I ... my homework.
A have done B haven't done C didn't
19 You're late! I ... for you since five o'clock.
A am waiting B have been waiting C wait
20 How long have you been going to school?
A Since six years. B By six years. C For six years.
21 Asif ... in London all his life.
A has lived B lived C is living

b) *Check your answers on p. 113 and add up your points – one point for each correct answer. 17 or more points? Well done! But do this page again after Unit 2 and see how much you remember. 16 points or fewer? It's a good idea to do some more work before you go on to the next unit. Where did you make mistakes? The chart below will tell you what you can do to improve your English.*

No.	Area	Find out more	Exercise(s)
1– 6	London facts	Unit 1 (pp. 12–19)	P 3, 5, 12 (pp. 21, 25), WB 1 (p. 8)
7– 9	Word field: transport	Unit 1 (p. 14)	P 1–3 (pp. 20–21), WB 2, 4 (pp. 9–10)
10	Word field: food	Unit 1 (p. 16)	P 6 (p. 22)
11–12	Words from Text	Unit 1 (pp. 26–28)	WB 18 (p. 18)
13–16	Writing better sentences	Unit 1, P 11 (p. 24)	WB 14 (p. 15)
17–18	Present perfect v. simple past	GF 1 (p. 149)	P 5 (p. 21), WB 9–10 (pp. 12–13)
19–21	Present perfect (simple/ progressive) with *since/for*	GF 2 (p. 150)	P 7–10 (pp. 22–23), WB 12–13 (pp. 13–14)

Island girl

A

1 Hoy

a) *These are photos of the Orkney Islands in Scotland, most of them of Hoy. On the map above, look for the islands of Hoy, Mainland, Flotta, the town of Kirkwall and the village of Lyness.*

b) *Read the captions on the right. If you don't know a word and can't guess it, look it up in an English–German dictionary. Then match the correct seven captions to the photos.*

c) **Extra** *What do you think life on Hoy is like? Compare it to life in your town, village, … Make notes and talk in a group. Here are some ideas:*

country • entertainment • jobs • nature • people • sport • wild animals • …

1 The fields of Hoy are full of cows and sheep.
2 From the cliffs near Rackwick there are wonderful views of the Old Man of Hoy. This huge rock is 137 metres high and the star of several films.
3 A tourist guide at work on his boat.
4 On the way from Mainland to Hoy you can see the tanks at Flotta's oil terminal.
5 Relax and enjoy your holiday in an old cottage.
6 Hoy has only one shop.
7 The island is a walker's paradise.
8 The salmon farmer's job is hard work.
9 You can see the sea cages of the salmon farms from every hill on Hoy.

B

C

D

E

F

G

2 Two views of Hoy

a) *Listen to the CD. When you know why the boy is on Hoy, tell your teacher to stop. Then do the same for the girl.*

b) *Look at the chart. Decide who is going to listen for what information (e.g. transport, Flotta, ...). Listen again. Exchange information in your group and fill in a copy of the chart. What do the boy and girl think about the different things?*

► *SF English–German dictionary (p. 135)* • *P 1 (p. 38)* • *WB 1–2 (pp. 20–21)*

Information	Boy	Girl
transport	*small plane to ...*	...
Flotta	...	*good: jobs*
no factories	...	
one shop		
free time		
farms		
scenery		
weather		
holiday homes		
school		
winter		

All about ... electronic media

1 Keeping in touch

Who needs modern media more – people in big towns and cities, or people in faraway places like the Orkney Islands?

Katrina McFadden lives with her family on Hoy. Her great-grandmother can remember when the boat brought the post to the island once a week. And her grandfather remembers when the first people on the island got a telephone. Today Katrina can't imagine life without chat, instant messages, social networking websites or text messages on her mobile.

2 Now you

a) *Look at the table to see what media Katrina uses and how often she uses them. Fill in a copy of the table for yourself and compare.*

MEDIA	Use?	Every day	Often	Sometimes
Mobile phone				
– make phone calls	Y		✓	
– send text messages	Y	✓		
– take photos or make videos	N			
– download and listen to music	Y			✓
– download/exchange logos and ringtones	Y			✓
Computer				
– do homework	Y			✓
– play games	N			
– surf the internet	Y		✓	
– watch videos	N			
– download, listen to, make or mix music	Y		✓	
– chat or send instant messages	Y	✓		
– talk over the internet	Y			✓
– visit social networking websites	Y		✓	

b) *Interview one or more partners and put their answers in your table in different colours. Answer your partners' questions.*
Have you got a mobile phone?
If yes, do you use it to ...?
And how often do you ...?

"On the internet, nobody knows you're a dog."

c) **Extra** *Katrina has texted her cousin in Edinburgh. What is she asking her? What is her cousin's answer?*

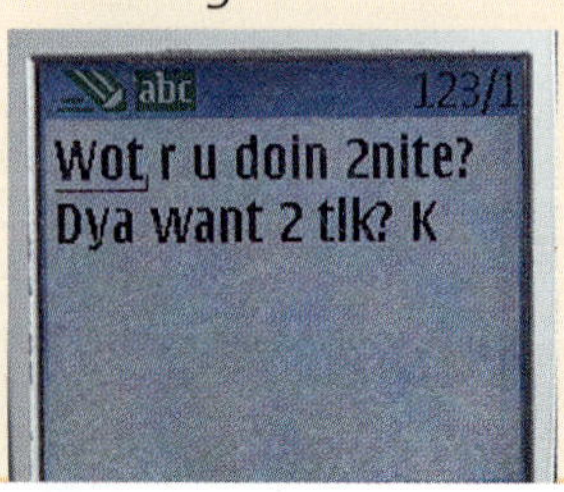

► P 2–3 (p. 38) • WB 3–4 (pp. 21–22) • Text File 3 (p. 118)

3 This Monday was different

It was a Monday morning and, as always, Katrina and her mum got in the car at 6.35 to drive to the ferry at Lyness. When they got there half an hour later, the ferry was just arriving.

'Dad's coming to get you on Friday, Katrina,' her mother said. 'Have a good week.'

'What are you doing on Friday, Mum? Why aren't you coming?' Katrina sounded unhappy.

'Och, I'm just helping with Saturday's ceilidh, love. So Dad's picking you up.'

At quarter to eight the ferry arrived in Houton on Mainland. Katrina waited there with the other kids for the school bus which took them to Kirkwall Grammar School. The same as every Monday morning.

But this Monday was different. A researcher was coming to interview some students for a TV documentary about the school. So at 10 o'clock Katrina was waiting outside the researcher's room for her interview.

The door opened and Fiona came out. Fiona was one of the 'Beauties', Katrina's name for a group of trendy girls in her class. Katrina went in and closed the door.

'Hello,' said the woman at the desk. She smiled and pointed to an empty chair. The film researcher's name was Jane and she already knew who Katrina was and where she lived.

'I see you're from Hoy, Katrina.'

'Aye, that's right,' Katrina answered.

'Why don't you go to school on Hoy?'

'Och, the school on Hoy only goes to Secondary 2,' Katrina explained. 'So I've been coming here to Kirkwall since last year.'

'I see. Do you come by ferry every day then?' Jane asked.

'No, I can't do that,' Katrina told her. 'It takes too long. I have to live in the hostel from Monday to Friday.'

Jane was surprised. 'Ah, that's interesting. The school has a hostel?'

'Aye,' Katrina told her. 'The students from the other islands live in the hostel during the week. I come over from Hoy early on Monday morning and I go home after school on Friday.'

Where does Katrina live during the week? Describe how Katrina gets to school. Compare it with your own way to school.

4 The rest of the interview

a) *Imagine you're Jane. Think of five questions for Katrina. Then listen and find out what Jane asked.*

b) *Look at these questions. Then listen again and take notes on the answers.*

1 What do we learn about Katrina's father and her brother?

2 What role does music play in Katrina's life?

Check your answers in a group.

c) **Extra** *Katrina talks about the view from her bedroom window. What can she see? Would you like that view? Why? Why not?*

5 Now you

Katrina is playing at a ceilidh next Saturday. What about you? What are you doing ...
- *after school today?*
- *tomorrow?*
- *in your next holidays?*

Talk to different partners.

A: I'm playing football after school today. What about you?
B: I'm going shopping with my mum.

► *GF 4: Talking about the future (p. 152) • P 4–7 (pp. 39–40) • WB 5–7 (pp. 22–24)*

6 The Beauties

Linda So, did the interview go well?
Fiona Aye, it did.
Alison If they choose you, you'll be a star.
Linda Then you'll be able to buy us tea every afternoon ...
Fiona ... and *you'll* be able to ask for my autograph.
Linda You wish!
Alison What are you doing after school?
Linda I don't know. Shall we walk down to the harbour, Fiona?
Fiona Och, no. I think I'll go to the wee shop in Albert Street.
Alison Oh, not shopping again.
Fiona I think they have those new bags from that magazine. I'll show you ... here, look – they're really trendy.
Alison Who needs a trendy bag in Kirkwall?
Fiona Well, not you, Alison, if you want to look like Fishface with her awful old rucksack.
Alison Do I look like Fishface, Linda?
Linda No, you don't. I mean, look at her hair: that awful ponytail!
Fiona Uh-oh, fish alert: here she comes.

What do the 'Beauties' think of Katrina? What phrases or sentences show this?

▸ *GF 5: will-future (spontaneous) (p. 153) • P 8 (p. 41) • GF 6a: Conditional sentences 1 (p. 153) • P 9 (p. 41) • WB 8–9 (pp. 24–25)*

7 Extra POEM Billy doesn't like school really

Billy doesn't like school really.
It's not because he can't do the work
but because some of the other kids
don't seem to like him that much.

They call him names
and make jokes about his mum.

Everyone laughs ... except Billy.
Everyone laughs ... except Billy.

by Paul Cookson

a) *Take turns. Read the poem on the left to the class. Find the right speed and stress. Use pauses.*

b) *Why doesn't Billy like school?*

c) *What links the poem to **6**? Explain.*

d) *Talk to a partner. What reasons do kids find to bully other kids? How do kids feel when others bully them?*

8 A Friday night chat

Katrina was tired and upset when she got back home on Friday evening. She went to her computer, found Latisha online and invited her to talk over the internet.

Katrina I'm so happy I found you online, Tish.
Latisha Why, what's wrong?
Katrina The 'Beauties' were horrible all week.
Latisha Hey, don't let them upset you.
Katrina If people called *you* 'Fishface', you would be upset too.
Latisha They're just bullies, Katrina. If they called *me* names, I'd just laugh.
Katrina Yes, but that's you, Tish. If I looked like you, they wouldn't call me names.

Latisha Katrina, you look great. Hey, you *are* great. What can these 'Beauties' do? Go shopping and gossip. Boring! I bet they can't play the fiddle like you. If I was you, I'd forget them.
Katrina I'd forget them if I knew how.

What does Latisha think of the Beauties? Why?

Looking at language

a) *Find the sentences with **if** in **8** and make a table like this:*

if-clause	*main clause*
If people called you 'Fishface',	*you would be upset too.*
If they ...	

b) *What verb forms appear in the two clauses?*

c) *Compare these two sentences. Which one is more likely to happen?*
If they call me names, I'll just laugh.
If they called me names, I'd just laugh.

▸ *GF 6b: Conditional sentences 2 (pp. 153–154) • P 10–11 (p. 42) • WB 10–13 (pp. 25–27)*

9 Feelings

a) *What did Latisha try to do for Katrina in **8**? Write down three possible answers – in German if you have to.*
Maybe you thought of 'aufmuntern' – but what's that in English? You can find out in a German–English dictionary. Look up your other words too.

aufmuntern *ermuntern* encourage [ɪn'kʌrɪdʒ]; *aufheitern* cheer up

STUDY SKILLS German–English dictionary

The dictionary entry on the left gives two English translations for 'aufmuntern'. The words in italics show the different meanings in German; the correct English translations follow them. Read all the entries before you decide which is the right meaning.

b) *Imagine you know Katrina. Write her an e-mail. You can find ideas in **8** or in the box (in German) on the right. If there are words that you don't know, you can look them up in a German–English dictionary.*

(nicht) beachten • (nicht) akzeptieren • um Rat fragen • aus dem Weg gehen • mit einem Lehrer/einer Lehrerin sprechen • ...

▸ *SF German–English dictionary (p. 136) • P 12–16 (pp. 42–44) • WB 14–16 (pp. 27–28)*

Extra | Background File | The Scotland game

1 Before you play
Read *The Scotland game* and for homework try to find out the answers to as many questions as you can. You can ask parents, look on the internet, in encyclopedias, etc.

2 How to play
You need three dice. Play in groups of 4–6. The youngest player starts.
Throw one, two, or three dice. How many did you get? 12? Then try to answer question 12.
The questions are all in blue.
You get one point for a correct answer. (Agree in your group or ask your teacher for correct answers.)
If you throw the dice and get a question that somebody has already answered correctly – bad luck!
The game ends when you have answered all the questions correctly (or when your teacher says 'Stop'). The player with the most points is the winner.

Tartans
Tartan is a traditional Scottish material and Scots often wear their tartans. But they don't buy a tartan just because they like the pattern. They wear the tartan of their family, or 'clan', and the patterns are often hundreds of years old.
1 *What is tartan made of?*

Highland Games
Every summer, towns and villages all over Scotland – but especially in the Highlands – have 'Highland Games'. There are competitions for ceilidh bands and dancers, bagpipers and this Scottish sport.
2 *What is the sport called?*

It's not a skirt!
For a special day or a traditional festival, the men in Scotland often get out their ...
3 *well, what do they call those 'skirts' which they wear?*
(PS Don't ever ask a Scot what he wears underneath – he'll tell you nothing.)

Food and drink
No special day in Scotland would be complete without haggis, shortbread and of course a glass of whisky.
4 *Now, is a haggis a kind of sausage or a cake?*
5 *Is shortbread a kind of bread or a biscuit?*
If Scots drink more than a glass or two of whisky, they might start to sing 'Auld Lang Syne'!
6 *When do people usually sing this song?*

A beautiful country

From the top of Ben Nevis to the bottom of Loch Morar, Scotland is a beautiful country. It's got wild mountains, lots of lakes and an exciting coast.

7 *How high is Ben Nevis?*

8 *And how deep is Loch Morar?*

Great Scots

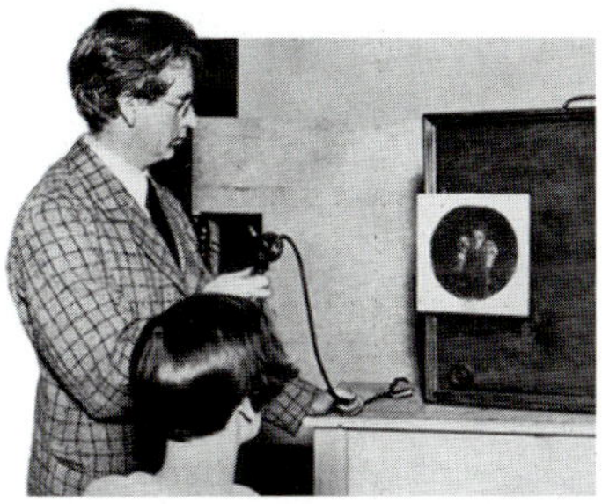

Every time you sit down on the sofa to watch your favourite programme, you should be grateful to the great Scot who invented television.

9 *What was his name?*

If it weren't for another great Scot, Alexander Fleming, you might not be alive today. In 1928 he discovered something that has saved the lives of millions of people.

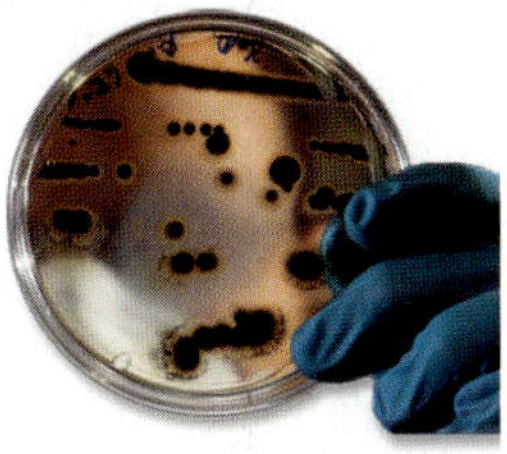

10 *What did he discover?*

Two Scottish actors

This Scottish actor became famous for his role as a very English spy: 'My name is Bond. James Bond.'

11 *What's his name?*

This much younger Scottish actor played Harry Potter's girlfriend, Cho Chang, and gave him his first screen kiss. 12 *What's her name?*

Technology

Lots of high-tech companies have opened in Scotland. Scientists there were the first in the world who cloned a sheep.

13 *Find out the sheep's name.*

Oil

When the big oil companies found oil in the North Sea, it brought a lot of money into the country. One city became the oil capital of Scotland.

14 *What's the name of the city: Aberdeen, Edinburgh or Dundee?*

Traditional music

It isn't just bagpipes. The Scots always enjoy a song – in English or in their own Celtic language.

15 *What is that language called?*

There's a famous Scottish song about 'Bonnie Prince Charlie', a 17th-century Scottish prince who had to leave Scotland to hide from the English. Perhaps you know the song.

16 *But do you also know what 'bonnie' means?*

Music scene

Scotland's biggest city is the place to go for clubs and to listen to the latest trends in music.

17 *But do you know which city is the biggest in Scotland?*

18 *And which of these four Scottish bands is not from this city: Belle & Sebastian, Franz Ferdinand, Travis, Wet Wet Wet?*

► **Text File 4** *(p. 119)* • *WB 17 (p. 29)*

1 WORDS Town and country

A

B

a) Which words go with which photo? Which go with both photos? Which don't fit either of the two? (The words with a + may be new. Only look them up if you have to.)

b) Look at the photos again. Where would you like to live? Why?

+bay • +busy • +canal • +car park • cathedral • church • city centre • coast • department store • dirty • +farmhouse • flat • forest • fun • +hilly • hotel • house • lake • mountain • noisy • park • post office • pub • restaurant • river • school • shop • +shopping precinct • station • theatre • valley • +waterfall

2 WORDS Electronic media

a) Complete the text below with these words:

chat • computer • download (2×) • exchange • logo • plays • ringtone • surf • text messages

Katrina has got her own ... in her room at home. She uses it to ... with friends and to ... the internet. It's cheaper for her to ... instant messages with her friends than to send ... on her mobile.

Katrina loves music, so she often spends her pocket money to ... her favourite songs. She hasn't got an MP3 player, but her mobile ... MP3s. The ... on her mobile is a picture of a fiddle, and of course her ... is fiddle music. But it isn't a ... – it's her on her own fiddle!

b) Choose five words from the box and make your own sentences.

3 PRONUNCIATION Stress in words with three or more syllables

a) Read the words in the box: do you think the stress is on the first, second or third syllable? Write the words down and underline the vowel with the stress:

accident, assistant, ...

b) Listen. Where do you hear the stress? Put a tick above the vowel with the stress. Were your ideas in a) correct?

✓accident, ass✓istant, ...

accident • assistant • cathedral • computer • disappear • discussion • electronic • expensive • helicopter • hospital • information • instrument • reality • telephone

4 WRITING Using paragraphs (Describing what happened)

a) *When you write something, use paragraphs – your text will be easier to understand. On a copy of this report on a trip to Orkney, mark where you think the paragraphs should go.*

Short report on the club trip to the Orkney Islands
Our trip to Orkney took place over the long weekend. We were very lucky with the weather so we were able to see a lot. We arrived by plane on Mainland – yes, the biggest island is really called Mainland. On our first two days we saw much of the island. The towns of Stromness and Kirkwall are interesting, but very quiet. Our visit to the stone circles of Brodgar and Stenness took us back thousands of years in time and was the highlight of the whole trip. On the third day we took a ferry from Kirkwall to the island of Hoy. There we did the famous walk to see the Old Man of Hoy. The big rock doesn't really look like an old man, but it is very impressive. All in all our trip was a lot of fun.

Click here for photos.

Always give your letter, e-mail, report etc. a structure. For example:

- Say at the beginning what the text is about (e.g. an exciting/strange/funny/... event).
- Start a new paragraph for each new idea.
- Start each paragraph with a topic sentence. The topic sentence gives the most important idea of the paragraph; the other sentences add details or examples.
- Finish with a general or personal sentence.
- Check: did you spell everything correctly? Is the grammar OK?

b) *In this letter there is a beginning and an ending. In the middle there are three paragraphs, each with a topic sentence. The parts are in the wrong order. Can you put them back together again?*

Dear Grandma and Grandpa,
Let me tell you about last Thursday, when I went to Edinburgh, Scotland's beautiful capital.

At lunchtime I had a delicious sandwich and then went shopping on the Royal Mile.

I spent most of the morning on a bus tour of the city.

I bought a nice hat for Mum and some souvenirs for some friends.

I saw all the sights and learned a lot about history.

It was a lovely journey and I arrived in Edinburgh at 9 am.

I took the train from Perth.

The best thing was the tour of Edinburgh Castle.

It started to rain in the afternoon, so I decided to get the train back home. Edinburgh is a wonderful city. I must go back soon.
Love,
Katie

c) *Now write an e-mail, letter or report about a real or imaginary day out. Maybe the words and phrases on the right will help you. Remember the tips from a).*

- Something amazing happened today.
- I'd like to give you a report on ...
- First, ... After that ...
- At lunch time ...
- Before we ..., we ...
- All in all, it was a very interesting day
- It was my best day out for a long time.

5 Katrina's plans for the weekend (Present progressive with future meaning)

Look at the pictures. Write down what Katrina is doing next weekend.

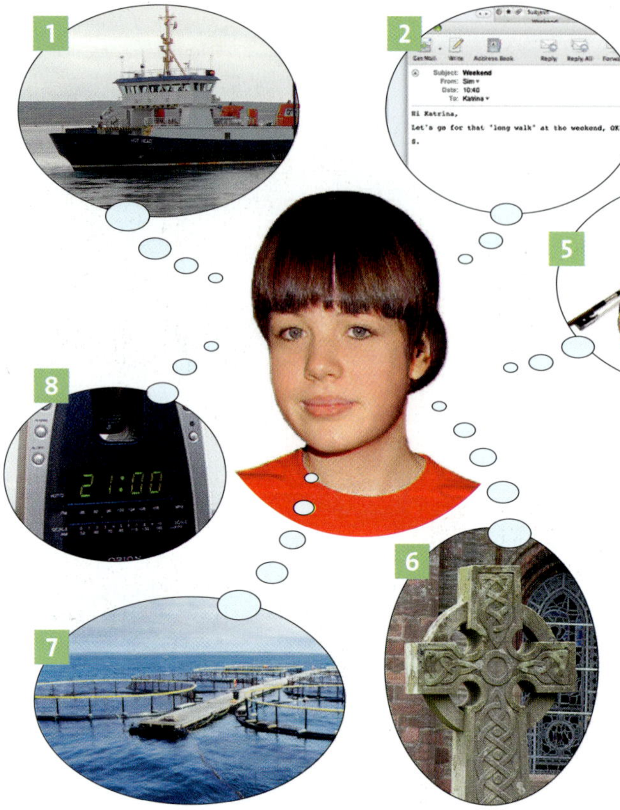

1 Fri: afternoon – take the ferry to Hoy
On Friday afternoon Katrina is taking the ferry to Hoy.
2 Fri: evening – check her e-mails
On Friday evening ...
3 Sat: morning – get up early
4 Sat: afternoon – go for a walk
5 Sat: evening – play at the ceilidh
6 Sun: morning – go to church
7 Sun: afternoon – help her dad at the salmon farm
8 Sun: night – go to bed early

6 REVISION More questions (Present perfect simple/progressive with since/for)

Here are some more questions the film researcher asked Katrina. How did she answer? Use **since** *or* **for**.

1 How long have you been coming here to Kirkwall? – last year
I've been coming here since last year.
2 How long has the school had a hostel? – 15 years, I think. But I don't really know.
3 How long has your dad been a salmon farmer? – about ten years
4 How long has he had his boat? – March
5 How long have you been playing the fiddle? – almost five years
6 How long have you had this fiddle? – my last birthday
7 How long have you known that tune? – my dad taught me it
8 How long have we been talking now? – half an hour

7 WORDS The prefix un- (Word formation)

You can add the prefix **un-** *to some adjectives and change their meaning. For example:*
fair – unfair: I always have to go to bed before my brother. That's unfair.
Now add **un-** *to these adjectives and write example sentences for each one.*

friendly • happy • healthy • important • safe • tidy

Be careful! You can't add **un-** *to every adjective. Check in a dictionary if you are unsure.*

8 I'll do it! (will-future, spontaneous decisions)

Look at the pictures. What can the people/animals say? Use the words under the pictures and the will-future.

1 give: *I'll give you a drink.*

2 open – door: *I'll ...*

3 not tell your parents

4 which – have?/have – the big one

5 jump – first

6 get

9 REVISION If it's sunny tomorrow, ... (Conditional sentences 1)

a) *Copy the network and complete it. Write a positive and negative statement for each bubble.*

What I will and won't do tomorrow

- If it doesn't rain tomorrow, ... – *... I'll go for a ride.* / *... I won't play video games.*
- If it's sunny tomorrow, ...
- If I've got lots of time tomorrow, ... – *I'll ...* / *I won't ...*
- If ... tomorrow, ...
- If I turn on the computer tomorrow, ...
- If a friend visits me tomorrow, ...
- If I'm at home without my family tomorrow, ...

b) **Extra** *Finish these sentences in the most interesting way you can. Read out the sentences in class. Who has got the best ones?*

1 I can call you on your mobile if ... *2 I won't do my homework if ...* *3 I must go home if ...*

10 Katrina's dreams (Conditional sentences 2)

Katrina sometimes dreams about what things would be like if she lived in London.

a) *Match the sentences.*

1 If I lived in London,	I would take them for a ride on the London Eye.
2 Maybe I would see the Queen	if an important film-maker saw me in a school play.
3 Maybe I would become a film star	I would take the underground.
4 If my parents visited me,	I would go to lots of musicals.
5 If I went shopping in town,	if I waited long enough at Buckingham Palace.

b) *Fill in the correct forms of the verbs in brackets.*

1 If my friends (come) to see me, I would show them all the famous sights.
2 I could see lots of new films if I (go) to Leicester Square.
3 If I wanted to see my family on the Orkney Islands, I (go) by plane.
4 I (miss) my friends and family if they (not/come) to visit me.

c) *What about you? What would you do if you lived in London? Write three sentences. Then compare them with your partner's sentences. Have you got the same or different ideas?*

11 What if ...? (Conditional sentences 2)

a) **Think:** *Complete these sentences.*

1 If I lived on the island of Hoy I'd chat on the internet every night / I'd ...
2 If I could have a new name, ...
3 If somebody called me 'Fishface', ...
4 If I didn't live in Germany, ...

b) **Pair:** *Read out your sentences. Together choose your three favourites.*

c) **Share:** *Join up with another pair. Choose your three favourites and read them to the class.*

If I was an apple

If I was an apple
And grew on a tree
I think I'd drop down
On a nice boy like me.

12 STUDY SKILLS Using a German–English dictionary

a) *Write the following words in alphabetical order. What do the words in **1** mean in English?*

1 Wildnis – Windel – Wiese – Windjacke – Windmühle – Wimper
2 Weile – Wein – Weide – weich – weiblich – Weintraube
3 Dachterrasse – Dach – Dachboden – Dackel – Dachrinne – Dachs

b) *Find the correct English words for the underlined German words in the following sentences.*

1 Katrina hat eine schöne Sicht von ihrem Fenster.
2 Die Sicht auf der Insel Hoy betrug gestern nur 10 Meter.
3 Um 8.05 kam die Fähre in Sicht.
4 Aus meiner Sicht ist Katrina altmodisch.
5 Auf lange Sicht wird sich das Leben auf Hoy verändern.

c) *Find the correct English translations for these German words and phrases.*

1 im Internet
2 ein Glas Marmelade
3 Wolken am Himmel
4 eine Brille
5 ihm aus dem Weg gehen
6 sich die Haare kämmen

13 Loch Ness and Edinburgh

a) *Partner B: Look at page 110.*
Partner A: A student has written a report on Loch Ness. There are seven mistakes in it. Read the report first quietly, then to your partner. He/She will correct the mistakes.

Loch Ness
Loch Ness is one of the most dangerous places in Scotland. It is a lake between the towns of Inverness and Fort Augustus in the north of Scotland. The word 'loch' is Scottish and means water. Loch Ness is 73 kilometres long. It is the longest lake in Britain. The water is so dark at the bottom that people can't see when they go down into the lake.

Everybody in Scotland says that there is a big monster in the lake. They have given it a name: Nessie. A small number of people think that Nessie is only a story, but every year hundreds of tourists come to Loch Ness to try and see her. There are even photos of her. But nobody can be sure if a big monster lives in the lake.

If you want to find out more about Nessie, you don't have to go to Scotland: there are lots of websites where you can see photos from helicopters over the lake.

b) *Now listen to your partner's report on Edinburgh. When you hear a mistake, correct it with facts from the box below.*

Facts about Edinburgh

1. Edinburgh is on the Scottish east coast.
2. Edinburgh is the second largest Scottish city.
3. More than 13 million tourists come to visit Edinburgh every year.
4. Visitors come to see famous places such as Edinburgh Castle, the Royal Mile or Princes Street.
5. Thousands of people visit the Edinburgh International Festival every summer.
6. Edinburgh was the home of famous people like Alexander Graham Bell, the 'father' of the telephone.
7. J. K. Rowling wrote her first 'Harry Potter' book in a café in Edinburgh.

14 Extra If I was 25 years old now

Use an empty piece of paper and design a page on one of these topics:

If I was 25 years old now, I would ...
If I had my own flat now, I would ...

a) *Think of things that you would like to do in these situations:*
– Where would you be?
– Would you live with somebody or live alone?
– Would you still go to school?
– If not, what would your job be?
– What would you do in your free time?
– ...

b) *Make a mind map with your ideas. Each idea completes the sentence If I was 25 years old now, I would ... or If I had my own flat, I would ...*

c) *Look for pictures for your page (magazines, brochures, internet, ...) and stick them on.*

d) *Bring your page to school and put it on the wall in your classroom. Look at everybody's pages. What are the most popular ideas? Talk to other people about them.*

15 MEDIATION The Ba' Game

You have found this tourist brochure about the Ba' Game in Kirkwall. First make notes in German on the most important information (you could highlight a copy of the article first). Only use a dictionary if you really have to. Now explain the Ba' Game for a family friend in three or four German sentences.

Every Christmas and New Year's Day the men and boys of Kirkwall, the capital of the Orkney Islands in Scotland, play the Ba' Game in the streets of their hometown. The game started in Kirkwall around 1850, but it's much older. There are two teams – the Uppies, who live in the hilly part of Kirkwall, and the Doonies (Downies), who live in the flat part by the sea.

There is really only one rule for this game: to win, the Uppies have to get the ba' – a three-pound leather ball – to a wall at the south end of the town, the Doonies have to get the ba' into the water of Kirkwall's harbour. Anything goes: you can kick and push people, punch, smash windows, run through houses or even over rooftops. Each team usually has between 200 and 300 players. The game goes on for about five to eight hours, sometimes even more.

The boys' Ba' Game begins at 10.30 am at the Market Cross opposite the Cathedral. The men's Ba' Game begins at one o'clock. As soon as the ba' lands in the crowd, the boys or the men start to fight for it and try to carry it towards their territories. An important player from the winning team usually hangs the ba' in his living room window.

▸ *SF Mediation (p. 143)*

16 EVERYDAY ENGLISH Talking about places

a) *Listen to the people on the CD. Each talks about where he or she lives. While you listen, fill in a copy of the table.*

	Glasgow	Stirling	Helmsdale
where?			
number of people			
what's special?			

b) *Look at the box below and list the phrases under these headings:*
– where places are
– what's special about a place

on the coast • in the Black Forest / ... • it's very green • in the Harz/... Mountains • where the famous sports cars / ... come from • quite near/not far from • in the north/... of Germany

Now try to add words and phrases from the table in a) to these lists.

c) *Compare your lists with a partner. Add to them or make changes if necessary.*

d) *Complete the dialogue about where you live.*
A: Where are you from?
B: I'm from a place called ..., in Germany.
A: Really? Where's that?
B: Well, it's in the ...
A: Is it a nice place?
B: Yes, I like it. It's got ..., and the people are ...

e) **Extra** *Make notes for a presentation about where you live. Follow the order below.*
– name of place: *Borgsdorf*
– kind of place: *village, part of Hohen Neuendorf*
– where it is: *few km north of Berlin*
– important thing(s) about it: *train station (trains to Berlin), own school, shopping centre*
– the people: *friendly, most work in Berlin*

f) **Extra** *Prepare and give a short talk about where you live and how you feel about it.*

Orkney Star

Look at the pictures of Katrina in this story. What is she doing in them? Who do you think the other people are? Then look at the other pictures. Who do you think these people are? Now, say in a few sentences what you think the story is about.

'And now for school announcements,' the head teacher of Kirkwall Grammar School said. 'I have a letter here from Scottish Television. As you all know, they're making one of their "Going to school in Scotland" documentaries here at KGS soon. And they've chosen a student from S3 to be "the star". It's ... Katrina McFadden. So, good luck to Katrina. And now ...'

Katrina didn't hear the rest of the announcements. There must be some mistake: why would they choose her? She couldn't believe it.

When she got back to her classroom most of the other kids were really excited.

'Great, Katrina!', 'You heard the head teacher, Katrina: soon you'll be a star!' Katrina began to feel very excited too.

At break, even the 'Beauties' came up to her: 'Congratulations, Katrina!' Alison said. 'Amazing!'

'Yes,' Fiona agreed, but she didn't look very happy about it. 'We thought you might need some help.'

'Help?' Katrina asked, 'Er ... with what?'

'With shopping,' said Linda. 'There are some nice wee shops in Kirkwall – we could help you buy some trendy new clothes ...'

'And a new bag!' added Fiona.

'But I don't need any new clothes, or a new bag,' said Katrina.

'Well, what about your hair? Alison's got this friend: she's a really good hairdresser,' said Fiona.

'Yes,' said Alison and smiled. 'I could ask her ... but only if you want.'

'Maybe the film crew would like to film you at the hairdresser's?' Linda went on.'You want to look nice on TV, don't you? You can't go on TV in that ponytail.'

Suddenly Katrina felt very angry.

'Listen,' she said. 'They chose me for the film the way I am. With my ponytail. Maybe you three like to spend all day at the hairdresser's. I've got better things to do.'

The 'Beauties' were shocked. Katrina never spoke to them like that. For a moment, they didn't know what to do or say. Then Fiona walked away.

'Once a fishface, always a fishface!' she said. Linda followed her. Before Alison joined her friends, she turned to Katrina and whispered, 'Good luck!'

The day the film crew came, it was cold and windy. Katrina walked across from the hostel in her wellies and anorak. She didn't know if she was more excited or more scared.

'Why did they choose me?' she thought. 'Film people are very trendy, aren't they? They probably all look like the 'Beauties'. And they'll probably think I'm really boring!'

'Ah, here she is!' said the head teacher. 'This is Katrina McFadden. Katrina, this is the director's assistant, Miss Burns.'

'Hi, Katrina. It's really nice to meet you. Call me Sheena.'

Katrina smiled: Sheena was about 25. She wore her jeans in her big green wellies and a green anorak. And she wore her hair in a ponytail.

'Hello, Sheena,' Katrina said.

'Now, I'm going to take you to meet the director – Bill. He's really nice.

We're planning to film in the school today and tomorrow and on Hoy on Friday and Saturday. The head teacher has said you don't have to come to school on Friday, OK?'

'OK!' smiled Katrina.

'We're going to start with an interview,' Bill explained, 'Just like the interview with the researcher, but this time we're going to film it!'

'Come and sit here,' said Sheena. Katrina sat down. The electrician smiled at her. 'I'm Fred,' he said, as he moved one of the lights to the right.

'And I'm Emma: I'm the sound assistant and I'm going to put this little microphone on your sweatshirt.'

'And I'm Alistair: I'm the real boss here,' laughed the cameraman. 'If you're nice to me, you'll look good in the film, if you aren't nice to me, well ...'

'Don't worry!' said Sheena, 'They always tease people. Is everybody ready?'

Katrina didn't feel ready, but Bill smiled at her and Sheena smiled at her ...

'Katrina's story: one, take one.' Bill began to ask questions. It all went well until he asked: 'Katrina, do you like living away from home?'

'No, I don't,' answered Katrina, 'The hostel's not bad, but I'd really like to be at home with my family. But the journey is just too ... Oh dear. Oh, no!'

'Cut!' called Bill. 'What's the matter, Katrina?' he asked.

'Oh dear, I'm sorry ...'

'You don't have to worry. We can just cut out that bit ...'

'People will think I don't like the hostel. I do, but I like home more. But they'll be upset at the hostel.'

Just then they heard the bell for break.

'OK, don't worry,' said Bill. 'Right, let's film the kids at break.'

*****

On Friday morning the film crew and Katrina took the ferry to Hoy. They filmed Katrina as she stood at the front of the boat with the wind in her hair.

When they arrived in Lyness, Bill was talking to the ferry captain. The film crew and the other passengers got off the boat, then Bill spoke to Katrina. 'OK, Katrina, back on the boat.'

Katrina was puzzled. 'What for?' she asked. 'We've only just got here.'

Bill explained: 'We're going to film the arrival of the ferry from the quay – with you at the front of the boat. The captain has agreed to go out and come back in again.'

*****

The next day and a half were like a dream for Katrina – but very hard work too. They filmed her in the fields with the cattle and sheep, in the island shop in Lyness, at home at breakfast with her family and in her room while she chatted online with Latisha and Asif. They filmed her when she went out to the salmon farm with her dad and checked the cages and fed the fish.

When Bill told her they also wanted to film her with the Old Man of Hoy in the background she said: 'Och, that's a very long walk with all your equipment. And I'm tired.'

Bill smiled. 'Oh, we're not walking,' he said. 'Look up there.'

Katrina heard the helicopter before she saw it. In next to no time, she was above the island and speeding towards the west coast. They set up their equipment on the cliffs opposite the Old Man and filmed Katrina in front of the Old Man with her arms above her head and a big smile on her face.

*****

On Saturday the crew had dinner with Katrina's family. Her mum made clapshot, a delicious Orkney stew.

And then it was time for the film crew's last job. They all drove together to the community hall for the Saturday evening ceilidh.

When they arrived, Katrina and her father grabbed their fiddles and went up on stage to join the band. Soon everybody was dancing – except Alistair, Emma and Fred. They had to film the ceilidh and Katrina.

When she had a break half an hour later, Katrina went outside for a minute. Suddenly somebody spoke to her.

'Hi, Katrina.'

Katrina turned round. She couldn't believe her eyes. It was Alison.

'Alison! What are you doing here?'

'Och, I'm staying with my uncle for the weekend. He lives on Hoy and he loves a ceilidh. You're a very good fiddle player, Katrina. OK, I should go back to my uncle.' Alison said and went back into the hall. Katrina smiled as she noticed that Alison had her hair in a ponytail.

Working with the text

1 What's the story about?

a) *Were your ideas about the story and the people in it correct?*

b) *Here are headings for different parts of the story. Put them in the right order and say where they should go (before line ...).*

1 At the ceilidh
2 Filming on Hoy
3 Katrina and the 'Beauties'
4 Congratulations, Katrina!
5 Alison in a ponytail
6 The ferry to Hoy
7 The film crew
8 The filming starts

c) *Write one or two sentences about each part.*

2 What did they mean?

Who made these statements? When? Why?

1 'They chose me for the film the way I am.' (ll. 43–44)
2 'Once a fishface, always a fishface.' (l. 51)
3 'I'd really like to be at home with my family.' (ll. 110–111)
4 'Oh, we're not walking.' (l. 152)
5 'You're a very good fiddle player.' (l. 181)

3 Katrina

a) *The film researcher chose Katrina. What do you think were her reasons?*

b) *Why were the 'Beauties' horrible to Katrina (A6, p. 34)? Why are they trying to be nice to her later? Are all three of them the same?*

c) *Katrina is angry with the 'Beauties' (ll. 42–46). Do you think she's right or wrong? Why?*

4 I can hear what you're thinking

Imagine you are one of the characters from the story and that you can hear what everybody else is thinking. What are the others thinking about you? Write a few sentences for each person:

You're Katrina – what are Fiona and Sheena thinking about you?

Fiona: Why did they choose Fishface for the film? I'm much more interesting. She ...

or

You're Alison – what are Katrina and Fiona thinking about you?

or

You're Fiona – what are Alison and Katrina thinking about you?

DOSSIER *Documentary*

Imagine you're going to make a documentary film for your partner school: 'Going to school in Karlsruhe/...'.
Write a description of 3–5 scenes for your film. These questions can help: What's special about your school? What will the star do/talk about? Where are you going to film the scenes?

5 Extra Make the film

In a group, agree on scenes for your film. Choose a star, a director, a cameraman or -woman, a sound assistant and a researcher. Make your documentary.

► *WB 18–19 (p. 30)* • **Checkpoint 2** *WB (p. 31)* • **Selbsteinschätzung 1–2** *WB (pp. 34–35)*

How am I doing?

► *SF Multiple-choice exercises (p. 139)*

a) *Fill in or choose the correct answers.*

Scotland

1 Hoy and Mainland are two of the ... Islands.

2 Kirkwall is the most important town and the ... of the islands.

3 Scotland is famous for a kind of fish. It usually comes from fish farms: ...

4 A kind of party where you can listen to Scottish music and dance is called a ...

5 It's not the largest city in Scotland but it is the capital: its name is ...

6 The Scottish word for lake is ...

Words

7 Which isn't a farm animal?
A cattle B chicken C fox D sheep

8 What are these four water words?
A esa B aby C leak D verri

9 It's usually cheaper to send somebody a ... than to make a phone call on your mobile.
A ringtone B text message C download D chat

10 'My friends and I often ... instant messages after school.'
A interchange B change C exchange D strange

11 Add the same letter to each word to make four words with similar meanings.
A hue B bi C lare D reat

German–English dictionary

12 Which word won't you find on a page between 'Perücke' and 'Pflaster'?
A pflanzlich B Pfannengericht C petzen D Perspektive

13 Where will you find the English translation for 'gehen' in the sentence, 'Sie sah ihn verärgert an und ging'? Under:
A laufen B weggehen C dauern D handeln

14 Imagine you need the English translation for a German word but the dictionary has three English words. What do you do?
A Look up all three in an English–German dictionary. B Use the first one – it's usually right. C Think of a different German word and look it up.

Grammar

15 If Tom ... to the party, I ... at home.
A will go, will stay B go, stayed C goes, will stay D would go, stay

16 If kids in my class ... horrible to me, I ... my teacher.
A were, would tell B would be, tell C would be, would tell D are, would tell

17 If I ... in his class, I ... careful.
A would be, was B was, would be C was, be D am, would be

b) *Check your answers on p. 113 and add up your points – one point for each correct answer (one point for each correct word in Nos. 8 and 11).*

c) *If you had 18 or more points, well done! Do page 29 again and see how much you still know. If you had 17 points or fewer, it's a good idea to do some more work before you go on to the next unit. Where did you make mistakes? The chart below will tell you what you can do to improve your English.*

No.	Area	Find out more	Exercise(s)
1– 6	Scotland facts	Unit 2 (pp. 30–37)	P 4, 13, 15, 16 (pp. 39–44), WB 1 (p. 20), 15 (p. 28)
7– 8	Word field: landscape	Unit 2 (pp. 30–31)	P 1 (p. 38), WB 2 (p. 21)
9–10	Word field: electronic media	Unit 2 (p. 32)	P 2 (p. 38), WB 3 (p. 21)
11	The German word 'groß'	Box (p. 176)	—
12–14	German–English dictionary	Unit 2, A9 (p. 35), SF (p. 136)	P 12 (p. 42), WB 14 (p. 27)
15	Conditional sentences 1	GF 6a (p. 153)	P 9 (p. 41), WB 9 (p. 25)
16–17	Conditional sentences 2	Unit 2, Looking at Language (p. 35), GF 6b (pp. 153–154)	P 10, 11, 14 (pp. 42–43), WB 11–13 (pp. 26–27)

1 WORDS In the country

Words about the country are important in the practice test on pages 52 and 53.

a) *Complete a copy of the mind map with country words and phrases.*

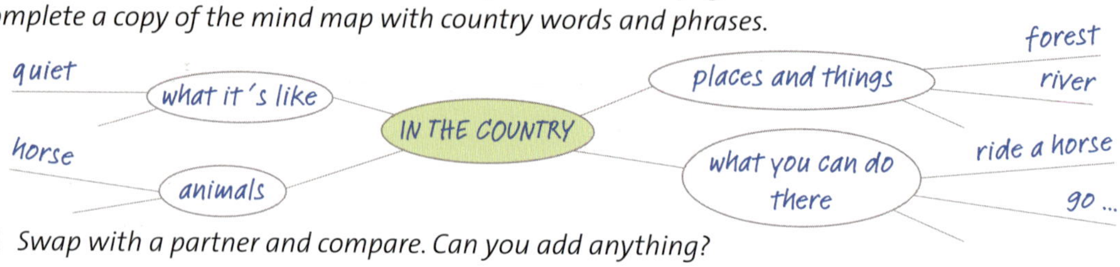

b) *Swap with a partner and compare. Can you add anything?*

2 STUDY SKILLS Describing pictures

▸ *Describing pictures (p. 137)*

In the test you will have to describe a picture.

Where are these people/things in the picture?

1 farmer 3 dog 5 boy 7 mountains
2 birds 4 horse 6 bike 8 farmhouse

at the top • in the background • on the left • in the foreground • in front of the farmhouse • in the middle • next to the field • between two trees • behind the horse

1) farmer – next to the field
2) dog – ...

3 The birds are flying (Present progressive)

You use the **present progressive** *to say what's happening in a picture.*

a) *Write the* **-ing form** *of the verbs in the box. Be careful with the spelling.*

arrive • chat • cycle • eat • fly • give • get • hide • meet • play • take • win • write

arrive	*arriving*
chat	*...*

b) *Complete the sentences with verbs from the box in a). Use the* **present progressive**.

1 I can see some birds. They*'re flying* through the air.
2 That must be the farmer next to the carrot field. He ... to somebody on his mobile.
3 The dog looks happy. It ... with a red ball.
4 The rabbits are happy too. They ... carrots.
5 I think the girl is the farmer's daughter. She ... the horse an apple.
6 That could be her little brother. He ... behind the horse.

4 Katrina's day (Simple past)

*In the practice test you will have to write a story. We usually do this in the **simple past**. Fill in the **simple past forms** of the verbs.*

1 Yesterday Katrina ... at ten to six. (get up)
Yesterday Katrina got up at ten to six.
2 Later she ... a hot breakfast. (have)
3 It ... windy and rainy when her mum ... her to the ferry at Lyness. (be, drive)
4 After two hours she ... at school. (arrive)
5 At Assembly there ... announcements. (be)
6 Katrina ... very surprised when she ... her name. (be, hear)
7 ... the other announcements. (not hear)
8 After school she ... her parents and ... them the news about the TV film. (call, tell)

5 Spelling (The plural of nouns)

Remember that nouns have different plural forms. Write the plural of the words from the box in a copy of the chart.

book • bookshelf • box • class • day • family • film • hobby • man • mouse • party • pen • sheep • teacher • watch • wife • woman

-s	-es	-ies	-ves	irregular
books			*bookshelves*	

6 Writing (Linking sentences) ▸ *Writing better sentences (p. 146)*

Time phrases and linking words can make stories and reports clearer and more interesting. Read this story. Choose the right word or phrase for each gap.

An appointment in Victoria Road

... (Every day in August/One day in August) when Asif was having breakfast he found a note from his brother:

> *Meet me at 73 Victoria Road*
> *at 11.45.*
> *I need your help.*
> *Hassan*

Asif looked at his watch. Only 8.55. He had enough time to do a few other things before he met Hassan. ... (First/The next day) he checked his e-mails. ... (After that/First) he tidied his room. ... (At two o'clock/Then) he packed two bottles of water into his bag, ... (because/so) it was very hot.

73 Victoria Road was a pet shop. 'What can Hassan want here?' Asif wondered. 'And where is he?' He drank some water and waited, but Hassan didn't come. ... (Two hours later/Two hours earlier) Asif picked up his bag and went home again.

'Where were you?' Hassan asked when Asif got home.

'I waited at that pet shop for hours,' Asif said.

'But 73 is a music shop,' Hassan answered. 'I had to get a big new drum for the band. And ... (although/that's why) I needed help.'

... (Suddenly/because) Asif had an idea. 'There's more than one Victoria Road in London, isn't there?' he asked.

'And you went to the wrong one!' Hassan said. Asif smiled, ... (although/so) he didn't really think that it was very funny.

'Listen,' he said. '... (if/then) you want my help again, just give me the full address.'

▸ *WB Getting ready for a test 1 (pp. 32–33)*

1 Reading

Robin Hood and Little John

Everybody knows that Robin Hood was a famous outlaw[1], and that he stole from the rich and gave the money to the poor. And everybody knows about 'Little' John, the big tall outlaw and Robin's number 2 man. But not so many people know the story of how the two men met.

One day Robin was fed up. He wanted something exciting to do, so he went out into the forest alone to see what he could find.

That same day, John Little, a shepherd[2], was unhappy too. The terrible Sheriff of Nottingham had taken away all his land, and so he had no place where he could keep his sheep. He gave all his sheep away and left his little village to look for work in the nearest town. The road took him through Sherwood Forest, where there were many thieves and robbers.

And so, at the same time, John and Robin arrived at the same place: a very narrow[3] bridge over a river. One man wanted to go one way; the other wanted to go the other way. And so they met in the middle.

Robin spoke first. 'Please go back, sir, so that I can cross the bridge. I was here before you.'

John was sure that that wasn't true, and he didn't want to go back. If he went back, he would have to turn round, and then he wouldn't be able to see the other man. 'What if he's a thief?' John thought. 'Maybe this is a trick, and he's going to steal my money.'

'No, sir,' John answered, 'I believe I was here first. You go back.'

Robin got his bow ready. When John saw this he said, 'You seem like a fair man, sir. As you can see, I haven't got a bow[4]. You don't want to kill a man who hasn't got a chance, do you?'

Robin agreed. 'You're carrying a staff[5], I see. If you wait here, I will quickly make a staff. Then we can have a fair fight[6].'

John waited on the bridge as Robin cut a tree and made a staff. Some minutes later Robin went back on the bridge and the fight began.

It didn't take long till Robin was in the water. John ran down to pull him out of the river.

'You saved me!' said Robin, surprised. 'You are a good man. What's your name, sir?'

'John Little,' answered the big man.

Robin thought that was a very funny name for a man as big as that, and he laughed. 'From now on, I will call you Little John. If you like, Little John, you can join me and my men and wear our green clothes.'

And so it happened that Robin Hood and Little John became best friends and had a lot of exciting adventures in their fight against the Sheriff of Nottingham.

a) *Choose the right answers:*

1 Robin Hood was ...
A a sheep farmer. B a friend of the poor.
C Little John's number 2 man.

2 Robin met John Little ...
A in a river. B on a bridge over a river.
C under a big tree.

3 When Robin met John, he first wanted to ...
A push him into the water. B kill him.
C cross the bridge and move on.

4 John ...
A gave Robin his staff. B killed Robin.
C pulled Robin out of the water.

b) *Are these statements true or false? Why?*

1 Robin thinks it's boring to spend time in the forest.
This statement is true/false because ...

2 John thinks that Sherwood Forest is a dangerous place.

3 Both John and Robin are fair men.

---

[1] outlaw ['aʊtlɔː] *Geächteter* [2] shepherd ['ʃepəd] *Schafhirte*
[3] narrow ['nærəʊ] *schmal* [4] bow [bəʊ] Bogen
[5] staff [stɑːf] *Stock* [6] fight [faɪt] *Kampf*

2 Speaking

a) *Describe the picture. Say:*
– what kind of place you can see,
– where the things/people are,
– what's happening.
It's a picture of the country. In the background you see the coast. There's …

b) *Say more about the two people in the foreground:*
– what kind of people you think they are,
– how you think they feel at the moment.
Give reasons for your ideas.
I think the woman is rich. She's checking her watch, so she's probably in a hurry.

c) *Work with a partner. Think about the following questions and make notes for a dialogue between the man and the woman. Use your notes to act out the dialogue.*
– Will the man decide to help the woman?
– Do the two become friends?

3 Writing

a) *Read the beginning of a story about the man and the woman in the picture above.*

★ A meeting on a country road

One hot day in June a young woman was driving along a country road. She was in a hurry because she was late for an appointment. Suddenly she saw lots of sheep on the road, so she had to stop. She jumped out of the car and went over to the shepherd.
'Good afternoon, young lady,' he said. 'Lovely weather today, isn't it?'

b) *Finish the story in about 80 words. Say if*
– the woman had an argument with the man,
– she arrived at her appointment in time,
– she ever saw the man again.

Remember

When you finish your story:
- count the words
- check the spelling
- check the grammar
- check for other mistakes you often make

Time for sport

1 A teenager's room

a) *Look at the room. What can you say about the person who lives there? What about his or her interests? Make notes. Then exchange ideas with your partner and add to your notes.*

b) *If you met the person who lives in this room, what questions would you ask? What could you both talk about?*

2 Extra A chat room profile

a) *Who is footie_girl? Use your notes from 1 and complete her profile.*

b) *Now write your own chat room profile. You can add a photo and put it in your DOSSIER.*

3 Now you

How is your room different from or similar to footie_girl's? Describe it. Explain what your interests are and how your room shows that. There are useful phrases in the box. You can use a German–English dictionary if you don't know a word.

- share a room with / room of my own /
- tidy/untidy/...
- furniture: bed/desk/chairs/...
- on the walls / in the corner / on the floor / ...
- family from ... so I ...
- My dream ... You can see that because ...

► *P 1 (p. 62) • WB 1–2 (pp. 36–37)*

All about ... sport

1 Girls' sports

2 Now you

What sports do you do or watch, at school or in your free time? Choose one and make a mind map about it. If you don't know a word, you can use a German–English dictionary.

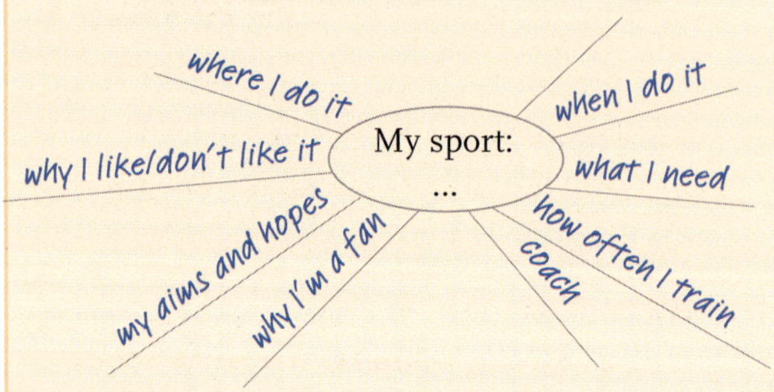

3 Extra ACTIVITY

a) *Present your sport on a mini-poster. Find photos of your sport or draw cartoons like the ones in 1. Use your mind map from 2 and write something to go with each picture.*

I love basketball because it is fun to run around a lot after school. I'm an Alba Berlin fan and ...

a) *Hang up your mini-posters in your classroom. Walk around and look at them all. Talk to classmates about the posters that you like or find interesting. Choose your favourite and guess who designed it.*
Later, you can put your work in your DOSSIER.

► **Text File 5** *(pp. 120–121)* • *P 2 (p. 62)* • *WB 3–4 (pp. 37–38)*

4 Dinner with the German girl

When Latisha got home from school on Friday afternoon, the German girl, Anna, was already there. She was another one of the exchange students who often stayed with them. Bad timing for Latisha – she had a big football match on Saturday. Latisha said hello and then disappeared into her room. 'There's some homework which I have to do,' she explained. An hour later Latisha was in a chat room with the friends that she met at the music festival. Suddenly she heard her mother's voice: 'Latisha! Dinner is on the table.' She said goodbye to the chat room and ran downstairs to the dining room.

Mrs Byrd There you are, Latisha. We've been waiting. The food is getting cold.
Latisha Sorry, Mum.
Anna Hi, Latisha.
Mrs Byrd Have you finished your homework?
Latisha Homework? Oh right. No. There's still some Maths I have to do.
Mrs Byrd Maybe you can do something with Anna after that.
Latisha But there's a new steel drum tune I want to practise for school, Mum.
Mrs Byrd Latisha, we have a guest. I'm sure that you can find some time for her.
Latisha Yes, Mum.
Mrs Byrd Well, Anna, I've made stewed chicken. It's a dish my grandma brought with her from Trinidad.
Anna Thank you, Mrs Byrd.
Mrs Byrd And these are plantains.
Anna Sorry? Plant...?
Latisha Plantains. Plantains are a sort of banana you have to cook.
Mrs Byrd Yes, that's right. Please start, Anna.
Anna OK. Er ... good appetite! Do you say that in English?
Mrs Byrd No, we don't, Anna. Sometimes we say 'Enjoy!', but we usually just eat.

> *Would you like to go to England and stay with an English family? Why? Why not? What would you look forward to most? What problems might you have?*

Looking at language

a) *Find the sentences with relative clauses in the first part of* ***4*** *(before the dialogue):*
She was another one of the exchange students who often stayed with them.
...

b) *Now look at this relative clause from the dialogue in* ***4****. What's missing?*
There's still some Maths I have to do.

c) *Find the other relative clauses in the dialogue. What relative pronouns are missing? What do you think: when can you leave out the relative pronoun?*

STUDY SKILLS Paraphrasing

Look again at **4**. How did Latisha explain 'plantain' to Anna?
To explain a word to somebody, you can use a **general word** and a relative clause or contact clause:
a **person** who ..., an **animal** that ...,
something which ..., the **thing** you use ...
Can you explain these words: **anorak**, **pet**, **rain**?

► *SF Paraphrasing (p. 144)* • *GF 7: Relative clauses (pp. 154–156)* • *P 3–6 (pp. 63–64)* • *WB 5–10 (pp. 38–41)* • **Text File 6** *(p. 122)*

5 At Salford Quays

On Saturday morning, Latisha and her mum made a deal. Latisha could play football in the afternoon if she showed Anna Manchester in the morning. So, at 10 am, the two girls were just getting off a tram at one of the sights.

'It's very pretty here,' Anna said.

'Pretty?' Latisha sounded surprised. 'Well, I suppose Salford Quays is pretty, yeah.'

'Keys? Like for the door?' Anna asked.

Latisha smiled for the first time. 'No,' she said, 'a quay is a place where they load and unload ships.'

'Oh. And what can we do here?' Anna asked.

'Er, I'm not sure. But there's an information centre at the Lowry. Let's ask there.'

The woman at the information centre told them more. 'The Lowry was opened in 2000. It's named after a famous painter from Manchester. It has two large theatres and a small one. Lowry's paintings are shown in the galleries with other modern art.'

'I like paintings,' said Anna. 'Let's go in.' Latisha wasn't so sure, but to her surprise, the Lowry had something for football fans too!

How do the two girls feel about their trip to Salford Quays this morning?

In 1953 a competition for football art was held by the Football Association. The first prize was won by L. S. Lowry, for his painting 'Going to the match'.

In 2006 the Lowry had another football art competition. Almost 900 entries were received and 100 were shown in the Lowry. On 30 November the winners were announced and the prizes were presented by football star Michael Owen.

Looking at language

a) *Compare these two sentences:*
Michael Owen presented the prizes.
The prizes were presented by Michael Owen.

In which sentence does the subject do something? In the first (active) or in the second (passive) sentence?

b) *Find more passive sentences on this page and write them down.*
The Lowry was opened in 2000.
It's named after a famous painter.

c) *What tenses are the passive forms in? How do you form the passive?*

▸ GF 8 a–c Passive (p. 156) • P 7–9 (pp. 64–65) • WB 11 (p. 41)

6 ACTIVITY

Make a 'passive' network. Choose one of the things in the box and write what is done with it.

bikes • football • homework • letters

7 The match

Listen to the CD to find out about Latisha's match. Then answer the questions below.

1 What's the name of the other team?
2 What's the score two minutes before the end of the game?
3 Who scores the last goal for Manchester?
4 What does Anna think at the end of the match?

8 The match report

Manchester

JUNIOR FOOTBALL NEWS

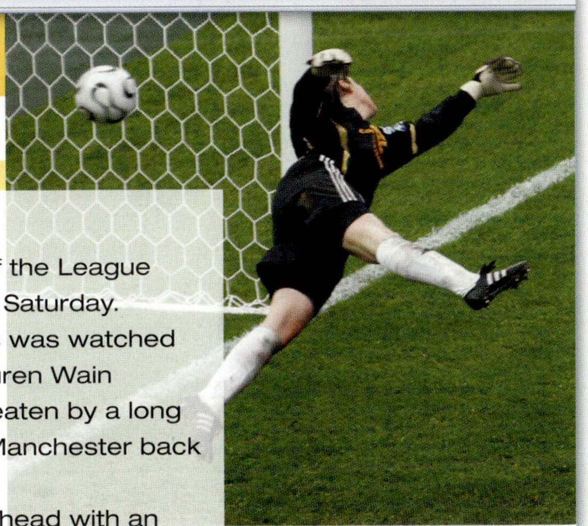

Rochdale beaten as United reach final

Manchester United U14 Girls reached the final of the League Cup after their exciting win against Rochdale on Saturday. The match between the league's two top teams was watched by a large crowd in Manchester. Rochdale's Lauren Wain scored first when Manchester's defence was beaten by a long ball. But a goal from Sandra O'Keefe soon put Manchester back in the game.

With the score 1–1 at half-time, Rochdale went ahead with an early second-half goal by Charlene Gordon. O'Keefe scored her second for Manchester with a penalty after Latisha Byrd was fouled by Rochdale's captain in the 80th minute. It then looked like a draw until Rochdale's goalkeeper Sue Waites was beaten by a last-minute shot from Byrd.

Rochdale keeper Sue Waites is beaten by Manchester's final goal.

TOP

9 The five Ws

Reports like this one usually answer 'the five Ws': the questions ***Who? What? When? Where?*** *and* ***Why?*** *Which does this report answer? Fill in a copy of the table below. Then find one more question for each question word and ask your partner. Add the answers to your table.*

Who played? / Who scored goals?	Manchester United U14 girls and Rochdale.
What is the report about?	...
When was the match?	...
Where was the match?	...
Why did Manchester win?	...

Looking at language

Look at these sentences:

Latisha Byrd was fouled.
Latisha Byrd was fouled by Rochdale's captain.

In which sentence do you know who did something? How do you show ***who*** *or* ***what*** *does something in a passive sentence? Find more examples in* ***8***.

► GF 8d: Passive with by (p. 157) • P 10–16 (pp. 65–68) • WB 12–17 (pp. 42–45) • **Text File 7** (p. 123)

Extra | **Background File**

MANCHESTER – a great city for young people

1 On the radio

a) *Look at the photos and captions and then listen to the radio programme 'Manchester – a great city for young people!'. Match each section of the programme to a caption number (1–4).*

b) *Listen again and write down one or two facts about each picture.*

1 Manchester is probably most famous for its very successful football team, Manchester United, and their stadium Old Trafford.

2 And let's not forget the other Old Trafford – the famous cricket ground.

3 Manchester is not all about sport. It has always been the city of textiles, like cotton and wool. The King Cotton City Trail is full of information on the city's history, including why it was once known as 'Cottonopolis'.

4 Music old and new – great bands and singers have always been found in Manchester, from the Hollies to Robbie Williams, 10CC to Oasis, Joy Division to Take That!

2 Now you

a) *Choose one picture. Find others who have chosen the same picture. Exchange all the information you have from 1 b).*

b) *Then use the information you have to talk to the class about your picture.*

▸ *WB 18 (p. 45)*

1 WORDS Spot the difference

Partner B: Go to page 111.
Partner A: Look at the picture. Tell your partner what you see in the rooms. Use words and phrases like ***next to, on the left, on the wall.*** *If you don't know a word in English, look it up in a dictionary. Ask about his/her picture. Your partner has to spot the differences. Take turns: listen to your partner's description and spot the differences.*

A: In my picture, there's a ... upstairs on the wall on the left. What about your picture?
B: Yes, in my picture it's there too. / No, in my picture it's on the wall on the right. – Now, in my picture, the ... is downstairs ...

2 WORDS Sports

a) *Look at the pictures 1–8. Something is missing from each one. Find the missing thing.*

Equipment:

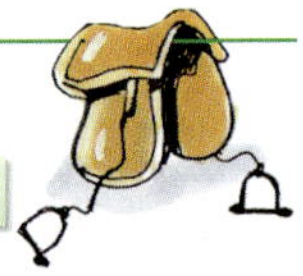
+saddle

badminton +racket

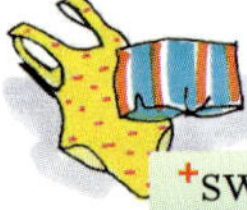
+swimming trunks/ +swimsuit

+skis

table tennis +bat

helmet

+running shoes

skates and +pads

b) *Now match a place to each sport:*

+bridle path • +court • +half-pipe • pitch • +running track • +ski slope • swimming pool • table

c) **Extra** *Write one or two sentences about each sport: Where do you do it, what do you need?*
1 You go skiing on a ski slope. You need ski boots and skis. If you want to play badminton you need ...

3 STUDY SKILLS Paraphrasing

a) *Partner B: Go to p. 111.*
Partner A: Explain the following words to your partner – but don't use the word.

coach • cooker • department store • lion • potato • shop assistant

It's somewhere/a place where ...
It's somebody/a person who ...
It's something/a vegetable/a ... that ...
It's something that you use to ...
It's a thing/an animal ...

Phrases from the box can help you.
A: It's a person who ...
B: Oh, do you mean a ...?

b) *Listen to your partner and guess his/her words.*

c) *Now try to explain the German words from the box on the right to your partner.*

Fernseher • Hausmeister • Pommes frites • Radweg • Tennisschläger • Verkäuferin

4 REVISION Who's that? (Relative clauses)

a) *Make sentences about these famous people who all have a connection with Manchester.*

1

- **Wayne Rooney**
- footballer
- first played for Everton in 2002

2

- **J. K. Rowling**
- writer
- the *Harry Potter* books made her rich and famous

3

- **Judi Dench**
- actor
- you can see her as *M* in the James Bond films

4

- **Mick Hucknall**
- singer
- sings with the band Simply Red

5

- **Alan Turing**
- scientist
- many people call him the father of computer science

6

- **Norman Foster**
- architect
- he designed the dome on the Reichstag in Berlin

7

- **Emmeline Pankhurst**
- activist
- she helped women to get the vote

1 Wayne Rooney is a footballer who first played ...
2 J. K. Rowling is a writer ...
3 ...

b) **Extra** *Find out what connection the people have to Manchester.*

5 Latisha and her friends (Contact clauses)

a) *Use the information in the boxes and make sentences about these things or people. Use contact clauses.*

Anna Robert Katrina Birmingham Manchester United Ice hockey The 'Beauties'	is are	a sport the football team the girls the Canadian kid the German girl a big city the girl from Hoy	the 'Beauties' think is very uncool. Asif invited to London. Latisha told her friends about. Latisha supports. Katrina doesn't like. Robert loves more than any other. Robert's dad lived in when he was a boy.

Anna is the German girl Latisha told ...

b) *Complete the sentences on the right with a contact clause.*

1 ... is the boy/girl I ...
2 ... is the TV programme I ...
3 ... is the person I ...
4 ... is the place I ...

6 Anna's photos (Full relative clauses or contact clauses)

Anna showed Latisha and Mrs Byrd some of the photos on her camera. What can she say about them? Use a relative clause with **who**, **which** *or* **that**, *or a contact clause when you can.*

1 photo of my parents – took at the airport
This is the photo of my parents I took at the airport.
2 little brother – came with us to the airport
3 house – live in in Chemnitz
4 teddy bear – lives on my bed
5 best friend – lives next door
6 old church – is in the centre of Chemnitz
7 plane – took me to Manchester
8 meal – had on the plane

7 REVISION If I lived in Manchester (Conditional sentences 2)

a) *What would Anna do if she lived in Manchester?*

If Anna lived in Manchester, she'd meet Latisha ...

b) **Extra** *What could Latisha do if she lived in Germany?*
Think *of five ideas.*
Pair: *exchange your ideas with a partner and decide on the five best ones.*
Share: *your ideas in a group and decide on the five best ones. Then tell the class.*
If Latisha lived in Germany she could play for a good football team.
If ...

8 Manchester news (Passive)

Look at yesterday's news headlines from Manchester. Write them out as complete sentences with the verbs in the simple past passive.

1 Man United beaten in cup match
2 Winner of football art prize announced
3 New school opened in east Manchester
4 Bus stolen from city centre
5 Library destroyed in early morning fire
6 Boy killed at dangerous corner
7 Salford Reds star hurt in big game

1 *Manchester United were beaten in a cup match.*
2 *The winner of the football art prize was ...*
3 ...

9 Manchester sights (Passive)

Complete the following information about some of the interesting places in Manchester. Use the passive in the simple past or simple present.

1 The Lowry Centre at Salford Quays – open – in 2000
The Lowry Centre at Salford Quays was opened in 2000.
2 Manchester United's home, Old Trafford – build – 1909
3 Cricket – play – at the other Old Trafford stadium
4 Roman fort – build – in Castlefield in 79 AD
5 Museum of Science and Industry – move to Castlefield – in 1983
6 The story of industrial Manchester – tell – at the museum
7 Chetham's Library, the oldest public library in the world – open – in 1653
8 Its oldest buildings – build – in the 15th century
9 In the 19th century – the library – use – by Karl Marx and Friedrich Engels

10 GAME Celebrity quiz

a) *Prepare a profile of a person you really like and who is well known – a celebrity – but don't use their name.*

b) *Present your profile to the class, sentence for sentence. Your class must try to guess who the celebrity is. Points: You get ten points for every sentence you say. If you use a passive, you get three points. If you use a relative clause, you get two points. You get five points for every wrong guess from the class.*

c) *Add the celebrity's name and a picture and put his or her profile in your DOSSIER.*

11 MEDIATION Where I'm from

Anna is from Chemnitz, Manchester's twin town. She has brought a brochure about the city with her. What can she tell the Byrd family about the places? The notes she has made will help you, so you can look the words up in a dictionary. Remember: don't try to translate the texts – just give an idea of what they're about.

Chemnitz auch für Kinder

Kosmonauten-zentrum „Sigmund Jähn"

Das Kosmonautenzentrum hat besondere Angebote für Kinder, z. B. in der Kabine einer 36 m hohen Rakete ins All fliegen. Als Mitglied des Kosmo-Stammpersonals beschäftigt man sich selbst mit Raumfahrt und testet Besucher auf Raumfahrt-tauglichkeit. Als Crew-Mitglied startet man mit ihnen zum simulierten Raumflug.

Wer wollte nicht schon einmal seinen Geburtstag an einem besonderen Ort feiern? Im Industriemuseum Chemnitz ist das möglich! Eine Stunde lang erleben das Geburtstagskind und seine Freundinnen und Freunde das Museum von seiner lustigen und geheimnisvollen Seite. Wie wird es sein, wenn die Glückwünsche per Fernschreiber oder Rohrpost beim Geburtstagskind eintreffen und wer schafft es, die große Stahltür des Tresors zu öffnen und eine Geburtstagsüberraschung sicher zu stellen? Neugierig geworden? Der nächste Geburtstag kommt bestimmt!

Industriemuseum Chemnitz

Kosmonaut
Angebot
Rakete
All / Weltraum
Raumfahrt
geheimnisvoll
Fernschreiber
Rohrpost
Tresor

12 Fun with history (Passive with by)

a) Think: *Take words from the three boxes and write down three funny sentences with them. Use the passive in the simple past with* ***by*** *...*

Subject or by-agent	Verb	Subject or by-agent
Troy cricket the Eiffel Tower Harry Potter the first plane the Mona Lisa Uranus	fly design discover find paint start write	the Wright brothers William Herschel J. K. Rowling Leonardo da Vinci Gustave Eiffel Heinrich Schliemann the English

Harry Potter was painted by the English.
The car was flown by ...
...

b) Pair: *Agree with a partner on your two funniest sentences.*

c) Share: *Join another pair. Agree on the two funniest sentences. Can you make seven correct sentences with the words?*

13 WRITING Collecting and organizing ideas (A report)

a) *A good report answers the '5 Ws' – **who? what? where? when? why?** – and sometimes **how?**, but not always in that order. It gives you the facts quickly, sometimes in the order they happened, sometimes with the important information first and the details later. Which of the following is the better report? Why?*

Manchester United beat Chelsea 2–1 in a fast and exciting match at the London club's Stamford Bridge stadium yesterday. There were no goals until the last minute of the first half, when United's Wayne Rooney beat Chelsea goalkeeper Petr Cech with a beautiful shot into the corner. Chelsea looked nervous but equalized just after

It was a nice and sunny day yesterday when Manchester United and Chelsea met for their big match. 'A great day for football,' I thought. 'Not too warm and not too cold.'
The match started one minute after 3 pm because the referee wasn't very happy with the ball and it was replaced with a new one. I was standing behind the Chelsea goal in the first half so I didn't get

b) *Here are some ideas for a report on a football match. How can you organize them for your own report?*

- Bristol South against Redcliffe ✓
- first match of year ✓
- first half finished 0–0 ✓
- slow start ✓
- boys' U14 football ✓
- final score: South 1, Redcliffe 0
- at Redcliffe's ground ✓
- 19 October ✓
- second half very fast ✓
- South's Tim Hooley best player, scored the goal ✓
- lots of mistakes by Redcliffe ✓

– You can collect your ideas in a mind map like this:

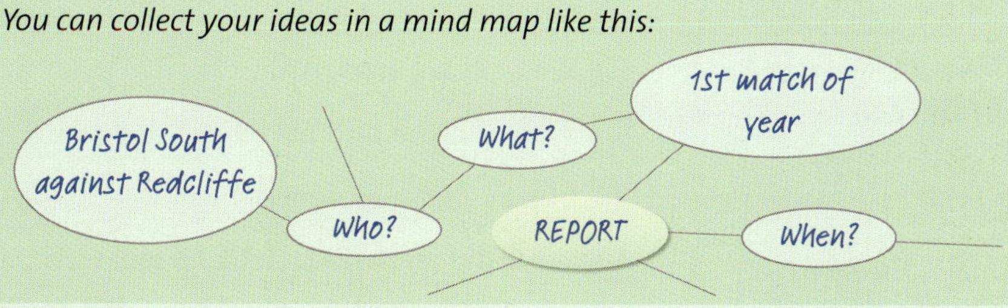

– Or maybe a table works better for you:

Who?	What?	When?	Where?	Why?	How?
		19th Oct			

Use one of the methods to organize the ideas. Add more ideas for a report if you want.

c) *Use your ideas from b) to write a short report (two or three paragraphs) on the match between Bristol South and Redcliffe.*

14 PRONUNCIATION Different stress in English and German words

a) *Copy the German words and the English words into your exercise book. Where is the stress in each word? Underline the stressed vowels.*

Appetit • April • brillant • Kathedrale • Instrument • Programm • Realität • Thermometer
appetite • April • brilliant • cathedral • instrument • programme • reality • thermometer

b) *Listen and check. Were you right?*

c) Extra *Choose five of the English words and write a sentence with each one. Read your sentences to your partner. Listen to your partner's sentences. Correct the pronunciation if necessary.*

15 LISTENING Sports quiz

a) *Listen to the CD and find out the names of the people on the show. Who is winning?*

b) *Listen again and note down as many of the questions and answers as you can. Then check and compare in class.*

c) Extra *Work in groups of five and put together six questions and six follow-up questions for your own sports quiz. Swap your quiz with another group. Decide who is the presenter and who are the teams and play the quiz.*

16 EVERYDAY ENGLISH Talking to people at meals

a) *This is how you can sound friendly when you talk to people:*

- Say 'please' and 'thank you'.
- Use the other person's name now and again.
- Don't answer with just one word.
- Don't just talk about yourself – ask questions too.
- Try and say something nice.

Now listen to the conversation at the Byrds' dinner table on Saturday night. Put the yellow phrases in the right order.
Listen again to check your answers.

A Well, we went to the Lowry.
B Would you like some more potatoes, Anna?
C Yes please, Mrs Byrd.
D Well, please start, Anna.
E What did you and Dad do all day, Mum?
F Mmm, that looks good.
G What did you and Latisha do today, Anna?
H Thank you. Enjoy!
I Thank you, dear.

b) *A foreign visitor is having dinner at Brendan's home. Write a dialogue in which everybody sounds friendly. Then act it out.*

Brendan __ I hope you like sausages, Michael.
Visitor __ I love sausages, thank you.
Brendan __ Well, please start.
Visitor __ ...

Who needs legs?

Partner B: Go to p. 70.
Partner A: Work with this text.

Nathan Stephens was born in a village in Wales on 11 April, 1988. When he was a baby he learned to walk early. 'He took his first steps when he was only ten months old,' says his mother Helen. 'He just got up and walked.'

Even as a little boy Nathan loved sport. At school he played football and rugby and in his free time he learned to ride. He loved animals. 'When I grow up, Mum,' he said, 'I'm going to work with animals.'

For his ninth birthday Nathan asked his parents for a pair of riding boots and a new riding hat. He was really excited when he came down to breakfast on 11 April, 1997, and there they were.

'Thanks, Mum and Dad! They're great!'

After school that day some cousins and friends came to tea. It was a sunny spring day so after tea the boys wanted to go down to the old railway line. There were no trains there any more so it was a favourite place for kids to play.

'Just remember to stay away from the new railway line,' called Nathan's mum as the boys ran into the woods.

Nathan remembers that afternoon. 'It was my ninth birthday. I went out to play with my friends. Our parents always said to us: "Don't go near the new railway line where the trains are" – but boys often do things they aren't allowed to do! Well, I saw this slow goods train. "I'll jump onto it and take a ride," I thought. I jumped, but I fell ... under the train. Both my legs were cut off.'

'A doctor and paramedics were already there when I arrived,' says Nathan's mum. 'I knew that he understood how bad it was because he asked, "Will I have to be in a wheelchair now?"'

'All he said to me as they put him in the ambulance was "Sorry, Mum!".'

Working with the text

1 Who is Nathan Stephens?

a) *Read the text again and take notes on these questions:*
- Where and when was Nathan born?
- What sports did he do as a little boy?
- Where did he play on his ninth birthday?
- What happened there?

b) *Answer your partner's questions about Nathan. Then ask him/her the following questions and take notes:*
- When did Nathan take his second 'first steps'?
- What sports did he do when he was ten?
- When did he win his first athletics medals?
- What are his hopes?

2 Nathan and you

a) *Imagine you're one of Nathan's friends. You keep a diary of your feelings. What did you write in your diary when ...*
- Nathan had the accident?
- he came back to school?
- you watched him at the World Sledge Hockey Championships?

b) *What are you doing next weekend? What would be different if you were in a wheelchair like Nathan?*

► *WB 19 (p. 46)* • **Checkpoint 3** *WB (p. 47)*

Who needs legs?

Partner B: Work with this text.

> Birthday boy Nathan Stephens was fighting for his life yesterday after a two-hour operation. His mother Helen is by his bed where last night he was very, very ill.

That was the report in the *Sunday Mirror*, a national newspaper, on 13 April, 1997. Three months later Nathan took his second 'first steps', this time with artificial legs. And soon after that he was back at school!
'Yes, Nathan has lost his legs, but he's as mad about sport as he was before,' his mum said a few months later. 'He still goes riding. And he plays football at school, as the keeper.'
When he was ten years old Nathan started to play sledge hockey – ice hockey for the disabled. Coaches quickly spotted his talent.

In April 2004, at the age of 16, Nathan was the youngest player at the World Sledge Hockey Championships, where he played for Great Britain. In 2006 he represented Wales at the Melbourne Commonwealth Games and Great Britain at the Winter Paralympics in Turin.
When he was 14 Nathan also began to do athletics in the summer. A year later he won gold medals for javelin, discus and shot put at the Junior British Championships.
The BBC asked Nathan Stephens what his hopes were. Nathan's answer: 'I hope I will be able to take part in the next Summer and Winter Paralympics. I hope we win more medals than last time and that the Paralympics are shown a lot on TV. That will make people more interested in what we do.'

Working with the text

1 Who is Nathan Stephens?

a) *Read the text and take notes on these questions:*
- When did Nathan take his second 'first steps'?
- What sports did he do when he was ten?
- When did he win his first athletics medals?
- What are his hopes?

b) *Ask your partner about Nathan's earlier life and take notes:*
- Where and when was Nathan born?
- What sports did he do as a little boy?
- Where did he play on his ninth birthday?
- What happened there?

Then answer your partner's questions.

2 Nathan and you

a) *Imagine you're one of Nathan's friends. You keep a diary of your feelings. What did you write in your diary when ...*
- Nathan had the accident?
- he came back to school?
- you watched him at the World Sledge Hockey Championships?

b) *What are you doing next weekend? What would be different if you were in a wheelchair like Nathan?*

► *WB 19 (p. 46)* • **Checkpoint 3** *WB (p. 47)*

How am I doing?

a) *Fill in or choose the correct answers.*

Facts from the unit

If you can't remember the answers to these questions, scan for them in the unit.

What's the name of

1 the instrument Latisha plays?
2 a Manchester art museum?
3 Manchester United's famous football stadium?
4 Manchester's twin town?
5 the young sports star who lost his legs when he was nine?

Paraphrasing

6 Paraphrase these words:
A a stadium B a gallery C a prize

Talking to people

7 Two of the most important words that help you to sound friendly are ...
A 'hello' and 'goodbye' B 'yes' and 'no'
C 'please' and 'thank you'
D 'what?' and 'why?'

8 Which of these is not a good idea when you talk to English people?
A Use the people's names now and again.
B Find something nice to say about England.
C Use complete sentences or short answers to answer questions – not just 'yes' or 'no'.
D Talk about yourself and don't ask questions about the other person.

Words

9 Which word doesn't fit?
A pitch B racket C stadium D court

10 Another word for 'fan' is ...
A supporter B score C match
D quay

11 Which word doesn't fit?
A racket B bat C pads D pool

12 Match the sports and the places:
1 tennis 2 ice hockey 3 rugby
4 skiing
A pitch B slope C ice rink D court

13 These places of learning are spelled wrongly. Write them down correctly.
A sumume B loosch C raribly
D regally

Grammar

14 In which of the following sentences can you leave out 'that'?
A Manchester is a city that I'd like to visit.
B Manchester is a city that gets a lot of tourists.

15 Link the sentences with a contact clause.
Latisha is an English girl. Anna stayed with her in Manchester.

16 Who won the game in this sentence?
Manchester United were beaten 2–1 by Arsenal.

17 How could you give the same information with a passive sentence?
The Romans built a fort here in AD 79.

b) *Check your answers on p. 113 and add up your points – one point for each correct answer (so you can get three points for No. 6, four points for No. 12 and four points for No. 13).*

c) *If you had 20 or more points, well done! Do page 49 again and see how much you still know. If you had 19 points or fewer, it's a good idea to do some more work before you go on to the next unit. Where did you make mistakes? The chart below will tell you what you can do to improve your English.*

No.	Area	Find out more	Exercise(s)
1– 5	Facts from the unit	Unit 3 (pp. 54–59, 65)	–
6	Paraphrasing	Unit 3 (p. 57)	P 3–4 (p. 63), WB 5 (p. 38)
7– 8	Talking to people	Unit 3, P 16 (p. 68)	P 16 (p. 68)
9–12	Word field: sports	Unit 3 (p. 56)	P 2, 4 (pp. 62–63), WB 3–4 (pp. 37)
13	Word field: places in town	Unit 3 (p. 58)	–
14–15	Contact clauses	GF 7b (pp. 155–156)	P 4–6 (pp. 63–64), WB 6–8 (pp. 39–40)
16–17	Passive	GF 8 (pp. 156–157)	P 5, 9, 12 (pp. 64–66), WB 11–12 (pp. 41–42)

Growing up in Canada

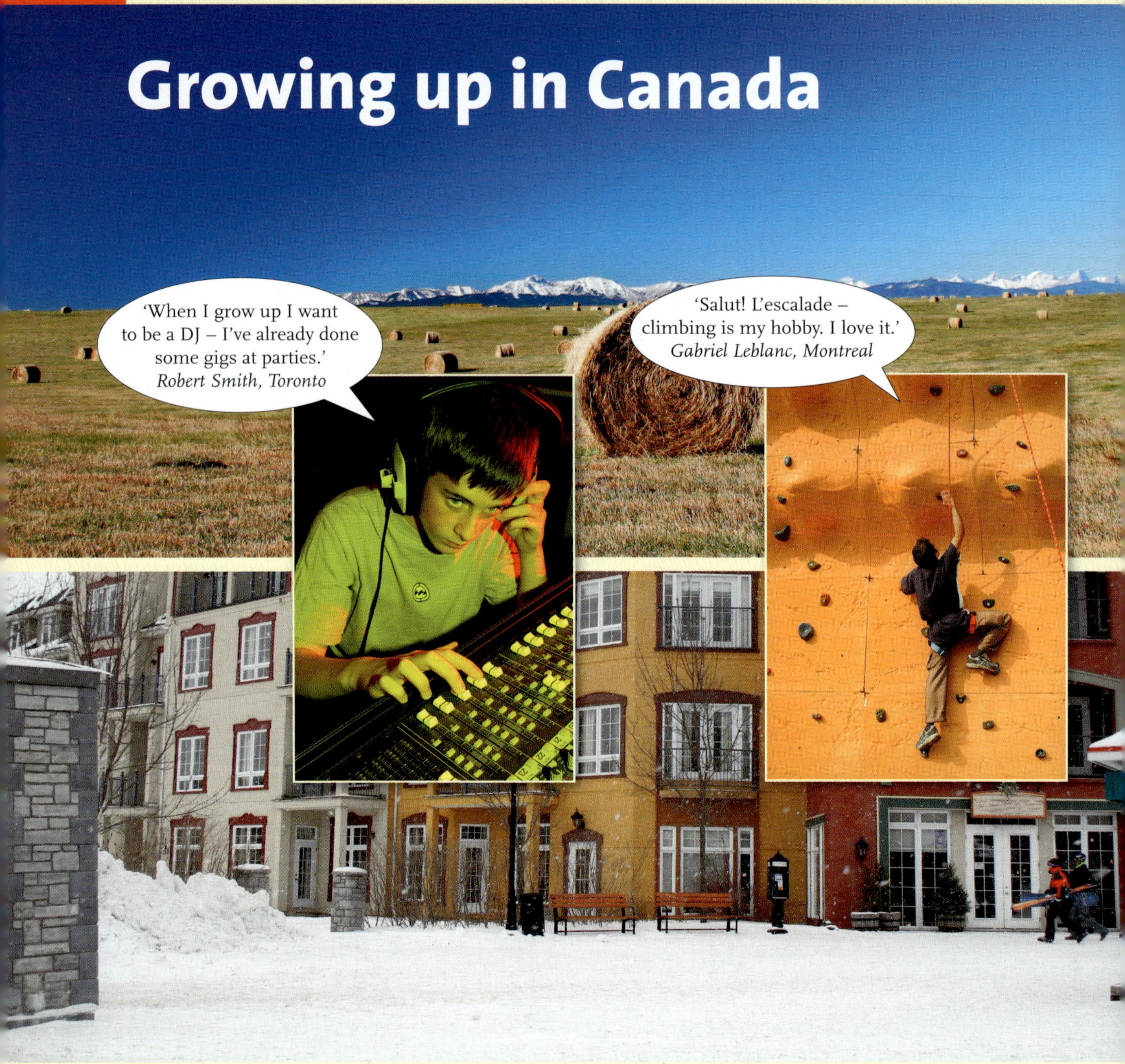

1 Canada

a) What do you know about Canada – language, geography, sports, animals, people, ...?

b) What do the table below and the four big photos tell you about Canada – area, population, weather, scenery, animals, ...?

	Land area	Population
Canada	9,984,670 sq km	33,098,932
Germany	357,021 sq km	82,422,299

	snow	coldest month	hottest month
Toronto	Nov – Mar	Feb (-4 °C)	July (22 °C)
Inuvik	Sep – May	Feb (-24 °C)	July (19 °C)
Berlin	Dec – Feb	Jan (2 °C)	June (23 °C)

2 Growing up in Canada

a) *Look at the smaller photos and statements. How do Canadian kids spend their free time?*

b) *Imagine you live in a country where life is what it 'should be like'. Describe that country: landscape, weather, animals, cities, how people behave, what you can do there, ...*
How is it different to Minnie Neeposh's Canada?

▸ P 1 (p. 80) • WB 1 (p. 48)

All about ... teenagers and adults

1 Different views

a) *What problems are these teenagers and their parents talking about?*

Turn the music down, Robert, please! It's too loud.

It's dance music, Mom. It has to be loud.

Dance music? How can anybody dance to that? It's not music, it's just noise!

Well, I don't like your music either, Mom.

You kids think money grows on trees! You want the latest fashions and cellphones. And you don't care how much it all costs.

I can't wear last year's clothes, Dad. And when my friends see my old cellphone, they just laugh!

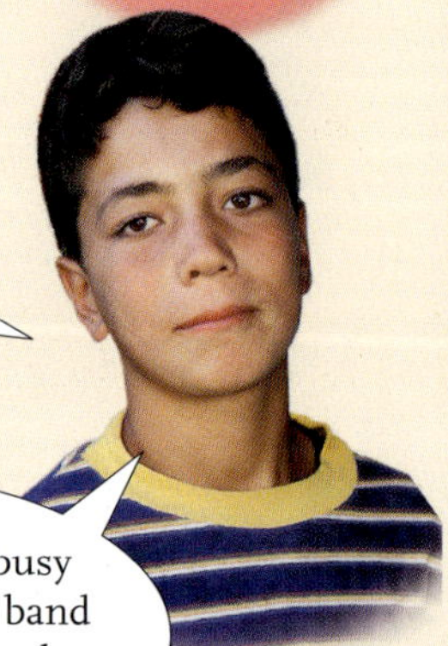

Have you done your homework, Jordan? And tidied your room?

No, not yet, Mom. I'm just texting Jessica.

Oh, Jordan! You're always texting or chatting or just hanging out. You waste so much time like that.

That's not fair, Mom. You know how busy I am after school. Judo, band practice, my volunteer work ... I need to relax sometimes.

b) *Which of these arguments have you had too? What did you say? Why?*

2 Now you

a) *Work in groups of four. Think of something that adults and teenagers argue about. On a piece of paper, write down what the adult might say. Then pass your piece of paper to the person on your left.*

b) *Look at the next piece of paper. Write down how a teenager might answer. Pass it to your left. Go on like this (adult–teenager–adult–...) until you have your piece of paper again.*

c) *With a partner, use the results of a) and b) and write two dialogues. In one dialogue the people just argue, in the other they find a compromise.*

Adult ___ Turn that radio down!
You ___ But it's a really good song!
Adult ___ But it's too loud.
You ___ I'll close the door, OK?
Adult ___ Thank you.

d) **Extra** *Act out your dialogues for the class.*

▸ **Text File 8** *(p. 124)* • *WB 2–3 (p. 49)*

3 Party presents

After school on Wednesday, Robert went to the local mall. He wanted to get a present for Ashley. She was having a birthday party on Friday evening. And he had planned to meet his friend Sam there too.

After he had walked up and down the mall, he went into the CD store. He had only been in there for a few minutes when Sam came in.

'Hey, Bobby. I knew I'd find you in here,' Sam said. 'Great lyrics'.

'Hey, Sam. Look at this.' Robert had just found a DVD and he showed it to his friend. 'What do you think? As a present for Ashley?'

'Sure. Everyone likes Nickelback, don't they?' Sam replied. 'Great lyrics.'

'My mom doesn't!' said Robert. He started to play air guitar and sing: 'If everyone cared ...'

Sam joined in: '... and nobody cried.'

Then Robert imitated his mum. 'Turn that noise off, Robert!' They both started to laugh.

'What are you getting Ashley?' Robert asked after they had left the shop. He was surprised by Sam's answer.

'Nothing,' Sam said. 'I can't go to the party.'

'But Sam, I'm DJing. You have to come.'

'Sorry. I can't. My uncle's coming from Ottawa. And you know how strict my parents are about family stuff.'

'What a bummer!' Robert said.

'Yeah. Oh, well. But there's something else I wanted to ask you about, Robert ...'

> *Why won't Sam be at the party? What does Robert think of that?*

Looking at language

a) *Look at this sentence from* ***3****:*
After he had walked up and down the mall, he went into the CD store.

What happened first, what second?

b) *Look for more examples of the new verb form that shows what happened first in* ***3****.*
How do you form it?

► *GF 9: Past perfect (p. 158) • GF 10: Talking about the past (p. 159)*

4 Dragon boat crew

a) *Look at the photo of a dragon boat race, then listen to Sam and Robert's conversation. What does Sam want to ask Robert?*

b) *Complete the statements below. Then listen again and check your answers.*

1 A dragon boat is a big ... that ... people paddle.
2 ... brought the dragon boats to Canada.
3 There are ... dragon boaters in Toronto.
4 Sam has to join the dragon boat crew because ...
5 Robert ... join the crew because ...

► *P 2–5 (pp. 80–81) • WB 4–7 (pp. 50–51)*

5 At Ashley's party

Robert Happy birthday, Ashley!
Ashley Thanks, Robert. Come in.
Robert Here's something for you. I hope you haven't already got it.
Ashley Oh, thanks. I love Nickelback!

Robert Great party, Ashley! Who's the girl with Jordan?
Ashley Her name's Jessica. She lives on his street.
Robert Where's Emily?
Ashley I don't know. She's not here.
Robert Not here? But Em and Jordan are still dating, aren't they?
Ashley I'm not sure. And I don't care anyway.
Robert Well, I care! I'll call Emily later and find out all about it.
Ashley You do that. What I care about is when you're going to play some music.
Robert How about right now? I can set up my computer and start straightaway.

Robert Hi, everybody. DJ Bobby here. I've got a mix of Canadian singers and groups for you this evening. The first is a slow song but it's great to dance to, so let's see you all on the dance floor. Here's Nickelback and 'If everyone cared'.

► P 6–7 (p. 82)

Explain why Robert plays the song 'If everyone cared'.

6 Dragon boat training

When Sam was in the dragon boat, he felt very nervous. Unlike Robert, he had never paddled a boat before. His uncle was speaking and Sam listened carefully.

What's the most important thing for a dragon boater to remember?

7 On the phone

On Saturday morning, Robert and his parents were going to their cabin near Ontario's Algonquin Park, about 200 km north of Toronto. Before they left, Robert called Sam.

Sam Hey, Robert. How was the party? Did Ashley like your present?
Robert Yes, she did. She said she loved Nickelback.
Sam Everyone does. Who else was there?
Robert Oh, the usual guys: Jordan ...
Sam Yeah. And Emily?
Robert No, Emily wasn't there. Jordan brought a different girl to the party.
Sam No way!
Robert Yes, her name's Jessica. Ashley said she lived on Jordan's street.
Sam So is she his new girlfriend?
Robert Maybe. Ashley said she wasn't sure and she didn't care anyway.
Sam Wow, that Ashley is one tough girl.
Robert Yeah, so I told her I would call Emily and find out all about it.
Sam So did you?
Robert No, I forgot all about it.
Sam Aha! So you didn't really care either. And how was the famous DJ Bobby?
Robert Great. Ashley said it was the best music she had ever danced to. A pity you couldn't be there. How was dragon boat training?
Sam It was fun. But, boy, it's hard work!
Robert Did you go out in a boat?
Sam Sure. There were about 15 of us in the boat and my uncle was talking all the time. First he said we didn't have to watch where we were going. That was his job. He said he would steer the boat.
Robert Wow! So you don't even see where you're going?
Sam No. He told us that all we had to do was watch the paddler in front of us. And paddle when he paddled.
Robert Sounds easy. Say, Sam, we're leaving soon. So, I'll call you when we're back.
Sam OK. And practise your paddling. You're going to need it.

Looking at language

a) *Robert and Sam are talking about what people said at the party and at dragon boat training. Find examples of this indirect speech in* ***7****.*
She said she loved Nickelback.
Ashley said ...

What is the tense of the reporting verbs (say, tell)?

b) *Now find what the people really said in* ***5*** *and* ***6*** *on p. 76, their direct speech.*
Ashley: I love Nickelback.
Ashley: She lives ...

Compare the sentences in a) and b). What happens to the tenses in indirect speech?

c) *Look at this example of indirect speech from* ***7****:*
Ashley said it was the best music she had ever danced to.

What were Ashley's words?

What did you find out in 7 about the party that you didn't know before?

8 ACTIVITY More reports

a) *Look at the last three speech bubbles in 6 (p. 76). How could Sam report them to Robert?*
Sam's uncle: We have to get the rhythm right.
We ...
My uncle said we had to get the rhythm right.
He told us that we had to ...
...

b) *Write down three more things people maybe said at the party. Swap with a partner and report his/her sentences.*
Ashley: Robert's a great DJ.
Ashley said Robert was a great DJ.

► *GF 11: Indirect speech (p. 160) • P 8–15 (pp. 83–86) • WB 8–16 (pp. 52–56)*

Extra Background File **CANADA**

	Canada	Germany
Head of state	British King or Queen	President
Capital	Ottawa	Berlin
Biggest city	Toronto (2,481,494)	Berlin (3,399,511)
Official language	English and French	German
Number of time zones	6	1

Aboriginal people in Canada

Aboriginal people – the Inuit, the First Nations (as the Indians of Canada are usually called) and the Métis – have lived in Canada for many thousands of years. Now only about 4.4% of the Canadian population are Aboriginals.

Aboriginals have tried to get many of their traditional lands back. In 1999 the Inuit were successful and Nunavut was founded. Nunavut means 'Our land' in the Inuit language. It is as big as Western Europe but only 30,000 people live there. Many First Nations live on reserves all across Canada.

Canadian settlers

The first Europeans who visited Canada were the Vikings, around the year 1000.

Later, in 1497, John Cabot left Bristol, crossed the Atlantic and landed in Newfoundland on the east coast of Canada.

In the 16th century the first French settlers in Canada lived near a mountain they called Mont Réal. Canada became a French colony, New France. In 1608 they founded the city of Québec. But in 1763 France lost Canada to the British.

Today, most people in Quebec speak French, the official language of the province, and Mont Réal has become Montréal, Canada's second biggest city.

Immigration to Canada

Most people in Canada are still of French or British descent, but people from many other parts of the world have also come to live there. Today the country really is a multicultural place. Vancouver, for example, is sometimes called 'Hongcouver' or 'Vankong' because of all the Chinese immigrants. In Toronto, 40 % of the people now belong to an ethnic minority and emergency calls can be made in 80 languages.

Canadian sports

Canadian First Nations invented the game of **lacrosse** hundreds of years ago. Today it is Canada's national summer sport.

The players have to get a small ball into a goal with the crosse – a stick with a net.

This very fast team sport is played all over North America and in Britain.

Ice hockey is Canada's national winter sport – Canadians just call it 'hockey'. Toronto's team – the Maple Leafs – plays in the American National Hockey League (NHL). In the cold winters, lots of people play hockey outside.

Two great Canadians

Margaret Atwood, born 1939, is sometimes called the greatest novelist of our times. Her complex but often funny novels are international bestsellers. Atwood is also a famous poet, critic and human rights activist.

Frederick Banting, 1891–1941, is known as the man who discovered insulin and brought hope to diabetics all over the world. His research in the early 1920s earned him Canada's first ever Nobel Prize.

▸ *WB 17 (p. 57)* • **Text File 9** *(p. 128)*

1 Interesting Canada

What do you find most interesting on these two pages? Why?

It was interesting to read that ... I thought Canada was ... / I didn't know Canada was ...

2 Your Canada

Choose one of these topics or another Canadian topic and find out more about it.

Produce a page about it (with pictures) and display it in class. Put it in your DOSSIER later.

1 WORDS Numbers

a) *Partner B: Go to p. 111.*
Partner A: Read out these numbers and dates to your partner:

17 • 76 • 104 • 1,516 • 100,000 • 21 January, 2010 • 6 June, 1999

Then write down the numbers and dates that your partner reads out to you.
Swap pieces of paper and check.

b) *Fill in the gaps with words and phrases from the box.*

million • 10-kilometre walk • twenty +per cent (20%) • 150 +kilograms • six point seven (6.7) • +thirteen-year-olds • +50 km per hour (kph)

1 The population of Canada is about 33 ...
2 The +speed limit in Canadian cities is ...
3 He took a ... in a Canadian park.
4 The bears in the Canadian woods can +weigh ...
5 Many ... in Toronto are untidy, just like everywhere.
6 French is the first language for ... million Canadians. That's about ... of the population.

2 REVISION Sam, a song and dragon boats (Passive)

a) *Use the words and write passive sentences.*

1 Sam – invite – Ashley's party
Sam was invited to Ashley's party.
2 Nickelback's songs – often hear – on Canadian radio
3 The video of their song 'If everyone cared' – make – in 2006
4 Dragon boats – bring – to Canada – the Chinese
5 Sam – take to dragon boat training – his uncle

b) *Put the verbs into the correct form of the simple past – active or passive.*

When a dragon boat (steal), (cut) in half, and one of its pieces (take), nobody (can) understand why somebody (want) half a boat. Now we know.
The missing half of the boat (find) by police at a motel in Maple Ridge on Wednesday.
It (paint) black and a man was trying to put a motor in it.
The man (tell) police: 'I (find) the boat.'

3 REVISION At my last party ... (Simple past)

a) *Copy and complete these sentences: What did and didn't you do?*

At my last party I ... I didn't ...	**When I was four** I ... I didn't ...
In my holidays I ... I didn't ...	**Two years ago** I ... I didn't ...

b) *How many people can you find in the class who did or didn't do the same things as you? Ask and find out:*

– Did you have a pizza at your last party?
– No, I didn't. Did you speak English at your last party?
– ...

c) *Your teacher is going to give you a dictation. Only write down the first and last letters of the words you hear.*

d) *With a partner, try to write out the dictation in correct English. Then check with your teacher.*

4 At the river (Past perfect)

a) *When Jack came home from a day at the river, he had done a lot of different things. Look at the pictures and use the past perfect to say what he had done.*

1 take some photos

2 sleep in the sun

3 finish his book

4 eat a sandwich

5 speak to a fisherman

6 catch a fish

7 swim in the river

8 make a fire

1 *When Jack came home, he had taken some photos.*
2 *When Jack came home, he had ...*
3 ...

b) *In what order do you think Jack did these things? Write it down like this:*
After Jack had taken some photos, he slept in the sun. After he had slept in the sun, he ...

5 When I was a kid (Simple past and past perfect)

David Simmons, a 70-year-old Canadian teacher, remembers his childhood. Put in the correct forms of the simple past or past perfect. Be careful – there is one passive form.

I ... (grow up) in a little village on Cape Breton Island. We often ... (go) to the beach after a storm to see what the sea ... (leave) there. There ... (be) parts of boats, dead fish and empty bottles. One day after a really big storm, I ... (find) one of these bottles – and it ... (have) a little piece of paper in it! I ... (be) very excited but I ...(not know) how to open the bottle.

I ... (take) the bottle home and after my father ... (come in), he ... (help) me to open it. It ... (be) hard to read the letter at the beginning, but after we ... (work) on it for half an hour, we ... (see) what it ... (be) – a love letter!

It ... (look) very old and it ... (write) beautifully by a man called John Peters. We ... (look) in the telephone book and ... (find) a man with that name on the island! We ... (call) his number and a woman ... (answer) the phone.

'Yes,' she ... (say) after my dad ... (tell) her about the letter in the bottle, 'John Peters is my husband! He ... (send) so many of those letters in bottles. After I ... (find) 25 of them, I ... (agree) to marry him. That was 35 years ago!'

6 Extra Listening to songs

a) *If you know the title of a song, it will often help you to understand it better. Look at the titles of these songs by Nickelback. What do you think they could be about?*

– PHOTOGRAPH	– HOW YOU REMIND ME
– FAR AWAY	– WHERE DO I HIDE?
– TOO BAD	– IF EVERYONE CARED

b) *If you can read the lyrics of a song, it will also be easier to understand. You can often find the lyrics on the CD cover or on the internet.*
Here are some of the lyrics of 'If everyone cared'. Read them and imagine the landscape the lovers are in and try to draw it.

If everyone cared

From underneath the trees, we watch the sky
Confusing stars for satellites
I never dreamed that you'd be mine
But here we are, we're here tonight

Singing Amen, I, I'm alive
Singing Amen, I, I'm alive

If everyone cared and nobody cried
If everyone loved and nobody lied
If everyone shared and swallowed their pride
Then we'd see the day when nobody died
...

And as we lie beneath the stars
We realize how small we are
If they could love like you and me
Imagine what the world could be

Chad Kroeger

c) *Now listen to the song.*
The chorus is often the most important part of a song. Which part of 'If everyone cared' is the chorus? How does the singer think we can change the world?

7 Extra Talking about songs

a) *Make notes on your favourite song: what kind of music is it? What do you know about the singer/group? Why do you like the song?*

b) *Make appointments with three other students. Meet them at their appointment times and tell them about your song. Listen to what they say about their songs.*

c) *Use your notes to prepare a DJ's introduction to the song. Bring your song to school and present it.*
- This song is rap/pop/rock/folk/...
- a nice/relaxing/an aggressive/... sound/ rhythm
- easy to listen to
- I always think of ... when I hear this song.
- The group/singer is Canadian/from ...
- great lyrics
- ...

8 EVERYDAY ENGLISH Teenager talk

***a)** Find English phrases that mean:*

1 als DJ auftreten (p. 75)
2 sehr interessiert an (p. 73)
3 eine SMS schicken (p. 74)
4 Schade! (p. 75)
5 einen Freund/eine Freundin haben (p. 76)
6 die üblichen Leute (p. 77)
7 Mensch!/Mann! (p. 77)

***b)** Complete the dialogue with phrases from a).*

A: Hey! I've got my first ... as a ... next weekend.
B: Are you playing any Asian fusion stuff? I'm ... that sort of music.
A: No, I'm doing it for my aunt and uncle. They want oldies.
B: ...! When is it?
A: Not sure yet. I'll ... you the place and time.

9 At the party (Indirect speech)

Report what Robert told people at the party.

Robert said Sam wasn't there. He was ...
He told them that Sam's uncle ...

10 What did he say? (Indirect speech)

Owen has been to Toronto to visit his grandparents. Back home in Winnipeg, he tells his mum about his trip. How does she report to her husband that evening what Owen has said?
Use reporting verbs in the simple past: **said**, **told**, ...

1 'I really enjoyed my visit.'
2 'I love Grandma's chocolate cake.'
3 'I'm reading one of Grandma's books.'
4 'We watched a hockey game.'
5 'The people in Toronto aren't very friendly.'
6 'They're much friendlier here in Winnipeg.'
7 'Grandpa didn't go to work and showed me the city.'
8 'We ate at a nice restaurant on my last evening.'
9 'The restaurant has a view over the lake.'
10 'I'll call them to say thank you tonight.'

11 All about you (Indirect speech)

a) ***Think*** *about these four questions and then write down your answers to them on a piece of paper.*

1 What was the last song that you sang?
2 What is the best film you have seen in the last three months?
3 What city will you live in when you're 25?
4 Who is your hero?

1 The last song I sang was 'Happy birthday'.
2 The best film I've seen is 'Spiderman'.
3 When I'm 25 I'll live in Vienna.
4 My hero is my big sister.

b) ***Pair:*** *Swap your answers with a partner. Look at your partner's answers and try to remember them.*

c) ***Share*** *your partner's answers with the class. Report what you can remember. Check if you're right.*

d) **Extra** *Find out why or when your classmates did what.*

– Why did you sing 'Happy birthday'?
– Because it was my mum's birthday.

Melissa said that the last song she had sung was 'Happy birthday'.

Then she said that the best film she had seen in the last three months was 'Titanic'. Is that right?

No, I said that the best film I had seen in the last three months was 'Spiderman'.

12 Stanley Park, Vancouver (Indirect speech)

Often when you report what someone said, you don't remember the exact words. So you just report the gist. Match the statements on the left to how they are reported on the right. Maybe you want to look up words you don't know in a dictionary.

a) Stanley Park is very close to downtown Vancouver.
b) There aren't many bigger parks in any city in North America.
c) You can walk round the place on foot but there are free buses too. They go to all the places you need to see.
d) One place you can't miss is the Aquarium.
e) There are animals from all over the world in the Aquarium, but I don't think they have any orcas.
f) The water is warm enough for swimming at the park's beaches in the summer.
g) The park is full of wildlife. You'll probably see raccoons, squirrels, geese, swans and ducks.
h) They even have some old Indian totem poles there.

Totem poles in Stanley Park, Vancouver

1 She said that we had to go to the Aquarium.
2 She said the park wasn't far from the city centre.
3 She told us that Stanley Park was one of the biggest city parks in North America.
4 She didn't think there were any orcas in the Aquarium.
5 She told us we could swim in the sea in summer.
6 She said we could see real totem poles there.
7 She told us that the free buses would take us to all the sights.
8 She thought we'd see lots of birds and animals.

13 WRITING The steps of writing (Telling a story)

a) *If you want to write a good, interesting or exciting story, for example about a strange event, you should follow these three steps:*

1 Prewriting
Before you write, brainstorm your ideas.

▸ *Writing course 3: Collecting and organizing ideas (p. 67)*

2 Writing
Your story should have these parts:
- **Beginning**
Try to make the beginning interesting, exciting, funny, so that people want to read on.
- **Middle**
Use adjectives and adverbs to make the story more interesting.
Use time and place phrases and linking words to make things clear.
Relative clauses or passive sentences might improve your style.
Start a new paragraph for each new idea.
- **Ending**
Try and find an interesting or funny way to finish your story and give it a title.

b) *On the right is part of the middle of a story. Find examples of the tips in Step 2 in it.*

▸ *Writing course 1: Writing better sentences (p. 24)* • *Writing course 2: Using paragraphs (p. 39)*

3 Revising
Read your story, check it and correct it:
– Is everything in the right order?
– Do you need more details?
– Is your story clear?
– Check the spelling, verbs, grammar, ...
Swap and check your partner's work.

c) **Extra** *Follow the steps and write a beginning and ending for the story about the strange boy in High Park. Start like this:*
You're not going to believe me, but this ...

d) *Write your own story about a strange event.*

STUDY SKILLS Brainstorming

You **brainstorm** a topic in two steps:
1 Write down every idea that comes into your head. Don't worry if they seem crazy at first.
2 Look at your ideas. Choose the ones you want to use and structure them in a mind map, or a chart with the 5 Ws and 'How', ...

▸ *SF Brainstorming (p. 145)*

'Look at that guy,' Jessica said to Emily on their day out in High Park. 'He's weird!'

The 'guy' was the strangest boy the two girls had ever seen. He looked about 14 years old but he was wearing an old man's clothes. He was standing in the middle of High Park with his mouth wide open as if he couldn't believe his eyes.

The two girls watched him for a few minutes and then began to walk away. Suddenly the boy turned his head and looked at them with scared eyes. 'Where am I?' he asked sadly. 'Where is this place?'

The girls were shocked by the fear in his voice.

Jessica told him he was in High Park. The boy just shook his head slowly.

'High Park ... Toronto ... Ontario ... Canada,' Emily explained.

14 LISTENING Crow brings daylight (An Inuit legend)

a) Do you know what these words or phrases mean? Check in a dictionary if you don't.

+chief • +crow • +daylight • +float • +speck of dust • +string

b) Before you listen to the legend, think about why daylight might be important to the Inuit.

c) Listen for the first time. Were your ideas right or wrong? Say in one sentence what the legend is about.

d) Before you listen for a second time, look at the questions below. Take notes to help you while you listen – remember: key words, not sentences.

1 What was the Inuit's world like when the world was young?
2 Who told them about daylight?
3 How did Crow get into the chief's house?
4 How did he get the ball of daylight?
5 Why is there half a year of daylight and half a year of darkness where the Inuit live?

e) Check your answers with a partner.

*f) **Extra** Do you know a legend? Tell it to the class.*

15 MEDIATION At Algonquin Park

a) Lisa, her little brother and her mother are at the Algonquin Park visitor centre. Her mother waits outside with her noisy little brother while Lisa goes in to get some information her mother wants.

Lisas Mutter will wissen
- wo man gut Elche sehen kann,
- ob es einen schönen Wanderweg in der Nähe gibt,
- ob man hier eine Taschenlampe kaufen kann, weil sie ihre im Hotel vergessen hat.

Imagine you're Lisa and explain what your mother wants to know.

Lisa ____ Excuse me, we're looking for ...

b) Now listen to the whole of Lisa's conversation. In the gaps, ask the assistant for the information her mother wants. Compare your answers with the ones on the CD.

c) Listen again. Take notes on the assistant's answers and explain them to Lisa's mother in German. Then listen and check.

STUDY SKILLS Mediation

If you don't know the English for a word you want to use, try to paraphrase it.

It's somebody/a person who ...
an animal/something that ...
something you use to ...
a place where ...

Try to paraphrase: Elch, Wanderweg, Taschenlampe

▸ *SF Mediation (p. 143)*

A fishing trip

Look at the pictures. Who are the people in them? Try and guess the right order of the pictures. How do you think the story will end? Now listen and check.

A

B

C

D

E

F

Working with the text

1 Your ideas about the story

Compare your ideas with the story. What is similar, what is different?

2 What's right?

Choose the correct answers (only one is correct).

1 Robert doesn't like the cabin
- A because they always have hot chocolate.
- B because there's no TV or internet.
- C because they have to paint the kitchen.

2 Robert and Mr Smith are getting up early
- A to go on a fishing trip.
- B to paint the kitchen.
- C to walk to the old bridge.

3 At the river, a man tells Robert and his dad
- A that there aren't many tourists at the campgrounds.
- B that there's a problem bear in the area.
- C that the rangers are feeding the bear.

4 This year the river is
- A slower.
- B colder.
- C higher.

5 The first fish is caught by
- A Mr Smith.
- B Robert.
- C the man at the river.

6 At the first rapids
- A they both fall into the water.
- B Mr Smith falls into the water.
- C Robert falls into the water.

7 In the rapids, Mr Smith hurts his
- A arm.
- B hand.
- C foot.

8 After the second rapids, they see
- A a deer.
- B a fish.
- C a bear.

9 When they go past the bear, Robert
- A paddles the canoe.
- B talks to the bear.
- C throws a fish at the bear.

10 Mr Smith
- A throws a fish to the bank.
- B talks to Robert.
- C paddles the canoe.

11 When they get to the old bridge
- A they phone Mrs Smith.
- B they see the bear again.
- C they eat their fish.

12 When Mrs Smith arrives, the bear
- A attacks Robert and his dad.
- B attacks the car.
- C runs away.

3 Extra Robert's story

Imagine you're Robert. When you get back to school after your weekend at the cabin, you have to write a story about your fishing trip. Look again at page 85 (Writing course) for help. Use the pictures on page 87 to make notes.
You can start like this:

At the weekend, my dad and I went on a fishing trip along a river near our cabin. After Mom had taken us to the river very early, we met ...

Put your story in your DOSSIER.

► *WB 18 (p. 58)* • **Checkpoint 4** *WB (p. 59)* • *WB* **Selbsteinschätzung 3–4** *(pp. 62–63)*

What the... MOM! This isn't deer! It's a yucky tourist again!!

How am I doing?

a) *Fill in or choose the correct answers.*

Canada

1 Canada is much ... than Germany, but it doesn't have ... people.
2 Name two outdoor activities in Canada, two Canadian cities, two Canadian singers, two parks in Canada, and a large wild animal you can see in Canada.
3 How many people take part in dragon boat races in Toronto?

Words

4 Most people want to wear the ... fashions.
A later B latest C last D late
5 I love that song. The music is good, but what I really like are the ...
A lyrics B texts C books D pages
6 If you text someone, they'll get your message
A in a letter. B on their computer.
C on their mobile.
7 If your parents won't let you do everything you want, they are
A strange B strict C strong
8 What do you call the people who work on a boat or a plane?
9 You drive a car, you ... a bike, you ... a canoe.
10 Fast water in a river is called ...
11 What's the British English for these American expressions?
A mom B cellphone C elevator

Writing

12 Every story needs three parts: a ..., a ... and an ...
13 Two ways to write down your ideas from brainstorming are a ... and a chart with the five ...
14 To make your sentences better you can add ...
15 After you have written a story you should ... it.

Grammar

16 Choose the correct answer for the gaps:
Robert ... (had been/was) in the shop for five minutes when Sam ... (came/had come) in.
17 In these sentences, what happened first and what happened second?
A Before he came to Canada, Sam's uncle had been a dragon boat coach in China.
B He had lived in Toronto for years when he got a job in Ottawa.
18 Report what these people said. Use a reporting verb (say, tell, ...) in the simple past and indirect speech:
A Robert: I met Jordan's new girlfriend at the party. B Sam: Dragon boat training is hard work. C Sam's uncle: You'll do well if you train hard. D Mr Smith: My foot is broken. I can't stand on it. E Mrs Smith: That bear will be hungry tonight.

b) *Check your answers on p. 114 and add up your points.*

c) *If you had 31 or more points, well done! Do page 49 again and see how much you still know. If you had 30 points or fewer, it's a good idea to do some more work before you go on to the next unit. Where did you make mistakes? The chart below will tell you what you can do to improve your English.*

No.	Area	Find out more	Exercise(s)
1– 3	Canada facts	Unit 4 (pp. 72–77, 84, 86)	WB 1–2 (pp. 48–49)
4–11	Words	Vocabulary Unit 4	WB 3 (p. 49), 11 (p. 53)
12–15	Writing	P 13 (p. 85)	WB 12 (p. 77)
16–17	Past perfect	GF 9 (p. 158)	P 4–5 (p. 81), WB 5–6 (pp. 50–51)
18	Indirect speech	GF 11 (p. 160)	P 9–12 (pp. 83–84), WB 8–10 (pp. 52–53)

1 STUDY SKILLS Understanding new words

▸ *SF Understanding new words (p. 134)*

If you read or hear a new word in a test, you can try and guess the meaning.
What do the green words mean?

1. North Rhine-Westphalia and Saxony are two of Germany's 16 states.
2. Beer is a traditional German product. Almost every part of Germany produces beer.
3. It's important to pack glasses and other breakable goods carefully.
4. Coconuts grow on some kinds of palm trees.
5. Greenpeace is an organization that tries to protect whales and other animals.
6. Recycling is easy: just take your old glass to the bottle bank.
7. It was a terrible storm. Almost everybody on the ship was seasick.
8. In this factory robots do all the work.

2 Spelling (Same sound, different words)

Different words sometimes sound the same. Be careful when you write them. It's easy to make mistakes.

Fill in the missing words

1. **hour, our** ['aʊə]
   The train was late. I waited for over an ...
   Is that ... train on platform 3?
2. **son, sun** [sʌn]
   The Browns have a ... and a daughter.
   They both wear hats when the ... shines.
3. **their, there** [ðeə]
   Who's ... ? – Oh, it's Malte and Hauke.
   They've got ... new bikes with them.
4. **know, no** [nəʊ]
   Do you ... our new teacher, Mrs Sprengel?
   ... , I haven't met her yet.
5. **hear, here** [hɪə]
   There are lots of birds ... in the forest.
   Can you ... the woodpecker?
6. **sea, see** [siː]
   We stayed in a caravan near the ...
   You could ... the beach from there.
7. **wear, where** [weə]
   ... is my new dress?
   I'd like to ... it at Matt's party.
8. **weak, week** [wiːk]
   This tea is too strong. I only drink ... tea.
   We spent a day in London and a ... at the coast.

3 Writing (The *5 Ws* and *How?*)

When you write a report, think about ***what***, ***when***, ***where***, ***who*** *and* ***why***. *Often it's also important to say* ***how***. *Complete the text on the right with phrases from the box. What kind of information do the different phrases give you?*

> Mum and Dad, Alex – my sister – and I • we went by bus • on a Sunday • our visit to the zoo • it was my little sister's birthday • only three miles from our house

1) our visit to the zoo = what
2) ...

▸ *Writing course 3 (p. 67)*

A great day in the school holidays

The best thing about my school holidays was ... (1). We don't often go there, because it's so expensive. But ... (2), so Dad asked her where she wanted to go, and she chose the zoo. Dad said that the whole family could go: ... (3).
I couldn't wait, but at last the day came. We went ... (4) because Dad didn't have to work.
I wanted to cycle because the zoo is ... (5), but Mum said it was too far, so ... (6).
When we arrived, we went to see the snakes first. After that it was the elephants, giraffes, lions and tigers. It took all day to see all the animals, but we enjoyed every minute of it.

4 Ashley's visit to Niagara Falls (Word order)

Remember that English word order is often different from German word order. Choose the right place in the sentences for the words in brackets.

1 Ashley and her dad went ... to Niagara Falls ... (last June)
... went to Niagara Falls last June.
2 Their bus left Toronto at six am, so they had ... to get up ... (very early)
3 And they almost missed the bus because Ashley ... her rucksack ... (forgot)
4 She hurried back to the house ... the rucksack... (to get)
5 When they got to Niagara, ... they ... the amazing falling waters. (watched)
6 They had ... lunch at one of the many restaurants ... (at 12.45)
7 Ashley's dad wanted ... to go for a walk ... after lunch. (in Victoria Park)
8 Everything was so interesting that Ashley wanted ... to stay there ... (all weekend)

5 I've always dreamed of ... (Prepositions)

Complete the sentences with the correct prepositions.

1 I have always dreamed ... a holiday in Canada. (from/of) *of*
2 There's something special ... Toronto – it's a fantastic city. (about/on)
3 I was really interested ... the railway museum. (for/in)
4 All the information was ... English. (in/of)
5 I had to translate it ... German. (in/into)
6 We listened to the weather report ... the radio. (in/on)
7 There wasn't a cloud ... the sky. (in/on)
8 There were lots of cars ... the city centre. (in/on)
9 Our friends had warned us ... the traffic. (about/for)
10 It was quicker to go ... foot than to go ... car. (on/to, by/with)
11 I was tired, so I slept ... the train. (in/on)
12 We left early ... the morning and arrived late ... night. (in/on, at/in)

6 If we go to Toronto ... (Conditional sentences 1 and 2)

a) *You're on holiday in Canada. You're planning a day trip to Toronto with a friend. Complete the conditional sentences (type 1).*

1 If we go to Toronto, we ... a good time. (have)
... we'll have ...
2 If we leave early, we ... more time in Toronto. (have)
3 We won't be able to explore the city, if we ... a good map. (not have)
4 If we take sandwiches with us, we ... them in a park. (can eat)
5 We ... something inside if it rains while we're there. (have to do)
6 If we check on the internet, we ... when the museums close. (find out)

b) *Tom's sister Susan thinks it would be better to take a day trip to Ottawa. Tom doesn't agree. Complete the conditional sentences (type 2).*

7 Tom: if we went to Ottawa, the journey ... much longer. (take)
... would take ...
8 Susan: You ... lots of time if you left early enough. (have)
9 Susan: And if you ... at a youth hostel, you could have a second day in Ottawa. (stay)
10 Tom: The trip ... more if you spent the night in Ottawa. (cost)
11 Susan: If you ... to Ottawa, you'd see the parliament building. (go)
12 Tom: But if we ... to Toronto, we wouldn't see the famous CN Tower! (not go)

► *WB Getting ready for a test 2 (pp. 60–61)*

1 Listening

A visit to Green Gables

Michael, a student, is working as a tour guide[1] on Prince Edward Island, Canada, during the summer. He's taking a tour group to Green Gables today.

Part 1:
The journey to Green Gables

Listen. Choose the correct answer for each question.

1 Lucy Maud Montgomery ...
A is a singer at a festival.
B wrote books for children.
C helped a young girl without parents.

2 Anne of Green Gables ...
A is the hero of a successful children's book.
B is a Canadian writer.
C comes from Ottawa.

3 Linda ...
A is a girl who has lost her parents.
B works as a bus tour guide.
C knows a lot about Anne of Green Gables.

4 Green Gables is ...
A the house where Linda lives.
B a place for children without parents.
C a farmhouse with a link to a famous book.

Part 2:
Lucy Maud Montgomery

a) *Read all the questions. Then listen and make notes about the dates and numbers you hear. Choose the correct answer for each question.*

1 Lucy Maud Montgomery was born in ...
A 1847.
B 1874.
C 1908.

2 You can find Montgomery's books in ...
A more than 50 languages.
B more than 20 languages.
C more than twelve languages.

3 Every year 'Green Gables' has ...
A 200,000 visitors.
B 2,200 visitors.
C 6,000 visitors.

b) *Are these statements true or false? Give a reason for your answer.*
1 'Montgomery left Prince Edward Island because she hated it.'
2 'Montgomery's books are important for people who have never been to Canada.'

I think statement 1 is true/false because ...

[1] tour guide [gaɪd] *Reiseleiter/in*

2 Reading

St. Jacobs Farmers' Market

Thurs. and Sat. 7 am to 3.30 pm. Fresh, healthy food. Great atmosphere. Mennonite farmers travel to market by horse and buggy to sell their vegetables, sausage and maple syrup.

Discover St. Jacobs

Explore St. Jacobs on foot with our new walking tour brochure. On sale at the Visitor Centre: **$2**

The Mennonite Farm Tour

On market days only. The 1 hour 15 min. tour starts and ends at the Farmers' Market. Travel in a horse-drawn trolley, see the farms at work and enjoy the country. ***Adults* $15**. ***Children* $7.50**

The Mennonite Story

Mennonites are a religious group that came from Europe to America to be free. Since 1800 they have lived on farms around St. Jacobs. What do they believe? Why do many of them use horses, not cars? At the Visitor Centre you can learn about Mennonite history and culture. See the 13-minute DVD presentation, lots of photos and other documents. **$3.** ***per person***

Read about St. Jacobs, a village near Toronto, Canada. Then finish the following sentences.

1. For $2 you can buy ...
2. Mennonites came to America because ...
3. Instead of cars, many Mennonites ...
4. At St. Jacobs Farmer's Market Mennonite farmers sell ...
5. At the Visitor Center you can see ...
6. The admission to the Visitor Center is ...

[1] buggy *Einspänner (Kutsche)*
[2] horse-drawn trolley *Pferdefuhrwerk*
[3] maple syrup ['meɪpl ˌsɪrəp] *Ahornsirup*

3 Speaking

Partner A and Partner B: You're planning a trip to St. Jacobs. Read the instructions below. You can make notes to help you with your dialogue. Then act out the dialogue.

Partner A	Partner B
Say you'd like to go to 'The Mennonite Story'. →	Ask what that is.
Answer. Say when and why Mennonites came to America. →	Tell your partner about the Mennonites and the Farmers' Market.
Say why you'd like to visit the market. →	Describe the Mennonite Farm Tour.
Say you'd like to stay in the village. Tell your partner about the walking tour brochure. →	Ask what your partner wants to see in the village.
Tell your partner about the Visitor Center. →	Say that two or three things are enough.
Agree. Say what you want to do and why.	Agree or disagree with your partner's ideas.

4 Writing

Yesterday you visited St. Jacobs. Write a report about your visit, about 90 words. Remember the 5 Ws.

A teen magazine

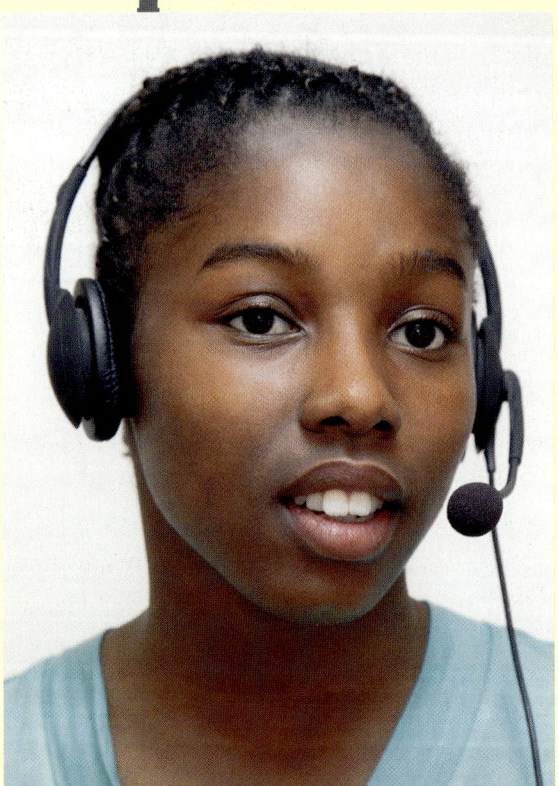

Harbourfront centre

Harbourfront Community Centre · Toronto · Youth Group

The Harbourfront Community Centre Youth Group announces its latest project:

A TEEN MAGAZINE !

WHAT'S IT ABOUT?

That's up to you!

So far our magazine has the following sections and editors:

sports Editor: Samantha Kowalski	**music** Editor: Robert Smith
movies Editor: Mitsu Nagora	**fashion** Editor: Natalie L'Estane

Look at the brochure. Describe the youth group's latest project.
Explain the difference between a magazine and an e-zine.

1 Now you

What teen magazines and/or e-zines do you read?
Which sections (fashion, music, problem pages, ...) interest you most?
Exchange information in your group.

JOIN IN!

Help us to produce this magazine.

Everybody who's interested can send an article. If it's interesting, we'll publish it!

Send your articles (with photos or drawings) to the editors. And if you want to start a new section, contact the Community Centre's manager.

WHAT'S NEXT?

If the magazine is a success, we'd like to do an **e-zine**, an **e**lectronic maga**zine** that you can read on the centre's website. The e-zine will have more photos – and of course sound files, videos and lots of links to other websites.

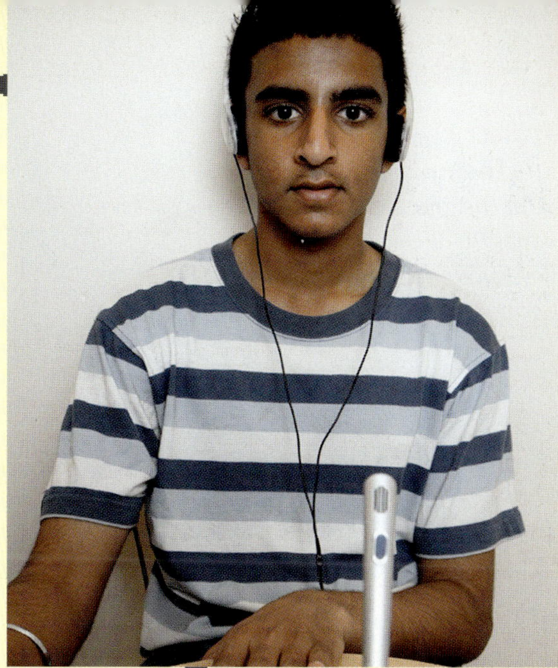

2 Talking about the photos

a) *Describe the photos. Say something about the rooms, the people and the equipment they're using. Here's some help:*

headphones • microphone • monitor • mouse • side of somebody's head • webcam

In the photo at the top of page 94, Robert is ...

b) *What do you remember about the people in the photos? Share your information in class.*

► SF Describing pictures (p. 137)

3 A video chat

a) *Listen to the CD and explain why Robert and his friends are having this video chat.*

b) *Listen again and find out what Asif, Katrina and Latisha think of Robert's suggestion. Take notes. Then compare your answers in a group.*

c) *From what you know about them, what might each of the four kids write for the magazine? Make notes in your exercise book.*

► P 1 (p. 100) • WB 1–2 (p. 64)

1 The music section

Skim the four texts for Robert's music section on pages 96–99.
Were your ideas for 3c) on page 95 right or wrong? Now read the texts in detail.

▸ SF Skimming (p. 141) • WB 3 (p. 65)

STUDY SKILLS **Skimming**

If you want to get a first idea of what a text is about, you can skim it.
- First look at the title and the pictures.
- Then read the first and the last paragraphs quickly.
- Now just let your eyes 'fly' over the rest of the text – don't try to read every word.

MUSIC Editor: Robert Smith

A riddle

by Katrina McFadden

I'm a musical instrument. I was born far, far away in Iran, over two thousand years ago.

From there I travelled all over Europe, but you probably know me best as an instrument from one part of Great Britain.

I look very interesting: my body is made of leather and lots of pipes stick out of me! You blow into a small one. The other ones let the air out. That's what makes the sounds.

How do you play me? Well, you have to be very clever to play me. First you have to blow air into me. I keep it in my body. Then you have to squeeze it out again – very carefully – through the pipes. One of these pipes has little holes in it. When you put your fingers over the different holes, I play different notes.

I bet you can't guess my name, can you?

I MUST BE GETTING GOOD, BECAUSE MY DAD TOLD ME TO GO PLAY FOR THE NEIGHBOURS!

▷ *What is the answer to Katrina's riddle?*

2 Extra Now you

Write a riddle for your favourite instrument. Katrina's riddle can help. You could write about:

- the history of the instrument (how old / where it was invented /...)
- what it looks like / what it is made of
- how it is played
- famous players of the instrument
- ...

▸ P 2–3 (pp. 100–101) • WB 4 (p. 65)

Mika – the story of a singer

by Asif Azad

Mika was born in Beirut, the capital of Lebanon, in 1983.

His dad was American, his mum Lebanese. When he was one year old, the family had to leave Lebanon because of the war there. They moved to Paris, and when Mika was nine, they moved again, this time to London.

He was very unhappy at his first school there, so his mum took him out of it. Mika was allowed to study classical music at home until they were able to find a new school for him.

At the age of 11 he had lessons from a Russian singing teacher. With this training and his fantastic voice, Mika was able to become a boy soprano with the Royal Opera at Covent Garden and had already sung there by the time he was 12.

Later Mika studied at the Royal College of Music, but it was pop music, not classical, that made him a star.

When he was 23, he released his first single – 'Relax, take it easy' – and it was sold out after two days. Next came his first album. He wrote and produced all the songs for it and one of its tracks, 'Grace Kelly', went to number one in the UK in its first week! **The rest is history!**

3 Mika's life

a) *Say what happened in Mika's life in 1983, 1984, 1992, 1994, 1995 and 2007. Think of two questions about Mika and ask a partner.*

b) Extra *Mika was very unhappy at first in London. How would you feel if you had to move to another country?*

Looking at language

a) *Find verb forms in* **3** *that go into this table:*

simple present	simple past
must	had to
can	...
may	...

b) *What are the* will-*future forms of these verbs? –* will have to, ...

4 Extra SONG Relax, take it easy

a) *Listen to the song. Explain why you like or don't like it. Think about the type of music, the singer's voice, the speed, the instruments, the sound, the lyrics, ...*

b) *If you liked it, write a DJ's introduction for it.*

5 Now you

a) *Write down your answers:*

1. Name something you were able to do when you were four but can't do now.
2. Name something you will be allowed to do when you are 18 that you can't do now.
3. Name something you will have to do when you're 18 that you don't have to do now.

b) *Compare your answers in a group. Tell the class the ideas that at least two of you had.*

► GF 12: Modals and their substitutes (p. 161) • P 4–5 (p. 101) • WB 5–6 (p. 66)

'School's out for summer' – my top five countdown

by Robert Smith ('DJ Bobby')

'School's out' 5

by Alice Cooper

This had to be on the list because it's the song you're always going to hear on the radio just before the summer vacation. It might be an oldie – my dad taught himself the lyrics and sang it when he was still at high school – but I think it's a goldie.

4 'The sea'

by Morcheeba

What do people want to do in their summer vacation? Right! Go to the sea: sunshine, fishing boats, clear water, ice cream, this song has it all. So find a friend, go down to the beach and send yourself to paradise with the soft, smooth sound of Morcheeba.

'Summer in the city' 3

by the Lovin' Spoonful

But what do you do if you can't go down to the seaside for the summer? I know what I do. I make myself comfortable, turn on the stereo and listen to the Lovin' Spoonful's classic song for folks who have to spend their long hot summers in the city.

2 'The sound of San Francisco'

by Global Deejays

Summer is the time to travel. A lot of us can't just jump on a plane, but we can take ourselves to London, Paris and San Francisco. How? Easy! Listen to this great dance mix and you'll have travelled to those cities in your mind by the end of the song.

'Come on over' 1

by Shania Twain

Vacation is a time to hang out with friends – that's what I like doing and it's what this song by Shania Twain is about. She's my number 1 Canadian singer – even though my mother likes her too. So ask a friend to come on over, put on this song and just chill out.

6 **Now you**

a) *Which of these songs would you like to listen to now? Explain why.*

b) *What's your own top five countdown? Alone, with a partner, or in a group, write a playlist like Robert's. Describe your five favourite songs and explain why you like them.*
Make a classroom display with all the playlists.

► *GF 13: Reflexive pronouns (p. 162) • P 6–7 (p. 102) • WB 7–8 (p. 67)*

Looking at language

Complete a copy of the chart with words from Robert's playlist above.

-self		-selves	
I	...	we	...
you	...	you	*yourselves*
he	...	they	*themselves*
she	*herself*		
it	*itself*		

The day the music died

by Latisha Byrd

When I woke up at 7 in the morning, they were playing that oldie on the radio, American Pie. Don McLean was singing '… the day the music died …' when the song stopped and this guy started talking. So I tried some other stations, but none of them were playing music.

'Well,' I said to myself, 'there's no music on the radio, so I'll listen to some on my MP3 player while I pack my bag for school.' I turned it on – and it crashed. I restarted it once, twice, but it crashed every time.

I was angry now. The MP3 player was new: if I had known it was such a bad one, I wouldn't have bought it. I turned round, picked up a drumstick and hit my steel drum but, to my horror, no sound came out. I played a couple of tunes on it but I couldn't hear anything! Had I gone deaf?

No, I hadn't. If I had gone deaf, I wouldn't have heard my mother's voice from the bathroom. She said I was late for school. But I hadn't had a shower yet, so I went to the bathroom.

I usually take the radio with me but there was no point that day as I couldn't listen to music. Mum had a newspaper in her hands. I said good morning and we both looked at ourselves in the mirror. I tried to sing but no sound came out.

I started to tell Mum about the music but she shook her head and stopped me. She already knew. She showed me the newspaper. This was the headline on the front page:

We looked at each other with fear in our eyes. 'No,' I shouted. 'I can't live without music! I can't!'

I ran downstairs and put a CD in the CD player and turned it up LOUD. Nothing! No sound at all. I started to cry.

Then I woke up again, with tears in my eyes. On the radio they were playing that oldie, American Pie. Don Maclean was singing '… the day the music died …'.

This time the music didn't stop.

What is the difference between the first and the second time Latisha hears the song 'American Pie'? Find all the examples of how the music 'died'. Which would be the scariest for you?

► *GF 14: each other (p. 163)* • *P 8 (p. 102)* • *WB 9 (p. 68)* •
Extra *GF 15: Conditional sentences 3 (p. 164)* •
P 9–12 (pp. 103–104) • *WB 10–16 (pp. 68–72)* •
Checkpoint 5 *WB (p. 73)*

7 Now you

a) *Note down what you know about Latisha and music from this text and from the other units.*

Music is very important for Latisha.
She went to the … festival.
She plays …

b) *What about you? How important is music in your life? When do you listen to or play music? Compare yourself to Latisha.*

► **Text File 10** *(p. 130)*

8 Extra My favourite article

Which of the four articles do you like best? Why?

interesting information • pictures/photos • layout • exciting/funny/fun to read/ strange/… • I really enjoyed/loved/… • …

Make notes, then talk to a partner.

I like Katrina's article best because it's fun to read.
– Oh, I don't like hers much. My favourite article is Asif's, because I'm a Mika fan.

1 WORDS All about music

a) *Read the definitions and find the music words.*

1 a group of people who sing together
2 a round instrument you hit to make music
3 a part of a song you sing more than once
4 a machine you can download music onto
5 the words of a song
6 a machine that plays CDs
7 a place where people dance to music
8 someone who can read and play music
9 someone who puts on the music at a party or club
10 another word for a group that plays rock or pop or jazz
11 a Scottish dance party

b) *Partner B: Go to page 112.*
Partner A: Read the text below and try to memorize it.

When the people stopped cheering, the musicians began to play the next piece. She was listening to a CD of a live concert on her computer. A choir was singing Mozart. After a few minutes, she stopped the CD and copied it to her MP3 player.

With your book closed, dictate your text to your partner from memory, while he/she writes it down. Then together try to correct the text. Check in the book when you have finished.
Now your partner dictates his/her text and you write it down. Then together try to correct the text. Check in the book when you have finished.

c) **Extra** *Describe your favourite music programme on radio or TV and say why you like it.*

2 REVISION Electric guitar men (Personal pronouns: subject/object)

Put in the subject form (I, you, he, ...) or object form (me, you, him, ...) of the personal pronouns.

Rock, pop, blues, jazz, heavy metal: what would ... sound like without the electric guitar? But have ... ever thought about where the electric guitar came from? Two Americans, Les Paul and Leo Fender, made ... popular in the middle of the 20th century.

Les Paul was a jazz musician and inventor. ... built his first modern electric guitar in 1941. Paul worked with the Gibson guitar company and together ... made the *Gibson Les Paul* in the early 1950s. ... became one of the most successful electric guitars. Paul once said: '... will be remembered in years from now. People will remember ... and my guitar.'

Leo Fender was the man who designed the most popular electric guitar of all time, the *Fender Stratocaster*. Even today many of the world's most famous guitarists play Stratocasters. ... were first produced in 1954 and the Fender company has been making ... since then. The most expensive *Stratocaster* in the world was sold for US$ 2.8 million. ... was signed by Bryan Adams, Eric Clapton, Keith Richards, Pete Townshend, Ray Davies, David Gilmour, Mark Knopfler, Paul McCartney, Sting and many other famous musicians. The money helped victims of the 2004 Asian Tsunami. 'With the money, ... will repair a school in Thailand,' Adams said. 'It will also help ... to build a sports hall for seven schools in Sri Lanka.'

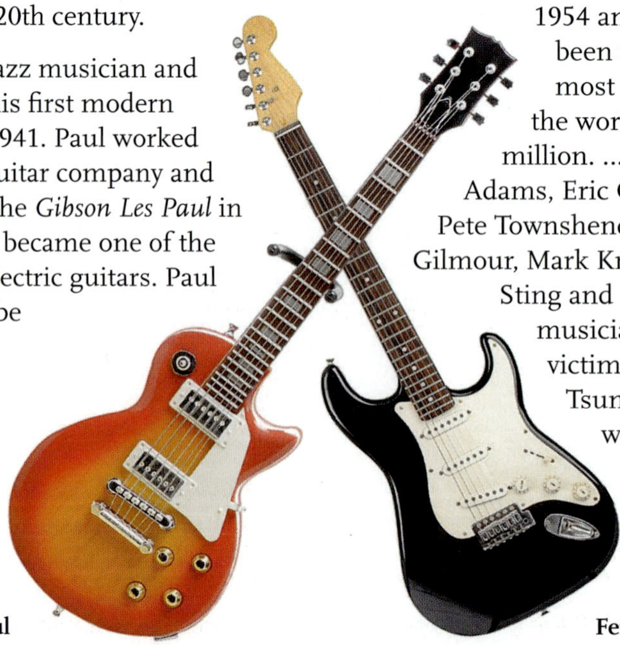

Gibson Les Paul **Fender Stratocaster**

3 Musical instruments (one/ones)

a) *Replace a word in each sentence by **one** or **ones**.*

1 Modern violins have four strings but earlier violins had only three.
Modern violins have four strings but earlier ones had only three.

2 Violin strings often break so players always carry extra strings with them.

3 Britain makes a lot of steel drums today but the first steel drum was made in Trinidad.

4 Latisha plays a British steel drum but she'd love to have a steel drum from the Caribbean.

5 Martin Block was the first person who was called a disc jockey and the first disc jockey who became famous.

b) *Listen to Katrina's conversation at the music shop. Which violin case does she like best?*

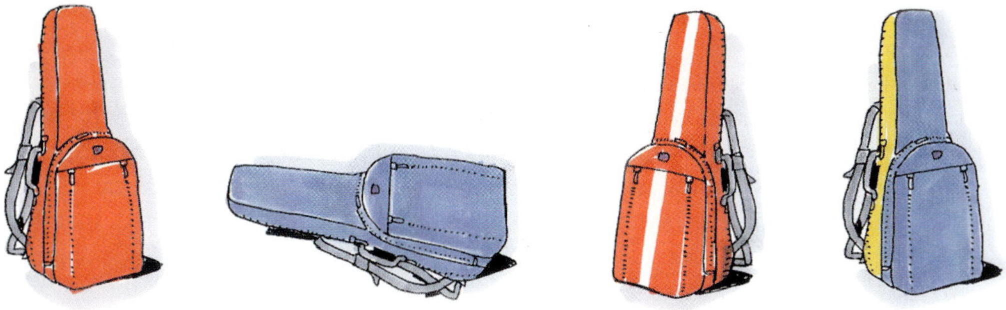

4 School rules (have to and be allowed to)

a) *Make sentences about some of the rules at one of the schools Mika went to.*

– arrive in time for lessons
– turn off mobile phones in the classroom
– tidy their desks
– be friendly to other students

Students had to arrive in time for lessons.

– wear caps in class
– cycle or skate in the school building
– smoke or drink alcohol at school
– bully other students

They weren't allowed to ...

b) Extra *Name some of the rules at your school. Which are OK? Which would you like to change?*

5 Robert wasn't able to ... (be able to and be allowed to)

a) *Make sentences about Robert. Use the information in the charts.*

be able to	*five years ago*	*in five years*
– speak French	–	+
– paddle a boat	+	+
– climb through small windows	+	–

Five years ago Robert wasn't able to speak French.
In five years he'll be able to speak French.

be allowed to	*five years ago*	*in five years*
– stay out late	–	+
– go to night clubs	–	+
– go on holiday without adults	–	+

Five years ago Robert wasn't allowed to ...
In five years ...

b) *Make sentences about yourself like the sentences in a). Give reasons for what you've written.*

6 Mum and Dad are on strike (Reflexive pronouns)

Complete the sentences with the reflexive pronouns.

1. Mr and Mrs Jones are on strike, so the children have to cook for themselves.
2. Mrs Jones usually teaches Jack the guitar, but he knows: 'Today I'll have to teach ...'
3. Jack usually talks to his mum and dad, but today he has to talk to ...
4. Mr and Mrs Jones usually shop for the children, but today Jack tells Jill: 'Mum and Dad are on strike, so we have to shop for ...'
5. Jill's mum usually puts her to bed, but today she tells her: 'You'll have to put ... to bed tonight.'
6. Mr Jones usually tells Jill a story, but today she'll have to tell ... one.
7. 'Why are you on strike?' the children ask them. But they only answer: 'Don't ask us. Ask ...!'

7 My not-so-lucky day (Reflexive pronouns)

Decide if you need a reflexive pronoun or not. You can look at the list of reflexive verbs on p. 194 for help.

Today has been an awful day. My friends and I wanted to meet ... after breakfast. But when I went into the bathroom to clean ... my teeth, there was no water. 'That's OK,' I said to ..., 'I can get water in the kitchen.' But then I remembered ... that there was a sign in the street about a water problem. So I got dressed and went to buy some water. I felt ... dirty and I was afraid that somebody would see me. So I walked home quickly. But when I put the key in the door, it didn't open ...! 'What can I do?' I wondered ... Then I remembered ... that my bedroom window wasn't closed. I was able to pull ... up to it, but it was so small that I wasn't able to get in! I had just decided ... to climb down again when the police came. Now I'm here at the police station. Oh well, I can only blame ... for that!

8 Are they looking at themselves or each other? (each other/themselves)

Partner B: Go to p. 112.
Partner A: Look at the following pictures. You and your partner have the same pictures, but in a different order. Talk to your partner about your pictures. Take turns.

1 look at

2 take photos of

3 think of

4 teach/English

5 think of

6 look at

7 take photos of

8 teach/English

A: In my picture 1 a boy and a girl are looking at themselves.

B: Oh, a boy and a girl are looking at themselves in my picture 6. In my picture 1 two girls are ...

9 REVISION What did Latisha say? (Indirect speech)

Look at what Latisha wrote in her article for Robert's magazine. Choose a sentence and read it to your partner. He/She has to put it into indirect speech. Be careful with the tenses.

I woke up at 7 in the morning.

This time the music didn't stop.

I can't live without music!

I heard my mother's voice.

There was an oldie on the radio: 'American Pie'.

I started to cry.

I'll listen to some music on my MP3 player.

I usually take the radio with me.

Latisha wrote that she had woken up at …

10 Extra What would or wouldn't have happened? (Conditional sentences 3)

a) *Match the if-clauses on the left to the clauses on the right.*

1 If Latisha had known it was a bad MP3 player,
2 If Robert hadn't gone to Birmingham,
3 If they hadn't been interested in music,
4 If Robert hadn't answered Asif's e-mail,
5 If Katrina had been like the Beauties,
6 If her dad hadn't taught her the fiddle,
7 If Asif hadn't liked Mika,
8 If the magazine hadn't been good,

a) Asif couldn't have shown him round London.
b) he wouldn't have met Asif, Katrina and Latisha.
c) he wouldn't have written about him.
d) Robert wouldn't have asked them to write something for his magazine.
e) she might never have played at a ceilidh.
f) she wouldn't have been the star of the film.
g) she wouldn't have bought it.
h) they would never have published the e-zine.

b) *Finish these sentences as if you were your partner. Then swap with your partner. What do you think of what he or she wrote?*

1 If I hadn't come to school today, I would/wouldn't have …
2 If I had flown to London last weekend, …
3 If my mum had been born in England, …
4 If my dad had been an astronaut, …

11 Extra What would have been different? (Conditional sentences 3)

Read about the following situations. Then imagine something different had happened in the past and say what the result would be today.

1 Latisha was a good steel drum player so she was allowed to go to the music festival in Birmingham. That's where she met Katrina. Now they're really good friends.
If Latisha hadn't gone to Birmingham, …

2 Robert's mum heard from the man at the store that the river was very high and fast. That's how she knew Robert and his dad would be at the old bridge quite early.

3 When Mika first went to school in London he was very unhappy. He was very different from the other kids and became a victim of bullies.

4 Katrina played the fiddle at her interview and told the researcher about her musical family. That was why they chose her for the film.

Part 5 WRITING COURSE

12 WRITING Correcting your text (A short biography)

a) *A student has written a short biography of Shakira but there are lots of mistakes in it. Use the checklist below to correct the biography. Write the text with your corrections in your exercise book.*

CHECKLIST
- Spelling – capital letters (1 mistake)
- Grammar – irregular verbs (1 mistake)
- Grammar – wrong tenses (1 mistake)
- Grammar – plural noun/singular verb (1 mistake)
- Vocabulary – word for word translations from German (2 mistakes)
- Vocabulary – wrong preposition (1 mistake)
- Vocabulary – missing preposition (1 mistake)

Shakira

Shakira was born 1977 in Colombia in south America. It is in the north. It gives coasts on the Atlantic and the Pacific. Shakira has six brothers and sisters. One of them is her road manager. She began writing music with eight years. When she was ten, she was in television every week in a competition for kids. When she was 13 she sang three songs. Some managers of a big music company was also there. They said she could make three albums. Shakira releases her first album 'Magia' ('Magic') when she was only 15. It only selled about 1,000 times.

b) Extra *Write the biography again. Try to improve it with this checklist:*
- Is there a paragraph for each new idea?
- Are some sentences too short? Are there enough linking words?
- Would more adjectives or adverbs improve the text?
- Are the beginning and ending interesting?
- Will the rest interest the reader?
- Is there anything that you don't need?
- Have you got any other ideas?

► *Writing course, Units 1–4 (pp. 24, 39, 67, 85)*

Tip
Make a list of the kinds of mistakes you often make. Use the list as your own personal checklist.

c) *Now write your own short biography of a star. In your biography you could write:*
- when and where your star was born
- about his/her family and school days
- how his/her career began
- about his/her first CD/video/film ...

Try to find interesting information for your biography. Make sure you start with an interesting point and finish with a good ending.

d) *Correct your biography carefully with the help of a partner and write it out again.*

13 STUDY SKILLS Research on the internet (Using key words and phrases)

a) *To find information on the internet, you will have to use a search engine. Read the tips for internet research. Then answer the questions on the right.*

STUDY SKILLS Internet research

- Think carefully: what are you looking for?
- Use key words or phrases and enter them in your search engine.
- To look for a phrase, use quotation marks, e.g. "interview with Shakira".
- If you don't find what you're looking for:
  – add more key words or phrases
  – use different key words.
- Check your spelling.
- Don't copy complete articles from the internet. Take notes and use your own words.
- Websites are not always accurate. If you can, check information on several web sites.

b) *What key words would you use to research the following questions? Write them down.*

1 How many strings are there on a banjo?
strings, banjo
2 When and where was Elvis Presley born?
"Elvis Presley", born
3 Where did George Frideric Handel live for most of his adult life?
4 Who wrote the poem that is used in Beethoven's 9th Symphony?
5 What was the name of the record company the Beatles started?
6 What's the name of Madonna's first child?
7 What is the English title of Mozart's opera *Die Zauberflöte*?
8 Who made the first real piano?

c) *If you can, try your key words from b) in an online search engine. Can you find the answers?*

► *Project Step 2 (p. 106) • SF Internet research (p. 138)*

14 Extra STUDY SKILLS Adapting a text

a) *You want to write a short biography of the British composer Benjamin Britten and have found this information on the internet. Mark up the information you need in a copy of the text and take notes.*
BB: born 22/11/1913 – Lowestoft, Eng.

Benjamin Britten
Born: November 22, 1913
Died: December 4, 1976
Benjamin Britten was born in Lowestoft, a town on the eastern coast of England on the saint day of St Cecilia, the patron saint of music. Benjamin's father was a dentist; his mother loved to sing, and had regular concerts in their home.

From the moment he started to play the piano, Britten knew he wanted to become a composer. He became an expert in three different areas of music – conducting, composing and playing the piano. The first money he ever got was from writing music for films.

In 1939 it became clear that there would be a war between Britain and Germany and the pacifist Britten left for America.

When the war was over, a gala took place to reopen the biggest opera company in England, and Britten was asked to write a new opera. Britten also composed an opera when Elizabeth II became Queen of the UK.

b) *Decide what information is missing that you still need (family, school days, famous works, ...). Look for it on the internet. Then write your own short biography.*
The British composer Benjamin Britten was born in Lowestoft ...

► *Project Step 3 (p. 107) • SF Marking up a text (p. 142)*

Extra Project: Our music section

In this project, each of you will write an article for the music section of a teen magazine or e-zine, then put the section together in your group. Everything you have learned in the **Writing course** *in this book will help you as you do the project.*

Of course you can make your magazine section about something else (sport, fashion, ...), but this book will help you to produce a music section.

1 Step 1: Choose your topic

a) *What would you like to write about? Brainstorm ideas. Make notes – you can use a list/a mind map/...*
When you have finished, mark your two favourite ideas in a different colour.

▸ SF Brainstorming (p. 145)

b) *Talk about all your ideas. Agree with your group who will write what and when the articles will be ready.*
- I'd like to write about ...
- We can't have two articles about ... What's your second favourite?
- ...

2 Step 2: Collect information

a) *Where can you get the information you need for your articles?*
The list on the right shows some sources of information. Can you think of more? Which ones will have the kind of information you need?

b) *Now collect your information. If you find too much, try skimming. That will help you to decide which information will be useful.*

▸ SF Using an English–German dictionary (p. 135) • P 13 (p. 105)

Sources of information	Good for
encyclopedia	facts about people, places, things, e. g. musical instruments
internet (be careful, not all sources are accurate)	song lyrics, popular groups, what's happening now, ...
music/youth magazines	interviews, photos, song lyrics, ...
library	...
...	...

Tip

If you can, use sources in English. (An English–German dictionary will help. So will your teacher.) Then you won't make as many mistakes.

3 Step 3: Decide how to write up your information

a) *Look again at the articles by Robert and his friends. How did they write up their ideas? Match the topics to the text types:*

topics	text types
music in my life	a biography
a favourite instrument	a story
a famous singer	a playlist
favourite songs	a riddle

Tip

Don't just copy texts you find in books and magazines or on the internet. You must take notes and use your own words.

b) *Match the following ideas to topics in the list in Step 1 on p. 106. (There could be more than one right answer.)*

- a 'How you do it' page with pictures
- a funny story about a man who goes crazy in a department store
- new lyrics to a famous song
- a report on a concert

► *P 14 (p. 105)*

4 Step 4: Write and correct your article

a) *Write your article. Find a good title and sub-headings. Remember to use paragraphs and leave room for pictures.*

► *Writing course: The steps of writing (p. 85)*

b) *Correct each other's work in your group.*

► *Writing course: Correcting your text (p. 104)*

Tip

Try a 'correcting circle'. It works like this:

1. Each person in your group will look for one kind of mistake, e. g.:
   - spelling
   - 'He, she, it, das "s" muss mit!'
   - new paragraph for new idea
   - ...

   Decide who is responsible for what.
2. Sit in a circle. Give your article to the person on your right.
3. Read the article that your partner has given you. Only look for the kind of mistake that you are responsible for. If you find one, correct it.
4. When you have finished, give the article to the person on your right. Now correct the new article. Go on until you have your own article back.
5. Correct your article if necessary.

Tip

If you don't know the words you need while you are writing, you might find some in the articles by Robert and his friends (pp. 96–99). For others you can use a German–English dictionary.

► *SF Using a German–English dictionary (p. 136)*

5 Step 5: Publish your music section

a) *Agree in your group how you will publish your music section.*

You can …
… write the articles by hand/on the computer
… do your music section as a poster/as an e-zine and put it on the school website

b) *What are the different jobs? Decide who will do what.*
Everyone should try to make the section look as attractive and interesting as possible: headings, pictures, colours, layout, …

Scan pictures – Marcel
Layout – Aischa & Elias
Design front page for section – Laura
Find photos and pictures – Linda
Make photocopies – Oleg

c) *Put your music section together and publish it. Maybe you want to give it to other classes, parents at parents' evenings, …*

Tip
Don't forget to keep a copy of your article for your DOSSIER.

6 Step 6: How did it go?

When you have finished your project, think about how it went, alone and then together in your group. Give yourself marks: ☺ good, 😐 OK, ☹ not so good.

Alone:
- Did brainstorming give me good ideas?
- Did I find enough information for my article?
- Did I choose the right text type for my article?
- Did I make many mistakes? Did I find and correct them?
- Did I finish my article on time?
- …

Group:
- Did we usually speak English in our group?
- Was it easy to agree on topics for the section?
- Did we find enough different sources of information?
- Did the 'correcting circle' work well?
- Did everybody work hard?
- Did our section look good?
- …

How am I doing? – Units 1–5

This page will help you to check what you have learned in the whole of this book, not just in the last unit.

a) *Fill in or choose the correct answers.*

Facts about Britain

1 The three countries on the main island of the United Kingdom are England, ... and ...
2 The capital of the UK is ... It's on the River ...
3 The quickest way to get round London is on the ...
4 ... is a group of islands north of Scotland.
5 Old Trafford is the name of the football stadium in the northern English city of ...

Words

Add at least three words to each of the word fields below. Name the word fields for extra points.

6 ticket, train, ferry, ride, ...
7 mobile phone, download, website, ...
8 car park, theatre, traffic, ...
9 train, supporter, draw, stadium, ...
10 gig, DJ, hip-hop, ...

Skills

What do you call these skills?

11 looking for a word or phrase in a long text
12 finding the main ideas of a long text quickly
13 explaining a word that you don't know the English for
14 collecting lots of ideas on a topic, alone or in a group
15 looking for the German translation of an English word that you don't know
16 finding information on the internet

Writing

17 The main idea of a paragraph is usually in the ...
18 Your writing will be clearer if you use adjectives, adverbs, time phrases and ...
19 What are the 5 Ws and what can you use them for?
20 Name two things you can do to correct mistakes in something you have written.

Grammar

21 I've been waiting here for you ... an hour, ... 5 o'clock.
22 If you ... (be) in London now, what ... (you, want) to do?
23 *Use a contact clause to make one sentence:* I haven't read the book. The teacher gave us the book.
24 *Complete with the correct form of the passive.* The London Eye ... (open) in 2000. About 10,000 visitors ... (take) on the 30-minute ride every day.
25 'I went to Toronto last summer.' – She said she ...
26 *Correct the mistakes:* The film was very exciting. It was about two spies who were trying to kill the other. My sister and I can't ride our bikes to school. Our mum is afraid we'll hurt us.

b) *Check your answers on p. 114 and add up your points – one point for each correct answer.*

c) *If you had 31 or more points, well done! Maybe you can help students who had fewer points. If you had 30 points or fewer, it's a good idea to do some more work in your holidays. Where did you make mistakes? The chart below will tell you what you can do to improve your English.*

No.	Area	Find out more
1– 5	Britain facts	Units 1–3
6–10	Word fields	All about ... (pp. 14, 32, 56, 74)
11–16	Skills	Skills File (pp. 133–147)
17–20	Writing	Writing course (pp. 24, 39, 67, 85, 104)
21–26	Grammar	Grammar File (pp. 148–167)

Unit 1

8 How long? (Present perfect simple with since/for)

*Partner B: Use the notes and answer your partner's questions about the people in the blue box. Be careful: do you need **since** or **for** in your answers? Then ask questions about the people in the yellow box.*

A: How long has Lisa had piano lessons?
B: Since/For ...

Lisa: have piano lessons – six months
Maggie: live with her sister – last weekend
Phil: be a fireman – last year
Asif: know Robert – ten days

Johnny: be a footballer – ??
Alicia: live in New Zealand – ??
Pia: know Alicia – ??
Chris: have his new car – ??

Unit 2

13 Loch Ness and Edinburgh

a) *Partner B: Listen to your partner's report on Loch Ness. When you hear a mistake, correct it with facts from the box below.*

Facts about Loch Ness

1. It is one of the most famous places in Scotland.
2. The word 'loch' means lake.
3. Loch Ness is 37 kilometres long.
4. Some people say there is a monster.
5. Most people think that Nessie is only a story.
6. Every year thousands of tourists come to Loch Ness.
7. There are lots of websites with webcams from around the lake.

b) *A student has written a report on Edinburgh. There are seven mistakes in it. Read the report first quietly, then to your partner. He/She will correct the mistakes.*

Edinburgh

Edinburgh is on the Scottish west coast. With about 500,000 people it is the largest and the most famous city in Scotland. It has been Scotland's capital since 1437.

Edinburgh is a very old town and it was the home of the Scottish queens and kings. Today more than 30 million tourists from all over the world come to visit Edinburgh every year. In the UK, only London gets more tourists than Edinburgh. Visitors come to see the famous old buildings and places such as Buckingham Palace, the Royal Mile or Princes Street. And thousands come for the Edinburgh International Festival every winter. Edinburgh was the home of some famous people, like Alexander Graham Bell, the 'father' of the computer, or Sean Connery, one of the famous James Bond actors. And only a few people know that J. K. Rowling wrote her first 'Harry Potter' book in her house in Edinburgh.

Unit 3

1 WORDS Spot the difference

Partner B: Look at the picture. Your partner will tell you what he/she can see in the rooms. Spot the differences in your picture.
Take turns: tell your partner about your picture. Use words and phrases like **next to**, **on the left**, **on the wall**. *If you don't know a word in English, look it up in a dictionary.*
Ask about his/her picture.

A: In my picture, the ... is upstairs on the wall on the left. What about your picture?
B: Yes, in my picture it's there too. / No, in my picture it's on the wall on the right. – Now, in my picture, the ... is downstairs ...

3 STUDY SKILLS Paraphrasing

a) *Listen to your partner and guess his/her words.*

b) *Explain the following words to your partner – but don't use the word.*

apple • breakfast • crocodile • doctor • teacher • underground

Phrases from the box can help you.
A: It's a person who ...
B: Oh, do you mean a ...?

c) *Now try to explain the German words from the box on the right to your partner.*

It's somewhere/a place where ...
It's somebody/a person who ...
It's something/a fruit/a ... that ...
It's something that you use to ...
It's a thing/an animal ...

Cousine • Erdbeere • Geschirrspülmaschine • Stammbaum • Torwart • Zeitung

Unit 4

1 WORDS Numbers

a) *Partner B: Write down the numbers and dates that your partner reads out to you. Then read out these numbers and dates to your partner:*

15 • 93 • 303 • 2,684 • 300,000 • 8 May, 2012 • 21 November, 1985

Swap pieces of paper and check.

Unit 5

1 WORDS All about music

b) *Partner B: Read the text below and try to memorize it.*

My brother is in a rock band. They practise in our garage. He plays the drums. They write all their own songs. The tunes are pretty good but the lyrics are terrible. They've already made a CD. It's OK because you can't understand the lyrics.

With your book closed, write down the text your partner dictates to you. Then together try to correct the text. Check in the book when you have finished.

Now, with your book closed again, dictate your text to your partner from memory, while he/she writes it down. Then together try to correct the text. Check in the book when you have finished.

8 Are they looking at themselves or each other? (each other/themselves)

Partner B: Look at the following pictures. You and your partner have the same pictures, but in a different order. Talk to your partner about your pictures. Take turns.

1 teach

2 think of

3 look at

4 take photos of

5 teach/English

6 look at

7 take photos of

8 think of

A: In my picture 1 a boy and a girl are looking at themselves.

B: Oh, a boy and a girl are looking at themselves in my picture 6. In my picture 1 two girls are ...

Key to the self-assessment tests

Unit 1 ▸ p. 29

1 Thames
2 Tube
3 boroughs
4 Covent Garden
5 Buckingham Palace
6 Science Museum
7 A ticket
8 C get
9 A change
10 B food
11 D risk
12 D plug
13 B so
14 A After I spoke to the teacher, I tried to work harder.
15 A I don't usually like trying foods from different countries, but I liked the food at the Bangladeshi café.
16 C Dear ...
17 C Yes, I have.
18 B haven't done
19 B have been waiting
20 C For six years.
21 A has lived

Unit 2 ▸ p. 49

1 Orkney
2 capital
3 salmon
4 ceilidh
5 Edinburgh
6 loch
7 C fox
8 A sea B bay
C lake D river
9 B text message
10 C exchange
11 Letter 'g': A huge B big
C large D great
12 D Perspektive
13 B weggehen
14 A Look up all three in an English–German dictionary.
15 C If Tom goes to the party, I will stay at home.
16 A If kids in my class were horrible to me, I would tell my teacher.
17 B If I was in his class, I would be careful.

Unit 3 ▸ p. 71

1 steel drum
2 the Lowry
3 Old Trafford
4 Chemnitz
5 Nathan Stephens
6 Suggestions:
A It's a place where people watch big sports events and matches.
B It's a place where people look at art.
C It's something you win or get when you do something very well.
7 C 'please' and 'thank you'
8 D Talk about yourself and don't ask questions about the other person.
9 B racket
10 A supporter
11 D pool
12 1 tennis – D court
2 ice hockey – C ice rink
3 rugby – A pitch
4 skiing – B slope
13 A museum B school
C library D gallery
14 A
15 Latisha is an English girl Anna stayed with in Manchester.
16 Arsenal
17 A fort was built here by the Romans in AD 79.

Unit 4 ▸ p. 89

1 Canada is much larger than Germany, but it doesn't have as many people.
2 Possible answers: hunting, fishing, canoeing, dragon boat racing, ...; Toronto, Ottawa, Vancouver, Winnipeg, ...; Shania Twain, Avril Lavigne, Nickelback/Chad Kroeger ...; Stanley Park, Algonquin Park, High Park, ...; bear max. 9 points
3 20,000
4 B latest
5 A lyrics
6 C on their mobile
7 B strict
8 crew
9 ride, paddle 2 points
10 rapids
11 A mum B mobile (phone) C lift
12 Every story needs three parts: a beginning, a middle and an ending.
13 Two ways to write down your ideas from brainstorming are a mind map and a chart with the five wh-questions.
14 To make your sentences better you can add adjectives and adverbs / linking words.
15 After you have written a story you should revise/correct/check it.
16 had been, came
17 A first: dragon boat trainer in China, second: came to Canada
B first: live in Toronto, second: got a job in Ottawa
18 Different reporting verbs are possible; tell must have an object.
A Robert said he had met Jordan's new girlfriend at the party.
B Sam said dragon boat training was hard work.
C Sam's uncle said they would do well if they trained hard.
D Mr Smith said his foot was broken. He couldn't stand on it.
E Mrs Smith said the bear would be hungry that night.

Unit 1–5 ▸ p. 109

1 Scotland, Wales 2 points
2 London, Thames 2 points
3 underground/Tube 1 point
4 Orkney Islands 1 point
5 Manchester 1 point
6 Word field: transport
1 point for three or more words,
1 point for the name of the word field
7 Word field: electronic media
1 point for three or more words,
1 point for the name of the word field
8 Word field: town/city
1 point for three or more words,
1 point for the name of the word field
9 Word field: sport
1 point for three or more words,
1 point for the name of the word field
10 Word field: music
1 point for three or more words,
1 point for the name of the word field
11 scanning 1 point
12 skimming 1 point
13 paraphrasing 1 point
14 brainstorming 1 point
15 Using an English-German dictionary 1 point
16 internet research 1 point
17 topic sentence/first sentence 1 point
18 linking words 1 point
19 who, what, when, where, why (and how); you can use them to write a report
1 point for all five Ws,
1 point for saying what you can use them for
20 Checking grammar, spelling, vocabulary (cf. Writing course, p. 100)
2 points possible
21 for – since 2 points
22 were – would you want 2 points
23 I haven't read the book the teacher gave us. 1 point
24 was opened – are taken 2 points
25 ... had gone to Toronto last summer. 1 point
26 The film was very exciting. It was about two spies who were trying to kill <u>each other</u>. 1 point
My sister and I can't ride our bikes to school. Our mum is afraid we'll hurt <u>ourselves</u>. 1 point

TF 1 Two Elizabeths

England has had two Queen Elizabeths.

Elizabeth I became Queen in 1558, when she was 25 years old. All through her life there was a lot of gossip[1] about her. The big question was: Who will the Queen marry?

Well, she never married anybody, but she had a number of 'favourites'. One of them was Walter Raleigh.

They met, so people say, one rainy evening at Shakespeare's Globe Theatre in London. The Queen wanted to get out of her carriage when she saw a large puddle.

'Why isn't she getting out?' people whispered. Walter Raleigh, a new face at court[2] – young and good-looking – saw why: the puddle. He quickly took off his very expensive new cloak and threw it onto the puddle.

The Queen smiled and allowed Mr Raleigh

to help her down. She went into the theatre with dry feet and Raleigh became her new 'favourite'.

Just a few years later the Queen made Walter into 'Sir Walter' and allowed him to start a colony in America.

And what did Sir Walter bring back from Virginia? Gold or jewels? No: a dirty vegetable called the 'potato' and a dry leaf called 'tobacco'.

Which brings us to the second Queen Elizabeth. She was also very young when she became Queen in 1952 – just 26 years old. But she married and had four children.

One night in 1982, a man called Michael Fagan climbed first into the garden of Buckingham Palace and then into the Palace. There he went into the Queen's bedroom. And when she woke up in the middle of the night she found a strange[3] man by her bed.

Queen Elizabeth II is famous for being very calm[4]. And that night was an example. She asked the man to sit down and started to talk to him. After a few minutes she asked him, 'Would you like a drink?' He said, 'Yes, please.' So she picked up the phone.

'I'd like two gin and tonics, please. Oh, and my cigarettes,' she said.

The person on the other end of the phone knew that there was something very wrong. Why? Because the Queen has never smoked!

In a few minutes the police were there and took Mr Fagan away.

> *Choose Walter Raleigh or Michael Fagan. Imagine what they were thinking when they were with the Queen. Or what Queen Elizabeth was thinking. Write it down.*

---

[1] gossip ['gɒsɪp] *Klatsch* [2] (at) court [kɔːt] *(am) Hof (der Königin)* [3] strange [streɪndʒ] *fremd* [4] calm [kɑːm] *ruhig*

TF 2 Class Four-D's trip to the British Museum

(adapted from *The secret diary of Adrian Mole aged 13 3/4* by Sue Townsend)

What can go wrong on a class trip? What has gone wrong on one of your class trips?

Wednesday September 16th

Our form are going to the British Museum on Friday. Pandora and I are going to sit together on the coach. She is bringing the newspaper from home so we can have some privacy.

Thursday September 17th

Ms Fossington-Gore gave us a talk on the British Museum. She said it was a 'treasure house[1] of world culture'. Nobody listened to the talk.

Friday September 18th

2 am Just got back from London. The coach driver went mad on the motorway. I am too shocked to write clearly or intelligently about the day.

Saturday September 19th

The school will want a clear report of what happened on the way to, during, and on the way back from our trip to London. I am the only person who can do it.

7 am Get on coach.
7.05 Eat packed lunch.
7.10 Coach stops – Barry Kent is sick[2].
7.20 Coach stops – Claire Neilson goes to the Ladies.
7.30 Coach leaves school.
7.35 Coach returns to school for Ms Fossington-Gore's handbag.
7.40 Coach driver is behaving strangely.
7.45 Coach stops – Barry Kent is sick again.
7.55 Approach[3] motorway.
8 am Coach driver stops coach and says to everyone: 'Stop giving 'V' signs to lorry drivers!'
8.10 Coach driver gets angry and refuses[4] to drive on 'until bloody teachers control kids'.
8.20 Ms Fossington-Gore makes everyone sit down.
8.25 Drive on to motorway.
8.30 Everyone is singing 'Ten Green Bottles'.
8.35 Everyone is singing 'Ten Green Snotrags[5]'.
8.45 Coach driver shouts very loudly and stops the singing.
9.15 Coach driver stops at service station. He drinks from a hip-flask[6].
9.30 Barry Kent hands around bars of chocolate that he has stolen from shop at service station. Ms Fossington-Gore chooses Bounty bar.
9.40 Barry Kent is sick in coach.
9.50 Two girls near Barry Kent are sick.
9.51 Coach driver refuses to stop on motorway.
9.55 Ms Fossington-Gore covers sick in sand.
9.56 Ms Fossington-Gore is sick.
10.30 Coach moves along very slowly on side of motorway, all other lanes are closed.
11.30 Fight starts on the back seat.

---

[1] treasure house ['treʒə haʊs] *Schatzkammer* [2] be sick *sich übergeben* [3] approach sb./sth. [ə'prəʊtʃ] *sich jm./etwas nähern*
[4] refuse to do sth. [rɪ'fjuːz] *sich weigern, etwas zu tun* [5] snot rag *„Rotzfahne" (Taschentuch)* [6] hip-flask *Taschenflasche, Flachmann*

11.45	Fight ends. Ms Fossington-Gore finds first-aid kit[1] and cares for wounds. As a punishment Barry Kent has to sit next to driver.
11.50	Coach breaks down at Swiss Cottage.
11.55	Coach driver cries in front of AA man[2].
12.30	Class Four-D catch London bus to St Pancras.
1 pm	Class Four-D walk from St Pancras through Bloomsbury.
1.30	Enter British Museum. Adrian Mole and Pandora Braithwaite marvel at the treasure house of world culture. Rest of Class Four-D go mad, laugh at nude[3] statues and run away from curators.
2.15	Ms Fossington-Gore collapses. Adrian Mole phones headmaster but can't reach him.
3 pm	Curators catch Class Four-D and make them sit on steps of museum.
3.05	American tourists photograph Adrian Mole and say he is a 'cute English schoolboy'.
3.15	Ms Fossington-Gore OK again. Takes Class Four-D on a sightseeing tour of London.
4 pm	Barry Kent jumps in fountain at Trafalgar Square, as Adrian Mole predicted[4].
4.30	Barry Kent disappears near Soho.
4.35	Police arrive, take Four-D to a police station, arrange for a coach back home. Phone parents about new arrival time. Phone headmaster at home.
6 pm	Police find Barry Kent in sex shop.
7 pm	Coach leaves police station with police car.
7.30	Police in police car wave goodbye.
7.35	Coach driver asks Pandora Braithwaite to keep order.
7.36	Pandora Braithwaite keeps order.
8.30	Coach driver goes mad on the motorway.
8.40	Arrive back. Tyres burning. Class Four-D silent with terror. Headmaster takes Ms Fossington-Gore away. Parents all angry. Police arrest coach driver.

1 What's going on here?

a) *Choose an incident from Class Four-D's trip. Do a freeze-frame for the incident. What is going on? Can the class guess which incident it is?*

b) *Choose another incident and mime the action. Can the class guess who you are?*

2 A trip to a museum

Look at the photos. Who is having most fun at these London museums? Which of these museums would you most like to visit? What fun things have you done at a museum?

At the British Museum

At the Natural History Museum

At the Science Museum

[1] first-aid kit *Erste-Hilfe-Kasten* [2] AA man *Kfz-Mechaniker der Automobile Association (britischer Automobilclub)* [3] nude [nju:d] *nackt*
[4] predict sth. [prɪ'dɪkt] *etwas voraussagen*

TF 3 ru alone ...?

1 The people

a) *Who are the people in the advert? What do you think they're planning to do?*

b) *Why can't we see the man's face? How do you feel about him?*

2 The message

a) *Write out the advert in proper English. Who is the message for?*

b) *What can you do to be smart online and stay safe offline?*

TF 4 The lost girl (A folk tale[1] from the Orkney Islands)

There was once a family on one of the north Orkney Islands, a father and mother with two sons and a daughter. One day the daughter went out to catch some little fish. The father wanted to use them to catch big fish. The girl went out ... but she never returned. Her family looked everywhere, but they couldn't find the girl.

Years later the father and his two sons went fishing. It was a fine day when they left, but then a thick fog came down and they had no idea which way to go home! After a while, they came to an island. The three men left the boat and followed a path to a beautiful house. They knocked on the door, and a handsome[2] man opened it. He invited them in and said they could stay until the fog was gone.

The men could not believe how beautiful everything inside the house was. The man introduced[3] them to his wife. It was the lost girl! She welcomed her father and brothers warmly, asked how they were and about everyone else back home. Her husband asked the girl's father if he had any cows to sell. He answered yes, he had one fine cow, and the man gave him a very good price for the cow. He paid in gold.

Now the old man thought that he could find out what island they were on. He said, 'Well, you'll have to tell me how to get here, or I will not be able to bring the cow to you.'

'Och!' said the man, 'Don't worry about that. I'll come and get the cow.'

One of the brothers said, 'Father, the fog is going away. We should be on our way.'

The girl asked, 'Is there anything in the house you would like to take home with you?'

Her husband said, 'Yes, choose anything that you would like[4] and take it with you.'

The girl looked at them hopefully, sure that her father would choose her. But he was looking at a large gold plate and he took that home with him instead.

As the father and his sons got to the boat, the handsome man said, 'Just go that way for a bit.' The three men took their boat into the fog. As they came out the other side, they found that they were near their own island.

When they got home, the wife was very upset. 'An awful thing has happened,' she said. 'Our cow is dead.'

But the old man smiled. 'Ach,' he said, 'that's all right. She fetched a good price.'

No one ever saw the island, the man or the girl again.

1 Understanding the story

Write five questions about the story. Swap them with a partner. Answer his or her questions.

What was the girl doing before she disappeared?
– She was looking for some little fish.

2 What do you think?

1 Who do you think the husband was?
2 What do you think of the girl's father?
3 What is the moral of the story?

3 Acting out the story

Write the story as a little play and act it out for the class. Or record it with music and sound effects.

---

[1] folk tale *Volksmärchen* [2] handsome ['hænsəm] *(bei Männern) gut aussehend* [3] (to) introduce sb. [ˌɪntrə'djuːs] *jn. vorstellen*
[4] choose anything that you would like *such dir aus, was (immer) du willst*

TF 5 Tim goes abseiling[1] (adapted from the novel *Cliffhanger* by Jacqueline Wilson)

What's the scariest thing that you have ever done? Make notes (who? what? where? when? why? how?) and tell the class about it.

Tim's father has sent him on an adventure holiday for children. Great fun, right? Well, here's what Tim wrote in one of his postcards:

Dear Mum and Dad
Maybe this will be the last postcard you will get. Because we are going abseiling today. It is very dangerous. I could easily fall to my death.
With love from
Tim
xxxxxxxx to Mum
x to Dad

Now read on.

'OK, Tim. You next.'

'No!'

'Yes,' said Jake, our team leader.

'No,' I said.

'You all have to go sooner or later,' said Jake.

'Later,' I said.

'No. Sooner,' said Jake.

'I can't,' I said.

'Yes you can, Tim,' said Jake and held my hand.

'He's scared,' said Giles.

'We're all scared,' said Jake. 'Especially the first time.' He looked me straight in the eye. 'But you'll see it's easy, Tim. Believe me. Now. Into the harness[2].'

Jake put me into the harness before I could get away. He was telling me things about this rope[3] in this hand, that rope in that hand, but I couldn't listen. All I could hear was this terrible noise inside my head.

'Don't let go of[4] the rope, OK?' said Jake.

The noise in my head got louder and louder.

This couldn't be real. If I closed my eyes maybe it would all be a bad dream and then I'd wake up in bed at home with my teddy bear.

'Tim?' said Jake. 'Open your eyes! Now, your friend Biscuits is waiting for you down there. Come on. Start to walk backwards towards the edge[5].'

I walked backwards one step. Then another. Then I stopped.

'I can't!'

'Yes you can,' said Jake. 'You'll see. Over the edge. Don't worry. You can't fall. You just have to remember, you don't let go of the rope.'

I looked at him and started to go back some more. Then my feet suddenly lost contact with the ground. I slipped[6] backwards and suddenly ... there I was! I was hanging. In the air.

'Help!'

I was desperate[7].

I had to hold on to something.

I grabbed at the rock.

I let go of the rope!

Suddenly I was sliding[8] backwards, backwards, backwards.

I screamed[9].

I grabbed the rock. I held on to it. I was crying.

I heard them up above me. They were shouting.

'He's fallen!'

'He's let go of the rope.'

'I knew he would.'

'Of course Tim had to do it wrong!'

'He's stuck[10].'

'Don't stop, Tim!' Biscuits called from below.

I turned my head and tried to look at him. The whole world started to move this way and that. Biscuits looked like he was millions and millions of miles below me. I was hanging by my hands in the air.

'Help!'

'It's OK, Tim. Don't panic,' Jake called down.

'Don't panic, Tim, don't panic!' Kelly shouted. 'He's panicking, isn't he, Jake?'

'Shhh, Kelly. All of you. Go back, eh?' Jake said. 'Now. Tim. Listen. You've let go of the rope.'

'I know!'

---

[1] (to) abseil ['æbseɪl] *(sich) abseilen* [2] harness ['hɑːnɪs] *(Kletter-)Gurt* [3] rope [rəʊp] *Seil* [4] (to) let go of sth. *etwas loslassen*
[5] edge [edʒ] *Rand, Kante* [6] (to) slip *(aus)rutschen* [7] desperate ['despərət] *verzweifelt* [8] (to) slide, slid, slid [slaɪd], [slɪd] *rutschen, gleiten*
[9] (to) scream [skriːm] *(auf)schreien* [10] (to) be stuck [stʌk] *festsitzen, feststecken*

'But it's OK. You can't fall. You're safe, believe me.'

'I don't feel safe. I feel sick[1].'

'Well, you can get down in a few seconds. All you have to do is grab the rope.'

'How???'

'Just let go of the rock and –'

'I can't!' Was Jake mad? If I let go of the rock I'd swing through the air. I couldn't let go.

'You're safe in your harness,' Jake called. 'You needn't hold on to the rock. You just have to grab the rope. See the rope? Tim! Open your eyes!'

'I can't look down.'

'Look up. At me,' said Jake.

I turned my head up and opened my eyes a little. Jake was leaning right over the edge, not too terribly far away. He gave me a thumbs-up sign.

'That's good. Now. It's OK. Have a break if you like. It's not so bad now, is it?'

'Yes!'

'You can hang there all day if you really want,' said Jake.

'No!'

'Or you can grab that rope and walk down, one foot at a time, easy-peasy[2]. Mmm?'

I looked up at him.

'Can't you pull me up? Please?' I asked.

'We're trying to get you down, Tim, not up!' said Jake. 'You can do it. You're a brave[3] boy, Tim.'

He had to be joking!

'So just reach out[4] –' Jake said.

I thought about it. My fingers were hurting terribly. I couldn't hang there forever. Maybe if I let go and grabbed the rope I could get down. So I let go of the rock, I reached out suddenly, I tried to grab ...

I swung round and it was so scary that I closed my eyes and grabbed the rock again.

The others were grumbling. But Jake didn't give up.

'Almost. Try again. Go on.'

So I tried again. I reached out. My hand was wet with sweat[5] but I got the rope – I held onto it – I had it safe!

'Well done!' Jake called. 'There! I knew you could. Just hold on to it this time, eh? Now walk down. One step.'

I tried to move my feet. I couldn't feel them inside my boots. I made a little mouse's step downwards.

'Great!' said Jake. 'Now another step.'

My other leg moved. And I moved too. I was going down.

'There we go,' said Jake. 'That's it. You're getting it now.'

'I'm doing it!' I said and I walked down as carefully as I could.

'That's right. You're doing it, Tim,' Jake called. 'You're nearly halfway down. Doing just great. Go on. Nice and easy. Good boy. Well done.'

'I'm doing it,' I whispered, 'I'm doing it. I'm doing it. It's awful. But I'm doing it.'

I went down quicker and quicker – and then suddenly I was at the bottom and Biscuits hit me on the back and congratulated me.

'You did it, you did it, you did it!' Biscuits sang.

Jake was cheering me from right up at the top of the rock.

'Well done, Tim! It wasn't so bad, was it? Do you want to do it again, eh?'

I shook[6] my head so hard that my helmet moved.

'Never ever ever again!'

> *Write Tim's next postcard to his parents.*

[1] I feel sick. [sɪk] *Mir ist schlecht.* [2] easy-peasy [ˌiːzi ˈpiːzi] *kinderleicht* [3] brave [breɪv] *mutig* [4] (to) reach out [riːtʃ] *die Hand ausstrecken*
[5] sweat [swet] *Schweiß* [6] (to) shake, shook, shaken [ʃeɪk], [ʃʊk], [ˈʃeɪkən] *schütteln*

TF 6 Steel drums

Listen to the story on the CD. Close your book while you listen and enjoy all the different types of music. Listen to the story again and read it if you want to.

The Caribbean is a great place for music. You'll find Jamaican reggae in the charts all over the world. Wim Wenders has made a great film about old Cuban musicians. People dance to salsa in all the great cities of the world. And Puerto Rican reggaeton is a favourite in the dance clubs on every continent. But only Trinidad has its own music and its own musical instrument. The steel drum, or steel pan, as it's called in the Caribbean, is the most important acoustic instrument that was invented[1] in the 20th century. Here's its story:

Rhythm has always been the most important thing about African music, so when Africans were taken to work as slaves in the Caribbean, they took their rhythm with them. In the little free time they had, they played traditional African drums and danced.

The year of 1837 saw the end of slavery in the British Empire. The slaves were free now and they still used their drums for dances and ceremonies and to 'talk' to each other. Most importantly the drums were used in their carnival parades.

But the British were afraid the blacks might talk to each other in secret with their drums and make trouble. So in 1883 drums were banned from street parades. After that the blacks in Trinidad could only use bamboo sticks as drums.

Many years later, a 12-year-old boy from Trinidad's capital, Port of Spain, decided the bamboo sticks weren't good enough.

'I need a drum that makes more noise!' thought Winston 'Spree' Simon. He looked around. There, at the side of the road, stood an old, empty oil drum.

'An oil drum,' thought Winston. 'Why can't that become a real drum?' He banged[2] the top of the old oil drum. A dent[3] appeared – and a bump[4]. He banged first the dent, then the bump. A great sound came out – well, actually, two great sounds. The sounds were different.

For weeks Winston banged and tested and banged again till the top of the drum was full of dents and bumps. And when he played on the dents and bumps, 14 different sounds came out: the steel drum was born!

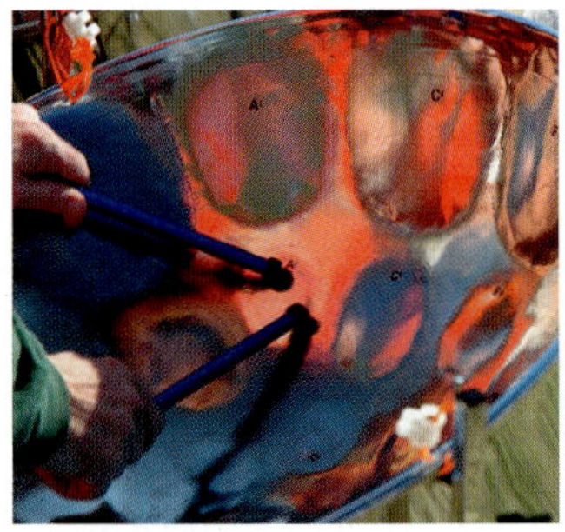

On Carnival Day 1946, Spree played his 14-note steel pan with two steelbands and the world heard this new instrument for the first time. And from that day, the drums of the Caribbean have played tunes, not just rhythms.

[1] invent [-'-] *erfinden* [2] (to) bang *schlagen* [3] dent *Delle* [4] bump *Beule*

TF 7 Football songs

1 The words of the songs

a) *Below are two songs that football supporters in Britain often sing. Perhaps you know them. There are some words missing. The vowel sound and the number of letters in the missing words are shown in blue. What could they be? Agree with your partner.*

You'll never walk alone

When you [ɔː] – 4 through the storm
Hold your [e] – 4 up high
And don't be afraid of the [ɑː] – 4.
At the end of the storm
There's a golden [aɪ] – 3
And the sweet silver song of the lark[1].

Walk on, through the [ɪ] – 4,
Walk on, through the [eɪ] – 4,
Though your dreams be tossed and blown[2].
Walk on, walk on, with hope in your heart,
And you'll never walk alone,
You'll never walk alone.

Walk on, walk on, with hope in your heart
And you'll never walk alone
You'll never walk alone.

by Oscar Hammerstein

We are the champions

I've paid my dues[3]
Time after [aɪ] – 4.
I've done my sentence[4]
But committed no crime[5].
And bad mistakes
I've made a [juː] – 3.
I've had my share[6] of sand kicked in my face
But I've come [uː] – 7.
And we mean[7] to go on, and on, and on, and on.

We are the champions, my [e] – 7
And we'll keep on fighting[8] till the [e] – 3.
We are the champions,
We are the champions.
No time for losers
'Cause we are the champions
Of the [ɜː] – 5.

by Freddie Mercury

b) *Now listen to the songs and check. Did you get the missing words right?*

2 Sing the songs

a) *Which song do you like better? Learn the words of that song.*

b) *Get together in a group with all the others who like the same song. Now imagine you are a football crowd and sing the song as loud as you can.*

---

[1] lark [lɑːk] *Lerche* [2] though your dreams be tossed and blown [tɒst] *etwa: auch wenn deine Träume in Gefahr geraten*
[3] (to) pay one's dues [djuːz] *seine Schulden zahlen* [4] sentence *Strafe* [5] crime *Verbrechen* [6] share *Anteil*
[7] (to) mean to do sth. *etwas vorhaben zu tun* [8] (to) keep on fighting ['faɪtɪŋ] *weiterkämpfen*

TF 8 Dawn (by Tim Wynne-Jones, abridged and adapted)

Barnsey met Dawn on the night bus to North Bay. His mother put him on at Ottawa. His parents owned a store and Christmas was busy, so as usual Barnsey was going up to Grandma Barrymore's, and his parents would follow Christmas Day.

'What if I have to sit beside someone weird[1] the whole way?' Barnsey asked his mother in the bus station.

'You are thirteen, Matthew,' she said. Her voice sounded different. 'Has anything bad happened to you yet?'

'I didn't say anything bad was going to happen. I'm just talking about someone weird.'

'For example?' said his mother.

'Someone who smells. Someone really, really fat who's half in my seat.'

'Come on,' said his mother. 'Or the only weird person you're going to be sitting beside is your mother on the way back to the store.'

In the line for the bus his mother suddenly gave him a big hug[2]. That wasn't like her. They weren't a hugging family. She looked him in the eyes.

'Matthew,' she said. 'It's not so long. Remember that.'

'I know,' said Barnsey. But he wasn't sure: did she mean the trip or the time before he'd see her again? He couldn't tell.

They moved through the line towards the driver at the door of the bus.

'Don't do the thing with the money,' Barnsey whispered to his mother.

'Why not?' she said. 'It's just good business. And anyway, young man, I'll do what I like.'

And she did. As Barnsey gave the driver his ticket, Barnsey's mother tore a twenty-dollar bill in half in front of the driver's face. She gave half the bill to Barnsey.

'Here, my good man,' said his mother to the bus driver in her store voice. 'My son will give you the other half when he arrives safely in North Bay. Merry Christmas.'

*

Then Barnsey was on the bus and there was Dawn.

There was no other seat. He looked at his mother through the window. She looked as miserable[3] as he felt. Sadly, he turned to Dawn.

'Is this seat taken?' he asked.

The girl took off her Walkman earphones and looked at the seat for a long time.

'Doesn't look like it.'

Barnsey sat down. He got out his own Walkman, arranged his CDs on his lap.

Then the driver got on the bus and they started. The girl beside Barnsey was just listening to what was coming through her earphones.

It was only the way she looked that he had a problem with. The nine earrings, the nose rings, and the mohawk haircut[4] – orange near her head and purple at the top, like her head was a planet and the sun was just coming up. She was about twenty and dressed all in black, with big black boots. But as long as she was just going to listen to her music, then Barnsey would listen to his and everything would be fine.

And it was for the first hour or so. But there isn't much room in a bus seat. And there wasn't much room on Barnsey's lap. Somehow a couple of his CDs fell down into the space between him and Dawn. The weird thing was, the same thing happened to her CDs. And the weirdest thing was that they both found out at the same time.

Barnsey put the new X.P. CD into his machine and turned it on. While he was waiting for the music to start, he looked at the CD cover. The band was standing under a dark sky around a gravestone[5]. Then if you moved the cover just right, there was a horrible monster full of dirt and worms where the gravestone had been. It was great.

It took Barnsey a minute to notice he wasn't hearing anything. He turned up the volume. Nothing. Then he realized there was

[1] weird [wiːəd] *seltsam* [2] hug [hʌg] *Umarmung* [3] miserable *traurig, elend* [4] mohawk haircut ['məʊhɔːk] *Irokesenhaarschnitt*
[5] gravestone *Grabstein*

something. A soft noise and then some rain and more soft noises.

Barnsey hit his Walkman. He thought the batteries were dying. Then Dawn changed CDs and suddenly shouted, as if she had just touched something hot. Both of them took the CDs out of their Walkmans and checked the titles.

'Rain Forest with Bells?' Barnsey read out loud.

'Scream for Your Supper!' Dawn read out loud.

Then they both laughed. They swapped CDs, but before Barnsey could even say thank you, the girl suddenly took his CD back.

'Tell you what,' she said. 'You listen to that for 'alf a minute, and I'll give this a try. Okay?'

She had a strong accent, British.

'Okay,' said Barnsey, 'but I think yours is broken or something.'

She took her CD back and tried it. She smiled and her smile was good.

'Naa,' she said. 'You just 'ave to listen, mate[1]. Carefully, like.'

So Barnsey listened carefully. There were some more soft sounds while he was waiting for the music. He didn't know what the music would be. Any moment a drum would start, then a guitar and a bass and, last of all, a voice, a voice would sing about saving the trees.

But no drum started. Maybe the CD was broken.

Then Dawn tapped him on the shoulder. She had his X.P. CD in her hand.

'This is killer-diller,' she said.

'You like X.P.?' he asked.

'It's rubbish[2].'

Barnsey laughed. Rubbish. What a great word. He pulled out Rain Forest with Bells.

'What you think?' she asked.

'It's rubbish.'

Then they both started to laugh. She held her hand out.

'Dawn,' she whispered.

'Barnsey,' he whispered back. He shook her hand.

*

When Barnsey woke up the bus was stopped.

'Will you look at that,' said Dawn with her nose against the window. Outside was nothing but white.

They were in a parking lot[3] with lots of other buses, trucks and cars. The road was blocked[4] by snow and they were at a big roadhouse[5] called the Cattle Yard. Still sleepy, Barnsey stayed in his seat as people started to walk past him. Dawn still had her nose against the glass.

'You know where I spent last Christmas?' she said. 'In Bethlehem.'

'The Bethlehem?'

'That's right,' she said. 'In a bar.'

Barnsey looked at Dawn. 'There are bars in Bethlehem?'

She laughed. 'Brilliant bars. Great little town is Bethlehem.'

Barnsey tried to imagine it.

Then the bus driver was beside him. 'Here, you might need this,' he said and gave Barnsey the half a twenty-dollar bill Barnsey's mother had given him.

'What's that then?' asked Dawn. Barnsey pulled the other half of the twenty out of his pocket and held them side by side.

'Hungry?' he said.

*

And she was hungry. She ate a grilled cheese sandwich in no time and two pieces of apple pie with cream. She ordered hot water and took a tea bag out of her black jacket.

'Ginseng, mate,' she said.

It was all so strange. Strange for Barnsey to walk into a place with her, as if they were on a date – a thirteen-year-old boy and a twenty-year-old. Perhaps people thought she was his sister. He could imagine what his parents would think of the way Dawn looked. She turned heads at the Cattle Yard.

It was a huge bar with moose[6] heads on the walls and two or three big TVs with country music on. There was a hockey game on the TV over the bar. Just about everyone was wearing a trucker's hat.

'I've got to go to the loo[7],' Dawn said. Barnsey watched her as she walked through

---

[1] mate *„Kumpel"* [2] rubbish *Mist* [3] parking lot *Parkplatz* [4] (to) be blocked *versperrt, unpassierbar sein* [5] roadhouse *Raststätte*
[6] moose [muːs] *Elch* [7] loo [luː] *Toilette*

the bar past all the truckers. He was full of admiration[1] for her. He picked up her tea cup and smelled the ginseng. It smelled deadly.

*

At around eleven word came that it was safe to leave and everyone got back on the bus. By then Barnsey knew that Dawn had just got back from Nepal where she was travelling with 'er mate. Before that she had been in Israel and worked on a kibbutz[2]. That was after Bloody Cairo where all her kit[3] was stolen. Before that she'd been in Ghana and before that art school. Barnsey didn't know what a kit was or a kibbutz. He wasn't sure where Nepal was or what or who 'er mate might be. But he didn't ask. She had called him mate too.

Finally Barnsey slept. And the next thing he knew, the bus was driving through the streets of North Bay. It was past 2:00 A.M.

'That'll be 'er,' said Dawn as they arrived at the bus station. Somehow she had recognized Grandma Barrymore in the group of people who were waiting.

'Go on,' said Dawn. And she made a big joke of it as she pushed Barnsey out of his seat as if he was Dumbo the elephant. Barnsey was weak with laughter. At the door he said goodbye and hoped her trip to Vancouver would be nothing but rubbish. Grandma Barrymore was standing at the bottom of the bus stairs. Dawn grabbed Barnsey by the head and rubbed it hard with her hand.

'Toodle-oo, mate,' said Dawn and blew him a kiss. She blew one at Grandma Barrymore too.

*

Then it was Christmas morning. It was a four-hour drive from Ottawa. His parents would arrive by 1 P.M. When he saw his father's Mustang at 10.30 A.M., Barnsey knew something was wrong.

He didn't go to the door. He watched from the window. Why weren't they in the big car? But there wasn't any they. Just his dad.

'Matthew, go help your dad,' said Grandma.

'No,' said Barnsey. He was remembering the last time he looked at his mother's face in the bus station, through the window. The look on her face. 'It won't be long,' she had said.

Everything was suddenly clear to him. He could see a trail of things that had led to this. You just had to move life a bit, and there was a whole other picture. Now he could hear in his head all the signs of this and they went back for months.

Then his father was in the living room. His face didn't look good but to Barnsey he didn't look bad enough. Grandma Barrymore was standing behind him with her hand on her son's shoulder. She looked very sad. They waited. Barnsey looked out the window. Then he turned and looked at his grandma.

'I wish you'd told me,' he said.

'She didn't know, Matthew,' said his father.

Barnsey stared out the window. There was a pair of skis on the top of the car.

'They're yours,' said his father. 'Your mother is hoping maybe you'll go on a skiing trip with her later in the holidays. Maybe Vermont.'

'That would be nice,' said Barnsey. Then he left the window and went to his room. His father didn't follow.

Barnsey stayed in his room and listened to the whole of the new X.P. CD. He moved the CD cover again and again. The monster appeared and disappeared. Appeared and disappeared.

Then his mother phoned. They had probably arranged all this too.

'Sure it was a terrible shock ...

'Decided it was best this way ...'

Barnsey listened. Said the right things.

'Do you think we could go down to Vermont for a long weekend?' said his mother. 'Give those new skis a workout[4]?'

Then, when the plans were made, Barnsey joined his father and his father's mother in the living room. They both gave him hugs.

'You okay?' his father asked.

'Yes.'

'You want to talk now? Or later?'

'Later.'

*

In bed Barnsey thought about where his mother would live. She was the one who was

[1] admiration *Bewunderung* [2] kibbutz [kɪˈbʊts] *Kibbuz (Gemeinschaftssiedlung in Israel)* [3] kit *Kleidung, Sachen*
[4] give sth. a workout *(hier:) etwas mal ausprobieren*

leaving. Would there be a room for him or would he sleep on the couch when he came to visit? Would his father stay in Ottawa or move back to the west coast? He tried to think of everything that could go wrong so that he wouldn't be surprised by anything.

'I just wish someone had told me,' he said.

In his sleep, Barnsey escaped. He was back on the bus. Dawn was saying 'Rubbish.' All of X.P. were also on the bus and were singing 'Rubbish. Rubbish. Rubbish.' Soon the whole bus sang 'Rubbish. Rubbish. Rubbish.'

Barnsey woke up. All he could think about was rubbish. He thought about the talk he had to have with his father that day. They would talk about everything openly. It would all be okay.

Rubbish.

So he left.

He only took his backpack. He didn't know what a ticket to Vancouver cost, but it didn't matter. He had his bank card. He had no idea what he was going to do and he didn't care. He would not run away like his mother. She had planned it carefully first. How far did that get you?

And so, by nine o'clock on Boxing Day[1] morning, he was waiting at the bus station. He had his Walkman and he pulled his CDs out of his backpack, one by one: X.P., Alice in Chains, Guns N' Roses, Nirvana, Rain Forest with Bells –

Rain Forest with Bells?

Barnsey stared[2] at the CD. There was a piece of paper inside the cover.

dear barnsey this is for the meal and for the fun and for when the rubbish gets to be too much. dawn xox[3]

Barnsey read the note again and again. He smelled it and then put it carefully back inside the CD cover. He took the CD out and put it on. He closed his eyes. The rain on the bells and the birds and the trees and the wind filled his ears.

Then suddenly a voice said, 'Matthew.' Barnsey opened his eyes and his father was sitting there beside him. His father was in his black coat but his hair was a mess. His eyes were the worst mess of all.

'You look scared,' said Barnsey. His father nodded. He didn't speak. Barnsey looked into his father's eyes and realized he didn't know what to say or do. Barnsey wanted to shake him, throw things at him, laugh and push him. Wake him up.

'Here,' he said. He took his earphones off and put them on his father.

'What is it?' his father asked. 'Is it broken?'

'No,' said Barnsey. 'Listen carefully.'

He watched his father as he listened. Barnsey listened too. He didn't need the earphones to hear it.

1 Understanding the story

Here are some of the main themes in the story 'Dawn':

– music
– 'weird' people
– parents who separate
– parents who don't tell you the truth
– how to deal with the 'rubbish' in life ...

What is the most important theme for you? Why?

2 The characters

a) *Take notes on the two main characters, Dawn and Barnsey (Matthew). Write short profiles for both of them. Find pictures (magazine, internet, ...) that you think could look like them.*

b) *Compare your ideas with a partner's.*

3 Beyond the story

Two people play Dawn and Barnsey. They write a short dialogue they have on the bus. The others are the passengers. They write down what they are thinking about Dawn and Barnsey. After Dawn and Barnsey act out their dialogue, the passengers tell the class about their thoughts.

[1] Boxing Day *26. Dezember* [2] (to) stare at sb./sth. *jn./etwas anstarren* [3] xox *(am Ende eines Briefes) Küsse*

TF 9 Poetry – out in the wilds

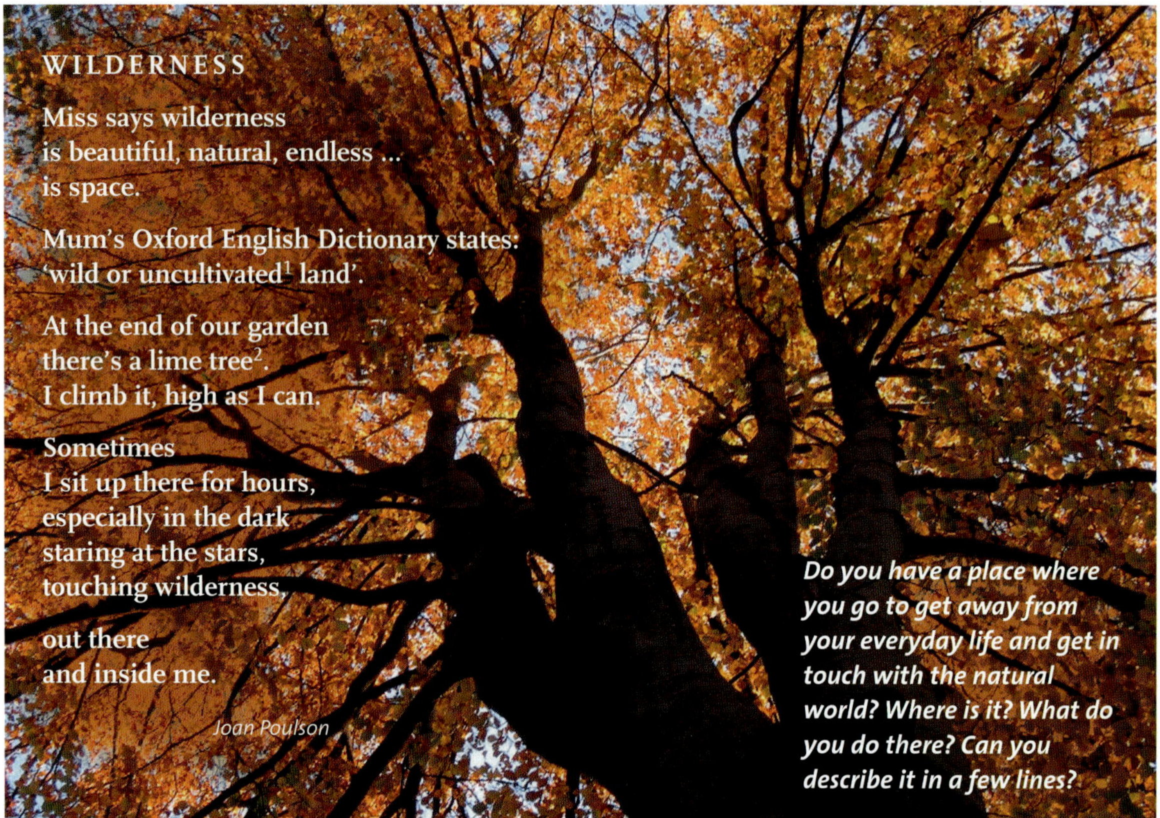

WILDERNESS

Miss says wilderness
is beautiful, natural, endless …
is space.

Mum's Oxford English Dictionary states:
'wild or uncultivated[1] land'.

At the end of our garden
there's a lime tree[2].
I climb it, high as I can.

Sometimes
I sit up there for hours,
especially in the dark
staring at the stars,
touching wilderness,

out there
and inside me.

Joan Poulson

Do you have a place where you go to get away from your everyday life and get in touch with the natural world? Where is it? What do you do there? Can you describe it in a few lines?

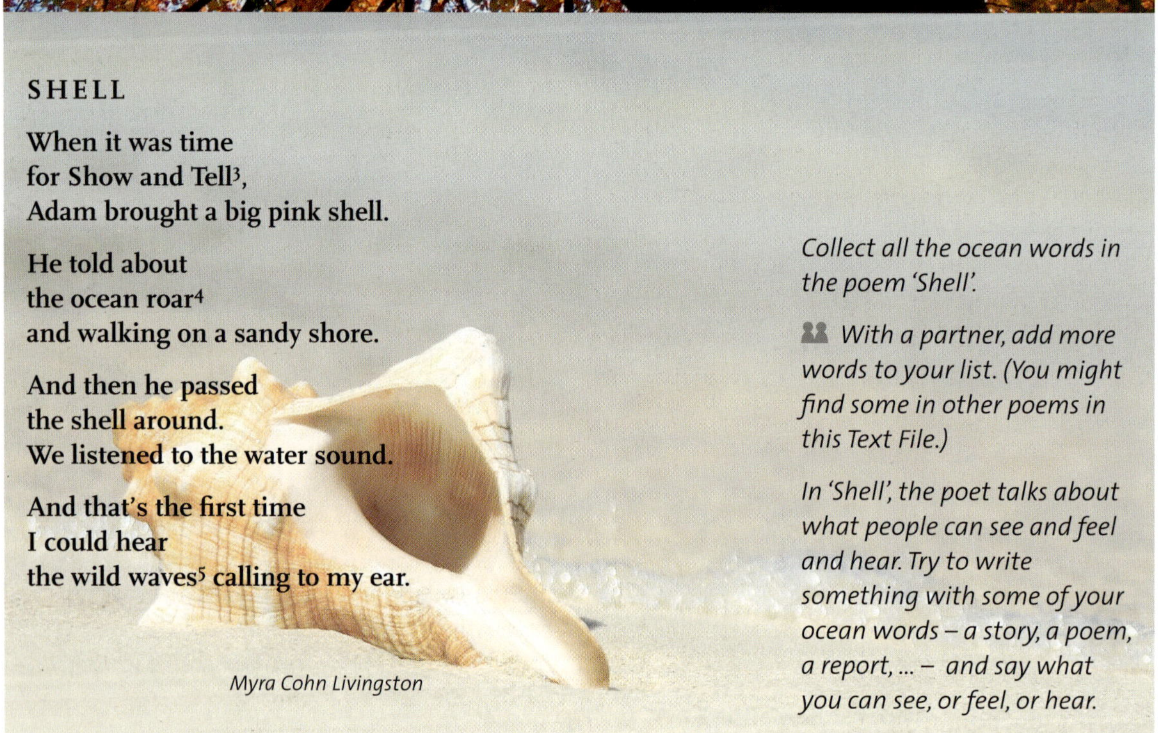

SHELL

When it was time
for Show and Tell[3],
Adam brought a big pink shell.

He told about
the ocean roar[4]
and walking on a sandy shore.

And then he passed
the shell around.
We listened to the water sound.

And that's the first time
I could hear
the wild waves[5] calling to my ear.

Myra Cohn Livingston

Collect all the ocean words in the poem 'Shell'.

With a partner, add more words to your list. (You might find some in other poems in this Text File.)

In 'Shell', the poet talks about what people can see and feel and hear. Try to write something with some of your ocean words – a story, a poem, a report, … – and say what you can see, or feel, or hear.

---

[1] uncultivated *unbebaut* [2] lime tree *Linde* [3] Show and Tell *Unterrichtsstunde, in der einzelne Schülerinnen und Schüler der Klasse etwas über einen mitgebrachten Gegenstand erzählen* [4] roar [rɔː] *Brüllen* [5] wave *Welle, Woge*

WHERE?

where do you hide a leaf?
in, if possible, a forest.

where do you hide a wind?
among straw[1] in dust.

where do you hide a horse?
within cloth or sea.

where do you hide the sun?
behind clouds, under horizons.

where do you hide water?
below a terrible flood[2].

where do you hide a storm?
inside a ghost or magician.

where do you hide a word?

Dave Calder

Look at how the poet hides his words in 'Where?' Can you do the same? Choose a word you like (not longer than eight letters). Hide your word between two other words and then write your own new verse for the poem, e.g.:
Where do you hide a cloud?
*In sky musi**c loud** and clear.*
Where do you hide thunder?
*In cool ear**th under** a tree.*

STORM

They're at it again
the wind and the rain
It all started
when the wind
took the window
by the collar[3]
and shook it
with all its might
Then the rain
butted in[4]
What a din[5]
they'll be at it all night
Serves them right
if they go home in the morning
and the sky won't let them in

Roger McGough

Try to imagine what the four characters in the poem look like: the wind, the rain, the window and the sky.

Draw a comic story of what happens in the poem. Give the characters some speech bubbles.

1 Out loud

Choose your favourite poem. Learn it by heart and practise saying it out loud. Think about the right speed and stress for the poem so that the listeners will understand it. Use pauses if they help.
Recite your poem to the class.

2 Collage

Make a collage of pictures that catch the atmosphere of one of the poems.
Stick the poem on to the collage. If you like, you can do all this on the computer.
Display the poem collages in class.

---

[1] straw *Stroh* [2] flood [flʌd] *Flut, Wassermenge* [3] (to) take sb. by the collar *jn. beim Kragen packen* [4] (to) butt in *sich einmischen* [5] din *Lärm*

TF 10 'Fans' – a play (by Ann Cartwright, abridged)

1 Before the play

Are you a fan of something or somebody? How serious are you? Are you a fanatic? Now read the play and find out how serious these four British fans are.

Scene:
Four friends are sitting in their form room. The three girls are looking at teen magazines. Tim is reading a computer magazine.

Kaz He's lovely.
Shaz He's got lovely hair.
Jaz Lovely eyes.
Kaz / Shaz / Jaz Ah!
Tim Are you talking about me again?
Kaz / Shaz / Jaz No!
Tim Now you know you are really.
Kaz / Shaz / Jaz We're not!
Tim Well, who ARE you on about[1], then?
Shaz Dermot Devlin!
Jaz From the band Celtic Nomads.
Tim Oh. Him. He's rubbish.
Kaz He is not!
Tim He looks like a girl.
Shaz He does not!
Tim He wears a dress!
Jaz It's a kaftan, actually. It's ethnic.

Tim You mean hippy. He's stupid. AND he can't sing.
Kaz I wish he'd walk into the room.
Shaz I wish he'd walk into the room right now.
Jaz I wish he'd walk into the room right now – and I'd – and I'd scream[2].
Kaz / Shaz Oo, and I would.
Tim What for?
Kaz Because he's lovely.
Shaz You just don't understand, Tim. Read your computer magazine.
Jaz Yeah. All those hard-drives and mega-nothings.

[1] (to) be on about ... *reden von/über ...* [2] (to) scream [skriːm] *schreien, kreischen*

Tim There's more point to this than what you do.

Jaz There isn't!

Tim There is. At least I can look at these pictures and buy something. You can't look at a picture of Dermot Drill-Head and buy him, can you?

Kaz Oo!

Shaz Buy Dermot Devlin!

Jaz Oo! You've started me off again[1] now!

Kaz I'd pay anything.

Tim But you can't! That's the point. You can't buy him.

Jaz We can buy his music.

Shaz And videos.

Kaz Did you see his latest one?

Shaz With him in the boat?

Jaz Sailing towards that woman with the flowers in her hair?

Kaz And the stars above their heads.

Shaz And the breeze flowing softly across the canal.

Jaz And he moves that oil-drum out of the way and that big bag of rubbish so that he can get to her.

Kaz He's so strong!

Shaz He's so romantic.

Jaz And singing to her at the same time!

Kaz, *Shaz*, *Jaz* Wow!

Tim I feel ill.

Kaz Oh, shut up.

Shaz Have you heard his latest song?

Jaz Oh, you mean 'Siren Dream'?

Shaz No, no, that was his last one.

Kaz Oh, I know the one! 'Tidal Wave Sensation'?

Shaz No! That's the CD album. I mean his very latest, 'Flowing From The Heart'.

Kaz Oh, yeah! I've heard that one! It's ever so romantic.

Tim Got a water fixation, hasn't he? Is that because he's a big drip[2]? You do waste your money on that sad singer.

Jaz He's not a sad singer! He's THE BUSINESS[3]!

Tim It's such a shame[4].

Kaz What is?

Tim You're just pitiful[5] and totally obsessed[6].

Shaz Let's have a look at YOUR magazine, then.

Tim Give us that back!

Kaz Yeah. Let's see how wonderful it is. Two pounds fifty?! Oh, you do waste your money on this sad computer stuff!

Tim It's not sad! A madman singer in a dress singing a song about jump-leads to his girlfriend whilst[7] sitting on an oil-drum! Now THAT'S sad!

Jaz Look at this! Page 14! Wow! New games!

Kaz 'Deadliest Mortality Blood-Spurt Revenge'[8]? What kind of game's that?

Tim A really good one.

Shaz About what?

Tim Gardening! What do you think?

Jaz What do you have to do?

Tim I'm not telling you.

Jaz Why not?

Tim 'Cause you'll make fun of me, that's why not.

Kaz Now why should we make fun of your very serious computer magazine just because you've ripped our beloved Dermot to pieces[9]?

Shaz We wouldn't do that, would we?

Jaz Certainly not. We're mature[10].

Kaz So go on, Tim.

---

[1] You've started me off again. *etwa: Jetzt bringst du mich wieder auf dieses Thema.* [2] a drip [drɪp] *ein Waschlappen, eine Flasche (wörtlich: ein Tropfen)* [3] the business ['bɪznəs] *etwa: DER HIT* [4] such a shame [ˌsʌtʃ‿ə 'ʃeɪm] *so ein Jammer, so eine Schande* [5] pitiful ['pɪtɪfl] *jämmerlich* [6] obsessed [əb'sest] *besessen* [7] whilst [waɪlst] *während* [8] deadliest mortality blood-spurt revenge (*Name eines Computerspiels, in dem viel Blut vergossen wird)* [9] (to) rip sth. to pieces [rɪp] *etwas in Stücke reißen* [10] mature [mə'tʃʊə] *reif, vernünftig*

Tim — All right, but you'd better not make fun of it 'cause it's really serious.

Jaz — We won't.

Tim — Well – There's two gangs – The Bloods and the Spurts – and you get to be in one of the gangs and fight the other one.

Kaz / *Shaz* / *Jaz* — What a load of rubbish!

Tim — I knew it! Shut up!

Kaz — Sounds really boring.

Tim — Boring?! It's brilliant! I've got the whole series.

Shaz — Series? There's more of them?

Tim — Yeah! There's 'Deadliest Mortality Blood-Spurt Revenge: The Beginning' followed by 'Deadliest Mortality Blood-Spurt Revenge: The Battle' followed by 'D.M.B-S.R.: The Hospitalization' followed by –

Jaz — Oh, don't tell me any more!

Kaz — How dreary!

Tim — I'm getting the next one for my birthday! You should see all the stuff I've got. And the posters! And what I really want is a virtual-reality set-up where I can really INTERACT with the gangs!

Pause.

Kaz — Shame, isn't it?

Shaz — Yeah. Pitiful.

Kaz — He's just totally obsessed.

Tim — Look who's talking[1]!

Kaz — Look out. Teacher's coming.

Shaz — She'll be in here with her X-Files magazine again.

Jaz — She's on about that stuff all the time.

Tim — Was Shakespeare an alien?

Kaz — Did Wordsworth have a Close Encounter whilst looking at those daffodils?

Shaz — Now she IS obsessed.

Kaz / *Shaz* / *Jaz* / *Tim* — She's such a fanatic!

2 The play

Describe in three or four sentences what the play is about.

3 Fans or fanatics?

a) *Find examples in the play that show the four school students as fans or fanatics.*

b) *Compare with a partner. Decide together who the biggest fanatic is. Tim? One of the girls? Or you?*

4 Performing the play

a) *Each student learns a role from part 1 (ll. 5–95) or part 2 (ll. 96–175) of the play.*

b) *Make groups of eight – four students who learned the first half of the play, four who learned the second half.*
Imagine what the characters do as they talk. Write stage directions into a copy of the play. They will help you to perform better.

Example:

Jaz / *Kaz* — Lovely eyes.

They all look into the air and smile.

Shaz / *Jaz* — Ah!

Tim — *(He looks over at the three girls.)* Are you talking about me again?

Perform the play for your class. Decide who is the best group.

[1] Look who's talking! *Das musst du/müsst ihr gerade sagen!*

Skills File – Inhalt

Im **Skills File** findest du Hinweise zu Arbeits- und Lerntechniken. Was du in den Skills-Kästen der Units gelernt hast, wird hier näher erläutert.

Was du bereits aus Band 2 von English G 21 kennst, ist mit **REVISION** gekennzeichnet,
z. B.
– **REVISION Learning words**, Seite 133
– **REVISION Describing pictures**, Seite 137

Viele neue Hinweise helfen dir bei der Arbeit mit Hör- und Lesetexten, beim Sprechen, beim Schreiben von eigenen Texten, bei der Sprachmittlung und beim Lernen von Methoden.

Manchmal gibt es auch Aufgaben dazu.

STUDY AND LANGUAGE SKILLS

SF REVISION Learning words

Worauf solltest du beim Lernen und Wiederholen von Vokabeln achten?

– Führe dein Vokabelverzeichnis, dein Vokabelheft oder deinen Karteikasten aus Klasse 6 weiter.
– Lerne immer 7–10 Vokabeln auf einmal.
– Lerne neue und wiederhole alte Vokabeln regelmäßig – am besten jeden Tag 5–10 Minuten.
– Lerne mit jemandem zusammen. Fragt euch gegenseitig ab oder übt die Wörter mit Lernspielen (z. B. Vokabel-Domino, Schiffe versenken, Quartett, *Vocabulary Action Sheets*).

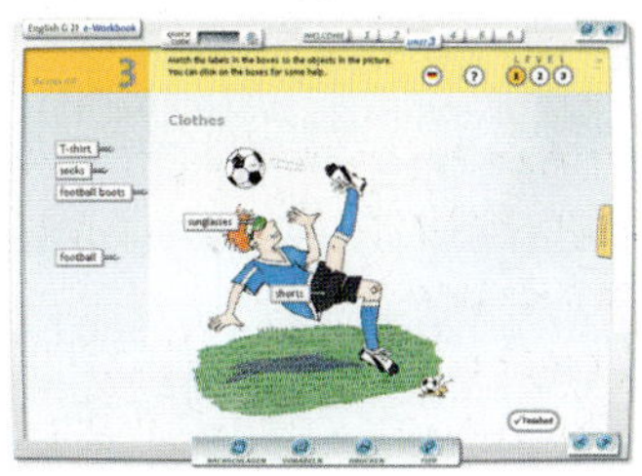

– Du weißt nach zwei Jahren Englischlernen wahrscheinlich, wie du am besten Vokabeln lernst: durch Hören und Nachsprechen, durch Bilder, am Computer (z. B. mit deinem e-Workbook oder dem *English Coach*) oder indem du dir eigene Geschichten um die neuen Vokabeln ausdenkst, sie in Texte bzw. Lieder einbaust oder dich beim Vokabellernen in deinem Zimmer oder der Wohnung bewegst.
– Schreib die neuen Wörter immer auch auf und überprüfe die Schreibweise mithilfe des *Dictionary* oder *Vocabulary*.

Wie kannst du Wörter besser behalten?

Wörter kannst du besser behalten, wenn du sie in Wortgruppen sammelst und ordnest. Dazu gibt es verschiedene Möglichkeiten.

Du kannst ...

- **Gegensatzpaare** sammeln, z.B.
  old-fashioned – modern,
  spicy – mild,
  forget – remember;

- Wörter mit **gleicher Bedeutung** sammeln, z.B.
  (to) train – (to) practise
- Wörter in **Wortfamilien** sammeln, z.B.
  (to) sing – song – singer
  shop, shopper, shopping, shopping list, shop assistant ...
  (to) ride (a horse/bike), (to) go riding, a bike ride, (to) take a ride, riding boots, riding hat
- Wörter in **Wortnetzen** (*networks*) oder **Wortfeldern** sammeln und ordnen.

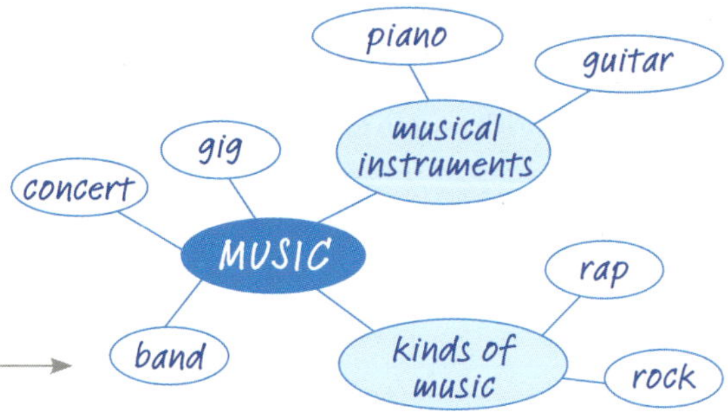

SF REVISION Understanding new words

Immer gleich im Wörterbuch nachschlagen?

Das Nachschlagen unbekannter Wörter im Wörterbuch kostet Zeit und nimmt auf Dauer den Spaß am Lesen. Oft geht es auch ohne Wörterbuch!

Was hilft mir, unbekannte Wörter zu verstehen?

1. Bilder zeigen oft die Dinge, die du im Text nicht verstehst. Schau sie dir deshalb vor dem Lesen genau an.
2. Oft hilft dir der Textzusammenhang, also die Wörter, die vor oder nach dem unbekannten Wort stehen,
   z.B. *We must hurry. Our train* **departs** *in ten minutes.*
3. Viele englische Wörter werden ähnlich wie im Deutschen geschrieben oder klingen ähnlich,
   z.B. brochure, electrician, president.
4. Manchmal stecken in neuen Wörtern bekannte Teile,
   z.B. arrival, a westbound train, snowshoes.

- Alles klar? Dann überlege, was diese Wörter bedeuten:
  hilly • imaginary • head of state • a winning shot • useful • canal • material • realistic • colony • official

SF Using an English–German dictionary

▸ Unit 1 (p. 16) • P 6 (p. 22)

Wann brauche ich ein englisch-deutsches Wörterbuch?

Du findest einen Text schwierig, weil er zu viele Wörter enthält, die dir unbekannt sind? Dann kann dir ein englisch-deutsches Wörterbuch weiterhelfen.
Im Text „Only a game“ auf S. 26 kommen eine Reihe von Wörtern vor, die du nicht kennst und die auch nicht in den EG 21-Wörterverzeichnissen aufgeführt sind, z. B. *experimental, at your own risk, lavender, Elizabethan, fog horn, brick, footstep*. Einige dieser Wörter kannst du sicherlich ableiten oder aus dem Zusammenhang erschließen. Wenn das nicht geht, hilft dir ein englisch-deutsches Wörterbuch.

Play at your own risk.

As they walked on, a fog came down on the street. They heard a fog horn.

All the boys could see were fog, dirty brick walls, blood – and the lavender.

Wie benutze ich ein englisch-deutsches Wörterbuch?

- Die **Leitwörter** (*running heads*) oben auf der Seite helfen dir, schneller zu finden, was du suchst. Auf der linken Seite steht das erste Stichwort, auf der rechten Seite das letzte Stichwort der Doppelseite.
- **rise** ist das **Stichwort** (*headword*). Stichwörter sind alphabetisch geordnet: **r** vor **s**, **ra** vor **re**, **rhe** vor **rhi** usw.
- Die ***kursiv* gedruckten** Hinweise helfen dir, die für deinen Text passende Bedeutung zu finden.
- Die **Ziffern 1**, **2** usw. zeigen, dass ein Stichwort unterschiedlichen Wortarten angehören kann (z. B. Adjektiv, Nomen, Verb).
- **Beispielsätze** und **Redewendungen** sind dem Stichwort zugeordnet. In den Beispielsätzen und Redewendungen ersetzt eine **Tilde** (~) das Stichwort.
- Die **Lautschrift** gibt Auskunft darüber, wie das Wort ausgesprochen und betont wird. (→ English sounds, S. 222)
- **Unregelmäßige Verbformen**, **besondere Pluralformen**, die **Steigerungsformen der Adjektive** und ähnliche Hinweise stehen in Klammern.

riveting

rink [rɪŋk] Eisbahn
rinse [rɪns] **1** *Nomen; für Haare* Tönung **2** *Verb mit Obj; Kleidung, Haare* ausspülen; *Geschirr* (ab)spülen

rise [raɪz] **1** *Verb ohne Obj* (**rose, risen**) *aus Stuhl o. Ä.* aufstehen, sich erheben; *von Sonne* aufgehen; *von Rakete* aufsteigen; *von Preis, Temperatur* ansteigen; *von Wasseroberfläche* (an)steigen **2** *Nomen; von Preis, Temperatur* Anstieg; *von Wasseroberfläche* (An)Steigen; *von Sozialismus* Aufstieg; *von Gehalt* Gehaltserhöhung; ***give ~ to*** verursachen
risen ['rɪzn] *Part. Perf.* ☞ ***rise***
riser ['raɪzə]: ***be an early / late ~*** ein Frühaufsteher / Langschläfer sein
risk [rɪsk] **1** *Nomen* Risiko; ***take a ~*** ein Risiko eingehen; ***at one's own ~*** auf eigene Gefahr **2** *Verb mit Obj* riskieren; ***let's ~ it*** das Risiko gehen wir ein!
risky ['rɪski] (***-ier, -iest***) riskant
ritual ['rɪtjʊəl] **1** *Nomen* Ritual **2** *Adj* rituell
rival ['raɪvl] **1** *Nomen* Rivale, Rivalin; *von Firma, Mannschaft* Konkurrent(in) **2** *Verb mit Obj* (**-ll-**, *AE* **-l-**) *Person* rivalisieren mit; *Firma, Mannschaft* konkurrieren mit; ***I can't ~ that*** da kann ich nicht mithalten
rivalry ['raɪvlri] (*Pl* ***-ies***) Rivalität; *zwi-*

• Finde nun heraus, was die folgenden Wörter und Wendungen bedeuten:
1. *at your own risk*
2. *'rose'* in *'The rocket rose in the early morning.'*
3. *'rises'* in *'The sun rises in the east.'*
4. *brick*
5. *lavender*
6. *footstep*

• In deinem Wörterbuch werden vermutlich viele Abkürzungen und Symbole verwende, wie z. B.
jn.
Obj
Pl
USA
Finde heraus, was sie bedeuten.

SF Using a German–English dictionary

▸ Unit 2 (p. 35) • P 12 (p. 42)

Wann brauche ich ein deutsch-englisches Wörterbuch?

Stell dir vor, du sollst einen Text über Katrina schreiben. Du findest, dass die Situation in der Schule schwer für sie ist. Aber was heißt in diesem Fall „schwer"? Hier hilft dir ein deutsch-englisches Wörterbuch.

Wie benutze ich ein deutsch-englisches Wörterbuch?

Viele Dinge sind dir wahrscheinlich vom *English–German dictionary* vertraut:

- **Leitwörter** (*running heads*) oben auf den Seiten helfen dir, das gesuchte Wort zu finden.
- Die **Stichwörter** (*headwords*) sind alphabetisch geordnet. **Beispielsätze** und **Redewendungen** sind den Stichwörtern zugeordnet. Die **Tilde** (~) ersetzt das Stichwort.
- Die ***kursiv* gedruckten** Hinweise helfen dir, die für deinen Text passende Bedeutung zu finden.
- Die **Ziffern 1**, **2** usw. zeigen, dass ein Stichwort unterschiedlichen Wortarten angehören kann (z.B. Adjektiv, Nomen, Verb).
- Bei schwierig auszusprechenden Wörtern stehen auch Hinweise zu Aussprache und Betonung.
- Bei kniffligen Wörtern gibt es in vielen Wörterbüchern weitere Hilfen und Hinweise.

Schwester

schwer 1 *Adj*; *gewichtsmäßig* heavy ['hevi] (*auch Musik, Parfüm*); *schwierig* difficult, hard (*auch Arbeit*); *Wein, Zigarre* strong; *Essen* rich; *Krankheit, Fehler, Unfall, Schaden* serious ['sɪəriəs]; *Strafe* severe; *Gewitter, Kämpfe, Ausschreitungen* heavy, violent; ***schwere Zeiten*** hard times; ***100 Pfund ~ sein*** weigh [weɪ] 100 pounds; ***es ~ haben*** have a hard time; ***das ist ~ zu sagen*** it's hard to say **2** *Adv*: ***~ arbeiten*** work hard; ***~ beschädigt*** *Haus o.Ä.* severely damaged; ***ich bin ~ erkältet*** I've got a bad cold; ***er ist ~ zu verstehen*** it's hard to understand what he's saying; ***~ enttäuscht sein*** be* bitterly disappointed; ***das will ich ~ hoffen*** I really hope so; ☞ **schwerfallen, schwertun**

Schwerkraft … ☞ **schwer ma**… ancholy ['mel… **Schwerpunkt** … *gen* (main) … *legen* put* th… **Schwert** sword **schwertun**: *sic*… culty with sth. **Schwerverbre**… offender **schwerverwun**… **schwerwiegen**… ['sɪəriəs] **Schwester** sist… *als Anrede*

schwer krank

schwer

Das deutsche **schwer** hat drei Hauptbedeutungen:
1) *schwer von Gewicht*: **heavy**;
2) *schwerwiegend, ernst*: **serious**, **bad**;
3) *schwierig*: **difficult**, **hard**, **tough**.

• Welche Entsprechung von **schwer** brauchst du in diesen Sätzen?

1. Das Leben im Internat ist schwer für Katrina.
2. Schultaschen sind für jüngere Schüler häufig zu schwer.
3. Heute Morgen war ein schwerer Unfall auf der Autobahn.
4. Die Matheaufgabe ist sehr schwer.
5. Nach einer schweren Krankheit kann er wieder zur Schule gehen.
6. Letzte Nacht gab es ein schweres Gewitter.

Tipp

Lies immer erst den **gesamten Wörterbucheintrag**, bevor du dich für eine bestimmte Übersetzung entscheidest. Nimm nicht einfach die erste Übersetzung, die dir angeboten wird!

SF REVISION Describing pictures

Wie kann ich Bilder beschreiben?

Wo?

- Um zu sagen, wo etwas abgebildet ist, benutze:
  at the top/bottom • in the foreground/background • in the middle • on the left/right
- Du kannst diese *phrases* auch kombinieren:
  at the bottom on the left • at the top on the right
- Diese Präpositionen sind auch hilfreich:
  behind • between • in front of • next to • under

Wie?

Geh bei der Beschreibung in einer bestimmten Reihenfolge vor, z. B. von links nach rechts, von oben nach unten oder vom Vordergrund zum Hintergrund.

Wie kann ich beschreiben, was die Personen auf dem Bild tun?

Um zu sagen, was die Personen auf dem Bild tun, verwendet man das **present progressive**.

Robert and Asif <u>are standing</u> inside the London Eye. Robert <u>is taking</u> a photo.

SF REVISION Giving a presentation

Wie mache ich eine gute Präsentation?

Vorbereitung

- Ordne deine Gedanken und notiere sie, z. B. auf nummerierten Karteikarten oder als Mindmap.
- Bereite ein Poster oder eine Folie vor. Schreib groß und für alle gut lesbar.
- Übe deine Präsentation zu Hause vor einem Spiegel. Sprich laut, deutlich und langsam, mach Pausen. Reicht die Zeit?

Durchführung

- Bevor du beginnst, bereite deine Medien vor und sortiere deine Vortragskarten.
- Warte, bis es ruhig ist. Schau die Zuhörer an.
- Erkläre zu Anfang, worüber du sprechen wirst.
  Lies nicht von deinen Karten ab, sondern sprich frei.
- Schreibe die Gliederung sowie unbekannten Wortschatz und Eigennamen an die Tafel.

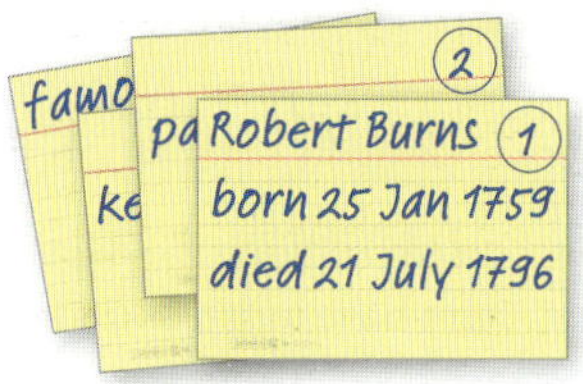

My presentation is about ...
First, I'd like to talk about ...
Second, ...

This picture/photo/... shows ...

Schluss

- Sag, dass du fertig bist.
- Frag die Zuhörenden, ob sie Fragen haben.
- Bedanke dich fürs Zuhören.

That's the end of my presentation. Thank you for listening. Have you got any questions?

SF Internet research ▸ *Unit 5, P 13 (p. 105)*

Es gibt inzwischen weit mehr Internetseiten, als Menschen auf der Welt leben. Wie findest du in diesem Dschungel die Informationen, die du brauchst? Wie kannst du sie sortieren und für dein Thema bearbeiten?

1. Überlege, welches die wichtigsten Stichwörter für dein Thema sind. Nimm an, du willst eine Kurzbiografie von Shakira schreiben. Passende Stichwörter sind dann z. B. **Shakira biography**.

2. Gib deine Stichwörter (ohne Satzzeichen) auf der Startseite deiner Suchmaschine ein.
3. Dann erhältst du eine Liste mit Webseiten, die alle diese Stichwörter enthalten. Je mehr Stichwörter du eingibst, desto zielgenauer ist deine Suche. Wenn du nach Wörtern suchst, die zusammengehören, setzt du sie in Anführungszeichen: **"Shakira songs in Spanish"**.
4. Achte bei der Auswahl der Seiten darauf, wer sie erstellt hat. Kannst du dich darauf verlassen, dass die Informationen zuverlässig sind (Online-Lexikon, bekannte Zeitschrift oder Organisation, ...)? Oder handelt es sich nur um persönliche Meinungen (Forum, Fan-Seite, ...)?
5. Sieh dir mehrere Websites an. Verschaffe dir einen schnellen Überblick, ob die betreffende Seite die von dir gesuchten Informationen enthält (vgl. SF **Skimming**, S. 141).
6. Du kannst mit deinem Stichwort in der Suchmaschine auch nach Bildern und Grafiken suchen.
7. Leg alle interessanten Artikel, Bilder, Songtexte, Podcasts usw. zu deinem Thema in einem eigenen Ordner ab. Dann kannst du sie dir später genauer ansehen und auswählen. Eine Liste kann dir helfen, die Übersicht zu bewahren:

Thema	*Shakira biography*
Webadresse	*http://en.wikipedia.org/wiki/Shakira*
Inhalt	*education, career*

8. Kopiere keine ganzen Artikel aus dem Internet. Mach dir Notizen und verwende deine eigenen Worte.
9. Setz dir ein Zeitlimit für deine Internetrecherche. Wenn du dein Material gesichtet hast, ordne es und prüfe, ob dir noch Informationen fehlen. Vielleicht findest du sie in anderen Quellen (Bücher, Zeitschriften, CD-ROMs usw.). Lösche überflüssige Informationen und Seiten, damit du die Übersicht bewahrst.

LISTENING AND READING SKILLS

SF Listening

► *Unit 1 (p. 13)* • *P 2 (p. 20)*

Vor dem Hören

- Frag dich, was du schon über das Thema weißt.
- Nutze Überschriften oder Bilder um zu erahnen, was dich z. B. bei einer Geschichte erwarten könnte.
- Bereite dich darauf vor, Notizen zu machen. Leg z. B. eine Tabelle oder Liste an.

Während des Hörens

Listening for gist:
Konzentriere dich beim ersten Hören auf allgemeine Informationen, z. B. die Personen (unterschiedliche Stimmen), das Thema, die Umgebung (Geräusche), die Atmosphäre (die Sprechweise der Leute).

Listening for detail:
- Mach dir bewusst, worauf du genau achten willst (Hörauftrag).
- Gerate nicht in Panik, wenn du meinst, du hättest gerade etwas Wichtiges verpasst. Konzentriere dich auf die nächste wichtige Information.
- Lass dich nicht von anderen Einzelheiten oder Geräuschen ablenken.
- Mach nur kurze Notizen, z. B. Anfangsbuchstaben, Symbole oder Stichworte.
- Manche Signalwörter machen es dir leichter, den Hörtext zu verstehen
- Aufzählung: **and**, **another**, **too**
- Gegensatz: **although**, **but**
- Grund, Folge: **because**, **so**, **so that**
- Vergleich: **larger/older/... than**, **as ... as**, **more**, **most**
- Reihenfolge: **before**, **after**, **then**, **next**, **later**, **when**, **at last**, **at the same time**

Nach dem Hören

- Vervollständige deine Notizen sofort.
- Wenn du den Text ein zweites Mal hören kannst, konzentriere dich auf das, was du nicht sicher verstanden hast.

SF REVISION Multiple-choice exercises

Worauf sollte ich bei Multiple-Choice-Aufgaben achten?

- Lies die Frage sehr genau durch.
- Bevor du dir die Lösungsangebote ansiehst, überlege dir, wie die richtige Antwort lauten könnte. Wenn diese dann auch als Lösung angeboten wird, könnte es die richtige sein.
- Lies aber erst alle vorgegebenen Lösungen, bevor du dich entscheidest.
- Sprich die Sätze mit den verschiedenen Lösungsmöglichkeiten leise nach. Oft hört man heraus, was richtig ist.
- Achte darauf, dass du nur **eine** Antwort ankreuzt.
- Mach erst die Aufgaben, die dir leicht fallen. Gehe dann zu den Fragen zurück, bei denen du unsicher bist.

1 Which is a famous London sight?
- A Brandenburg Gate
- B the Eiffel Tower
- C Buckingham Palace
- D the Orkney Islands

2 What did Robert and Asif do at the Trocadero?
- A play football
- B eat Indian food
- C visit Asif's family
- D play a new game

SF REVISION Scanning

Lesen, um nach Informationen zu suchen

Du musst einen Text manchmal gar nicht ganz lesen, wenn du nur bestimmte Informationen (für eine spezielle Aufgabe) brauchst. Stattdessen kannst du den Text nach Schlüsselwörtern (**key words**) absuchen und nur dort lesen, wo du diese findest.
Manchmal sind in Aufgaben bereits Schlüsselwörter vorgegeben, nach denen du in einem Text suchen sollst. So möchte Asif z. B. in A5 auf S. 16 *„something spicy or very spicy"* essen. Auf der Speisekarte findest du solche Speisen unter „Tikka dishes" und „Jalfredi dishes", d. h. du brauchst nur dort weiterzusuchen.

Wie gehe ich vor?

Schritt 1: Bevor du auf den Text schaust
Denk an das Schlüsselwort, nach dem du suchst. Du kannst es dir auch aufschreiben.

Schritt 2: Das Schlüsselwort finden
Geh mit deinen Augen sehr schnell durch den Text. Dabei hast du das Schriftbild oder das Bild des gesuchten Wortes vor Augen. Das Wort wird dir sofort „ins Auge springen".
Du kannst auch mit dem Finger in breiten Schlingen oder Bewegungen wie bei einem „S" durch die Mitte des Texts von oben bis unten gehen. Wenn du das Schlüsselwort gefunden hast, lies nur dort weiter, um Näheres zu erfahren.

Schritt 3: Gegebenenfalls neue Schlüsselwörter finden
Es kann sein, dass das Schlüsselwort, nach dem du suchst, nicht im Text vorkommt. Dann musst du dir überlegen, welche anderen Wörter mit den benötigten Informationen zu tun haben, und nach diesen Wörtern suchen. Stell dir z. B. vor, du suchst auf einer Speisekarte ein Gericht mit Fleisch. Das Wort *meat* steht aber nirgends. Dann versuch es z. B. mit *lamb*, *chicken* oder *pork*.

Tipp

Wenn du wie bei Aufgabe 5 auf S. 16 nach mehreren Schlüsselwörtern suchen musst (*mild, nuts, spicy* ...), scanne den Text nach jedem Schlüsselwort einzeln.

SF Skimming

▸ Unit 5 (p. 96)

Lesen, um sich einen Überblick zu verschaffen

„Skimming" bedeutet, dass du einen Text überfliegst, um schnell einen Überblick zu bekommen, worum es geht. Das ist z. B. sehr nützlich, wenn du herausfinden willst, ob ein Text, den du im Internet oder in einem Buch gefunden hast, überhaupt die Informationen enthält, nach denen du suchst.

Wie gehe ich vor?

Beim Überfliegen des Textes helfen dir

- die **Überschrift**
- **hervorgehobene** Wörter oder Sätze
- die **Bilder** und **Bildunterschriften**
- die **Zwischenüberschriften**
- der **erste Satz** jedes Absatzes
- der **letzte Satz** des Textes
- **Grafiken** und **Statistiken**
- die **Quelle** des Textes

'Hello Glasgow! It's good to be home!'

Franz Ferdinand play fantastic gig in their home town

Review by J. Colthorpe

Franz Ferdinand get Glasgow dancing

They have come a long way since they started out playing gigs in Glasgow's local indie clubs back in 2001. Two successful albums and a world tour later, Franz Ferdinand are one of the most popular bands in the world today. But last night they were back playing in their hometown, Glasgow, and this time to a much larger audience than they did six years ago.

Electric atmosphere

The atmosphere outside the concert hall was electric. The crowd were excited and many fans were already singing their favourite Franz Ferdinand songs. Inside the place was full and noisy; people were pushing through the crowds, hoping to get down near the stage. Soon the support band had finished and it was time for Franz Ferdinand to take to the stage.

All the favourite hits

'Hello Glasgow! It's good to be home!' shouted singer Alex Kapranos as he ran onto the stage. The crowd cheered as Alex started with "Jacqueline", the first song off their first album. He was soon joined by Bob Hardy on bass guitar as the song kicked in followed by Paul Thomsen on the drums. All of their popular songs followed to make up a 16-song, 90-minute set. They finished with their classic "Take Me Out" – the perfect song to end an excellent show.

Not only girls

Franz Ferdinand once said that they want to make music that girls can dance to. Well, they have certainly done that. Last night everbody was dancing, girls and boys.

New Amsterdam Music Review 18th December 2007

- Überflieg den Artikel um herauszufinden, worum es darin geht.
- Dann mach die Aufgabe 1 auf Seite 96.

SF REVISION Taking notes

Worum geht es beim Notizenmachen?

Wenn du beim Lesen oder Zuhören Notizen machst, kannst du dich später besser daran erinnern, wenn du etwas vortragen, nacherzählen oder einen Bericht schreiben sollst.

Wie mache ich Notizen?

In Texten oder Gesprächen gibt es immer wichtige und unwichtige Wörter. Die wichtigen Wörter werden Schlüsselwörter (**key words**) genannt und nur die solltest du notieren. Meist sind das Substantive und Verben, manchmal auch Adjektive oder Zahlen.

Tipp

- Verwende Ziffern (z. B. „7" statt „seven").
- Verwende Symbole und Abkürzungen, z. B. ✔ (für Ja) und + (für und) oder GB für Great Britain, K für Katrina.
  Du kannst auch eigene Symbole erfinden.
- Verwende not oder statt „doesn't" oder „don't".

SF REVISION Marking up a text

Wann sollte ich einen Text markieren?

Du hast einen Text mit vielen Fakten vor dir liegen und sollst später über bestimmte Dinge berichten. Dann wird es dir helfen, die für dich wichtigen Informationen im Text zu markieren.

Wie gehe ich am besten vor?

Lies den Text und markiere nur die für dein Thema wichtigen Informationen. Nicht jeder Satz enthält Wörter, die für deine Aufgabe wichtig sind und oft reicht es aus, nur ein oder zwei Wörter in einem Satz zu markieren.

– Du kannst wichtige Wörter einkreisen.

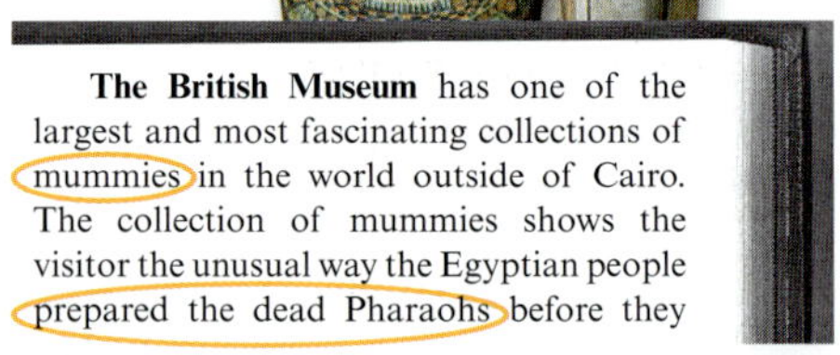

The British Museum has one of the largest and most fascinating collections of mummies in the world outside of Cairo. The collection of mummies shows the visitor the unusual way the Egyptian people prepared the dead Pharaohs before they

– Du kannst sie unterstreichen.

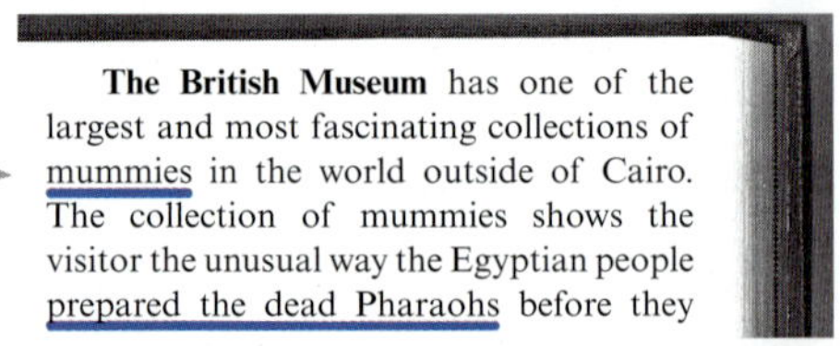

The British Museum has one of the largest and most fascinating collections of mummies in the world outside of Cairo. The collection of mummies shows the visitor the unusual way the Egyptian people prepared the dead Pharaohs before they

– Du kannst sie mit einem Textmarker hervorheben.

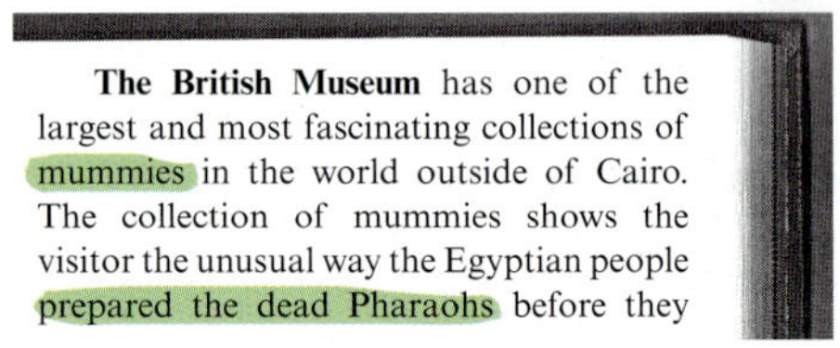

The British Museum has one of the largest and most fascinating collections of mummies in the world outside of Cairo. The collection of mummies shows the visitor the unusual way the Egyptian people prepared the dead Pharaohs before they

ABER:
Markiere nur auf Fotokopien von Texten oder in deinen eigenen Büchern.

MEDIATION SKILLS

SF Mediation

▸ *Unit 4, P 15 (p. 86)*

REVISION Wann muss ich zwischen zwei Sprachen vermitteln?

Manchmal musst du zwischen zwei Sprachen vermitteln. Das nennt man **mediation**.

1. Du gibst englische Informationen auf Deutsch weiter:
   Du fährst z. B. mit deiner Familie nach Großbritannien und deine Eltern oder Geschwister wollen wissen, was jemand in einem Café gesagt hat oder was an einer Informationstafel steht.
2. Du gibst deutsche Informationen auf Englisch weiter:
   Vielleicht ist bei dir zu Hause eine Austauschschülerin aus England oder Dänemark zu Gast, die kein Deutsch spricht und Hilfe braucht.
3. In schriftlichen Prüfungen musst du manchmal in einem englischen Text gezielt nach Informationen suchen und diese auf Deutsch wiedergeben. Oder du sollst Informationen aus einem deutschen Text auf Englisch wiedergeben.

REVISION Worauf muss ich bei *mediation* achten?

- Übersetze nicht alles wörtlich, sondern gib den Sinn wieder.
- Gib nur das Wesentliche weiter, lass Unwichtiges weg.
- Verwende kurze und einfache Sätze.
- Wenn du ein Wort nicht kennst, umschreibe es oder ersetze es durch ein anderes Wort.

Was kann ich tun, wenn ich ein wichtiges Wort nicht kenne?

Vielleicht findest du es manchmal schwer, mündliche Aussagen oder schriftliche Textvorlagen in die andere Sprache zu übertragen, z. B. weil
- dein Wortschatz nicht ausreicht
- dir bekannte Wörter „im Stress" nicht einfallen
- spezielle Fachbegriffe auftauchen.

Manche Wörter kannst du umschreiben, z. B. mithilfe von Relativsätzen wie:
It's somebody/a person who ...
It's something that you use to ...
It's an animal that ...
It's a place that/where ...

▸ *Paraphrasing (S. 144)*

SPEAKING AND WRITING SKILLS

SF Paraphrasing

▸ *Unit 3 (p. 57)* • *P 3 (p. 63)*

Worum geht es beim Paraphrasing?

„Paraphrasing" bedeutet, etwas mit anderen Worten zu erklären. Man kann vieles umschreiben, z. B. einen Gegenstand, eine Tätigkeit oder eine Person. Paraphrasing ist auch besonders nützlich für **Mediation**. (▸ *Mediation, p. 143)*

Wie gehe ich beim Paraphrasing vor?

- Man kann mit einem Wort umschreiben, das dieselbe Bedeutung hat:
  To begin is the same as to start.
  Oder man sagt das Gegenteil:
  To win is the opposite of to lose.
- Manchmal braucht man mehrere Wörter, z. B. wenn man etwas beschreibt oder erklären will, wie man es verwendet. Dabei benutzt man ein allgemeines Wort (**general word**) und nennt weitere Eigenschaften.
  A half-pipe is a location for skateboarders.
- Oder du beginnst mit **It's like ...**
  It's like a path through the woods or the fields and you can ride your horse on it. (*a bridle path*)
- Du kannst zum Umschreiben auch einen Relativsatz (**relative clause**) verwenden:
  A coach is a person who trains sports teams.
  A swimsuit is something that girls wear when they go swimming.
- Natürlich kannst du auch mehrere Methoden gleichzeitig anwenden:
  A hanger is something that you use to hang clothes on.
  A desert is a large piece of land that has very little water.

1. Umschreibe ein Wort aus der linken Spalte mit einem Wort aus der rechten Spalte. Benutze **the same as** oder **the opposite of**.

sad	parents
white	happy
clean	black
wonderful	dirty
mother/father	great

2. Schau dir diese Umschreibungen an. Findest du ein passendes Wort dafür? Dann erkläre einem Partner, wie das Wort umschrieben wurde.
- **It's a man who looks funny and works in a circus.**
- **It's something you put food on.**
- **It's a place where you watch films.**
- **It's an animal like a rat, but smaller.**

3. What's wrong here? Correct the sentences.
- **A horse is a place where people can drink beer.**
- **A pub is a meal that you eat in the evening.**
- **A dinner is an animal you can ride on.**

SF Brainstorming

▸ Unit 4, P 13 (p. 85)

Was ist Brainstorming und wofür ist es gut?

Write a text about your perfect weekend oder *Prepare a presentation on …* – so oder ähnlich lauten viele Aufgaben, die dir im Unterricht gestellt werden. Ob mündliche Präsentation oder das Schreiben eines längeren Textes – bei beiden Aufgaben ist es nützlich, wenn du im ersten Schritt möglichst viele Ideen zum Thema sammelst. Dafür gibt es verschiedene Techniken: Du kannst eine Mindmap anlegen oder auch eine Liste. Dabei schreibst du alles auf, was dir zu einem Thema einfällt, ohne es gleich zu ordnen.

Auswertung der Ergebnisse deines Brainstormings

Working with a list

1. Schreib all deine Ideen so auf, wie sie dir einfallen. Es gibt dabei keine falschen oder verrückten Ideen – alles ist erlaubt! Schreib jede Idee auf eine neue Zeile.
2. Überlege, welche Ideen du für dein Thema verwenden willst. Unterstreiche sie. Ideen, die du gar nicht verwenden möchtest, kannst du durchstreichen.
3. Nummeriere deine Ideen nach Wichtigkeit, als würdest du eine Hitliste anlegen. Die Nummer 1 markiert deine wichtigste Idee.

6. watch DVDs
3. swimming pool
no jobs for parents
parents not at home
1. sleep late – every morning
~~hang out~~
2. no homework
5. disco/party with friends
watch TV
4. see friends cinema

Working with a mindmap

1. Überlege dir, welche Oberbegriffe zu deinem Thema passen. Verwende unterschiedliche Farben.
2. Ergänze jede Idee, die zu einem Oberbegriff passt, auf einem Nebenast.
3. Du kannst statt Wörtern auch Symbole oder Bilder ergänzen.

Working with the 5 Ws

Schreib die Fragewörter **Who? What? When? Where? Why?** in eine Tabelle. Die Ideen, die dir zu der jeweiligen Frage kommen, werden darunter geschrieben.

who	what	when	where	why
I + friends	do sports	Friday	at home	no homework
no parents	go to disco	Saturday	at friends'	no jobs to do
	chat		swimming pool	have fun
	sleep late			

WRITING COURSE – ZUSAMMENFASSUNG

The steps of writing

1. Brainstorming – Ideen sammeln und ordnen (s. S.145)
2. Schreiben. Dabei achte darauf,
   - deine Sätze zu verbinden und auszubauen (*Writing better sentences*)
   - deinen Text gut zu strukturieren (*Using paragraphs*)
   - bei einem Bericht die 5 Ws abzudecken (*Writing a report*).
3. Deinen Text inhaltlich und sprachlich überprüfen (*Correcting your text*)

Writing better sentences ▸ *Unit 1, P 11 (p. 24)*

REVISION Linking words and phrases

Eine Geschichte klingt interessanter, wenn man die Sätze mit **linking words** miteinander verbindet. Dabei gibt es mehrere Möglichkeiten:

- **Time phrases** wie at 7 o'clock, every morning, in the afternoons, a few minutes later, suddenly, then, next ...
- **Konjunktionen** wie although, and, because, but, so ... that, that, when, while
- **Relativpronomen** wie who, which und that.

Adjektive und Adverbien

- Mit Adjektiven kannst du eine Person, einen Ort, einen Gegenstand oder ein Erlebnis genauer beschreiben und interessanter gestalten. Vergleiche:
  The man looked into the room. → The young man looked into the empty room.
- Mit Adverbien kannst du beschreiben, **wie** jemand etwas macht:
  The young man looked nervously into the empty room.

Using paragraphs ▸ *Unit 2, P 4 (p. 39)*

REVISION Structuring a text

Ein Text ist viel besser zu verstehen, wenn er mehrere Absätze enthält:

- eine Einleitung (**beginning**) – hier schreibst du, worum es geht
- einen Mittelteil (**middle**) – hier schreibst du mehr über dein Thema
- einen Schluss (**end**) – hier bringst du den Text zu einem interessanten Ende.

REVISION Topic sentences

Am Anfang eines Absatzes sind kurze, einleitende Sätze (**topic sentences**) gut, die den Lesern sofort sagen, worum es geht, z. B.

1. Orte: My trip to ... was fantastic./... is famous for .../... is a great place.
2. Personen: ... is great/funny/interesting/clever ...
3. Aktivitäten: ... is great fun./Lots of people ... every day.

Wie kann ich meine Absätze interessant gestalten?

- Beginne mit einem interessanten Einstiegssatz:
  Guess what happened to me today!/Did I tell you that ...?
- Fang für jeden neuen Aspekt einen neuen Absatz an.
- Beende deinen Text mit einer Zusammenfassung oder etwas Persönlichem.

Writing a report – organizing ideas

▸ *Unit 3, P 13 (p. 67)*

Worauf kommt es bei einem Bericht an?

Wenn du einen Bericht über ein Ereignis oder ein Spiel schreibst, beachte:

- Gib dem Leser **eine schnelle Orientierung**, was passiert ist.
- Beginne mit **wichtigen Informationen** und gib erst dann Detailinformationen.
- Ein Bericht gibt immer Antworten auf die **5 Ws**: **Who? What? When? Where? Why?** und manchmal auch **How?** Achte darauf, dass du diese fünf (bzw. sechs) Fragen möglichst beantwortest.

Correcting your text

▸ *Unit 5, P 12 (p. 104)*

Ein Text ist noch nicht „fertig“, wenn du ihn zu Ende geschrieben hast. Du solltest ihn immer mehrmals durchlesen:

- einmal, um zu sehen, ob er vollständig und gut verständlich ist
- noch einmal, um ihn auf Fehler zu überprüfen, z. B. **Rechtschreibfehler (*spelling mistakes*)** oder **Grammatikfehler (*grammar mistakes*)**.

tomato [tə'mɑːtəʊ], *pl* tomatoes Tomate II

wife [waɪf], *pl* wives [waɪvz] Ehefrau II

drop (-pp-) [drɒp] fallen lassen I

forget (-tt-) [fə'get] vergessen I

REVISION Spelling mistakes

Lies deinen Text langsam, Wort für Wort, Buchstabe für Buchstabe. Wenn du unsicher bist, hilft dir ein Wörterbuch. Beachte folgende Regeln:

Tipp

- Manche Wörter haben Buchstaben, die man nicht spricht, aber schreibt, z. B. **walk**, **know**.
- Manchmal ändert sich die Schreibweise, wenn ein Wort eine Endung erhält, z. B. **take** → **taking**, **grumble** → **grumbled**, **happy** → **happily**, **fly** → **flies** (**aber stay** → **stays**), **run** → **running**, **plan** → **planned**.
- Beim Plural muss manchmal noch ein *-e* zum *-s*, z. B. **box** → **boxes**.

Grammar mistakes

Diese Tipps helfen dir, typische Fehler zu vermeiden:

Tipp

- Im **simple present** wird in der 3. Person Singular **-s** angehängt: **she knows**.
- **Unregelmäßige Verben**: Manche Verben bilden die Formen des *simple past* und des Partizip Perfekt (*past participle*) unregelmäßig. Die unregelmäßigen Formen musst du lernen. Die Liste steht auf S. 168–169.
  go – went – gone; buy – bought – bought
- **Verneinung**: Im *simple present* werden Vollverben mit **don't/doesn't** verneint, im *simple past* mit **didn't**.
- **Satzstellung**: Im Englischen gilt immer (auch im Nebensatz):
  a) subject – verb – object (SVO) … when **I saw my brother**.
  als **ich meinen Bruder sah**.
  b) Orts- vor Zeitangabe **I bought a nice book <u>in the city yesterday</u>**.

Grammar File – Inhalt

Im **Grammar File** (S. 148–167) wird zusammengefasst, was du in den fünf Units **über die englische Sprache** lernst.

In der **linken Spalte** findest du **Beispielsätze** und **Übersichten**, z.B.

Reflexive pronouns

Singular		Plu…
myself	(ich) mir/mich	
yourself	(du) dir/dich	
himself	(er) sich	
herself	(sie) sich	
itself	(er/sie/es) sich	

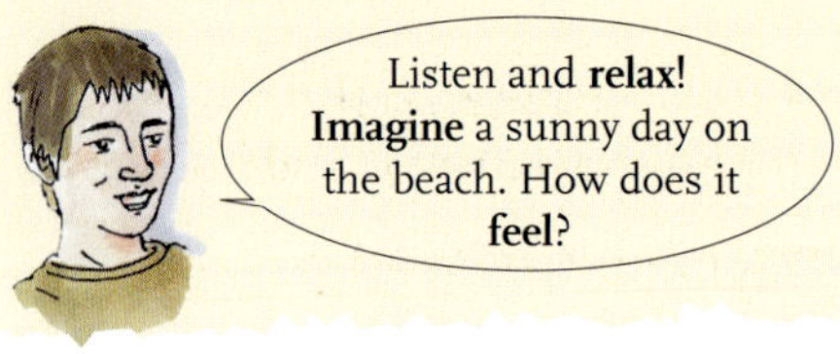

In der **rechten Spalte** stehen **Erklärungen** und nützliche **Hinweise**. Das **rote Ausrufezeichen** (**!**) macht dich auf besondere Fehlerquellen aufmerksam.

Hinweise wie ▸ *Unit 1 (p. 17)* • *P 7–8 (p. 22)* zeigen dir, zu welcher Unit und welcher Seite ein **Grammar-File-**Abschnitt gehört und welche Übungen du dazu im Practice-Teil findest.

Die **grammatischen Fachbegriffe** (*grammatical terms*) kannst du auf den Seiten 165–166 nachschlagen.

Am Ende der Abschnitte stehen wieder kleine Aufgaben zur Selbstkontrolle. Schreib die Lösungen in dein Heft. Überprüfe sie dann auf Seite 167.

Unit 1

GF 1 The present perfect and the simple past in contrast

Das *present perfect* und das *simple past* im Vergleich

a) REVISION The simple past

Last weekend Robert **went** to London with his parents.

Asif **met** them at the London Eye and they all **had** a great time.

On Sunday they **visited** the Tower, and then they **took** the Tube to Waterloo.

▸ *Unit 1 (p. 16)*

Die einfache Form der Vergangenheit

Mit dem ***simple past*** berichtest du über Vergangenes – z. B., wenn du eine Geschichte erzählst.
Das *simple past* drückt aus, dass etwas zu einem **bestimmten Zeitpunkt** oder **in einem bestimmten abgeschlossenen Zeitraum** in der Vergangenheit geschah. (Frage: **Wann?**)
Daher findest du in *simple past*-Sätzen oft **genaue Zeitangaben** wie *last weekend, yesterday, a week ago, in 2005.*

b) REVISION The present perfect

Asif **has** already **visited** the London Trocadero.
... hat schon mal ... besucht

He **has** always **wanted** to go on the London Eye, but he **hasn't done** that yet.
... hat schon immer ... gehen wollen
... hat ... noch nicht getan

He and his friends **have** often **been** to Brick Lane Market.
... sind schon oft ... gewesen

▸ *Unit 1 (p. 16)* • *P 5 (p. 21)*

Das *present perfect*

Mit dem ***present perfect*** drückst du aus, dass etwas **irgendwann in der Vergangenheit** geschehen ist.
Daher findest du oft **Adverbien der unbestimmten Zeit** in *present perfect*-Sätzen, z. B.

already	schon (mal)	*always*	(schon) immer
just	gerade (eben)	*never*	(noch) nie
not ... yet	noch nicht	*often*	(schon) oft
ever?	jemals?	*yet?*	schon?

! Beim ***present perfect*** ist der genaue Zeitpunkt des Geschehens nicht wichtig oder nicht bekannt.

c) Present perfect or simple past?

▸ *Unit 1 (p. 16)*

Present perfect oder *simple past*?

◂ 1 Asif fragt, ob Robert **überhaupt schon mal** türkisch gegessen hat – also ***present perfect***:

***Have** you ever **tried** Turkish food?*

◂ 2 Dann möchte er wissen, **wann** das war, und er fragt daher im ***simple past***:

*And when **did** you **try** it?*

◂ 3 Robert antwortet im ***simple past***, weil er den **genauen Zeitpunkt** nennt:

*We **went** to a Turkish restaurant last Saturday.*

GF 2 The present perfect with *since* and *for* — Das *present perfect* mit *since* und *for*

Du kannst das *present perfect* verwenden, um über einen **Zustand** zu sprechen, der in der Vergangenheit begonnen hat und jetzt noch andauert.

Oft findest du dabei Zeitangaben mit ***since*** oder ***for***:

1 Robert and his parents **have been** in England since September 1st.
Robert und seine Eltern **sind** seit dem 1. September in England.

◄ 1 Mit ***since*** („seit") gibst du einen **Zeitpunkt** an *(since September 1st; since 2006; since 12 o'clock).* ***since*** **+ Zeitpunkt** drückt also aus, **seit wann** ein Zustand andauert.

2 Robert and his parents **have been** in England for ten days.
Robert und seine Eltern **sind** seit zehn Tagen in England.

◄ 2 Mit ***for*** („seit") gibst du einen **Zeitraum** an *(for ten days; for years; for a long time).* ***for*** **+ Zeitraum** drückt also aus, **wie lange** ein Zustand bereits andauert.

since **+ Zeitpunkt** — ***for*** **+ Zeitraum**

Robert and Asif are in a restaurant in Tower Hamlets. **It's 2 o'clock.**

They'**ve been** there since 1 o'clock. — ... seit 13 Uhr ...

They'**ve been** there for an hour. — ... seit einer Stunde ...

Robert has known Asif since the music festival.
Robert kennt Asif seit dem Musikfestival.
But he feels like he has known him for years.
..., als ob er ihn seit Jahren kennt.

! Achtung:
Im **Deutschen** benutzt man meist das **Präsens**:
*Er **kennt** ihn seit ...*
Im **Englischen** muss das ***present perfect*** stehen:
*He **has known** him since/for ...*

How long **have** you **lived** in this part of town?
– Since last month. / For a few weeks.
Wie lange **wohnt** ihr in diesem Teil der Stadt?
– Seit letztem Monat. / Seit ein paar Wochen.

Mit ***How long ...?*** + *present perfect* kannst du fragen, seit wann oder wie lange ein Zustand schon andauert.

▸ *Unit 1 (p. 17)* • *P 7–8 (p. 22)*

Since *oder* for? *Schreib die vollständigen Sätze in dein Heft.*

1 Nora has been in London ... ten days.
2 Eric hasn't seen his parents ... last May.
3 Asif's family have lived in Tower Hamlets ... ten years.
4 Robert has known Asif ... the festival in July.
5 My mother has been a teacher ... 1996.
6 How long have you lived in your house?
– ... three years, I think.

GF 3 The present perfect progressive — Die Verlaufsform des *present perfect*

a) Use — Gebrauch

Robert I've **been watching** the acrobat for a few minutes.
Ich **schaue** seit einigen Minuten dem Akrobaten zu.

Mr Smith And we**'ve been walking** around since lunchtime.
Und wir **laufen** seit Mittag umher.

Mit dem *present perfect progressive* kannst du ausdrücken, dass eine **Handlung** oder ein **Vorgang** in der Vergangenheit begonnen hat und bis jetzt andauert.

Zeitangaben mit ***since*** und ***for*** werden genauso verwendet wie bei der einfachen Form des *present perfect*:

***since* + Zeitpunkt** (seit wann?)	***for* + Zeitraum** (wie lange?)

! Auch in diesen Fällen benutzt man im **Deutschen** meist das **Präsens**:
*Wir **laufen** umher seit ...*
Im **Englischen** steht das ***present perfect progressive***:
*We**'ve been walking** around since/for ...*

b) Form — Form

Present perfect progressive

Statements

+	I/You/We/They	**have been waiting**
	He/She/It	**has been waiting**
–	I/You/We/They	**haven't been waiting**
	He/She/It	**hasn't been waiting**

Questions

Have you **been waiting** long?
Has she **been waiting** long?

How long **have** you **been waiting**?
How long **has** she **been waiting**?

What **have** you **been doing**?
Who **has** Robert **been watching**?

Das *present perfect progressive* bildest du mit ***have/has been*** + ***ing*-Form**.

How long **has** Asif **known** Robert?

not: How long ~~has Asif been knowing~~ Robert?

▸ *Unit 1 (p. 17)* • *P 9–10 (p. 23)*

Verben, die nicht Tätigkeiten, sondern **Zustände** beschreiben, werden meist **in der einfachen Form** und nicht in der Verlaufsform verwendet.
Zu den **Zustandsverben** gehören
be, mean, need, seem, sound sowie
- Verben des Meinens und Wissens wie *agree, know, remember, understand,*
- Verben des Mögens und Wollens wie *hate, like, love, want,*
- Verben der Sinneswahrnehmung wie *feel, hear, see.*

Sieh dir die Bilder an und schreib die dazu passenden Sätze in dein Heft.

1 
They – wait – a long time

2 
She – read – lunchtime

3 
He – play – an hour

Unit 2

GF 4 Talking about the future Über die Zukunft sprechen

a) The *going to*-future

Jane, a researcher, **is going to interview** some students for a TV documentary.
Jane ... hat vor/plant, einige Schüler und Schülerinnen ... zu interviewen.

Das Futur mit *going to*

Wie du weißt, benutzt du das Futur mit ***am/are/is going to* + Infinitiv**, wenn du über **Vorhaben** und **Pläne** für die Zukunft sprechen willst.

Mit ***going to* + Infinitiv** kannst du auch ausdrücken, dass etwas **wahrscheinlich gleich passieren** wird.
Es gibt dafür schon deutliche **Anzeichen** (hier: das Kabel, das sich um das Bein des Assistenten gewickelt hat).

b) The *will*-future

Das Futur mit *will*

Mit ***will/won't* + Infinitiv** kannst du Vermutungen und Vorhersagen über die Zukunft äußern.

Maybe Katrina **will talk** about the school band.
Vielleicht wird Katrina über die Schülerband sprechen.

◂ Eine **Vermutung** fängt oft mit *I think, I'm sure* oder *maybe* an.

Katrina **will be** 14 next year.
Katrina wird nächstes Jahr 14.

◂ Bei einer **Vorhersage** geht es oft um Dinge, die man nicht beeinflussen kann, z.B. das Wetter oder das Alter.

c) The present progressive with future meaning

Katrina's mum Your dad **is picking** you up from school on Friday.
Dein Vater holt dich am Freitag von der Schule ab. / ... wird dich ... abholen.

Katrina What **are** you **doing** on Friday? Why **aren't** you **coming**?
Was machst du am Freitag? Warum kommst du nicht?

▸ *Unit 2 (p. 33)* • *P 5 (p. 40)*

Das *present progressive* mit futurischer Bedeutung

Feste Pläne und **Verabredungen** kannst du auch mit dem *present progressive* ausdrücken. Dabei muss klar sein, dass es sich um etwas Zukünftiges handelt, z.B. durch eine Zeitangabe wie *on Friday, next week, at the weekend, tomorrow*.
(Manchmal wird diese Verwendung des *present progressive* auch ***diary future***, deutsch „Kalender-Zukunft", genannt, weil es sich um Verabredungen handelt, die man schon in seinen Terminkalender eingetragen hat.)

Welche festen Termine und Verabredungen hat Katrina nächste Woche nach der Schule? Schreib die Sätze in dein Heft.

1 On Monday Katrina is meeting ...
2 On Tuesday ...
...

GF 5 The *will*-future for spontaneous decisions
Das Futur mit *will* für spontane Entschlüsse

Alison Which bags do you mean, Fiona?

Linda The bags from the magazine.
I'**ll show** you ... here, look.
... Ich zeig sie dir ... hier, schau.

I'm thirsty. – I'**ll get** you a drink.
(Angebot)

What a lot of work! – I'**ll help** you. I promise.
(Versprechen)

▸ *Unit 2 (p. 34) • P 8 (p. 41)*

Das *will-future* verwendest du auch, wenn du einen spontanen (nicht geplanten) Entschluss fasst.
Oft handelt es sich dabei um Hilfsangebote oder Versprechen.

! Im Deutschen steht bei einem spontanen Entschluss meist die Gegenwart. Im Englischen muss das *will-future* stehen:
I'll show you ...
Ich zeig sie dir ...

GF 6 Conditional sentences (type 2) Bedingungssätze (Typ 2)

a) REVISION Conditional sentences (type 1)

Alison **If** they **choose** you, you'**ll be** a star.
Wenn sie dich wählen, bist du ... /
Wenn sie dich wählen, wirst du ... sein.

Linda **If** I **don't get** to the shop soon, they **won't have** those trendy new bags any more.

▸ *Unit 2 (p. 34) • P 9 (p. 41)*

Bedingungssätze (Typ 1)

Du kennst bereits Bedingungssätze vom Typ 1 (**„Was ist, wenn ..."-Sätze**).
Sie sagen aus, was unter bestimmten Bedingungen geschieht oder nicht geschieht:

***if*-Satz (Bedingung)**	**Hauptsatz (Folge)**
*If they **choose** you,*	*you'**ll be** a star.*
simple present	***will-future***

b) Conditional sentences (type 2)

If a film-maker **discovered** me, I **would be** famous.

Wenn mich ein Filmemacher entdecken würde, wäre ich berühmt / würde ich berühmt.

I **wouldn't live** here if I **was** rich and famous.

Ich würde nicht hier wohnen, wenn ich reich und berühmt wäre.

Bedingungssätze (Typ 2)

Bedingungssätze vom Typ 2 sind **„Was wäre, wenn ..."-Sätze**.
Sie drücken aus, was unter bestimmten Bedingungen **sein würde**, aber doch eher unwahrscheinlich ist (oder sogar unmöglich):

Es ist unwahrscheinlich, dass Fiona von einem Filmemacher entdeckt werden wird. Also wird sie wahrscheinlich auch nicht berühmt.

***if*-Satz (Bedingung)**	**Hauptsatz (Folge)**
*If a film-maker **discovered** me,*	*I **would be** famous.*
simple past	***would + infinitive***

(Kurzform von *I/you/he/... would: I'd / you'd / he'd / ...*)

If a film-maker **discovered** me, ...
Wenn mich ein Filmemacher entdecken würde, ...

! Im *if*-Satz steht **kein *would***.
Also nicht: *If a film-maker ~~would discover~~ me, ...*

If I **had** enough money, I could **buy** a new bike.
Wenn ich genug Geld hätte, könnte ich mir ein neues Rad kaufen.

Im Hauptsatz kann auch *could* („könnte") stehen.

▸ *Unit 2 (p. 35) • P 10–11 (p. 42)*

Vervollständige die Sätze in deinem Heft. Achte auf die richtige Form der Verben.

1 If the other girls ... (call) Latisha names, she would laugh.
2 Latisha would forget the girls if she ... (be) Katrina.
3 Katrina ... (be) much happier if the girls ... (not call) her 'Fishface'.
4 If the girls ... (be) friendly to her, she ... (not be) upset.
5 If people ... (call) you 'Fishface', you ... (be) upset too. Right?
6 What would you do if classmates ... (call) you names?

Unit 3

GF 7 Relative clauses Relativsätze

a) REVISION Relative pronouns

Relativpronomen

Mit Relativsätzen sagst du genauer, wen oder was du meinst.

The girl who plays for United U14s is Latisha.
Das Mädchen, das für die U14 von *United* spielt, ...

Asif is **a boy** who Latisha knows from the festival in Birmingham.
... ein Junge, den Latisha vom Festival ... kennt.

◂ In Relativsätzen, die **Personen** beschreiben, verwendest du ***who***:
***the man / the woman / people** who ...*
der Mann, der ... / die Frau, die ... / Leute, die ...

Do you know **a shop** which sells cheap CDs?
... einen Laden, der billige CDs verkauft?

Mrs Byrd has cooked **a dish** which Anna likes.
... ein Gericht, das Anna mag.

◂ In Relativsätzen, die **Dinge** (und Tiere) beschreiben, verwendest du ***which***:
***the shop / the dish / an animal** which ...*
der Laden, der ... / das Gericht, das ... / ein Tier, das ...

... **the friends** that Latisha met at the festival
... **a shop** that sells cheap CDs

◂ Das Relativpronomen ***that*** wird für Personen und Dinge verwendet.

The girl **who plays** football ...

Das Mädchen, **das** Fußball **spielt** ...

! Beachte die unterschiedliche Wortstellung in englischen und deutschen Relativsätzen.

▸ *Unit 3 (p. 57) • P 4 (p. 63)*

Wo brauchst du who, *wo brauchst du* which?

1 Anna is the German girl ... is staying with Latisha.
2 Latisha thinks training is something ... is great fun.
3 What's the name of the player ... scored both goals in United U14s' last match?
4 Stewed chicken is a dish ... comes from Trinidad, isn't it?

b) Contact clauses

Relativsätze ohne Relativpronomen

Das Relativpronomen kann **Subjekt** oder **Objekt** sein.

1 Anna is a girl **who** is staying with the Byrds.
..., **das** bei den Byrds wohnt.

1 Das Relativpronomen ist **Subjekt des Relativsatzes** (es steht direkt vor dem Verb):

	Subjekt	
Anna is a girl	***who***	*is staying with the Byrds.*
Anna ist ein Mädchen,	***das***	*bei den Byrds wohnt.*
Plantains are bananas	***that***	*grow in Trinidad.*
Plantains sind Bananen,	***die***	*auf Trinidad wachsen.*

2 Beckham is the only player who Anna knows.
..., den Anna kennt.

2 Das Relativpronomen ist Objekt **des Relativsatzes**:

	Objekt	Subjekt	
Beckham is the only player	*who*	*Anna*	*knows.*
Beckham ist der einzige Spieler,	*den*	*Anna*	*kennt.*
Football is a sport	*that*	*Latisha*	*loves.*
Fußball ist ein Sport,	*den*	*Latisha*	*liebt.*

Mrs Byrd is somebody who likes cooking.

(*not:* Mrs Byrd is ~~somebody likes cooking~~.)

◀ Wenn das Relativpronomen **Objekt** des Relativsatzes ist, wird es manchmal **weggelassen** – wie in den Beispielen links.
Relativsätze ohne Relativpronomen nennt man *contact clauses.*

! Achtung:
Wenn das **Relativpronomen direkt vor dem Verb** steht, ist es Subjekt – dann darfst du es **nicht weglassen**!

The girl **Latisha is chatting** with is Katrina.
Das Mädchen, mit dem Latisha chattet, ist Katrina.

The stadium **they are looking** at is Old Trafford.

▸ *Unit 3 (p. 57) • P 5–6 (p. 64)*

! Beachte die Stellung der Präposition in Relativsätzen mit Verben wie *talk to, chat with, look at, stay with.* Die Präposition steht an derselben Stelle wie im Hauptsatz:

	Latisha is** chatting with* ***Katrina.
The girl	***Latisha is** chatting with* ***is Katrina.***

Wo kannst du das Relativpronomen weglassen? Schreib die Sätze als contact clauses *in dein Heft.*

1 Anna is the girl **who** is staying with the Byrds.
2 Which is the instrument **that** Latisha plays?
3 Football is a sport **which** Latisha likes a lot.
4 David Beckham is a football star **who** everybody knows.
5 Mrs Byrd's grandmother is somebody **who** came from Trinidad.
6 Let's do something **that** we both want to do.

GF 8 The passive — Das Passiv

a) Active and passive

Active: Kids play football all over the world.

Passive: Football is played all over the world.
Fußball wird überall auf der Welt gespielt.

Aktiv und Passiv

Mit einem **Aktivsatz** drückst du aus, **wer oder was etwas tut**. Das Subjekt des Aktivsatzes führt die Handlung aus:

Subjekt	**Verb** (aktiv)	**Objekt**	**...**
Kids	*play*	*football*	...
Jugendliche	*spielen*	*Fußball*	...

Mit einem **Passivsatz** drückst du aus, **mit wem oder womit etwas geschieht**. Das Objekt des Aktivsatzes *(football)* wird Subjekt des Passivsatzes:

Subjekt	**Verb** (passiv)	**...**
Football	*is played*	...
Fußball	*wird gespielt*	...

b) Form

... ist nach einem berühmten Maler ... benannt.
... wurde im Jahr 2000 eröffnet.
Viele Gemälde werden ... ausgestellt/gezeigt.

Form

Das Passiv bildest du mit einer **Form von *be*** und der 3. Form des Verbs. Die 3. Form des Verbs heißt **Partizip Perfekt** *(past participle)*.

Simple present: *am/are/is* + ***past participle***
*The Lowry is **named** ...*
*Lowry's paintings are **shown** ...*

Simple past: *was/were* + ***past participle***
*The Lowry was **opened** ...*

c) Use

At 8.45 yesterday morning a 12-year-old boy <u>was hurt</u> in a car accident on Duke Street. The police <u>were called</u> and the boy <u>was taken</u> to hospital.

▸ *Unit 3 (p. 58) • P 8–9 (p. 65)*

Gebrauch

Mit einem Passivsatz kannst du Handlungen beschreiben, ohne zu sagen, wer die Handlung ausführt. Oft ist gar nicht bekannt oder nicht wichtig, wer die Handlung ausführt.
Du findest daher das Passiv oft in Nachrichten und in Zeitungsberichten (z.B. über Unfälle, Verbrechen) oder auf Schildern.

Ein englischer Passivsatz wird im Deutschen oft durch einen Aktivsatz mit „man" wiedergegeben:

*The boy **was taken** to hospital.*
***Man brachte** den Jungen ins Krankenhaus.*

d) Passive sentences with *by* ...

The planet Uranus **was discovered** by William Herschel in 1781.
... wurde 1781 von William Herschel entdeckt.

The final goal **was scored** by Latisha Byrd.
... wurde von Latisha Byrd geschossen.

My parents' house **was destroyed** by fire.
... wurde durch ein Feuer zerstört.

▸ *Unit 3 (p. 59) • P 12 (p. 66)*

Passivsätze mit *by* ...

Wenn du in einem Passivsatz den „Täter" oder „Verursacher" nennen willst, verwendest du die Präposition ***by*** („von", „durch").

Sieh dir die Bilder, die Verben und die Namen an. Schreib die richtigen Passivsätze in dein Heft.

1

2

3

1 The telephone was ... by ...
2 'We will rock you!' was ...
3 Clifton Suspension Bridge ...

build • invent • sing
Alexander Bell • Brunel • Queen

Unit 4

GF 9 The past perfect   Das *past perfect*

a) Use

Gebrauch

After school Robert **went** to the mall. ... ging ...
He **wanted** to buy a birthday present. ... wollte ...

◀ Du benutzt das *simple past* für **Handlungen, Ereignisse und Zustände in der Vergangenheit**.

Robert went to the mall because he had planned to meet Sam there.
..., weil er ausgemacht hatte, Sam dort zu treffen.

Robert had already chosen a present when Sam came in.
Robert hatte bereits ein Geschenk ausgesucht, ...

◀ Mit dem ***past perfect*** (Plusquamperfekt, Vorvergangenheit) drückst du aus, dass eine Handlung noch **vor einer anderen Handlung in der Vergangenheit** stattgefunden hatte. Die Handlung im *past perfect* geschah zuerst:

2	1
*Robert **went** to the mall*	*because he had planned to ...*

1	2
He had already chosen a present	*when Sam **came** in.*

Past perfect
When Sam arrived, Robert had bought a DVD for Ashley.
Als Sam eintraf, hatte Robert (bereits) eine DVD für Ashley gekauft. *(der Kauf geschah vor Sams Eintreffen)*

Simple past
When Sam arrived, Robert bought a DVD for Ashley.
Als Sam eintraf, kaufte Robert eine DVD für Ashley.
(der Kauf geschah erst nach Sams Eintreffen)

! Beachte die Bedeutungsunterschiede zwischen *past perfect* und *simple past*.

b) Form

Form

Robert knew where there was a big DVD shop because he'd been there before.
..., weil er schon einmal dort gewesen war.

Had he bought the present when Sam arrived?   Hatte er das Geschenk schon gekauft, ...?

▸ *Unit 4 (p. 75) • P 4–5 (p. 81)*

Das *past perfect* bildest du mit ***had*** (Kurzform: *'d*) und der 3. Form des Verbs. Die 3. Form des Verbs heißt **Partizip Perfekt** *(past participle)*.

! Beim *past perfect* musst du immer ***had*** verwenden, egal ob im Deutschen „hatte" oder „war" steht.

Simple past *oder* past perfect? *Sieh dir die Bilder an und vervollständige die Sätze.*

1 The band (start) to play when I arrived.

2 The band (start) to play when I arrived.

3 When his mum came home from work, Jason ... (make) tea.

4 When his mum came home from work, Jason ... (make) tea.

GF 10 Talking about the past Über die Vergangenheit sprechen

a) Simple past, past perfect, past progressive

Simple past, past perfect, past progressive

Simple past

Active: Robert went to Ashley's party **last Friday**. He gave her a DVD.
Robert ist letzten Freitag auf Ashleys Party gegangen. Er hat ihr eine DVD geschenkt.

Passive: Sam was invited too.
Sam war/wurde auch eingeladen.

Wenn du über Vergangenes berichtest – z.B., wenn du eine Geschichte erzählst –, benutzt du überwiegend das ***simple past***. Mit dem ***simple past*** beschreibst du Handlungen, Ereignisse und Zustände, die zu einem bestimmten Zeitpunkt in der Vergangenheit *(yesterday, last Friday, two years ago, in 2003, ...)* stattfanden.

! Im Deutschen wird dafür oft das Perfekt verwendet, im Englischen jedoch nicht.

Past perfect

When Robert **got** to the party, all the other guests had already arrived.
Als Robert ankam, waren alle anderen Gäste schon eingetroffen.

Wenn du sagen willst, dass etwas noch vor etwas anderem in der Vergangenheit stattgefunden hatte, dann benutzt du das ***past perfect***.

Past progressive

The other guests were laughing and talking when Robert **arrived**.
Die anderen Gäste lachten und unterhielten sich, als Robert eintraf.

Wenn du sagen willst, dass etwas zu einem bestimmten Zeitpunkt in der Vergangenheit im Gange war, dann benutzt du das ***past progressive***.

b) Present perfect (progressive)

Present perfect (progressive)

Present perfect und ***present perfect progressive*** haben mit der Vergangenheit und mit der Gegenwart zu tun:

Die **einfache Form des *present perfect*** benutzt du ...

Present perfect

Robert has set up his computer.
Robert hat seinen Computer aufgestellt.
But he hasn't played any music **yet**.
Aber er hat noch keine Musik gespielt.

◄ wenn du sagen willst, dass etwas (irgendwann) geschehen ist. Oft hat die Handlung Auswirkungen auf die Gegenwart (Robert hat den Rechner aufgestellt und kann daher jetzt mit dem Auflegen beginnen).
Ein genauer Zeitpunkt wird nicht genannt. Aber das *present perfect* steht oft mit Adverbien der unbestimmten Zeit wie *just, already, never, not ... yet*.

Ashley has liked Nickelback **since** their first hit.
Ashley mag Nickelback seit ihrem ersten Hit.

◄ für **Zustände**, die in der Vergangenheit begonnen haben und jetzt noch andauern (oft mit ***since*** bzw. ***for***).

! Im Deutschen steht hier meist das Präsens, im Englischen muss das *present perfect* stehen.

Present perfect progressive

Robert has been DJing at parties **for** over a year.
Robert legt seit über einem Jahr auf Partys auf.

Die **Verlaufsform des *present perfect*** (das *present perfect progressive*) benutzt du für **Vorgänge** und **Handlungen**, die in der Vergangenheit begonnen haben und jetzt noch andauern (oft mit ***since*** bzw. ***for***).

! Auch hier steht im Deutschen meist das Präsens – aber im Englischen das *present perfect progressive*.

► *Unit 4 (p. 75)*

GF 11 Indirect speech Die indirekte Rede

a) Direct and indirect speech

Direkte und indirekte Rede

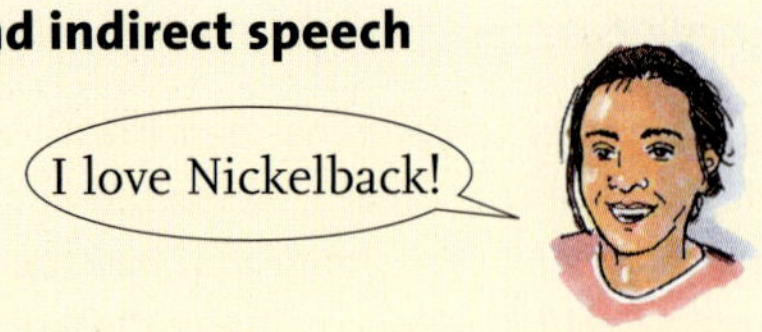

Das, was jemand sagt (oder gesagt hat), kannst du direkt oder indirekt wiedergeben.

Direct speech Ashley says, 'I love Nickelback!'
Ashley sagt: „Ich liebe Nickelback!"

◄ In der **direkten Rede** *(direct speech)* gibst du **wörtlich** wieder, was jemand sagt oder schreibt.
Direkte Rede steht in der Regel in Anführungszeichen.

Indirect speech Ashley **says** (that) she loves Nickelback.
Ashley sagt, dass sie Nickelback liebt.

◄ In der **indirekten Rede** (*indirect speech* oder *reported speech*) berichtest du, was jemand sagt oder schreibt.
Die indirekte Rede wird mit Verben wie *say, tell sb., answer, explain, write* eingeleitet.

! Im Englischen steht vor der indirekten Rede **kein Komma**.
Das Wort *that* wird oft weggelassen.

b) Indirect speech: tense changes

Indirekte Rede: Veränderungen der Zeitform

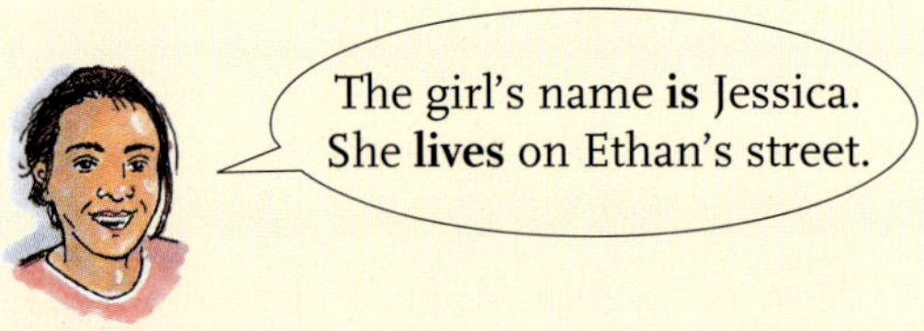

Wenn das einleitende Verb im ***simple past*** steht (*she **said**, he **wrote*** usw.), werden in der indirekten Rede meist andere Zeitformen verwendet als in der direkten Rede:

Die Zeitformen der direkten Rede werden um eine Zeitstufe in die Vergangenheit „zurückverschoben" *(backshift of tenses)*.

Indirect speech
Ashley **said** (that) the girl's name was Jessica.
She **told** me (that) she lived on Ethan's street.

◄ So wird z.B. das *simple present* der direkten Rede in der indirekten Rede zum *simple past*.

Tense changes

	Direct speech	Indirect speech
present ► past	*Ashley* 'I'm not sure.' 'I'm waiting for Robert.'	Ashley **said** she wasn't sure. Ashley **said** she was waiting for Robert.
past ► past perfect	*Robert* 'It was a great party.'	Robert **told** Sam it had been a great party.
present perfect ► past perfect	*Robert* 'I haven't called Emily.'	Robert **told** Sam he hadn't called Emily.
***will*-future ► *would* + infinitive**	*Sam* 'I'll call Ashley.'	Sam **said** he would call Ashley.
***going to*-future ► *was/were going to* + infinitive**	*Sam* 'I'm going to practise paddling.'	Sam **said** he was going to practise paddling.

– Verben im *past perfect* bleiben unverändert, da man sie nicht weiter „zurückverschieben" kann.
– In der Umgangssprache werden *simple past*-Formen der direkten Rede oft nicht ins *past perfect* verändert.

c) Indirect speech: changes of pronouns

Robert 'Sam, **I**'ll call **you** when **we**'re back.'
„Sam, ich rufe dich an, wenn wir zurück sind."

(Sam berichtet seinem Onkel:)
Robert told me that he would call me when they were back.
Robert sagte mir, er würde mich anrufen, sobald sie zurück wären.

(Robert berichtet Ashley:)
I told Sam that I would call him when we were back.
Ich sagte Sam, ich würde ihn anrufen, sobald wir zurück wären.

▸ *Unit 4 (p. 77) • P 9–12 (pp. 83–84)*

Indirekte Rede: Veränderungen der Pronomen

Wie im Deutschen hängt die Veränderung der Pronomen in der indirekten Rede davon ab, wer wem berichtet.

Berichte, was Sam gesagt hat. Schreib die Sätze in der indirekten Rede in dein Heft.

1 'Paddling isn't as difficult as it looks.' — Sam said paddling ...
2 'I didn't feel very nervous.' — He told Robert that he ...
3 'I have learned quite a lot about boats.' — He also said he ...
4 'I had never paddled a boat before.' — He explained that he ...
5 'I'll have to practise more often.' — He told his uncle that he ...
6 'I really hope we'll win the race.' — He said he ...

Unit 5

GF 12 Modals and their substitutes — Modale Hilfsverben und ihre Ersatzverben

a) REVISION *can – may – must*

Latisha can play football very well.
Can/May I go to the match, Mum?
Latisha must do her homework first.

can – may – must

Can, may und ***must*** sind modale Hilfsverben (*modal auxiliaries* oder kurz: *modals*). Sie drücken aus, dass jemand etwas tun **kann, darf** oder **muss**.

b) (to) be able to – (to) be allowed to – (to) have to

Jack was ill on Friday, but he was able to **go** to the disco on Saturday. ... konnte gehen ...

Holly didn't have much time yesterday, but she will be able to **buy** a present for her dad tomorrow. ... wird kaufen können ...

(to) be able to – (to) be allowed to – (to) have to

Wenn es um „können/dürfen/müssen" in der Vergangenheit oder der Zukunft geht, werden meist **Ersatzverben** verwendet:

„können": *(to) be able to*

- **Vergangenheit** (wenn jemand etwas tun **konnte**): ***was/were able to***
- **Zukunft** (wenn jemand etwas tun **können wird**): ***will be able to***

Jodie wasn't allowed to **go** to the school disco last month. ... durfte nicht gehen ...

She won't be allowed to **go** to Lauren's party on Saturday. ... wird nicht gehen dürfen...

„dürfen": *(to) be allowed to*
- **Vergangenheit** (wenn jemand etwas tun **durfte**): ***was/were allowed to***
- **Zukunft** (wenn jemand etwas tun **dürfen wird**): ***will be allowed to***

Holly had to **clean** her room yesterday. ... musste putzen ...

She can go to the party, but she will have to **be** home by ten. ... wird sein müssen ...

„müssen": *(to) have to*
- **Vergangenheit** (wenn jemand etwas tun **musste**): ***had to***
- **Zukunft** (wenn jemand etwas tun **müssen wird**): ***will have to***

Robert doesn't play an instrument, but he's able to DJ.

Jodie I'm not allowed to **go** to parties!

Sam Hey Robert, I have to **talk** to you.

! Alle Ersatzverben werden auch im *simple present* verwendet.

I could **hear** music, but I couldn't **see** anybody.

Zu *can* gibt es auch die Vergangenheitsform *could* („konnte"). Sie steht vor allem in verneinten Sätzen und Fragen und mit Verben der Wahrnehmung *(see, hear, ...)*.

▸ *Unit 5 (p. 97) • P 4–5 (p. 101)*

Vervollständige den Dialog mit Formen von be able to, be allowed to *und* have to.

Holly My mother is so strict. Yesterday I wanted to buy a present for my dad, but I ... (have to) tidy my room.
Jodie My parents are strict too. I'm sure I ... (not be allowed to) go to Lauren's party.
Holly Well, I'm sure I ... (have to) be home by ten again, as always.
Jack I ... (not be able to) go to the party because I'm going to visit my cousins.

GF 13 Reflexive pronouns Reflexivpronomen

Reflexivpronomen *(himself, ourselves, themselves, ...)* bezeichnen dieselbe Person oder Sache wie das Subjekt *(my dad, we, they, ...)*:

Subjekt		Reflexivpronomen	
My dad	*taught*	*himself*	*the lyrics.*
We	*will send*	*ourselves*	*to paradise.*

Mein Vater brachte sich den Text bei.
Wir werden uns ins Paradies schicken.

Reflexive pronouns

Singular		Plural	
myself	(ich) mir/mich	**ourselves**	(wir) uns
yourself	(du) dir/dich	**yourselves**	(ihr) euch
himself	(er) sich	**themselves**	(sie) sich
herself	(sie) sich		
itself	(er/sie/es) sich		

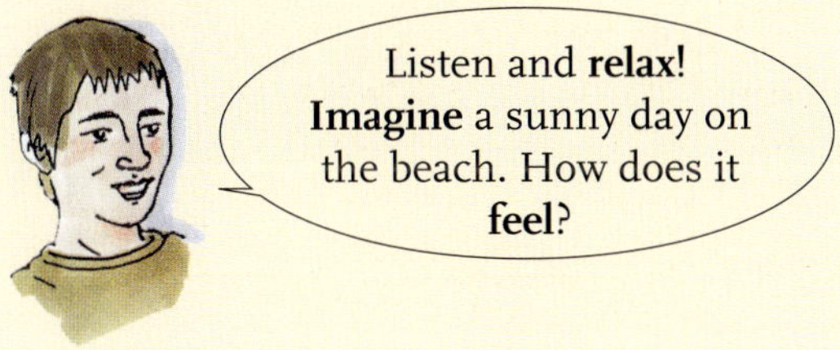

▸ *Unit 5 (p. 98)* • *P 6–7 (p. 102)*

! Es gibt eine Reihe von Verben, die im Deutschen mit „sich" gebraucht werden, im Englischen aber ohne Reflexivpronomen.

Beispiele:	
(to) argue	sich streiten
(to) feel	sich (an)fühlen
(to) imagine sth.	sich etwas vorstellen
(to) relax	sich entspannen

(Weitere Beispiele ▸ *Vocabulary, S. 194*)

Schreib die Sätze in dein Heft. Wo brauchst du ein Reflexivpronomen?

1 Today my friends and I wanted to meet ... after breakfast.
2 But when I went into the bathroom to clean ... my teeth, there was no water.
3 Then I remembered ... that there had been a sign in the street about a water problem.
4 So I went into the living room, sat ... down and made ... comfortable.

GF 14 Reflexive pronoun or *each other*? Reflexivpronomen oder *each other*?

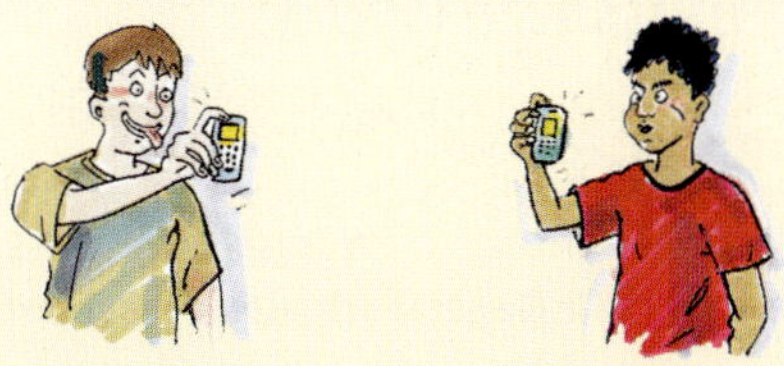

Robert and Asif are taking photos of themselves.
Robert und Asif machen Fotos von sich (selbst).

Für **„sich"** im Sinne von **„sich selbst"** benutzt du die Pronomen auf ***-self/-selves***:
I – myself, we – ourselves, they – themselves usw.

◂ Robert und Asif machen Fotos von sich selbst – Robert fotografiert sich selbst, und Asif fotografiert sich selbst.

Now they are taking photos of each other.
Jetzt fotografieren sie sich gegenseitig. /
Jetzt machen sie Fotos voneinander.

▸ *Unit 5 (p. 99)* • *P 8 (p. 102)*

Für **„sich"** im Sinne von **„sich gegenseitig"** oder **„einander"** benutzt du ***each other***.

◂ Robert und Asif fotografieren sich gegenseitig – Robert fotografiert Asif, und Asif fotografiert Robert.

(Statt *each other* wird auch *one another* verwendet: *Now they are taking photos of one another.*)

Sieh dir die Bilder an. Schreib zu jedem Bild einen kurzen Satz. Brauchst du themselves *oder* each other?

1 (laugh at)
They're laughing ...

2 (teach – German)
They're teaching ...

3 (hurt)
They've hurt ...

4 (talk to)
They're ...

They understand each other ...

GF 15 Extra Conditional sentences (type 3) Bedingungssätze (Typ 3)

a) REVISION Conditional sentences (type 1)

Asif If Katrina **comes** to London,
I'**ll show** her the sights.
Wenn Katrina nach London **kommt**,
zeige ich ihr die Sehenswürdigkeiten /
werde ich ihr die Sehenswürdigkeiten **zeigen**.

Bedingungssätze (Typ 1)

Bedingungssätze vom Typ 1 (**„Was ist, wenn ..."-Sätze**) beziehen sich auf die **Gegenwart** oder die **Zukunft**. Sie sagen aus, was unter bestimmten Bedingungen **geschieht** oder **nicht geschieht**.

b) REVISION Conditional sentences (type 2)

Asif If Katrina **came** to London,
I **would show** her the sights.
Wenn Katrina nach London **käme**,
würde ich ihr die Sehenswürdigkeiten **zeigen**.

Bedingungssätze (Typ 2)

Bedingungssätze vom Typ 2 (**„Was wäre, wenn ..."-Sätze**) beziehen sich auch auf die **Gegenwart** oder die **Zukunft**.
Sie drücken aus, was unter bestimmten Bedingungen **geschehen** oder **nicht geschehen würde**.
(Bedingungssätze vom Typ 2: siehe auch GF 6, S. 153)

c) Conditional sentences (type 3)

Bedingungssätze (Typ 3)

Asif — If Katrina **had come** to London,
I **would have shown** her the sights.
Wenn Katrina nach London **gekommen wäre**,
hätte ich ihr die Sehenswürdigkeiten **gezeigt**.

Bedingungssätze vom Typ 3 sind
„Was wäre gewesen, wenn …"-Sätze.
Sie beziehen sich auf die **Vergangenheit**.
Sie drücken aus, was **geschehen** oder **nicht geschehen wäre**, wenn eine Bedingung eingetreten wäre.

If Katrina had come to London, …

◀ Der ***if*-Satz** nennt eine Bedingung, die nicht eingetreten ist: Katrina ist nicht nach London gekommen.

… Asif would have shown her the sights.

◀ Der **Hauptsatz** drückt aus, was geschehen wäre oder hätte sein können, wenn die Bedingung eingetreten wäre: Wenn Katrina nach London gekommen wäre, dann hätte Asif ihr die Sehenswürdigkeiten zeigen können.

- Im ***if*-Satz** steht das ***past perfect***: *had come.*
- Im **Hauptsatz** steht ***would + have +* Partizip Perfekt**: *would have shown.*

If she'd **come** … = If she had **come** …
… he'd **have shown** … = … he would **have shown**

! Beachte:
Die Kurzform *'d* steht im *if*-Satz für *had*,
im Hauptsatz aber für *would*.

If Mika hadn't taken singing lessons,
he couldn't **have sung** at the opera.
Wenn Mika nicht Gesangsstunden genommen hätte,
hätte er nicht an der Oper singen können.

If Latisha had known her MP3 player was bad,
she might **have bought** a different one.
Wenn Latisha gewusst hätte, dass ihr MP3-Player schlecht war, hätte sie vielleicht einen anderen gekauft.

Im Hauptsatz können statt ***would have + past participle*** auch ***could have*** oder ***might have + past participle*** stehen.

▸ *Unit 5 (p. 99) • P 10–11 (p. 103)*

Grammatical terms (Grammatische Fachbegriffe)

active ['æktɪv]	Aktiv	*Beckham **scored** the final goal.*
adjective ['ædʒɪktɪv]	Adjektiv	*good, red, new, boring, …*
adverb ['ædvɜːb]	Adverb	*always, badly, here, really, today*
adverb of frequency ['friːkwənsi]	Häufigkeitsadverb	*always, often, never, …*
adverb of indefinite time [ɪnˌdefɪnət 'taɪm]	Adverb der unbestimmten Zeit	*already, ever, just, never, …*
adverb of manner ['mænə]	Adverb der Art und Weise	*badly, happily, quietly, well, …*
auxiliary [ɔːg'zɪliəri]	Hilfsverb	*be, have, do; will, can, must, …*
backshift of tenses ['bækʃɪft]	Verschiebung der Zeitformen *(bei der indirekten Rede)*	*'**I'm** sorry.'* ▸ *Sam said he **was** sorry.*
comparison [kəm'pærɪsn]	Steigerung	*old – older – oldest*
conditional sentence [kənˌdɪʃənl 'sentəns]	Bedingungssatz	*I'd call him if I knew his number.*
conjunction [kən'dʒʌŋkʃn]	Konjunktion	*and, or, but; because, before, …*
contact clause ['kɒntækt klɔːz]	Relativsatz ohne Relativpronomen	*She's the girl **I love**.*
direct speech [ˌdaɪrekt 'spiːtʃ]	direkte Rede, wörtliche Rede	***'I'm sorry.'***
***going to*-future**	Futur mit *going to*	*I'm **going to watch** TV tonight.*
***if*-clause** ['ɪf klɔːz]	*if*-Satz, Nebensatz mit *if*	***If I see Jack**, I'll tell him.*

imperative [ɪm'perətɪv]	Imperativ (Befehlsform)	*Open your books. Don't talk.*
indirect speech [ˌɪndərekt 'spi:tʃ]	indirekte Rede	*Sam said* ***(that) he was sorry****.*
infinitive [ɪn'fɪnətɪv]	Infinitiv (Grundform des Verbs)	*(to) open, (to) see, (to) read, ...*
irregular verb [ɪˌregjələ 'vɜ:b]	unregelmäßiges Verb	*(to) go – went – gone*
main clause	Hauptsatz	***I like Scruffy*** *because I like dogs.*
modal, modal auxiliary [ˌməʊdl‿ɔ:g'zɪliəri]	modales Hilfsverb, Modalverb	*can, could, may, must, ...*
negative statement [ˌnegətɪv 'steɪtmənt]	verneinter Aussagesatz	*I don't like bananas.*
noun [naʊn]	Nomen, Substantiv	*Sophie, girl, brother, time, ...*
object ['ɒbdʒɪkt]	Objekt	*My sister is writing* ***a letter****.*
object form ['ɒbdʒɪkt fɔ:m]	Objektform (der Personalpronomen)	*me, you, him, her, it, us, them*
passive ['pæsɪv]	Passiv	*The final goal* ***was scored*** *by Beckham.*
past participle [ˌpɑ:st 'pɑ:tɪsɪpl]	Partizip Perfekt	*cleaned, planned, gone, seen, ...*
past perfect [ˌpɑ:st 'pɜ:fɪkt]	Plusquamperfekt, Vorvergangenheit	*He was late because he* ***had missed*** *the bus.*
past progressive [ˌpɑ:st prə'gresɪv]	Verlaufsform der Vergangenheit	*At 7.30 I* ***was having*** *dinner.*
personal pronoun [ˌpɜ:sənl 'prəʊnaʊn]	Personalpronomen (persönliches Fürwort)	*I, you, he, she, it, we, they; me, you, him, her, it, us, them*
plural ['plʊərəl]	Plural, Mehrzahl	
positive statement [ˌpɒzətɪv 'steɪtmənt]	bejahter Aussagesatz	*I like oranges.*
possessive determiner [pəˌzesɪv dɪ'tɜ:mɪnə]	Possessivbegleiter (besitzanzeigender Begleiter)	*my, your, his, her, its, our, their*
possessive form [pəˌzesɪv fɔ:m]	*s*-Genitiv	*Jo's brother; my sister's room*
possessive pronoun [pəˌzesɪv 'prəʊnaʊn]	Possessivpronomen	*mine, yours, his, hers, ours, theirs*
preposition [ˌprepə'zɪʃn]	Präposition	*after, at, in, next to, under, ...*
present perfect [ˌpreznt 'pɜ:fɪkt]	*present perfect*	*We****'ve made*** *a cake for you.*
present perfect progressive [ˌpreznt ˌpɜ:fɪkt prə'gresɪv]	Verlaufsform des *present perfect*	*We****'ve been waiting*** *for an hour.*
present progressive [ˌpreznt prə'gresɪv]	Verlaufsform der Gegenwart	*The Hansons* ***are having*** *lunch.*
pronoun ['prəʊnaʊn]	Pronomen, Fürwort	
question tag ['kwestʃən tæg]	Frageanhängsel	*This place is great,* ***isn't it?***
question word ['kwestʃən wɜ:d]	Fragewort	*what?, when?, where?, how?, ...*
regular verb [ˌregjələ 'vɜ:b]	regelmäßiges Verb	*(to) help – helped – helped*
reflexive pronoun [rɪˌfleksɪv 'prəʊnaʊn]	Reflexivpronomen	*myself, yourself, themselves, ...*
relative clause [ˌrelətɪv 'klɔ:z]	Relativsatz	*There's the girl* ***who helped me****.*
relative pronoun [ˌrelətɪv 'prəʊnaʊn]	Relativpronomen	*who, that, which, whose*
reported speech [rɪˌpɔ:tɪd 'spi:tʃ]	indirekte Rede	*Sam said* ***(that) he was sorry****.*
short answer [ˌʃɔ:t‿'ɑ:nsə]	Kurzantwort	*Yes, I am. / No, I don't. / ...*
simple past [ˌsɪmpl 'pɑ:st]	einfache Form der Vergangenheit	*Jo* ***wrote*** *two letters yesterday.*
simple present [ˌsɪmpl 'preznt]	einfache Form der Gegenwart	*I always* ***go*** *to school by bike.*
singular ['sɪŋgjələ]	Singular, Einzahl	
subject ['sʌbdʒɪkt]	Subjekt	***My sister*** *is writing a letter.*
subject form ['sʌbdʒɪkt fɔ:m]	Subjektform (der Personalpronomen)	*I, you, he, she, it, we, they*
subordinate clause [səˌbɔ:dɪnət 'klɔ:z]	Nebensatz	*I like Scruffy* ***because I like dogs****.*
verb [vɜ:b]	Verb	*hear, open, help, go, ...*
***will*-future**	Futur mit *will*	*I think it* ***will be*** *cold tonight.*
word order ['wɜ:d‿ˌɔ:də]	Wortstellung	
yes/no question	Entscheidungsfrage	*Are you 13? Do you like comics?*

Lösungen der Grammar-File-Aufgaben

p. 150
1 Nora has been in London **for** ten days.
2 Eric hasn't seen his parents **since** last May.
3 Asif's family have lived in Tower Hamlets **for** ten years.
4 Robert has known Asif **since** the festival in July.
5 My mother has been a teacher **since** 1996.
6 How long have you lived in your house? – **For** three years, I think.

p. 151
1 They **have been waiting for** a long time.
2 She **has been reading since** lunchtime.
3 He **has been playing for** an hour.

p. 152
1 On Monday Katrina **is meeting** Jane.
2 On Tuesday she **is practising** the fiddle.
3 On Wednesday she **is chatting** with Latisha.
4 On Thursday she **is calling** Mum about the weekend.

p. 154
1 If the other girls **called** Latisha names, she would laugh.
2 Latisha would forget the girls if she **was** Katrina.
3 Katrina **would be** much happier if the girls **didn't call** her 'Fishface'.
4 If the girls **were** friendly to her, she **wouldn't be** upset.
5 If people **called** you 'Fishface', you **would be** upset too. Right?
6 What would you do if classmates **called** you names?

p. 155
1 Anna is the German girl **who** is staying with Latisha.
2 Latisha thinks training is something **which** is great fun.
3 What's the name of the player **who** scored both goals in United U14s' last match?
4 Stewed chicken is a dish **which** comes from Trinidad, isn't it?

p. 156
2 Which is the instrument Latisha plays?
3 Football is a sport Latisha likes a lot.
4 David Beckham is a football star everybody knows.
6 Let's do something we both want to do.

p. 157
1 The telephone **was invented by Alexander Bell**.
2 'We will rock you!' **was sung by Queen**.
3 Clifton Suspension Bridge **was built by Brunel**.

p. 158
1 The band **started** to play when I arrived.
2 The band **had started** to play when I arrived.
3 When his mum came home from work, Jason **had made** tea.
4 When his mum came home from work, Jason **made** tea.

p. 161
1 Sam said paddling **wasn't as difficult as it looked**.
2 He told Robert that he **hadn't felt very nervous**. *or*
He told Robert that he **didn't feel very nervous**.
3 He also said he **had learned quite a lot about boats**.
4 He explained that he **had never paddled a boat before**.
5 He told his uncle that he **would have to practise more often**.
6 He said he **really hoped they would win the race**.

p. 162
My mother is so strict. Yesterday I wanted to buy a present for my dad, but I **had to** tidy my room.
My parents are strict too. I'm sure I **won't be allowed to** go to Lauren's party.
Well, I'm sure I **will have to** be home by ten again, as always.
I **won't be able to** go to the party because I'm going to visit my cousins.

p. 163
1 Today my friends and I wanted to meet after breakfast.
2 But when I went into the bathroom to clean my teeth, there was no water.
3 Then I remembered that there had been a sign in the street about a water problem.
4 So I went into the living room, sat down and made **myself** comfortable.

p. 164
1 They're laughing at **each other**.
2 They're teaching **themselves** German.
3 They've hurt **themselves**.
4 They're talking to **each other**.

Diese Wörterverzeichnisse findest du in deinem Englischbuch:

- Das **Vocabulary** (Vokabelverzeichnis – S.168–194) enthält alle Wörter und Wendungen, die du lernen musst. Sie stehen in der Reihenfolge, in der sie in den Units vorkommen.
- Das **Dictionary** besteht aus zwei alphabetischen Wörterlisten zum Nachschlagen:
  Englisch – Deutsch: S.195–222
  Deutsch – Englisch: S.223–246.

So ist das Vocabulary aufgebaut:

- Hier siehst du, wo die Wörter vorkommen.
  p.54/A 1 = Seite 54, Abschnitt 1
  p.60/P 2 = Seite 60, Übung 2
- Die Lautschrift zeigt dir, wie ein Wort ausgesprochen und betont wird. (→ Englische Laute: S.222)
- Eingerückte Wörter lernst du am besten zusammen mit dem vorausgehenden Wort, weil die beiden zusammengehören.
- Diese Kästen solltest du dir besonders gut ansehen.

Tipps zum Wörterlernen findest du im Skills File auf Seite 133.

p.54/A 1	(to) **spot (-tt-)** [spɒt]	entdecken	I can't fin
	2 all	2 beide (2:2 unentschieden)	
p.60/P 2	(to) **score (a goal)** [skɔː], [gəʊl]	ein Tor schießen, einen Treffer erzielen	We won : – Smith ·
	score [skɔː]	Spielstand; Punktestand	

A football match

What's the score now? – 2–0. *(you say: **two nil**)* Wie steht e:
What was the final score? – Chelsea 2, Arsenal 1. Wie war der End:
Our last match was a draw, 2–2. *(you say: **two all**)* Unser letz

Word field: Sports

EQUIPMENT [ɪ'kwɪpmənt] Ausrüstung LO

skis [skiːz]

Abkürzungen:

n = *noun*		*v* = *verb*	
adj = *adjective*		*adv* = *adverb*	
prep = *preposition*		*conj* = *conjunction*	
pl = *plural*		*no pl* = *no plural*	
p. = page		pp. = pages	
sb. = somebody		sth. = something	
jn. = jemanden		jm. = jemandem	
AE = *American English*		*BE* = *British English*	

infml = *informal* (umgangssprachlich, informell)

Symbole:

! Hier stehen Hinweise auf Besonderheiten, bei denen man leicht Fehler machen kann.

◄► ist das „Gegenteil"-Zeichen: **slow ◄► fast** (**slow** ist das Gegenteil von **fast**)

~ Die Tilde in den Beispielsätzen steht für das neue Wort.

* Wörter mit einem **Sternchen** sind nur für Schüler/innen neu, die bisher mit D2 gearbeitet haben.

(F) verwandtes Wort im Französischen
(L) verwandtes Wort im Lateinischen

Introduction

p.6	**introduction (to)** [ˌɪntrə'dʌkʃn]	Einführung (in)	This book is a good ~ **to** a difficult topic. (F) introduction
	youth [juːθ]	Jugend	the time when you are young In her ~ my grandma was very beautiful. (L) iuventus
	national ['næʃnəl]	national, National-	**national ◄► international** (F) national
	musician [mjuː'zɪʃn]	Musiker/in	somebody who makes music (F) le musicien (L) musicus

	(to) **take part in** sth.	an etwas teilnehmen, bei etwas mitmachen	500 singers **took ~ in** the concert. (to) join other people in an activity
	the United Kingdom (UK) [juˌnaɪtɪd ˈkɪŋdəm], [ˌjuː ˈkeɪ]	das Vereinigte Königreich	! **the UK** = Great Britain (England, Scotland, Wales) and Northern Ireland *(Nordirland)*
	from **all over** the UK / the world / England	aus dem gesamten Vereinigten Königreich / aus der ganzen Welt / aus ganz England	Madonna is famous **~ ~ the world**. (= auf der ganzen Welt)
	kind of [kaɪnd]	Art (von)	What **~ of** music do you like? – Pop music. ! <u>Was für ein</u> Auto ...? = <u>What **kind of**</u> car ...?
	classical [ˈklæsɪkl]	klassisch	Do you like Mozart? – No, I don't like ~ music. Ⓕ classique
	drum [drʌm]	Trommel; Schlagzeug	! (to) **play <u>the</u> drums** *(pl)* = Schlagzeug spielen
	violin [ˌvaɪəˈlɪn]	Violine, Geige	! Klavier/Geige spielen = (to) **play <u>the</u> piano/violin**
p.7	**fiddle** [ˈfɪdl] *(infml)*	Fiedel, Geige	 a **violin** or **fiddle** ! (to) **play <u>the</u> fiddle** = Geige spielen
	(to) **be into** sth. *(infml)*	etwas mögen; voll auf etwas abfahren	My brother **is ~** reggae at the moment.
	by the way [ˌbaɪ ðə ˈweɪ]	übrigens; nebenbei (bemerkt)	**By the way**, I've bought a new computer game.
	***concert** [ˈkɒnsət]	Konzert	! Betonung auf der ersten Silbe: **<u>con</u>cert** [ˈkɒnsət]
p.8	**hostel** [ˈhɒstl]	Herberge, Wohnheim	youth **hostel** = Jugendherberge
	instrument [ˈɪnstrəmənt]	Instrument	! Betonung auf der ersten Silbe: **<u>i</u>nstrument** [ˈɪnstrəmənt]
	steel drum [ˌstiːl ˈdrʌm]	Steeldrum	**steel drums** 
	steel [stiːl]	Stahl	
	tune [tjuːn]	Melodie	
	gig [gɪg] *(infml)*	Gig, Auftritt	(to) **do a gig** = einen Auftritt haben, ein Konzert geben
p.9	**box office** [ˈbɒks‿ˌɒfɪs]	(Theater-, Kino-)Kasse	ticket office in a theatre, cinema, etc.
	*(to) **suppose** [səˈpəʊz]	annehmen, vermuten	She's the boss, so I ~ she's right.
	mixture [ˈmɪkstʃə]	Mischung	Ⓛ mixtura
	western [ˈwestən]	westlich, West-	***north** [nɔːθ] **northern** [ˈnɔːðən] ***west** [west] **western** [ˈwestən] ***east** [iːst] **eastern** [ˈiːstən] ***south** [saʊθ] **southern** ! [ˈsʌðən] Spain is one of the biggest countries in ~ Europe.
p.10	**the United States (US)** [juˌnaɪtɪd ˈsteɪts], [ˌjuː‿ˈes]	die Vereinigten Staaten (von Amerika)	
	***hungry** [ˈhʌŋgri]	hungrig	! Ich <u>habe</u> **Hunger**. = I<u>'m</u> **hungry**.
	***thirsty** [ˈθɜːstɪ]	durstig	! Ich <u>habe</u> **Durst**. = I<u>'m</u> **thirsty**.

	(to) **DJ** ['di:dʒeɪ]	(Musik/CDs/Platten) auflegen *(in der Disko)*	noun: **DJ (disc jockey)** – verb: (to) **DJ**
	workshop ['wɜ:kʃɒp]	Workshop, Lehrgang	
	Nice to meet you. [ˌnaɪs tə 'mi:t ju]	Nett, dich/euch/Sie kennenzulernen.	! Mit **Nice to meet you** grüßt man, wenn man jemanden das erste Mal trifft. John, this is Ben. – Hello, Ben. **Nice to meet you**.
p.11	* **half an hour** [ˌhɑ:f‿ən‿'aʊə]	eine halbe Stunde	! Word order: **half <u>an</u> hour** – **<u>eine</u> halbe Stunde**
	half [hɑ:f], *pl* **halves** [hɑ:vz]	Hälfte	I felt ill and spent ~ of the day in bed.
	(to) **mail** sb. sth. [meɪl]	jm. etwas schicken, senden *(vor allem per E-Mail)*	You can ~ us the answer at survey@cornelsen.de.
	* **wonderful** ['wʌndəfəl]	wunderbar	= very nice, fantastic
	(to) **keep in touch** [tʌtʃ]	in Verbindung bleiben, Kontakt halten	It was nice to meet you. – Yes, let's **keep in ~**.
	Wait and see!	Wart's ab!	What's for dinner this evening? – **Wait and ~**!
	recording [rɪ'kɔ:dɪŋ]	Aufnahme, Aufzeichnung	noun: **recording** – verb: (to) **record** [rɪ'kɔ:d]
	(to) **go with**	gehören zu, passen zu	The first text **goes ~** the third picture.

bass [beɪs]	Kontrabass; Bassgitarre
cello ['tʃeləʊ]	Cello
clarinet [ˌklærɪ'net]	Klarinette
flute [flu:t]	Querflöte
electric [ɪ'lektrɪk]	elektrisch, Elektro-
recorder [rɪ'kɔ:də]	Blockflöte
saxophone ['sæksəfəʊn]	Saxophon
trumpet ['trʌmpɪt]	Trompete
trombone [trɒm'bəʊn]	Posaune

Unit 1: My London

Places without articles

p.12	I go **to school** in London. My friends **at school/from school** are nice.	Ich gehe in London zur Schule. Meine Freunde in der/aus der Schule ...
	My dad's ill. He's gone **to hospital**. He has to stay **in hospital** for three weeks.	ins Krankenhaus im Krankenhaus
	We go **to church** every Sunday. I know him **from church**.	in die Kirche von/aus der Kirche
	the centre **of town** / his part **of town** Let's go shopping **in town**. We went **into town** to watch a film.	die Mitte der Stadt; sein Teil der Stadt in der Stadt in die Stadt

capital ['kæpɪtl]	Hauptstadt	Berlin is the ~ of Germany. Ⓕ la capitale
(to) **show** sb. **around**	jn. *(in der Stadt/im Museum/...)* herumführen	
PS [ˌpiː‿'es] **(postscript** ['pəʊstskrɪpt]**)**	PS, Postskript *(Nachschrift unter Briefen)*	
big wheel [ˌbɪɡ 'wiːl]	Riesenrad	
wheel [wiːl]	Rad	A bike has two ~s. 
you	man	How do ~ say 'once more' in German? (= Wie sagt man ...?)
They say ...	Man sagt, ...	**They say** a monster lives in that lake.
sound file ['saʊnd faɪl]	Tondatei, Soundfile	
although [ɔːl'ðəʊ]	obwohl	I went to bed early ~ I wasn't really tired.
queen [kwiːn]	Königin	
***royal** ['rɔɪəl]	königlich, Königs-	Tourists love the British ~ family.
***air** [eə]	Luft	Please open the window and let some ~ in.
(to) **dream (of, about)** [driːm]	träumen (von)	verb: (to) **dream** – noun: **dream**

on („weiter")

You want to be a rock star? **Dream on**!	... Träum weiter!
It started to rain, but we **walked on**.	..., aber wir gingen weiter.
Read on. You'll find the information on the next few pages.	Lies weiter. ...
He stopped talking for a moment. Then he **went on**.	... Dann redete er weiter.

p.13 **quite** [kwaɪt]	ziemlich; ganz	I play football ~ well, but I'm not ~ good enough for the school team.
borough ['bʌrə]	Bezirk	
flea market ['fliː ˌmɑːkɪt]	Flohmarkt	

second-hand [ˌsekənd 'hænd]	gebraucht; aus zweiter Hand	! I bought it **second-hand**. = ... aus zweiter Hand
(to) **listen for** sth.	auf etwas horchen, achten	I'm going to have a bath. Can you **listen** ~ the doorbell, please?
gist [dʒɪst]	*das* Wesentliche	Did you understand everything that he said? – No, but I understood the ~ of it.
***time(s)** [taɪm, taɪmz]	Mal(e); -mal	We played football four **~s** last week.
***for the first time**	zum ersten Mal	On Saturday I saw the film *Casablanca* **for the** tenth **~**.
generally ['dʒenrəli]	im Allgemeinen	
detail ['diːteɪl]	Detail, Einzelheit	! Betonung auf der 1. Silbe: **detail** ['diːteɪl]
exact [ɪɡ'zækt]	genau	What is the ~ size of London? Ⓕ exact/e Ⓛ exactus

Buildings and places in a town

		Examples in London:
cathedral [kə'θi:drəl]	Kathedrale, Dom	**St Paul's Cathedral** [sənt 'pɔ:lz]
circus ['sɜ:kəs]	(runder) Platz	**Piccadilly Circus** [ˌpɪkədɪli 'sɜ:kəs]
column ['kɒləm]	Säule	**Nelson's Column** [ˌnelsnz 'kɒləm]
lane [leɪn]	Gasse, Weg	**Brick Lane** [ˌbrɪk 'leɪn]
lock [lɒk]	Schleuse	**Camden Lock** [ˌkæmdən 'lɒk]
palace ['pæləs]	Palast, Schloss	**Buckingham Palace** [ˌbʌkɪŋəm 'pæləs]
parliament ['pɑ:ləmənt] ! Schreibung: **parl<u>ia</u>ment**	Parlament	**the Houses of Parliament** ! Betonung auf der 1. Silbe: **p<u>a</u>rliament**
square [skweə]	Platz	**Leicester Square** ! [ˌlestə 'skweə]; **Trafalgar Square** [trəˌfælgə 'skweə]

	(to) **panic** ['pænɪk]	in Panik geraten	! -ing form: **pani<u>ck</u>ing**; simple past: **pani<u>ck</u>ed**
	* (to) **be called** [kɔ:ld]	heißen, genannt werden	Asterix has got a big friend. He**'s ~** 'Obelix'. (= His name is 'Obelix'.)
	tip [tɪp]	Tipp	
	* **cheap** [tʃi:p]	preiswert	**cheap ◄► expensive**
p. 14/A 1	**ticket** ['tɪkɪt]	Fahrkarte	
	zone [zəʊn]	Zone, Bereich	(F) la zone (L) zona
	Travelcard ['trævlkɑ:d]	Tages-/Wochen-/Monats-fahrkarte *(der Londoner Verkehrsbetriebe)*	
	central ['sentrəl]	Zentral-, Mittel-	! Betonung auf der 1. Silbe: **c<u>e</u>ntral** ['sentrəl]
	the Tube [tju:b] *(BE)*	die Londoner U-Bahn	underground (in London)
	What's the best way to get there?	Wie komme ich am besten dahin?	
	line [laɪn]	(U-Bahn-)Linie	(F) la ligne
	eastbound ['i:stbaʊnd]	Richtung Osten	**northbound** **westbound** ◄ ▲▼ ► **eastbound** **southbound**
	(to) **change** [tʃeɪndʒ]	umsteigen	Take the Central Line eastbound and ~ to the Bakerloo Line southbound at Oxford Circus.
p. 15/A 3	**high** [haɪ]	hoch	What's the **~est** mountain in the world?
	fact [fækt]	Tatsache, Fakt	I've found lots of interesting **~s** for my essay on the Music for Youth Festival. (F) le fait (L) factum
p. 16/A 4	(to) **walk** [wɔ:k]	(zu Fuß) gehen, laufen; spazieren gehen	I never ride my bike to school. I always ~. At the weekend we often ~ in the woods.
	mom [mɑ:m] *(AE)*	Mutti, Mama; Mutter	= *BE* **mum**
	cellphone ['selfəʊn] *(AE)*	Mobiltelefon, Handy	= *BE* **mobile phone**
	surprise (for/to) [sə'praɪz]	Überraschung für	A present? For me? That's a nice ~! (F) la surprise
	mosque [mɒsk]	Moschee	(F) la mosquée

	synagogue ['sɪnəgɒg]	Synagoge	! Betonung auf der 1. Silbe: **synagogue** ['sɪnəgɒg] (F) la synagogue
	***we could ...** [kʊd]	wir könnten ...	What can we do tonight? – We ~ watch TV. **Could** I have a hamburger with chips, please? **could** = **1.** konnte(n); **2.** könnte(n)
	meal [mi:l]	Mahlzeit, Essen	We like to eat a hot ~ in the evenings.
	takeaway ['teɪkəweɪ]	*Restaurant, das auch Essen zum Mitnehmen verkauft;* *Essen zum Mitnehmen*	There's a good Chinese ~ near our house. We sometimes get an Indian ~ on Fridays.
.16/Study	* (to) **guess** [ges]	raten, erraten, schätzen	**Guess** how old I am! – 15?
	menu ['menju:]	Speisekarte; Menü *(Computer)*	Look! There are 125 different pizzas on the ~. ! Ich nehme das **Menü**. = I'll have the **set meal**.
	(to) **look up words**	Wörter nachschlagen	
	***whole** [həʊl]	ganze(r, s), gesamte(r, s)	We played cards the ~ day. (= all day) John was in Berlin for the ~ of 2007.
	entry ['entri]	Eintrag, Eintragung *(in Wörterbuch/Tagebuch)*	I've got a new dictionary. It has 200,000 **entries**. There's no ~ in Jane's diary for 12th June.
	***meaning** ['mi:nɪŋ]	Bedeutung	
p.16/A 5	**mild** [maɪld]	mild	! Pronunciation: **mild** [maɪld]
	medium ['mi:diəm]	mittel-, mittlere(r, s); mittelgroß	
	spicy ['spaɪsi]	würzig, scharf gewürzt	**spicy ◄► mild**
	dish [dɪʃ]	Gericht *(Speise)*	What's your favourite ~? – Spaghetti.
	allergic (to sth.**)** [ə'lɜ:dʒɪk]	allergisch (gegen etwas)	
	nut [nʌt]	Nuss	
	vegetable ['vedʒtəbl]	*(ein)* Gemüse	! **Vegetables are** good for me. = Gemüse ist gut ...
	lentil ['lentəl]	Linse *(Hülsenfrucht)*	
	dry [draɪ]	trocken	**dry ◄► wet**
	sauce [sɔ:s]	Soße	(F) la sauce
p.17/A 6	**(street) performer** [pə'fɔ:mə]	Straßenkünstler/in	
	since September [sɪns]	seit September	John has lived in Bristol **since** 2006. ! *Not:* ~~lives in~~
	(to) **seem** (to be/to do) [si:m]	(zu sein/zu tun) scheinen	He's got three cars. He **~s** to be very rich.
	***guy** [gaɪ]	Typ, Kerl	! Der Plural **guys** („Leute") wird auch für Frauen und Mädchen verwendet.
	like [laɪk] *(infml)*	als ob	What's that boy doing? – He looks ~ he's waiting for somebody.
	for years	seit Jahren	Laura has lived in Bristol **for** three months. ! *Not:* ~~lives in~~
	area ['eəriə]	Gebiet, Gegend; Bereich	I live in an ~ with a lot of restaurants. Grammar is my problem ~. (L) area
	yummy ['jʌmi] *(infml)*	lecker	= **delicious**
	(to) **get lost**	sich verlaufen	
	neat [ni:t] *(AE, infml)*	großartig, toll, klasse	= *BE* **fantastic, great**
	***busy** ['bɪzi]	beschäftigt	Can you help me? Or are you ~?

	a couple of ['kʌpl]	ein Paar/paar	two; some, a few
p.17/A 7	**crowd** [kraʊd]	(Menschen-)Menge	
	acrobat ['ækrəbæt]	Akrobat/in	❗ Betonung auf der 1. Silbe: **a**crobat ['ækrəbæt]
	(to) **walk around**	herumlaufen	Let's **walk** ~ for a bit and look for some nice shops.
	***I don't think so.**	Das finde/glaube ich nicht.	This is a great book. – **I don't ~ so.** I think it's boring.
	***I think so.**	Ich glaube (ja).	Is he from Germany? – **I ~ so**, but I'm not sure.
p.20/P 1	**transport** *(no pl)* ['trænspɔːt]	Transport(wesen)	❗ Betonung auf der 1. Silbe: **tra**nsport ['trænspɔːt]

Word field: Transport

1 **bus stop** ['bʌs stɒp]
2 **ticket machine** ['tɪkɪt məˌʃiːn]
3 **bus pass** ['bʌs pɑːs]
4 **gate** [geɪt] Flugsteig
5 **taxi** ['tæksi]
6 **tram** [træm]
7 **airport** ['eəpɔːt]
8 **ferry** ['feri]

	land [lænd]	Land	After the long plane trip, it was good to be on ~ again.
	ground [graʊnd]	(Erd-)Boden	This railway tunnel is 20 metres under the ~. ❗ Erdboden = **ground** – Fußboden = **floor**
p.20/P 2	**announcement** [ə'naʊnsmənt]	Durchsage	This is an important ~. Please keep your bags with you at all times.
p.21/P 4	***coast** [kəʊst]	Küste	Aberdeen is a town on the ~ of Scotland.
p.24/P 11	**course** [kɔːs]	Kurs, Lehrgang	My mum does an English ~ on Tuesday evenings. (F) le cours (L) cursus
	(to) **have a suntan** ['sʌntæn]	sonnengebräunt sein	
	*(to) **make friends (with)**	Freunde finden; sich anfreunden (mit)	He's a nice boy and **makes friends** easily. I **made friends with** John in 2004.
	crowded ['kraʊdɪd]	voller Menschen, überfüllt	The city centre is often ~ with tourists in the summer.
	(to) **wish** sth. [wɪʃ]	sich etwas wünschen	I ~ I had lots of money.

(to) wish

I **wish** I **knew** the answer to this question. — Ich wünschte, ich wüsste die Antwort …

I **wish** it **wasn't raining**. — Ich wünschte, es regnete nicht/würde nicht regnen.

In Wunschsätzen mit **I wish** (= „Ich wünschte") steht das folgende Verb im *simple past* oder im *past progressive*, obwohl sich die Sätze nicht auf die Vergangenheit beziehen, sondern auf die Gegenwart oder die Zukunft. Im Deutschen steht der Konjunktiv.

	***friendly** ['frendli]	freundlich	

p.25/P 12	***directions** *(pl)* [də'rekʃnz]	Wegbeschreibung(en)	I couldn't find the station, but then a nice woman gave me ~.
	***I didn't get that.**	Das habe ich nicht verstanden/kapiert.	Look, it's very easy: if x is 52 , y has to be 13. – **I don't get it**.
p.25/P 13	**everyday** *(adj)* ['evrideɪ]	Alltags-; alltäglich	Are you going to wear anything special tonight? – No, just my ~ clothes: jeans and a T-shirt.

Only a game

p.26	(to) **work** [wɜːk]	funktionieren	I need your help. My computer doesn't ~.
	helmet ['helmɪt]	Helm	**helmets** 

around

herum... / umher...	We walked **around** till we found a nice café.	herumlaufen, umherspazieren
	It's fun to run and jump **around** in the park after school.	herumrennen; herumspringen
in ... umher, durch	We walked **around** the town and looked at the sights.	in der Stadt umher, durch die Stadt
	They rode their bikes **around** the village.	im Dorf umher, durch das Dorf
um ... (herum)	There was water all **around** them.	ganz um sie herum
	Let's run **around** the lake and see who is fastest.	um den See (herum)
	! *(auch zeitlich:)* I'll see you **around** six.	um sechs Uhr herum, gegen sechs

action ['ækʃn]	spannendes Geschehen; Handlung, Tat	I want to see ~**s**, not words! Ⓕ une action
sign [saɪn]	Schild; Zeichen	The ~ says it's only a mile to the city centre. I'll wait till you give me a ~. Then I'll come.
(to) look at sth. **closely** ['kləʊsli]	etwas genau anschauen	
button ['bʌtn]	Knopf	**buttons**  Which ~ do I push to turn the MP3 player on? Ⓕ le bouton
(to) **appear** [ə'pɪə]	erscheinen, auftauchen	(to) **appear** ◄► (to) **disappear** Ⓛ apparere
kind of scary *(infml)* [kaɪnd]	irgendwie unheimlich	! **kind of + noun:** What **kind of music** ... = Welche **Art** Musik ... **kind of + adjective: kind of scary** = **irgendwie** unheimlich
murder ['mɜːdə]	Mord	
(to) **murder** ['mɜːdə]	(er)morden	(to) kill
murderer ['mɜːdərə]	Mörder/in	! **Mord** = murder **Mörder/in** = murderer
***voice** [vɔɪs]	Stimme	
victim ['vɪktɪm]	Opfer	The dead man was the ~ of a murder. Ⓕ la victime Ⓛ victima

p.27	**blood** [blʌd]	Blut	
	***flower** ['flaʊə]	Blume; Blüte	
	rat [ræt]	Ratte	Ⓕ le rat
	realistic [ˌriːə'lɪstɪk]	realistisch, wirklichkeitsnah	I want to see all the sights in London. – Be ~. We've only got two days.
	just [dʒʌst]	einfach	

just

They call you names? **Just** don't listen to them.	... Hör **einfach** nicht hin.
It's **just** a game.	Es ist **nur/bloß** ein Spiel.
They're **just** leaving. / They've **just** left.	Sie gehen **gerade**. / Sie sind **gerade (eben)** gegangen.
Just then the phone rang.	**Genau in dem Moment / Gerade dann** klingelte das Telefon.
You look **just like** your mother.	Du siehst **genau wie** deine Mutter aus.

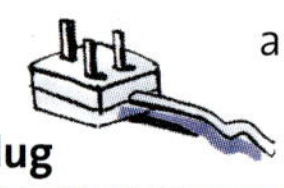
a British **plug**

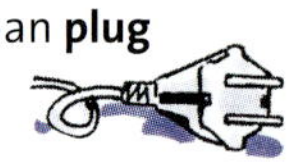
a German **plug**

	plug [plʌg]	Stecker	a British **plug** / a German **plug**
	electricity [ɪˌlek'trɪsəti]	Strom, Elektrizität	noun: **electricity** – adjective: **electric** Ⓕ l'électricité *(f)*
	flash [flæʃ]	Lichtblitz	
	***strange** [streɪndʒ]	seltsam, sonderbar	
	close (to) [kləʊs]	nahe (bei, an)	The café isn't far: it's very ~ to our home ! Pronunciation: (to) **close** [kləʊz] schließen; **close** *(adj)* [kləʊs] nahe
	shadow ['ʃædəʊ]	Schatten	I woke up and saw the ~ of a man on the wall. 
	knife [naɪf], *pl* **knives** [naɪvz]	Messer	! Silent letter **k**: **knife** [naɪf] 
	* (to) **realize** ['rɪəlaɪz]	erkennen, merken	
p.28	**light** [laɪt]	Licht	
	(to) **take care of** sth./sb. [keə]	sich um etwas/jn. kümmern	
	(to) **get away from** sth./sb.	von etwas/jm. weggehen; sich von etwas/jm. entfernen	**Get ~ from** the window! You'll fall out!
	* (to) **cry** [kraɪ]	schreien	'I love you!' he **cried**.
	ending ['endɪŋ]	Ende, (Ab-)Schluss *(einer Geschichte, eines Films usw.)*	Not every story can have a happy ~. ! German: Happyend – English: **happy ending**
	view [vjuː]	Ansicht, Meinung	Jo doesn't like folk music, but in my ~ it's fantastic.

	***not (...) any more**	nicht mehr	The Greens do**n't** live here **any ~**. They're in London now.

How am I doing?

p.29	**How am I doing?**	Wie komme ich voran? *(Wie sind meine Fortschritte?)*	
	***danger** ['deɪndʒə]	Gefahr	

Unit 2: Island girl

p.30	**huge** [hjuːdʒ]	riesig, sehr groß	

big – large – huge

big / large	**big** und **large** sind oft austauschbar.	a **big/large** family; a **big/large** house
	big ist umgangssprachlicher als **large**, daher solltest du in eher förmlichen Texten besser **large** schreiben.	
	large wird in der Regel nicht verwendet, um Menschen zu beschreiben.	a very **big** man
huge	**huge** bedeutet „riesig“, „sehr groß“.	a **huge** bag

	salmon ['sæmən], *pl* **salmon**	Lachs	**!** Silent letter **l**: **sa<u>l</u>mon** ['sæmən] Ⓛ salmo
p.31	**scenery** ['siːnəri]	Landschaft	
p.32/A 1	**electronic** [ɪˌlek'trɒnɪk]	elektronisch	Ⓕ électronique
	media *(pl)* ['miːdiə]	Medien	It's faster to use **~** like the phone or e-mail than to write letters.
	faraway ['fɑːrəweɪ]	fern; abgelegen	
	great-grandmother/-father	Urgroßmutter/-vater	
	post [pəʊst]	Post *(Briefe, Päckchen, ...)*	**!** die Post, das Postamt = the **post office**
	once [wʌns]	einmal	
	twice [twaɪs]	zweimal	**!** **once** (1x) – **twice** (2x) – **three times** (3x)
	(once/twice) **a** week	(einmal/zweimal) pro Woche	Our band practises once **~** week.
	(to) **imagine** sth. [ɪ'mædʒɪn]	sich etwas vorstellen	Ⓕ imaginer Ⓛ imaginari
	instant messages *(pl)* [ˌɪnstənt 'mesɪdʒɪz]	*Nachrichten, die man im Internet austauscht (in Echtzeit)*	
	***text message** ['tekst ˌmesɪdʒ]	SMS	I get about twenty **~ ~s** a day.
	*(to) **text** sb. [tekst]	jm. eine SMS schicken	Have a good trip. **Text** me when you get there.

p.32/A 2	**use** [ju:s]	Gebrauch	! Pronunciation: (to) **use** [ju:z] gebrauchen **use** *(noun)* [ju:s] Gebrauch
	(to) **exchange** [ɪks'tʃeɪndʒ]	austauschen	
	ringtone ['rɪŋtəʊn]	Klingelton	
	(to) **mix** [mɪks]	mischen, mixen	If you ~ blue and yellow, you get green. (L) miscere
p.33/A 3	* **as**	wie	Traffic is a problem here, ~ in all big cities. Bristol, ~ you know, is a city in England.
	ceilidh ['keɪli]	*Musik- und Tanzveranstaltung, vor allem in Schottland und Irland*	
	(to) **pick** sb. **up** [ˌpɪk‿'ʌp]	jn. abholen	He's **~ing up** Mr Brown.
	grammar school ['græmə ˌsku:l]	Gymnasium	
	researcher [rɪ'sɜ:tʃə, 'ri:sɜ:tʃə]	Rechercheur/in	
	* **documentary** [ˌdɒkju'mentri]	Dokumentarfilm	! Betonung: **documentary** [ˌdɒkju'mentri]
	beauty ['bju:ti]	Schönheit	adjective: **beautiful** – noun: **beauty** (F) la beauté
	trendy ['trendi]	modisch, schick	
	(to) **take** [teɪk], **took** [tʊk], **taken** ['teɪkən]	dauern, *(Zeit)* brauchen	It **~s** about 15 minutes to get home from here. How long does your journey to school ~?
	from Monday **to** Friday	von Montag bis Freitag	My father usually works ~ 9 am **to** 5.30 pm.
	during *(prep)* ['djʊərɪŋ]	während	I met her ~ my visit to London.
	surprised (**at** sth.) [sə'praɪzd]	überrascht (über etwas)	I was ~ **at** the size of their house. It was bigger than I thought.
	(to) **surprise** sb. [sə'praɪz]	jn. überraschen	Don't tell Jo about the party. We want to ~ him. noun: **surprise** – verb: (to) **surprise**
	role [rəʊl]	Rolle	What's your ~ in the play? – I'm the detective. (F) le rôle
p.34/A 6	* (to) **be able to** do sth.	etwas tun können; fähig sein/in der Lage sein, etwas zu tun	Sandra **wasn't ~ to** come to my party last Saturday. (= Sandra couldn't come ...)
	You wish!	*etwa:* Das hättest du wohl gerne!	
	Shall we ...? [ʃæl]	Wollen wir ...? / Sollen wir ...?	I'm bored. **Shall we** watch TV? It's hot in here. **Shall I** open the window?
	rucksack ['rʌksæk]	Rucksack	! Pronunciation: **rucksack** ['rʌksæk]
	ponytail ['pəʊniteɪl]	Pferdeschwanz *(Frisur)*	a **ponytail**

p. 35/A 8	**upset (about)** [ˌʌp'set]	aufgebracht, gekränkt, mitgenommen (wegen)	John was ~ because his sister didn't remember his birthday.
	(to) **upset** sb. **(-tt-)** [ʌp'set], **upset, upset**	jn. ärgern, kränken, aus der Fassung bringen	It **~s** me when people are rude to me. The bad news about her father ~ her a lot.
	(to) **let** sb. **do** sth. **(-tt-)** [let], **let, let**	jm. erlauben, etwas zu tun; zulassen, dass jd. etwas tut	My parents never ~ me watch late films. You look hungry. **Let** me make you a sandwich.
	bully ['bʊli]	(Schul-)Tyrann	verb: (to) **bully** – noun: **bully**
	(to) **call** sb. **names**	jn. mit Schimpfwörtern hänseln, jm. Schimpfwörter nachrufen	He felt upset because the other kids always **~ed him names** like Carrot-Nose or Rabbit-Ears.
	(to) **gossip** ['gɒsɪp]	schwatzen, klatschen, tratschen	
	(to) **bet (-tt-)** [bet], **bet, bet**	wetten	I ~ my bike is faster than yours.
	(to) **forget (-tt-)** [fə'get], **forgot** [fə'gɒt], **forgotten** [fə'gɒtn]	vergessen	Tomorrow is Grandpa's birthday. Don't ~ it! (to) **forget** ◄► (to) **remember**
	main [meɪn]	Haupt-	the **main** information/clause/road/thing = the **most important** ...
p. 35/A 9	**feeling** ['fi:lɪŋ]	Gefühl	verb: (to) **feel** – noun: **feeling**
	translation [træns'leɪʃn]	Übersetzung	Ⓛ translatio
	(to) **translate** [træns'leɪt]	übersetzen	We had to ~ the text from English into German.
	* (to) **decide (on** sth.**)** [dɪ'saɪd]	sich entscheiden (für etwas), (etwas) beschließen	We **~d on** a project about the sea. (= We **~d to do** a project ...)

Word field: Town and country

p. 38/P 1

canal [kə'næl]

* **coast** [kəʊst] Küste

hilly ['hɪli] hügelig

bay [beɪ] Bucht

shopping precinct ['pri:sɪŋkt] Einkaufsviertel, Einkaufsstraße *(autofrei)*

car park ['kɑ: pɑ:k]

busy ['bɪzi] belebt, verkehrsreich; hektisch

a **busy** street

p. 38/P 3	**stress** [stres]	Betonung	Where's the ~ in 'stupid'? – On the first syllable.
p. 39/P 4	* (to) **take place**	stattfinden	Our next school trip will **take** ~ next month.
	(to) **be lucky** ['lʌki]	Glück haben	! She is **happy**. = Sie ist glücklich. She is **lucky**. = Sie hat Glück.

	circle ['sɜːkl]	Kreis	(F) le cercle (L) circulus
	highlight ['haɪlaɪt]	Höhepunkt	
	***rock** [rɒk]	Fels	
	impressive [ɪm'presɪv]	beeindruckend, eindrucksvoll	
	structure ['strʌktʃə]	Struktur; Gliederung	! Stress: **structure** ['strʌktʃə] (F) la structure (L) structura
	***for example** [fər‿ɪg'zɑːmpl]	zum Beispiel	
	beginning [bɪ'gɪnɪŋ]	Anfang, Beginn	**beginning** ◄► **ending**
	***event** [ɪ'vent]	Ereignis	The first day at school is a big ~ in a child's life.
	general ['dʒenrəl]	allgemeine(r, s)	! Stress: **general** ['dʒenrəl] (F) général/e
	personal ['pɜːsənl]	persönlich	! Stress: **personal** ['pɜːsənl] (F) personnel/le (L) personalis
	souvenir [ˌsuːvə'nɪə]	Andenken, Souvenir	(F) le souvenir
	***lovely** ['lʌvli]	schön, hübsch, wunderbar	
	journey ['dʒɜːni]	Reise, Fahrt	
p.40/P 6	***almost** ['ɔːlməʊst]	fast, beinahe	
p.42/P 11	*(to) **grow** [grəʊ], **grew** [gruː], **grown** [grəʊn]	wachsen	Orange trees ~ only in hot countries.
p.43/P 13	**loch** [lɒx]	(Binnen-)See in Schottland	! Pronunciation: like German „Loch" (hole)
	kilometre (km) ['kɪləmiːtə]	Kilometer	1,000 metres = 1 ~ (F) le kilomètre
	centimetre (cm) ['sentɪmiːtə]	Zentimeter	100 **~s** = 1 **metre** (F) le centimètre
	million ['mɪljən]	Million	! one **million** cars (eine Million Autos) – two **million** cars (zwei Millionen Autos) *But:* **millions of** cars (Millionen von Autos) (F) le million

Orkney Star

p.45	**(and) now for ...**	und jetzt ... *(kündigt ein neues Thema an)*	That's the end of the news. **Now for** the weather ...
	announcement [ə'naʊnsmənt]	Durchsage, Ansage; Ankündigung, Bekanntgabe	I have an ~ for you all: I'm going to have a baby! (F) une annonce
	head teacher [ˌhed 'tiːtʃə]	Schulleiter/in	
	(to) **believe** [bɪ'liːv]	glauben	That can't be true! I don't ~ it.
	***excited** [ɪk'saɪtɪd]	aufgeregt, begeistert	She was **excited** about the trip. (aufgeregt) It was an **exciting** trip. (aufregend)
	Congratulations! [kənˌgrætʃu'leɪʃnz]	Herzlichen Glückwunsch!	! Mit **Congratulations!** gratuliert man jemandem zu einem Erfolg. Zum Geburtstag wünscht man aber **Happy birthday**.
	you **might** need help [maɪt]	du könntest (vielleicht) Hilfe brauchen	If you wait outside Buckingham Palace, you ~ see the Queen.
	hairdresser ['heədresə]	Friseur/in	
	shocked [ʃɒkt]	schockiert	

at the hairdresser's / to the doctor's / ...

Wenn der **Ort** gemeint ist, an dem jemand seinen Beruf ausübt – z.B. ein Friseurgeschäft oder eine Arztpraxis –, wird oft der **s-Genitiv** benutzt:

My father is **at the hairdresser's**.	Mein Vater ist beim Friseur.
She felt ill and went **to the doctor's**.	Sie fühlte sich krank und ging zum Arzt.
I met Grandpa **at the chemist's** this morning.	Ich habe Opa heute Morgen beim Apotheker getroffen.

	they didn't know **what to do**	sie wussten nicht, was sie tun sollten; sie wussten nicht, was zu tun war	= they didn't know **what they should do**
	across [ə'krɒs]	hinüber, herüber	Look at that river. How can we get ~?
	anorak ['ænəræk]	Anorak, Windjacke	(F) un anorak
p.46	***just like**	genau wie	
	(to) **tease** [ti:z]	necken, auf den Arm nehmen	Don't ~ the dog. He might get angry.
	until [ən'tɪl]	bis	= till
	*(to) **cut (-tt-), cut, cut** [kʌt]	schneiden	**Cut** the paper into four pieces.
	*(to) **cut out**	ausschneiden	
	***bell** [bel]	Klingel, Glocke	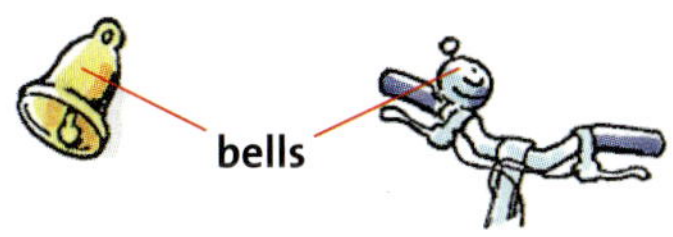
	at the **front** [frʌnt]	vorne, im vorderen Teil	The board is at the ~ of our classroom.
	*at the **back** [bæk]	hinten, im hinteren Teil	**front ◄► back**
	captain ['kæptɪn]	Kapitän/in	(F) le capitaine
	passenger ['pæsɪndʒə]	Passagier/in, Fahrgast	(F) le passager
	arrival [ə'raɪvl]	Ankunft	verb: (to) **arrive** – noun: **arrival** (F) l'arrivée *(f)*
	quay [ki:]	Kai	! Pronunciation: **quay** [ki:] (F) le quai
p.47	**while** *(conj)* [waɪl]	während	I met her ~ I was in London.

German 'während'

before a noun: **during** *(preposition)*

John phoned **during** the football match.	John rief während des Fußballspiels an.

before a clause: **as/while** *(conjunction)*

John phoned **as/while** we were watching the football match.	John rief an, während wir das Fußballspiel schauten.

equipment [ɪ'kwɪpmənt]	Ausrüstung	(F) l'équipment *(m)*
in next to no time	im Nu	The exercise was easy. I did it **in next to no time**.
above [ə'bʌv]	über, oberhalb (von)	Your eyes are ~ your nose.
below [bɪ'ləʊ]	unter, unterhalb (von)	Your mouth is ~ your nose. **below ◄► above**
(to) **speed** [spi:d]	rasen; *hier:* schnell fliegen	He said bye and **~ed** away on his bike.
(to) **set up (-tt-)** [set], **set, set**	aufstellen, aufbauen	(to) make something ready (for use)

cliff [klɪf]	Klippe	
stew [stjuː]	Eintopf(gericht)	
community hall [kəˈmjuːnəti]	Gemeinschaftshalle, -saal / Gemeindehalle, -saal	(L) communitas
(to) **grab** **(-bb-)** [græb]	schnappen, packen	I was late, so I **grabbed** my school bag and ran to the station.
***stage** [steɪdʒ]	Bühne	The band went on ~ and started to play.
She **couldn't believe** her **eyes.**	Sie traute ihren Augen kaum.	When I saw my present, I **couldn't ~ my eyes**. It was so beautiful!
***I should** [ʃəd, ʃʊd]	ich sollte	You ~ ask me first before you go out.

Unit 3: Time for sport

p. 54	**final** [ˈfaɪnl]	Finale, Endspiel	! Pronunciation and stress: **final** [ˈfaɪnl]
	final [ˈfaɪnl]	letzte(r, s); End-	The hero saved the girl in the ~ minute of the film. (F) final/e
	semi-final [ˌsemiˈfaɪnl]	Halbfinale	
	training session [ˈseʃn]	Trainingsstunde, -einheit	
	(to) **train** [treɪn]	trainieren	(F) entraîner
p. 55	**furniture** *(no pl)* [ˈfɜːnɪtʃə]	Möbel	! Die **Möbel sind** neu. = The **furniture is** new. (*Never:* The ~~furnitures are~~ new.) ein Möbel(stück) = **a piece of furniture**

Words without a plural

This new **furniture is** very nice. **Was it** expensive?	**Diese** neuen **Möbel sind** sehr hübsch. **Waren sie** teuer?
I think your **hair is** too long. Why don't you cut **it**?	... deine **Haare sind** zu lang. Warum schneidest du **sie** nicht?
That's too much **homework**.	**Das sind** zu viele **Hausaufgaben**.
All **this information is** very interesting.	All **diese Informationen sind** sehr interessant.
OK, **that's** the bad **news**. And what **is** the good **news**?	OK, **das ist/sind** die schlechte(n) **Nachricht(en)**. Und was **ist/sind** die gute(n) **Nachricht(en)**?

p. 56/A 1	**supporter** [səˈpɔːtə]	Anhänger/in, Fan	
	(to) **support** a team [səˈpɔːt]	eine Mannschaft unterstützen; Fan einer Mannschaft sein	Which football team do you ~? – Manchester United.
	such good pitches [sʌtʃ]	so gute (Fußball-)Felder	
	***football/hockey pitch** [pɪtʃ]	Fußball-/Hockeyplatz, -feld	

German 'so'

with noun: **such**	Helen is **such** a nice **person**.	... so ein netter Mensch.
	Helen and Mark are **such** nice **people**.	... so nette Menschen.
with adjective: **so**	Helen is **so nice**.	... so nett.

(to) **score (a goal)** [skɔː], [gəʊl]	ein Tor schießen, einen Treffer erzielen	We won 3–2. – Oh, great! Who **~d**? – Smith **~d** all three **~s**.
score [skɔː]	Spielstand; Punktestand	

	goal [gəʊl]	Tor *(im Sport)*	

A football match

What's the score now? – 2–0. *(you say: **two nil**)*	Wie steht es jetzt? – 2:0.
What was the **final score**? – Chelsea 2, Arsenal 1.	Wie war der Endstand? – 2:1 für Chelsea.
Our last match was a **draw**, 2–2. *(you say: **two all**)*	Unser letztes Spiel war ein Unentschieden, 2:2.

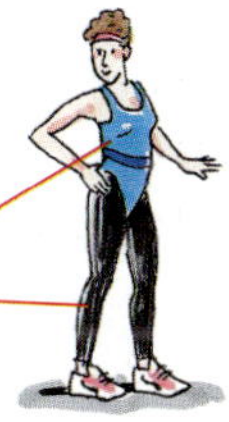

	coach [kəʊtʃ]	Trainer/in	
	Music is for dancing.	*etwa:* Musik ist zum Tanzen da.	
	leotard ['li:ətɑ:d]	Gymnastikanzug; Turnanzug	a **leotard**
	tights *(pl)* [taɪts]	Strumpfhose	**tights**
p.56/A 2	**aim** [eɪm]	Ziel	What is your ~ in life? – To be happy.
	hope [həʊp]	Hoffnung	verb: (to) **hope** – noun: **hope**
p.57/A 4	**exchange** [ɪks'tʃeɪndʒ]	Austausch	Our teacher set up an ~ between students in our class and students at a school in England.
	(to) **exchange** [ɪks'tʃeɪndʒ]	aus-, umtauschen; *(Geld)* wechseln	First think, then ~ your ideas with a partner. These trousers don't fit. I need to ~ them. Where can I ~ euros for dollars? Ⓕ échanger
	bad timing ['taɪmɪŋ]	schlechtes Timing, schlechte Wahl des Zeitpunkts	
	appetite ['æpɪtaɪt]	Appetit	**!** Manchmal sagt man **Enjoy!**, wenn man gemeinsam isst. Aber nie ~~Good appetite~~!
	(to) **paraphrase** ['pærəfreɪz]	umschreiben, anders ausdrücken	Ⓕ paraphraser
p.58/A 5	(to) **make a deal** [di:l]	ein Abkommen/eine Abmachung treffen	Help me with my Maths, and I'll help you with English. – OK, it's a **deal**! (= Abgemacht!)
	(to) **load** [ləʊd]	beladen	I **~ed** the car at the supermarket ...
	(to) **unload** [ʌn'ləʊd]	entladen	... so please can you help me to ~ it?
	painting ['peɪntɪŋ]	Gemälde, Bild; Malerei	a **painting** <u>**by**</u> a boy <u>**of**</u> his mother 
	gallery ['gæləri]	Galerie	**!** Spelling: **ga<u>ll</u>ery** Stress: **<u>ga</u>llery** ['gæləri]
	competition [ˌkɒmpə'tɪʃn]	Wettbewerb	(to) **hold a ~** = einen Wettbewerb veranstalten (to) **take part in a ~** = an einem Wettbewerb teilnehmen
	entry ['entri]	Einsendung, Beitrag *(zu einem Wettbewerb)*	There were only 13 **entries** for our competition.
	(to) **receive** [rɪ'si:v]	erhalten	a more formal word for (to) **get** (to) **receive** a letter ◄► (to) **send** a letter Ⓛ recipere
	(to) **announce** [ə'naʊns]	bekanntgeben	verb: (to) **announce** – noun: **announcement** Ⓕ annoncer Ⓛ annuntiare

	*(to) **present** sth. **(to** sb.**)** [prɪ'zent]	(jm.) etwas präsentieren, vorstellen; überreichen	He **~ed** his ideas to the class. The Queen **~ed** the prizes to the winners.
p. 59/A 8	***news** *(no pl)* [nju:z]	Nachrichten	! Hier **sind** die Nachrichten. = Here **is** the news.
	(to) **beat** [bi:t]**, beat, beaten** ['bi:tn]	schlagen; besiegen	I ~ my brother at tennis last Sunday.
	(to) **reach** [ri:tʃ]	erreichen	If we leave now, we'll ~ London before dinner.
	win [wɪn]	Sieg	verb: (to) **win** – noun: **win**
	***against** [ə'genst]	gegen	**against ◄► for**
	top *(adj)* [tɒp]	Spitzen-, oberste(r, s)	the ~ team = the best team
	defence [dɪ'fens]	Verteidigung	(F) la défense (L) defensio
	half-time [ˌhɑ:f 'taɪm]	Halbzeit(pause)	the break between the first and the second half of a match ! the first **half** = die erste Halbzeit
	(to) **go ahead** [ə'hed]	in Führung gehen	Bayern Munich **went ~** after six minutes and stayed **ahead** until the last two minutes of the game. Then United scored twice and won.
	penalty ['penəlti]	Strafstoß; Elfmeter *(Fußball)*	Gerrard took the ~ and scored.
	goalkeeper ['gəʊlki:pə]	Torwart, Torfrau	
	shot [ʃɒt]	Schuss	

goalkeeper

p. 62/P 1	(to) **spot (-tt-)** [spɒt]	entdecken	I can't find my key. If you ~ it, please tell me.
	difference ['dɪfrəns]	Unterschied	! Stress: **difference** ['dɪfrəns] adjective: **different** – noun: **difference** (F) la différence (L) differentia

Word field: Sports

p. 62/P 2

EQUIPMENT

skis [ski:z]

table tennis bat [bæt]

badminton racket ['rækɪt]

LOCATION [ləʊ'keɪʃn] (Einsatz-)Ort, Platz

ski slope [sləʊp] Skipiste

sports hall

court [kɔ:t] Platz, Court

Word field: Sports

EQUIPMENT

running shoes

swimming trunks *(pl)* [trʌŋks] Badehose / **swimsuit** ['swɪmsuːt] Badeanzug
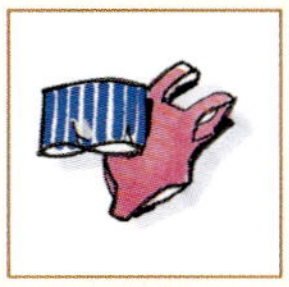

saddle ['sædl]
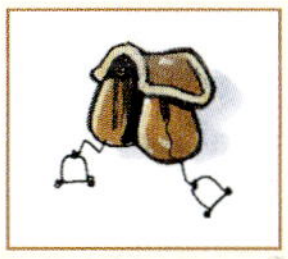

helmet, pads [pædz] (Knie-usw.)Schützer

helmet, pads Schulterpolster

LOCATION

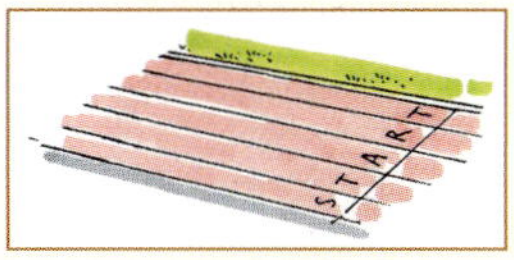

running track [træk] Laufbahn

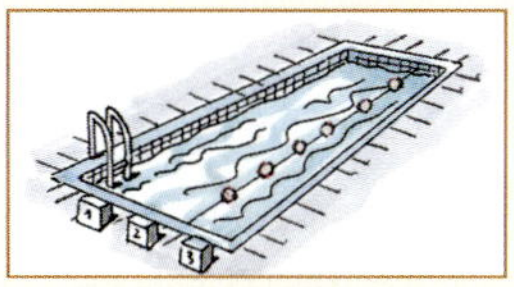
(swimming) pool

bridle path ['braɪdl pɑːθ] Reitweg

half-pipe ['hɑːfpaɪp]

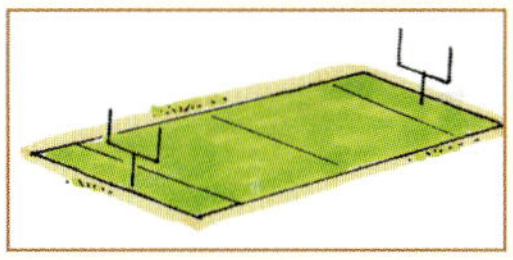
pitch

p.63/P 4	**vote** [vəʊt]	Stimme; Stimmrecht	There were 55 **~s** for the idea and 44 against. German women got the ~ in 1919.
p.65/P 8	**cup** [kʌp]	Pokal	 two **cups** 
	(to) **destroy** [dɪ'strɔɪ]	zerstören	(L) destruere
p.65/P 9	**industry** ['ɪndəstri]	Industrie	! Stress: **industry** ['ɪndəstri]
	industrial [ɪn'dʌstriəl]	industriell	! Stress: **industrial** [ɪn'dʌstriəl]
p.65/P 10	**celebrity** [sə'lebrəti]	berühmte Persönlichkeit, Prominente(r)	If you lived in London, you might see **celebrities**.
p.66/P 12	* (to) **discover** [dɪ'skʌvə]	entdecken; herausfinden	
p.67/P 13	(to) **organize** ['ɔːgənaɪz]	organisieren, veranstalten	to plan something and get ready for it
	stadium ['steɪdiəm]	Stadion	(F) le stade (L) stadium
	(to) **equalize** ['iːkwəlaɪz]	ausgleichen; das Ausgleichstor erzielen	Walcott **~d** in the last minute, so it was a draw.
	referee [ˌrefə'riː]	Schiedsrichter/in	
	(to) **replace** sth. **(with)** [rɪ'pleɪs]	etwas ersetzen (durch)	In this exercise, you have to ~ all the nouns **with** pronouns.
p.68/P 16	**now and again**	ab und zu, von Zeit zu Zeit	I don't see my grandma very often, just ~ and ~.
	about yourself [jə'self, jɔː'self]	über dich selbst	You're so boring: you always talk **about ~**.

Who needs legs?

p.69	**even** ['iːvn]	(sogar) schon	I wanted to be a doctor ~ when I was little.
	(to) **grow up** [ˌɡrəʊ_ˈʌp], **grew up** [ˌɡruː_ˈʌp], **grown up** [ˌɡrəʊn_ˈʌp]	erwachsen werden; aufwachsen	Dave wants to be a doctor when he **~s up**. When my grandparents were **~ing up**, they had no television.
	* **woods** *(pl)* [wʊdz]	Wald, Wälder	Let's go for a walk in the ~.
	* (to) **be allowed to** do sth. [əˈlaʊd]	etwas tun dürfen	**Were** you **~ to** use dictionaries in your English tests?
	* **may** [meɪ]	dürfen	**May** I come in? (*höflich für:* Can I come in?)
	onto [ˈɒntə, ˈɒntʊ]	auf (... hinauf)	The cat saw the dog and jumped ~ the table.
	(to) **take a ride**	eine Spritztour/Fahrt machen	
	ambulance [ˈæmbjələns]	Krankenwagen	! Pronunciation and stress: **a**mbulance [ˈæmbjələns] Ⓕ une ambulance  an **ambulance**
	athletics [æθˈletɪks]	Leichtathletik	I'm an ~ fan. I love sports like running and jumping. Ⓕ l'athlétisme *(m)*
	medal [ˈmedl]	Medaille	! Stress: **me**dal [ˈmedl] Ⓕ la médaille
	sledge [sledʒ]	Schlitten	 a **sledge**
	championship [ˈtʃæmpiənʃɪp]	Meisterschaft	Ⓕ le championnat
p.70	(to) **fight (for)** [faɪt], **fought** [fɔːt], **fought**	kämpfen (für, um)	Nathan had to ~ **for** his life after his accident.
	operation (on) [ˌɒpəˈreɪʃn]	Operation (an)	He had an ~ **on** his knee after he was hurt in the match. Ⓕ une opération
	artificial [ˌɑːtɪˈfɪʃl]	künstlich, Kunst-	Are those flowers real or ~? Ⓕ artificiel/le Ⓛ artificialis
	disabled [dɪsˈeɪbld]	(körper)behindert	Mr Hanson is ~. He has to use a wheelchair.
	talent [ˈtælənt]	Talent, Begabung	! Stress: **ta**lent [ˈtælənt] Ⓕ le talent
	age [eɪdʒ]	Alter	I'm 14. What ~ are you? – 15.
	at (the age of) 16 [eɪdʒ]	mit 16; im Alter von 16	Scots are allowed to marry ~ **the age of** 16.
	(to) **represent** [ˌreprɪˈzent]	repräsentieren, vertreten	There were groups from all over Europe at the festival. A group from Frankfurt **~ed** Germany. Ⓕ représenter
	the Commonwealth [ˈkɒmənwelθ]	*Gemeinschaft der Länder des ehemaligen Britischen Weltreichs*	
	(to) **be interested (in)** [ˈɪntrəstɪd]	sich interessieren (für); interessiert sein (an)	! (to) be **interest<u>ed</u>** (in) = interessiert sein (an) an **interest<u>ing</u>** book = ein interessantes Buch

Unit 4: Growing up in Canada

p.72	**population** [ˌpɒpju'leɪʃn]	Bevölkerung, Einwohner(zahl)	With a ~ of 2.5 million, Toronto is Canada's largest city. (F) la population (L) populus
	square km **(sq** km**)** [skweə]	Quadratkilometer	
p.73	**First Nations** [ˌfɜːst 'neɪʃnz]	die Ersten Nationen *(indianische Ureinwohner/innen Kanadas)*	
	nation ['neɪʃn]	Nation	
	(to) **hunt** [hʌnt]	jagen	Do people still ~ lions in Africa?

Verbs and nouns with the same form

(to) **fish**	fischen, angeln	(to) **sleep**	schlafen
fish	Fisch	**sleep**	Schlaf
(to) **hunt**	jagen	(to) **speed**	rasen
hunt	Jagd	**speed**	Geschwindigkeit
(to) **link**	verbinden	(to) **trap (-pp-)**	(mit einer Falle) fangen
link	Verbindung	**trap**	Falle

	traditional [trə'dɪʃənl]	traditionell	(F) traditionel/le
	way of life	Lebensart	People say the Queen, red buses and rain are all part of the British **~ of ~**.
	sleepover ['sliːpəʊvə]	Schlafparty	
	real late ['riːəl] *(AE, infml)*	wirklich spät, echt spät	= really late
p.74/A 1	**adult** ['ædʌlt]	Erwachsene(r)	Children pay 50 p, **~s** £ 1.50. (F) un/e adulte (L) adultus
	(to) **turn** sth. **down/up** [tɜːn]	etwas leiser/lauter stellen	Please **~ up** the radio. I want to hear the news.
	* **not** (...) **either**	auch nicht	Jack isn't going to Jo's party. Lucy is**n't** going **~**.
	Money doesn't grow on trees.	*Redensart:* Geld wächst nicht auf Bäumen; Geld liegt nicht auf der Straße.	
	latest ['leɪtɪst]	neueste(r, s)	I've just downloaded Billy Talent's ~ song. The band is Canadian, you know. ! not: ~~newest~~
	(to) **care** about sth. [keə]	etwas wichtig nehmen	

(to) care

I **don't care** about money.	Geld ist mir egal.
She **doesn't care** if it rains.	Ob es regnet, ist ihr egal.
My dad **doesn't care** what I do.	Es ist meinem Vater egal, was ich mache.
But my mum **cares**!	Aber meiner Mutter ist es nicht egal!
I really **care** about recycling.	Recycling liegt mir sehr am Herzen.
Her parents are rich. – Who **cares**?	... Wen interessiert das?/Was soll's?/Ist doch egal!/Na und?

	(to) **cost, cost, cost** [kɒst]	kosten	How much did your new computer ~? – A lot. It ~ more than £900.
	(to) **hang out** [ˌhæŋ‿ˈaʊt], **hung** [hʌŋ], **hung** *(infml)*	rumhängen, abhängen	
	(to) **waste** sth. **(on)** [weɪst]	etwas verschwenden, vergeuden (für)	'Don't ~ your time and money **on** computer games,' my dad said.
	volunteer work [ˌvɒlənˈtɪə]	Arbeit als Freiwillige(r)	= the work you do for no money
p. 75/A 3	**local** [ˈləʊkl]	örtlich, Lokal-; am/vom Ort	Find out what's happening in your town! Buy your ~ newspaper! Ⓕ local/e, Ⓛ localis
	(shopping) mall [mɔːl, *BE auch:* mæl]	(großes) Einkaufszentrum	a **mall**
	everyone [ˈevriwʌn]	jeder; alle	

-body / -one

everybody/everyone [ˈevriwʌn]	jeder, alle
somebody/someone [ˈsʌmwʌn]	jemand
anybody/anyone [ˈeniwʌn]	(irgend)jemand
nobody/no one [ˈnəʊ wʌn]	niemand

! Schreibung: zwei Wörter – **no one**

(to) **reply (to)** [rɪˈplaɪ]	antworten (auf), beantworten; erwidern	= (to) **answer**
lyrics *(pl)* [ˈlɪrɪks]	Liedtext(e)	This song is nice. I don't understand the ~ but I like the tune.
(to) **join in** [ˌdʒɔɪn‿ˈɪn]	mitmachen	
(to) **cry** [kraɪ]	weinen	
(to) **imitate** [ˈɪmɪteɪt]	nachmachen	The class laughed as Will **~d** the teacher's voice.
strict [strɪkt]	streng	Peter isn't allowed to watch TV after 8 o'clock. His parents are very ~ about that.
What a bummer! [ˈbʌmə] *(infml)*	So ein Mist! / Wie schade!	It's a real ~ that you can't come.
something **else** [els]	etwas anderes	

... else

I met Jo at the party. – Did you meet **anyone else**?	... – Hast du **sonst noch jemanden** getroffen?
Do you need **anything else** from the shop?	Brauchst du **sonst noch etwas** ...?
So you went to Paris. Did you go **anywhere else**?	... Bist du **sonst noch irgendwo** hingefahren?
I'm tired. **Someone else** will have to tidy up.	... **Jemand anders** muss aufräumen.
Let's play football. – Can't we do **something else**?	... – Können wir nicht **etwas anderes** machen?
We always go there. Let's go **somewhere else**.	... Lasst uns **woanders** hingehen.
Who else did you meet?	**Wen** hast du **(sonst) noch** getroffen?
What else do you know about Scotland?	**Was** weißt du **(sonst) noch** über Schottland?

p.75/A 4	**dragon** ['drægən]	Drache	(F) le dragon
	(to) **paddle** ['pædl]	paddeln	
	paddle ['pædl]	Paddel	
p.76/A 5	She lives **on** his street.	Sie wohnt in seiner Straße.	! Ananda lives **at** 13 Paul Road. *(with number)* Tony lives **on/in** Oxford Street/London Road.
	(to) **date** sb. [deɪt] *(besonders AE)*	mit jm. (aus)gehen; sich (regelmäßig) mit jm. treffen	Dad **~d** Mom for years before they got married.
	straightaway [ˌstreɪtə'weɪ]	sofort, gleich	
	dance floor ['dɑːns flɔː]	Tanzfläche	
p.76/A 6	**unlike** [ˌʌn'laɪk]	im Gegensatz zu	I'm not a good swimmer, ~ my sister. She swims very well.
	(to) **steer** [stɪə]	lenken	
	(to) **get** sth. **right**	etwas richtig machen	I tried lots of times and finally **got** it ~. (to) **get** sth. **right** ◄► (to) **get** sth. **wrong**
	rhythm ['rɪðəm]	Rhythmus	
p.77/A 7	**cabin** ['kæbɪn]	Hütte	
	No way! [ˌnəʊ 'weɪ]	*etwa:* Was du nicht sagst! / Das kann nicht dein Ernst sein!	
	one tough girl *(AE, infml)*	*etwa:* ein wirklich toughes Mädchen	! **one** wird als Betonung verwendet.
	tough [tʌf]	tough, selbstsicher, zäh	
	Boy! *(AE, infml)*	Mann! Mensch!	
	***It's a pity (that ...)** ['pɪti]	Es ist schade, dass ...	**It was a ~ that** Mary wasn't there.
p.80/P 1	**speed limit** ['spiːd ˌlɪmɪt]	Geschwindigkeitsbegrenzung, -beschränkung	**speed limit** 
	(to) **weigh** [weɪ]	wiegen	
	***everywhere** ['evriweə]	überall	
	per cent (%) [pə'sent]	Prozent	20 ~ ~ of 200 is 40. (F) pour cent
	per [pɜː, pə]	pro	50 miles ~ hour = 50 miles an hour
	kilogram ['kɪləgræm], **kilo** ['kiːləʊ] **(kg)**	Kilogramm, Kilo	We need two **kilograms/kilos <u>of</u>** oranges for the orange juice.

a three-pound ball / a 150-kilogram bear

a **three-pound** ball	ein drei Pfund schwerer Ball
a **150-kilogram** bear	ein 150 Kilogramm schwerer Bär
a **ten-kilometre** walk	eine Zehn-Kilometer-Wanderung
a **two-hour** operation	eine zweistündige Operation
a **24-hour** supermarket	ein Supermarkt, der 24 Stunden geöffnet ist
a **three-week** holiday	ein dreiwöchiger Urlaub
a **30-minute** ride	eine 30-minütige Fahrt
a **70-year-old** teacher	ein 70-jähriger Lehrer

! Im Englischen steht das Nomen im Singular:
a **two-<u>hour</u>** operation
(*nicht:* a two-~~hours~~ operation)

p.81/P 4	**fisherman** ['fɪʃəmən], *pl* **fishermen** ['fɪʃəmən]	Angler, Fischer	
p.81/P 5	(to) **marry** ['mæri]	heiraten	Ⓕ marier Ⓛ maritare
p.84/P 11	***hero,** *pl* **heroes** ['hɪərəʊ], ['hɪərəʊz]	Held/in	
p.84/P 12	*(to) **miss** [mɪs]	verpassen	She got up late, so she **~ed** the bus. (to) **miss** = **1.** vermissen – I ~ my friends. **2.** verpassen – I **~ed** the bus.
p.85/P 13	**prewriting exercise** [ˌpriː'raɪtɪŋ]	Übung vor dem Schreiben	
	(to) **brainstorm** ['breɪnstɔːm]	brainstormen *(so viele Ideen wie möglich sammeln)*	(to) collect as many ideas as possible
	so that	sodass, damit	I'm saving money ~ ~ I can buy a new bike.
	***phrase** [freɪz]	Ausdruck, (Rede-)Wendung	
	(to) **improve** [ɪm'pruːv]	verbessern; sich verbessern	
	style [staɪl]	Stil	Ⓕ le style
	crazy ['kreɪzi]	verrückt	You want to go out in this rain? You must be ~.
	weird [wɪəd]	seltsam	
	wide [waɪd]	weit, breit	The river is too ~; we can't get across. The doctor said I should open ~ and say ah.
	fear (of) [fɪə]	Furcht, Angst (vor)	I was afraid but didn't show my ~. **!** Angst haben vor = (to) be afraid/scared of
	(to) **shake your head** [ʃeɪk], **shook** [ʃʊk], **shaken** ['ʃeɪkn]	den Kopf schütteln	In most countries, people **shake their ~** to say 'No' ...
	(to) **nod (your head) (-dd-)** [nɒd]	(mit dem Kopf) nicken	... and they **nod their ~** to say 'Yes.'

A fishing trip

p.88	**campground** ['kæmpgraʊnd] *(AE)*	Zeltplatz	= *BE* **campsite**
	(to) **camp** [kæmp]	zelten	We asked the farmer if we could ~ in his field.
	ranger ['reɪndʒə]	Ranger/in, Aufseher/in	
	rapids *(pl)* ['ræpɪdz]	Stromschnellen	
	canoe [kə'nuː]	Kanu	
	(to) **canoe** [kə'nuː]	paddeln, Kanu fahren	

They're **canoeing** through the **rapids.**

	(to) **attack** [ə'tæk]	angreifen	verb: (to) **attack** – noun: **attack** Ⓕ attaquer
p.89	**outdoor** ['aʊtdɔː]	im Freien, Außen-	~ activities, an ~ swimming pool („Freibad“)
	expression [ɪk'spreʃn]	Ausdruck	Ⓕ une expression

Unit 5: A teen magazine

p.94	**That's up to you.**	Das liegt bei dir. / Das kannst/musst du (selbst) entscheiden.	Will I be on the football team? – **That's ~ ~ you**. If you practise hard, you'll have a good chance.
	so far	bis jetzt, bis hierher	
	the following ...	die folgenden ...	
	section ['sekʃn]	Abschnitt, Teil, (Themen-)Bereich	! Stress: **section** ['sekʃn] (F) la section
	editor ['edɪtə]	Redakteur/in	(F) un éditeur/une éditrice
p.95	* (to) **produce** [prə'dju:s]	produzieren, erzeugen, herstellen	Germany **~s** more cheese than France.
	* **article** ['ɑ:tɪkl]	(Zeitungs-)Artikel	
	(to) **publish** ['pʌblɪʃ]	veröffentlichen	J. K. Rowling **~ed** her first Harry Potter book in 1997. (F) publier (L) publicare
	drawing ['drɔ:ɪŋ]	Zeichnung	
	(to) **draw** [drɔ:], **drew** [dru:], **drawn** [drɔ:n]	zeichnen	I'll ~ a little map to help you find my flat.
	(to) **contact** sb. ['kɒntækt]	sich mit jm. in Verbindung setzen; mit jm. Kontakt aufnehmen	If you want to ~ me, you can phone me or send me an e-mail. ! Stress: **contact** ['kɒntækt] (F) contacter
	success [sək'ses]	Erfolg	The party was a big ~. Everybody enjoyed it. (F) le succès (L) successus
	headphones *(pl)* ['hedfəʊnz]	Kopfhörer	
	microphone ['maɪkrəfəʊn]	Mikrofon	
	monitor ['mɒnɪtə]	Bildschirm, Monitor	
p.96/A1	(to) **skim** a text **(-mm-)** [skɪm]	einen Text überfliegen *(um den Inhalt grob zu erfassen)*	(to) read a text quickly in order to find out the main information
	riddle ['rɪdl]	Rätsel, Scherzfrage	

Adverb oder Adjektiv nach bestimmten Verben?

Verb + Adverb

Wie du weißt, werden nach Verben **Adverbien der Art und Weise** verwendet, um zu sagen, **wie jemand etwas tut**:

She shouted **angrily** at me.
Sie schrie mich wütend an.
The choir sang **beautifully**.
Der Chor sang wunderschön.
The man looked around **nervously**.
Der Mann sah sich nervös um.

Verb + Adjektiv

Verben wie **feel, sound, look, smell, seem** beschreiben keine Tätigkeit, sondern einen **Zustand oder eine Eigenschaft (wie jemand oder etwas ist)**. Nach diesen Verben stehen **Adjektive**:

She felt **angry** and a bit **sad**.
Sie fühlte sich wütend und ein bisschen traurig.

The song sounded **beautiful**.	*Das Lied klang wunderschön.*
The man looked **nervous**.	*Der Mann sah nervös aus.*
The soup smells **delicious**.	*Die Suppe riecht lecker.*
Everybody seemed **happy**.	*Alle schienen glücklich zu sein.*

(to) **be made of** sth.	aus etwas (gemacht) sein	**Is** the bottle **~ of** glass?
leather ['leðə]	Leder	

	pipe [paɪp]	Pfeife	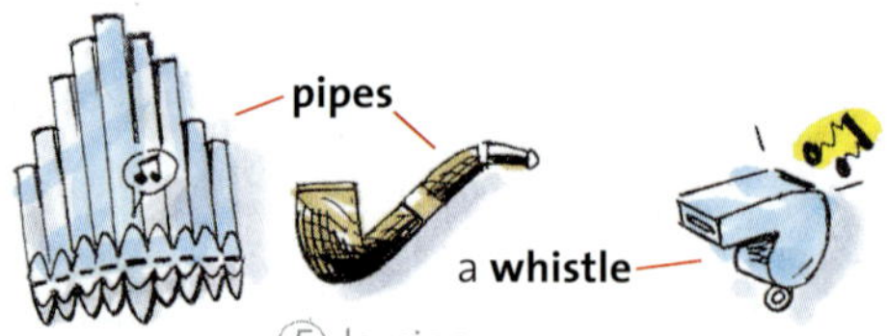 Ⓕ la pipe
	(to) **stick out of** sth. [stɪk], **stuck, stuck** [stʌk]	aus etwas herausragen, heraussstehen	A long pipe **stuck ~ of** the old man's mouth.
	(to) **blow** [bləʊ], **blew** [blu:], **blown** [bləʊn]	pusten, blasen; wehen	I **blew** into the trumpet but couldn't get a sound. The wind was **~ing** all night.
	(to) **keep** [ki:p], **kept, kept** [kept]	(be)halten; aufbewahren	**Keep** your eyes open when you're on the road. You can ~ the book, I don't need it any more. Where do you ~ your drawings? – In my dossier.
	(to) **squeeze** [skwi:z]	drücken; (aus)pressen	She said thank you and **~d** my arm. For one glass of juice, ~ three or four oranges. 
	note [nəʊt]	Ton	! **note** = **1.** Notiz – (to) take **~s** **2.** Ton – the first four **~s** of a tune ! German „Noten" = English **music**: Ich kann Noten lesen. = I can read music.
p.97/A1	**war** [wɔ:]	Krieg	
	(to) **study** ['stʌdi]	lernen; studieren	There's a test tomorrow so I have to ~ tonight. She's a professor now, but she had to ~ a long time.
	opera ['ɒprə]	Oper	We saw the ~ *Tannhäuser* at the Semper Opera House. Ⓕ l'opéra *(m)*
	college ['kɒlɪdʒ]	Hochschule, Fachschule	After school my sister went to ~ to study music.
	(to) **make** sb. sth.	jn. zu etwas machen	The film studio promised to ~ her a star.
	(to) **release** [rɪ'li:s]	*(CD, Film usw.)* herausbringen, auf den Markt bringen	
	(to) **be sold out**	ausverkauft sein, vergriffen sein	The concert tickets **were ~ out** after only three hours.
	track [træk]	Stück, Titel, Track *(auf einer CD)*	Now we'll hear a ~ from their new album.
p.98/A1	**vacation** [və'keɪʃn, *AE:* veɪ'keɪʃn] *(AE)*	Urlaub, Ferien	= *BE* **holiday** Ⓕ les vacances *(m)*
	paradise ['pærədaɪs]	Paradies	! Stress: **paradise** ['pærədaɪs] Ⓕ le paradis
	soft [sɒft]	weich, sanft	I love your pullover. It feels so ~.
	***comfortable** ['kʌmftəbl]	bequem	
	stereo ['steriəʊ]	Stereoanlage	
	classic ['klæsɪk]	klassisch	My dad loves the ~ songs of the 1970s.
	folks [fəʊks] *(infml, besonders AE)*	Leute	The ~ in my town are the friendliest in America.
	you**'ll have travelled**	du wirst gereist sein	
	by the end of the song	(spätestens) bis zum Ende des Lieds	Please be home ~ ten. (= not later than ten) We need your report ~ Friday. (= on or before Friday)

The future perfect: *will have* + past participle

Mit ***will have*** **+ past participle** kannst du ausdrücken, dass etwas zu einem bestimmten Zeitpunkt in der Zukunft geschehen oder getan sein wird:

... will have happened „... *wird geschehen sein*"
... will have done „... *wird getan haben*".

Diese Zeit wird *future perfect* genannt (deutsch: „Futur II" oder „vollendete Zukunft").

Next year my brother **will have finished** school.
... wird mein Bruder die Schule abgeschlossen haben.

The train **will have left** when we get to the station.
Der Zug wird abgefahren sein, wenn ...

You can't phone my mother at 11 pm. She **will have gone** to bed by then.
... Bis dahin wird sie (schon) ins Bett gegangen sein.

	(to) **chill out** [ˌtʃɪl_ˈaʊt] *(infml)*	sich entspannen, relaxen	
p.99/A1	(to) **wake up** [ˌweɪk_ˈʌp], **woke** [wəʊk], **woken** [ˈwəʊkən]	aufwachen	Yesterday I didn't ~ ~ till 8 o'clock and was late for school.
	(to) **wake** sb. **(up), woke, woken**	jn. (auf)wecken	This morning my mother **woke** me ~ at 7.
	(radio, pop) station [ˈsteɪʃn]	(Radio-, Pop-)Sender	
	(to) **crash** [kræʃ]	abstürzen	My computer **~es** too often. I need a new one.
	(to) **pick** sth. **up** [ˌpɪk_ˈʌp]	etwas aufheben *(vom Boden)*	**!** **1.** jn. abholen – (to) **pick** sb. **up** **2.** etwas aufheben – (to) **pick** sth. **up** They're **~ing up** rubbish.
	(drum-)stick [stɪk]	Trommelstock	
	horror [ˈhɒrə]	Entsetzen, Grauen, Horror	To my ~ I saw that she was dead. My brother loves ~ films.
	deaf [def]	taub, gehörlos	

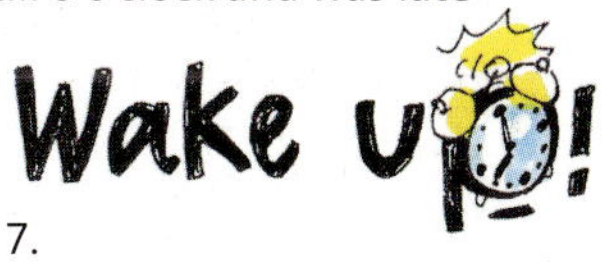

German 'werden'

We use (to) **get** and (to) **become** to mean 'werden'.
(to) **become/get** angry/tired/nervous/old/...
cold/windy/dark/...
boring/funny/more interesting/...

We use (to) **get** more in informal English.

With nouns, we only use (to) **become**:
She **became** a doctor/a football fan/...

When something gets worse, we can also use (to) **go**.

(to) **go hard** (e.g. bread)	hart werden
(to) **go bad** (e.g. fish, eggs)	schlecht werden
(to) **go deaf**	taub werden
(to) **go blind** [blaɪnd]	blind werden
(to) **go crazy/mad**	verrückt werden

	There was no point. [pɔɪnt]	Es hatte keinen Sinn.	**What's the point?** = Was soll das?
	headline [ˈhedlaɪn]	Schlagzeile	
	each other [iːtʃ_ˈʌðə]	einander, sich (gegenseitig)	David loves Victoria and Victoria loves David. = David and Victoria love **each** ~.
	***tear** [tɪə]	Träne	He was so sad that his eyes were full of **~s**.
p.100/P 1	(to) **hit (-tt-)** [hɪt], **hit, hit**	schlagen	He ~ me very hard on the nose.
	***machine** [məˈʃiːn]	Maschine, Gerät	
p.100/P 2	**popular** [ˈpɒpjələ]	populär, beliebt	Handball is very ~ in Germany, but almost nobody knows it in the UK. (F) populaire
	inventor [ɪnˈventə]	Erfinder/in	(F) un inventeur (L) inventor

Nouns with -or

(to) **act**	spielen	**actor**	Schauspieler/in	(to) **edit**	redigieren	**editor**	Redakteur/in
(to) **collect**	sammeln	**collector**	Sammler/in	(to) **invent**	erfinden	**inventor**	Erfinder/in
(to) **direct**	Regie führen	**director**	Regisseur	(to) **visit**	besuchen	**visitor**	Besucher/in

	company ['kʌmpəni]	Firma, Gesellschaft	My uncle works for an oil ~ in Scotland. Ⓕ la compagnie
	(to) **sign** [saɪn]	unterschreiben	He finished the letter and **~ed** it. Ⓕ signer
	(to) **repair** [rɪ'peə]	reparieren, ausbessern	This road's terrible. When are they going to ~ it? Ⓕ réparer
	string [strɪŋ]	Saite	Violins have four **~s** and guitars have six.
p.101/P 4	**rule** [ru:l]	Regel, Vorschrift	I don't understand the game. Can you explain the **~s**, please?
	alcohol ['ælkəhɒl]	Alkohol	Ⓕ l'alcohol *(m)*
p.102/P 6	**strike** [straɪk]	Streik	! (to) **be on strike** = streiken, sich im Streik befinden (to) **go on strike** = streiken, in den Streik treten

Reflexiv im Deutschen – nicht reflexiv im Englischen

p.102/P 7

(to) **calm down**	sich beruhigen	(to) **open**	sich öffnen
(to) **clean one's teeth**	sich die Zähne putzen	(to) **prepare**	sich vorbereiten
(to) **feel**	sich fühlen; sich anfühlen	(to) **relax**	sich entspannen, sich ausruhen
(to) **get dressed**	sich anziehen	(to) **remember sth.**	sich an etwas erinnern; sich etwas merken
(to) **get ready**	sich fertig machen	(to) **sit down**	sich hinsetzen
(to) **hide**	sich verstecken	(to) **turn**	sich umdrehen
(to) **imagine sth.**	sich etwas vorstellen	(to) **wonder**	sich fragen
(to) **meet**	sich treffen	(to) **worry**	sich Sorgen machen
(to) **move**	sich bewegen		

	(to) **blame** sb. **(for)** [bleɪm]	jm. die Schuld geben (an); jm. Vorwürfe machen (wegen)	Don't ~ me. It wasn't my mistake.
p.104/P 12	**biography** [baɪ'ɒgrəfi]	Biografie	! Stress: **biography** [baɪ'ɒgrəfi] Ⓕ la biographie
	capital letters	Großbuchstaben	**CAPITAL LETTERS ◄► small letters**
	irregular [ɪ'regjələ]	unregelmäßig	Ⓕ irrégulier/-ière
	regular ['regjələ]	regelmäßig	Ⓕ régulier/-ière
	tense [tens]	(grammatische) Zeit, Tempus	
	career [kə'rɪə]	Karriere	! Spelling: **career**
p.105/P 13	**research** *(no pl)* [rɪ'sɜ:tʃ, 'ri:sɜ:tʃ]	Recherche, Forschung(en)	I've got to do some ~ on Africa for homework.
	* (to) **enter** sth. ['entə]	etwas eingeben, eintragen	Please ~ your name on this list.
	quotation marks [kwəʊ'teɪʃn ˌmɑ:ks]	Anführungszeichen, -striche	! In German „like this"; in English 'like this' or **"like this".**
	accurate ['ækjərət]	genau, akkurat	What's the time? – It's about 2 pm. I don't know exactly because my watch isn't very ~. ! Stress: **accurate** ['ækjərət] Ⓛ accuratus

Tipps zum Wörterlernen → S.133 · Englische Laute → S.222 · Alphabetische Wörterverzeichnisse → S.195–222 / S.223–246

Das Dictionary besteht aus zwei alphabetischen Wörterlisten:

Englisch – Deutsch (S. 195–222)
Deutsch – Englisch (S. 223–246).

Das **English – German Dictionary** enthält den Wortschatz der Bände 1 bis 3 von *English G 21*.
Wenn du wissen möchtest, was ein Wort bedeutet, wie man es ausspricht oder wie es genau geschrieben wird, kannst du hier nachschlagen.

Im **English – German Dictionary** werden folgende **Abkürzungen und Symbole** verwendet:

jm. = jemandem	sb. = somebody	*pl* = *plural* (Mehrzahl)	*AE* = *American English*
jn. = jemanden	sth. = something	*no pl* = *no plural*	*infml* = *informal*

° Mit diesem Kringel sind Wörter markiert, die nicht zum Lernwortschatz gehören.
► Der Pfeil verweist auf Kästchen im Vocabulary (S. 168–194), in denen du weitere Informationen zu diesem Wort findest.

Die **Fundstellenangaben** zeigen, wo ein Wort zum ersten Mal vorkommt.
Die Ziffern in Klammern bezeichnen Seitenzahlen:

I = Band A1 • II = Band A2 • III = Band A3

III Intro (6)	= Band 3, Introduction, Seite 6
III Intro (6/168)	= Band 3, Introduction, Seite 168 (im Vocabulary, zu Seite 6)
III 1 (12)	= Band 3, Unit 1, Seite 12
III 1 (12/169)	= Band 3, Unit 1, Seite 169 (im Vocabulary, zu Seite 12)

Tipps zur Arbeit mit dem English – German Dictionary findest du im Skills File auf Seite 133.

1

1950s [ˌnaɪntiːnˈfɪftiz] die Fünfzigerjahre (des 20. Jahrhunderts) III 5 (100)

A

a [ə]
1. ein, eine I
2. once/twice a week einmal/zweimal pro Woche III 2 (32) • **a bit** ein bisschen, etwas II • **a few** ein paar, einige II • **a lot (of)** eine Menge, viel, viele II • **He likes her a lot.** Er mag sie sehr. I
abbey [ˈæbi] Abtei II
able [ˈeɪbl]: **be able to do sth.** etwas tun können; fähig sein/in der Lage sein, etwas zu tun II
°**aboriginal people** [ˌæbəˈrɪdʒənl] Ureinwohner/innen
about [əˈbaʊt]
1. über I
2. ungefähr II
ask about sth. nach etwas fragen I • **know about sth.** von etwas wissen; über etwas Bescheid wissen II • **learn about sth.** etwas über etwas erfahren, etwas über etwas herausfinden II • **This is about Mr Green.** Es geht um Mr Green. I • **What about ...? 1.** Was ist mit ...? / Und ...? I; **2.** Wie wär's mit ...? I • **What are you talking about?** Wovon redest du? I **What was the best thing about ...?** Was war das Beste an ...? II
above [əˈbʌv] über, oberhalb (von) III 2 (47)
abroad [əˈbrɔːd] im Ausland II • **go abroad** ins Ausland gehen/fahren II
accent [ˈæksənt] Akzent II
accident [ˈæksɪdənt] Unfall II
accurate [ˈækjərət] genau, akkurat III 5 (105)
acrobat [ˈækrəbæt] Akrobat/in III 1 (17)
across [əˈkrɒs]
1. (quer) über II
2. hinüber, herüber III 2 (45)
act [ækt] aufführen, spielen I
°**Act out ...** Spiele/Spielt ... vor.
action [ˈækʃn] Action; Handlung, Tat III 1 (26)
active [ˈæktɪv] aktiv III 3 (58)
activity [ækˈtɪvəti] Aktivität, Tätigkeit I
actor [ˈæktə] Schauspieler/in II
AD [ˌeɪ ˈdiː] *(from Latin: Anno Domini)* nach Christus III 3 (65)
°**adapt** [əˈdæpt] anpassen
°**add up** [ˌæd_ˈʌp] addieren, zusammenzählen
add (to) [æd] hinzufügen, ergänzen, addieren (zu) I
address [əˈdres] Anschrift, Adresse II
adult [ˈædʌlt] Erwachsene(r) III 4 (74) • **adult life** das Leben als Erwachsene/r III 5 (105)
adventure [ədˈventʃə] Abenteuer II
advert [ˈædvɜːt] Anzeige, Inserat; *(im Fernsehen)* Werbespot II
afraid [əˈfreɪd]
1. be afraid (of) Angst haben (vor) I
2. I'm afraid leider II
after [ˈɑːftə] nach *(zeitlich)* I
after that danach I
after [ˈɑːftə] nachdem II
afternoon [ˌɑːftəˈnuːn] Nachmittag I • **in the afternoon** nachmittags, am Nachmittag I • **on Friday afternoon** freitagnachmittags, am Freitagnachmittag I
°**afterwards** [ˈɑːftəwədz] danach
again [əˈgen] wieder; noch einmal I • **now and again** ab und zu, von Zeit zu Zeit III 3 (68)
against [əˈgenst] gegen I
age [eɪdʒ] Alter III 3 (70) • **at (the age of) 16** mit 16; im Alter von 16 III 3 (70)
°**aggressive** [əˈgresɪv] aggressiv
ago [əˈgəʊ]: **a minute ago** vor einer Minute I

agree [ə'gri:]: **agree (on)** sich einigen (auf) I • **agree (with sb.)** (jm.) zustimmen I
aim [eɪm] Ziel III 3 (56)
air [eə] Luft II
airport ['eəpɔ:t] Flughafen III 1 (20/174)
alarm clock [ə'lɑ:m klɒk] Wecker I
album ['ælbəm] Album II
alcohol ['ælkəhɒl] Alkohol III 5 (100)
°**alive: be alive** [ə'laɪv] leben, am Leben sein
all [ɔ:l] alle; alles I • **2 all** 2 beide (2:2 unentschieden) III 3 (55/183)
all day den ganzen Tag (lang) I
all over the world auf der ganzen Welt III Intro (6) • **all right** [ɔ:l 'raɪt] gut, in Ordnung II • **all the time** die ganze Zeit I • **all we have to do now …** alles, was wir jetzt (noch) tun müssen, … II • **from all over the world** aus der ganzen Welt II • **This is all wrong.** Das ist ganz falsch. I
allergic (to sth.) [ə'lɜ:dʒɪk] allergisch (gegen etwas) III 1 (16)
allow [ə'laʊ] erlauben, zulassen II
be allowed to do sth. [ə'laʊd] etwas tun dürfen II
almost ['ɔ:lməʊst] fast, beinahe II
alone [ə'ləʊn] allein I
along the road [ə'lɒŋ] entlang der Straße / die Straße entlang II
alphabet ['ælfəbet] Alphabet I
°**alphabetical** [,ælfə'betɪkl] alphabetisch
already [ɔ:l'redi] schon, bereits II
°**also** ['ɔ:lsəʊ] auch
although [ɔ:l'ðəʊ] obwohl III 1 (12)
always ['ɔ:lweɪz] immer I
am [,eɪ‿'em]: **7 am** 7 Uhr morgens/vormittags I
amazing [ə'meɪzɪŋ] erstaunlich, unglaublich II
ambulance ['æmbjələns] Krankenwagen III 3 (69)
°**amen** [ɑ:'men, eɪ'men] amen
American football [ə,merɪkən 'fʊtbɔ:l] Football I
an [ən] ein, eine I
and [ənd, ænd] und I • **and now for** und jetzt … *(kündigt ein neues Thema an)* III 2 (45) • **nice and cool/clean/…** schön kühl/sauber/… I
angel ['eɪndʒl] Engel II
angry (about sth./with sb.) ['æŋgri] wütend, böse (über etwas/auf jn.) II
animal ['ænɪml] Tier I
announce [ə'naʊns] bekanntgeben III 3 (58)
announcement [ə'naʊnsmənt] Bekanntgabe, Ankündigung; Durchsage; Ansage III 1 (20)
anorak ['ænəræk] Anorak, Windjacke III 2 (45)
another [ə'nʌðə] ein(e) andere(r, s); noch ein(e) I • **another 70 metres** weitere 70 Meter, noch 70 Meter II
answer ['ɑ:nsə] (be)antworten I
answer (to) ['ɑ:nsə] Antwort (auf) I
any ['eni]: **any …?** (irgend)welche …? I • **not (…) any** kein(e) I
not (…) any more nicht mehr II
anybody ['enibɒdi]: **anybody?** (irgend)jemand? II • **not (…) anybody** niemand II
anyone ['eniwʌn]: **anyone?** (irgend)jemand? III 4 (75/188) • **not (…) anyone** niemand III 4 (75/188)
anything ['eniθɪŋ]: **anything?** (irgend)etwas? II • **Did you do anything special?** Habt ihr irgendetwas Besonderes gemacht? I
not (…) anything nichts II
anyway ['eniweɪ]
1. sowieso I
2. trotzdem II
anywhere ['eniweə]: **anywhere?** irgendwo(hin)? II • **not (…) anywhere** nirgendwo(hin) II
appear [ə'pɪə] erscheinen, auftauchen III 1 (26)
appetite ['æpɪtaɪt] Appetit III 3 (57)
apple ['æpl] Apfel I
appointment [ə'pɔɪntmənt] Termin, Verabredung I
April ['eɪprəl] April I
architect ['ɑ:kɪtekt] Architekt/in III 3 (63)
are [ɑ:] bist; sind; seid I • **How are you?** Wie geht es dir/Ihnen/euch? II • **The pencils are 35 p.** Die Bleistifte kosten 35 Pence. I
area ['eəriə] Gebiet, Gegend; Bereich III 1 (17)
argue ['ɑ:gju:] sich streiten, sich zanken I
argument ['ɑ:gjumənt] Streit, Auseinandersetzung II • **have an argument** eine Auseinandersetzung haben, sich streiten II
arm [ɑ:m] Arm I
armchair ['ɑ:mtʃeə] Sessel I
around [ə'raʊnd] in … umher, durch, um … (herum) III 1 (26/175) • **around six** um sechs Uhr herum, gegen sechs III 1 (26/175) • **around the lake** um den See (herum) III 1 (26/175)
around the town in der Stadt umher, durch die Stadt III 1 (26/175)
look around sich umsehen III 1 (26/175) • **walk/run/jump around** herumgehen/-rennen/-springen, umhergehen/-rennen/-springen III 1 (26/175)
► S.175 around
arrival [ə'raɪvl] Ankunft III 2 (46)
arrive [ə'raɪv] ankommen, eintreffen II
art [ɑ:t] Kunst I
article ['ɑ:tɪkl] (Zeitungs-)Artikel I
artificial [,ɑ:tɪ'fɪʃl] künstlich, Kunst- III 3 (70)
as [əz, æz]
1. als, während II
► S.181 German „während"
2. wie II • **as you know** wie du weißt II
3. **as nice/big/exciting as** so schön/groß/aufregend wie II
as soon as sobald, sowie II
4. °**as a little boy** als kleiner Junge
ask [ɑ:sk] fragen I • **ask about sth.** nach etwas fragen I • **ask questions** Fragen stellen I • **ask sb. for sth.** jn. um etwas bitten II • **ask sb. the way** jn. nach dem Weg fragen II
asleep [ə'sli:p]: **be asleep** schlafen II
assistant [ə'sɪstənt]
1. Verkäufer/in I
°2. Assistent/in
at [ət, æt]: **at 7 Hamilton Street** in der Hamiltonstraße 7 I • **at 8.45** um 8.45 I • **at (the age of) 16** mit 16; im Alter von 16 III 3 (70)
at break in der Pause *(zwischen Schulstunden)* II • **at home** daheim, zu Hause I • **at last** endlich, schließlich I • **at least** zumindest, wenigstens I • **at night** nachts, in der Nacht I • **at school** in der Schule I • **at sea** auf See II • **at that table** an dem Tisch (dort) / an den Tisch (dort) I • **at the back (of the room)** hinten, im hinteren Teil (des Zimmers) II • **at the bottom (of)** unten, am unteren Ende (von) II • **at the chemist's/doctor's/hairdresser's** beim Apotheker/Arzt/Friseur III 2 (45/181) • **at the end (of)** am Ende (von) I • **at the moment** im Moment, gerade, zurzeit I
at the Shaws' house im Haus der Shaws / bei den Shaws zu Hause I • **at the station** am Bahnhof I • **at the top (of)** oben, am oberen Ende, an der Spitze (von) I
at the weekend am Wochenende I • **at work** bei der Arbeit / am Arbeitsplatz I
ate [et, eɪt] *siehe* **eat**

athletics [æθ'letɪks] Leichtathletik III 3 (69)
attack [ə'tæk] Angriff III 4 (88)
attack [ə'tæk] angreifen III 4 (88)
°**attractive** [ə'træktɪv] attraktiv
August ['ɔ:gəst] August I
aunt [ɑ:nt] Tante I • **auntie** ['ɑ:nti] Tante II
°**autograph** ['ɔ:təgrɑ:f] Autogramm
autumn ['ɔ:təm] Herbst I
away [ə'weɪ] weg, fort I • **get away from sth./sb.** von etwas/jm. weggehen, sich entfernen III 1 (28)
awful ['ɔ:fl] furchtbar, schrecklich II
°**Aye.** [aɪ] Ja. *(besonders in Schottland und Irland gebräuchlich)*

B

baby ['beɪbi] Baby I • **have a baby** ein Baby/Kind bekommen II
back [bæk]**: at the back (of the room)** hinten, im hinteren Teil (des Zimmers) II • °**put sb. back in the game** jn.zurück ins Spiel bringen
back door [ˌbæk 'dɔ:] Hintertür II
background ['bækgraʊnd] Hintergrund II • **background file** *etwa:* Hintergrundinformation II
bacon ['beɪkən] Schinkenspeck II
bad [bæd] schlecht, schlimm I
bad timing schlechtes Timing, schlechte Wahl des Zeitpunkts III 3 (57)
badminton ['bædmɪntən] Badminton, Federball I • **badminton racket** Federballschläger III 3 (62)
bag [bæg] Tasche, Beutel, Tüte I • Handtasche III 2 (34)
°**bagpipes** *(pl)* ['bægpaɪps] Dudelsack
°**bagpiper** ['bægpaɪpə] Dudelsackpfeifer/in
ball [bɔ:l]
1. Ball *(zum Sport)* I
2. Ball *(Tanz)* II
balloon [bə'lu:n] Heißluftballon; Luftballon II
banana [bə'nɑ:nə] Banane I
band [bænd] Band, (Musik-)Gruppe I
°**Bangladeshi** [ˌbæŋglə'deʃi] bangladeschisch
banjo ['bændʒəʊ] Banjo III 5 (105)
bank [bæŋk]
1. Bank, Sparkasse I • **bank robber** ['bæŋk ˌrɒbə] Bankräuber/in I
°**2.** Ufer
bar [bɑ:] Bar II
bark [bɑ:k] bellen II

baseball ['beɪsbɔ:l] Baseball I
baseball cap Baseballmütze II
basket ['bɑ:skɪt] Korb I • **a basket of apples** ein Korb Äpfel I
basketball ['bɑ:skɪtbɔ:l] Basketball I
bass [beɪs] Kontrabass; Bassgitarre III Intro (11) • **bass guitar** Bassgitarre III Intro (11) • **double bass** Kontrabass III Intro (11)
bat: table tennis bat [bæt] Tischtennisschläger III 3 (62)
bath [bɑ:θ] Bad, Badewanne II
have a bath baden, ein Bad nehmen II
bathroom ['bɑ:θru:m; 'bɑ:θrʊm] Badezimmer I
bay [beɪ] Bucht III 2 (38/179)
be [bi:]**, was/were, been** sein I
be into sth. *(infml)* etwas mögen III Intro (7)
beach [bi:tʃ] Strand II • **on the beach** [bi:tʃ] am Strand II
bear [beə] Bär II • **teddy bear** Teddybär III 3 (64)
beat [bi:t]**, beat, beaten** schlagen; besiegen III 3 (59)
beaten ['bi:tn] *siehe* **beat**
beautiful ['bju:tɪfl] schön I
beauty ['bju:ti] Schönheit III 2 (33)
became [bɪ'keɪm] *siehe* **become**
because [bɪ'kɒz] weil I
become [bɪ'kʌm]**, became, become** werden II
► S.193 German „werden"
bed [bed] Bett I • **Bed and Breakfast (B&B)** [ˌbed‿ən 'brekfəst] Frühstückspension I • **go to bed** ins Bett gehen I • **put sb. to bed** jn. ins Bett bringen III 5 (102)
bedroom ['bedru:m; 'bedrʊm] Schlafzimmer I
been [bi:n] *siehe* **be**
before [bɪ'fɔ:] vor *(zeitlich)* I • **the day before yesterday** vorgestern II
before [bɪ'fɔ:] bevor II
before [bɪ'fɔ:] (vorher) schon mal II
began [bɪ'gæn] *siehe* **begin**
begin (-nn-) [bɪ'gɪn]**, began, begun** beginnen, anfangen (mit) I
beginning [bɪ'gɪnɪŋ] Anfang, Beginn III 2 (39)
begun [bɪ'gʌn] *siehe* **begin**
°**behave** [bɪ'heɪv] sich benehmen
behind [bɪ'haɪnd] hinter I
bell [bel] Klingel, Glocke I
believe [bɪ'li:v] glauben III 2 (45) • **She couldn't believe her eyes.** Sie traute ihren Augen kaum. III 2 (48)
belong (to) [bɪ'lɒŋ] gehören (zu) II

below [bɪ'ləʊ]
1. unter, unterhalb (von) III 2 (47)
°**2.** unten
°**beneath** *(prep)* [bɪ'ni:θ] unter
best [best] am besten II • **the best …** der/die/das beste …; die besten … I • **What was the best thing about …?** Was war das Beste an …? II
°**bestseller** ['bestselə] Bestseller
bet (-tt-) [bet]**, bet, bet** wetten III 2 (35)
better ['betə] besser I • **like sth. better** etwas lieber mögen II
between [bɪ'twi:n] zwischen II
big [bɪg] groß I • **big wheel** Riesenrad III 1 (12)
► S.177 big – large – huge
bike [baɪk] Fahrrad I • **bike tour** Radtour II • **ride a bike** Rad fahren I
bin [bɪn] Mülltonne II
biography [baɪ'ɒgrəfi] Biografie III 5 (103)
biology [baɪ'ɒlədʒi] Biologie I
bird [bɜ:d] Vogel I
birthday ['bɜ:θdeɪ] Geburtstag I
Happy birthday. Herzlichen Glückwunsch zum Geburtstag. I • **My birthday is in May.** Ich habe im Mai Geburtstag. I • **My birthday is on 13th June.** Ich habe am 13. Juni Geburtstag. I • **When's your birthday?** Wann hast du Geburtstag? I • **for his birthday** zu seinem Geburtstag III 3 (69)
biscuit ['bɪskɪt] Keks, Plätzchen I
bit [bɪt]**: a bit** ein bisschen, etwas II
black [blæk] schwarz I
blame sb. (for) [bleɪm] jm. die Schuld geben (an); jm. Vorwürfe machen (wegen) III 5 (102)
bleep [bli:p] piepsen II
bleep [bli:p] Piepton II
blew [blu:] *siehe* **blow**
blind [blaɪnd] blind III 5 (99/193)
blood [blʌd] Blut III 1 (27)
blouse [blaʊz] Bluse II
blow [bləʊ]**, blew, blown** pusten, blasen; wehen III 5 (96)
blown [bləʊn] *siehe* **blow**
blue [blu:] blau I
blues [blu:z] Blues III 5 (100)
board [bɔ:d] (Wand-)Tafel I • **on the board** an der/die Tafel I
boat [bəʊt] Boot, Schiff I
body ['bɒdi] Körper I
°**bonnie** ['bɒni] hübsch *(besonders in Schottland gebräuchlich)*
book [bʊk] Buch I
booklet ['bʊklət] Broschüre II

boot [buːt] Stiefel I
boring ['bɔːrɪŋ] langweilig I
born [bɔːn]**: be born** geboren sein/ werden II
borough ['bʌrə] Bezirk III 1 (13)
borrow sth. ['bɒrəʊ] sich etwas (aus)leihen, etwas entleihen II
boss [bɒs] Boss, Chef/in I
both [bəʊθ] beide I • **°both my legs** meine beiden Beine
bottle ['bɒtl] Flasche I • **a bottle of milk** eine Flasche Milch I
bottom ['bɒtəm] unteres Ende II • **at the bottom (of)** unten, am unteren Ende (von) II
bought [bɔːt] *siehe* **buy**
bowl [bəʊl] Schüssel I • **a bowl of cornflakes** eine Schale Cornflakes I
box [bɒks] Kasten, Kästchen, Kiste I
box office ['bɒks‿ˌɒfɪs] (Theater-, Kino-)Kasse III Intro (9)
boy [bɔɪ] Junge I • **boy!** *(AE, infml)* Mann! Mensch! III 4 (77)
°bracket ['brækɪt] Klammer *(in Texten)*
brainstorm ['breɪnstɔːm] brainstormen *(so viele Ideen wie möglich sammeln)* III 4 (85)
bread *(no pl)* [bred] Brot I
break [breɪk]**, broke, broken** (zer)brechen; kaputt machen; kaputt gehen II
break [breɪk] Pause I • **at break** in der Pause *(zwischen Schulstunden)* II
breakfast ['brekfəst] Frühstück I **have breakfast** frühstücken I
bridge [brɪdʒ] Brücke I
bridle path ['braɪdl ˌpɑːθ] Reitweg III 3 (62)
bright [braɪt] hell, leuchtend II
bring [brɪŋ]**, brought, brought** (mit-, her)bringen I
British ['brɪtɪʃ] britisch; Brite, Britin II
°brochure ['brəʊʃə] Prospekt, Broschüre
broke [brəʊk] *siehe* **break**
broken ['brəʊkən] *siehe* **break**
broken ['brəʊkən] gebrochen; zerbrochen, kaputt II
brother ['brʌðə] Bruder I
brought [brɔːt] *siehe* **bring**
brown [braʊn] braun I
°budget: be on a budget ['bʌdʒɪt] mit wenig Geld auskommen müssen
budgie ['bʌdʒi] Wellensittich I
build [bɪld]**, built, built** bauen II • **the ship was built in Bristol** das Schiff wurde in Bristol gebaut II
building ['bɪldɪŋ] Gebäude II
built [bɪlt] *siehe* **build**
bully ['bʊli] einschüchtern, tyrannisieren II
bully ['bʊli] (Schul-)Tyrann III 2 (35)
bummer: What a bummer! ['bʌmə] *(infml)* So ein Mist! Wie schade! III 4 (75)
bunk (bed) [bʌŋk] Etagenbett, Koje II
bus [bʌs] Bus I
bus pass ['bʌs pɑːs] Bus-Monatskarte III 1 (20/174)
bus stop ['bʌs stɒp] Bushaltestelle III 1 (20/174)
business: Mind your own business. [ˌmaɪnd jər‿ˌəʊn 'bɪznəs] Das geht dich nichts an! / Kümmere dich um deine eigenen Angelegenheiten! II
busy ['bɪzi]
1. beschäftigt I
2. belebt, verkehrsreich; hektisch III 2 (38)
but [bət, bʌt] aber I
button ['bʌtn] Knopf III 1 (26)
buy [baɪ]**, bought, bought** kaufen I
°buzz [bʌz] *hier:* den Summer/die Glocke betätigen
by [baɪ]
1. von I
2. an; (nahe) bei II
by car/bike/... mit dem Auto/ Rad/... II • **by the end of the song** (spätestens) bis zum Ende des Lieds III 5 (98) • **by the way** übrigens; nebenbei (bemerkt) III Intro (7)
Bye. [baɪ] Tschüs! I

C

°caber ['keɪbə]**: tossing the caber** Baumstammwerfen
cabin ['kæbɪn] Hütte III 4 (77)
café ['kæfeɪ] *(kleines)* Restaurant, Imbissstube, Café I
cafeteria [ˌkæfə'tɪəriə] Cafeteria, Selbstbedienungsrestaurant II
cage [keɪdʒ] Käfig I
cake [keɪk] Kuchen, Torte I
calendar ['kælɪndə] Kalender I
call [kɔːl] rufen; anrufen; nennen I **be called** heißen, genannt werden II • **call sb. names** jn. mit Schimpfwörtern hänseln, jm. Schimpfwörter nachrufen III 2 (35)
call [kɔːl] Ruf, Schrei; Anruf II **make a call** ein Telefongespräch führen, telefonieren II
calm down [ˌkɑːm 'daʊn] sich beruhigen II • **calm sb. down** jn. beruhigen II
came [keɪm] *siehe* **come**
camel ['kæml] Kamel II
camera ['kæmərə] Kamera, Fotoapparat I • **°cameraman/-woman** Kameramann/-frau
camp [kæmp] zelten III 4 (88)
campground ['kæmpˌgraʊnd] *(AE)* Zeltplatz III 4 (88)
campsite ['kæmpsaɪt] Zeltplatz III 4 (88/190)
can [kən, kæn]
1. können I
2. dürfen I
Can I help you? Kann ich Ihnen helfen? / Was kann ich für Sie tun? *(im Geschäft)* I
canal [kə'næl] Kanal III 2 (38/179)
canoe [kə'nuː] Kanu III 4 (88)
canoe [kə'nuː] paddeln, Kanu fahren III 4 (88)
cap [kæp] Mütze, Kappe II
capital ['kæpɪtl] Hauptstadt III 1 (12)
capital letter [ˌkæpɪtl 'letə] Großbuchstabe III 5 (103)
°capsule ['kæpsjuːl] Kapsel, Kabine
captain ['kæptɪn] Kapitän/in III 2 (46)
°caption ['kæpʃn] Bildunterschrift
car [kɑː] Auto I
car park ['kɑː pɑːk] Parkplatz III 2 (38)
caravan ['kærəvæn] Wohnwagen II
card [kɑːd] (Spiel-, Post-)Karte I
care (about) [keə] sich interessieren (für); sich kümmern (um); wichtig nehmen III 4 (74) • **I care about the environment.** Die Umwelt liegt mir am Herzen. III 4 (74/187) • **I don't care about money.** Geld ist mir egal. III 4 (74/187) • **Who cares?** Ist doch egal! / Na und? III 4 (74/187)
► S.187 (to) care
care [keə]**: take care of sth.** sich um etwas kümmern III 1 (28)
career [kə'rɪə] Karriere III 5 (103)
careful ['keəfl] vorsichtig I
caretaker ['keəteɪkə] Hausmeister/ in II
carrot ['kærət] Möhre, Karotte I
cartoon [kɑː'tuːn] Cartoon (Zeichentrickfilm; Bilderwitz) II
case [keɪs] Fall II
castle ['kɑːsl] Burg, Schloss II
cat [kæt] Katze I
catch [kætʃ]**, caught, caught** fangen; erwischen II
cathedral [kə'θiːdrəl] Kathedrale, Dom III 1 (13)

caught [kɔːt] *siehe* **catch**
CD [ˌsiːˈdiː] CD I • **CD player** CD-Spieler I
ceilidh [ˈkeɪli] *Musik- und Tanzveranstaltung, vor allem in Schottland und Irland* III 2 (33)
celebrity [səˈlebrəti] berühmte Persönlichkeit, Prominente(r) III 3 (65)
cello [ˈtʃeləʊ] Cello III Intro (11)
cellphone [ˈselfəʊn] *(AE)* Mobiltelefon, Handy III 1 (16)
°**Celtic** [ˈkeltɪk] keltisch
cent (c) [sent] Cent I
cent: per cent [pəˈsent] Prozent III 4 (80)
centimetre (cm) [ˈsentɪmiːtə] Zentimeter III 2 (43)
central [ˈsentrəl] Zentral-, Mittel- III 1 (14)
centre [ˈsentə] Zentrum, Mitte I
century [ˈsentʃəri] Jahrhundert II
°**chain** [tʃeɪn] Kette
chair [tʃeə] Stuhl I
champion [ˈtʃæmpiən] Meister/in, Champion I
championship [ˈtʃæmpiənʃɪp] Meisterschaft III 3 (69)
chance [tʃɑːns] Chance II
change [tʃeɪndʒ]
1. Wechselgeld I
°2. (Ver-)Änderung
change [tʃeɪndʒ]
1. umsteigen III 1 (14)
°2. (ver-)ändern
°**Changing of the Guard** [gɑːd] Wachablösung III 1 (19)
°**chant** [tʃɑːnt] Sprechchor *(z.B. von Fußballfans)*
°**character** [ˈkærəktə] Person, Figur *(in Roman, Film, Englischbuch)*
charity [ˈtʃærəti] Wohlfahrtsorganisation II
°**chart** [tʃɑːt] Schaubild, Diagramm, Tabelle
chat (-tt-) [tʃæt] chatten, plaudern II
chat [tʃæt] Chat, Unterhaltung II
chat room [ˈtʃæt ruːm] Chatroom III 3 (57)
chat show Talkshow II
cheap [tʃiːp] billig, preiswert II
check [tʃek] (über)prüfen, kontrollieren I
checklist [ˈtʃeklɪst] Checkliste III 5 (104)
checkpoint [ˈtʃekpɔɪnt] Kontrollpunkt *(hier: zur Selbstüberprüfung)* I
cheer [tʃɪə] jubeln, Beifall klatschen II
cheese [tʃiːz] Käse I
chemist [ˈkemɪst] Drogerie, Apotheke II • **at the chemist's** beim Apotheker III 2 (45/181)
chicken [ˈtʃɪkɪn] Huhn; (Brat-)Hähnchen I • °**stewed chicken** [stjuːd] geschmortes Hühnchen
child [tʃaɪld], *pl* **children** [ˈtʃɪldrən] Kind I
°**childhood** [ˈtʃaɪldhʊd] Kindheit
chill out [ˌtʃɪl‿ˈaʊt] *(infml)* sich entspannen, relaxen III 5 (98)
chips *(pl)* [tʃɪps] Pommes frites I
chocolate [ˈtʃɒklət] Schokolade I
°**choice** [tʃɔɪs] (Aus-)Wahl, Entscheidung
choir [ˈkwaɪə] Chor I
choose [tʃuːz], **chose, chosen** (sich) aussuchen, (aus)wählen I
°**chorus** [ˈkɔːrəs] Refrain
chose [tʃəʊz] *siehe* **choose**
chosen [ˈtʃəʊzn] *siehe* **choose**
church [tʃɜːtʃ] Kirche I • **go to church** in die Kirche gehen III 1 (12/170)
► S.170 Places without articles
cinema [ˈsɪnəmə] Kino II • **go to the cinema** ins Kino gehen II
circle [ˈsɜːkl] Kreis III 2 (39)
circus [ˈsɜːkəs] (runder) Platz III 1 (13)
city [ˈsɪti] Stadt, Großstadt I
city centre [ˌsɪti ˈsentə] Stadtzentrum, Innenstadt I
°**clan** [klæn] Clan, Sippe
°**clapshot** [ˈklæpʃɒt] schottisches Eintopfgericht
clarinet [ˌklærɪˈnet] Klarinette III Intro (11)
class [klɑːs] (Schul-)Klasse I
class teacher Klassenlehrer/in I
classic [klæsɪk] klassisch III 5 (98)
classical [ˈklæsɪkl] klassisch III Intro (6)
classmate [ˈklɑːsmeɪt] Klassenkamerad/in, Mitschüler/in I
classroom [ˈklɑːsruːm; ˈklɑːsrʊm] Klassenzimmer I
clause [klɔːz] (Teil-, Glied-)Satz III 2 (35)
clean [kliːn] sauber II
clean [kliːn] sauber machen, putzen I • **clean one's teeth** sich die Zähne putzen III 5 (102)
cleaner [ˈkliːnə] Putzfrau, -mann II
clear [klɪə] klar, deutlich I
clever [ˈklevə] klug, schlau I
click on sth. [klɪk] etwas anklicken II
cliff [klɪf] Klippe III 2 (48)
climb [klaɪm] klettern; hinaufklettern (auf) I • **Climb a tree.** Klettere auf einen Baum. I
clinic [ˈklɪnɪk] Klinik II
clock [klɒk] (Wand-, Stand-, Turm-) Uhr I
°**clone** [kləʊn] klonen
close (to) [kləʊs] nahe (bei, an) III 1 (27) • **That was close.** Das war knapp. II
close [kləʊz] schließen, zumachen I
closely: look closely at sth. [ˈkləʊsli] etw. genau anschauen III 1 (26)
°**closing phrase** [ˈkləʊzɪŋ freɪz] Schlussworte, Grußformel *(am Briefende)*
closed [kləʊzd] geschlossen II
clothes *(pl)* [kləʊðz, kləʊz] Kleider, Kleidungsstücke I
cloud [klaʊd] Wolke II
cloudy [ˈklaʊdi] bewölkt II
clown [klaʊn] Clown/in I
club [klʌb] Klub; Verein I
coach [kəʊtʃ] Trainer/in III 3 (56)
coast [kəʊst] Küste II
cola [ˈkəʊlə] Cola I
cold [kəʊld] kalt I • **be cold** frieren I
cold [kəʊld] Erkältung II • **have a cold** erkältet sein, eine Erkältung haben II
collect [kəˈlekt] sammeln I
collector [kəˈlektə] Sammler/in II
college [ˈkɒlɪdʒ] Hochschule, Fachschule III 5 (97)
°**colony** [ˈkɒləni] Kolonie
colour [ˈkʌlə] Farbe I • **What colour is ...?** Welche Farbe hat ...? I
column [ˈkɒləm]
1. Säule III 1 (13)
°2. Spalte *(auf Buchseite)*
°**combination** [ˌkɒmbɪˈneɪʃn] Kombination, Verbindung
come [kʌm], **came, come** kommen I • **come home** nach Hause kommen I • **come in** hereinkommen I • **Come on. 1.** Na los, komm. II; **2.** Ach komm! / Na hör mal! II
come true wahr werden II
comedy [ˈkɒmədi] Comedyshow, Komödie II
comfortable [ˈkʌmftəbl] bequem I
comic [ˈkɒmɪk] Comic-Heft I
Commonwealth [ˈkɒmənwelθ]**: the Commonwealth** *Gemeinschaft der Länder des ehemaligen Britischen Weltreichs* III 3 (70)
community hall [kəˈmjuːnəti] Gemeinschaftshalle, -saal / Gemeindehalle, -saal III 2 (47)
company [ˈkʌmpəni] Firma, Gesellschaft III 5 (100)
compare [kəmˈpeə] vergleichen II
comparison [kəmˈpærɪsn] Steigerung; Vergleich II • °**make**

comparisons Vergleiche anstellen, vergleichen
competition [ˌkɒmpəˈtɪʃn] Wettbewerb III 3 (58)
°complete [kəmˈpliːt] vollständig, komplett
°complex [ˈkɒmpleks] komplex
°compliment [ˈkɒmplɪmənt] Kompliment
°compose [kəmˈpəʊz] komponieren
°composer [kəmˈpəʊzə] Komponist/in
°compromise [ˈkɒmprəmaɪz] Kompromiss
computer [kəmˈpjuːtə] Computer I • **computer science** [kəmˌpjuːtə ˈsaɪəns] Computerwissenschaft, Informatik III 3 (63)
concert [ˈkɒnsət] Konzert II
°conduct [kənˈdʌkt] dirigieren
°confuse [kənˈfjuːz] verwechseln
Congratulations! [kənˌɡrætʃuˈleɪʃnz] Herzlichen Glückwunsch! III 2 (45)
contact sb. [ˈkɒntækt] sich mit jm. in Verbindung setzen; mit jm. Kontakt aufnehmen III 5 (94)
continue [kənˈtɪnjuː] weitermachen (mit); weiterreden; weitergehen II
conversation [ˌkɒnvəˈseɪʃn] Gespräch, Unterhaltung II
cook [kʊk] kochen, zubereiten II
cook [kʊk] Koch, Köchin II
cooker [ˈkʊkə] Herd I
cool [kuːl]
1. kühl I
2. cool I
copy [ˈkɒpi] kopieren II
°copy [ˈkɒpi] Kopie, Abschrift
corner [ˈkɔːnə] Ecke I • **on the corner of Sand Street and London Road** Sand Street, Ecke London Road II
cornflakes [ˈkɔːnfleɪks] Cornflakes I
correct [kəˈrekt] korrigieren, verbessern II
correct [kəˈrekt] richtig, korrekt II
°correction [kəˈrekʃn] Verbesserung, Korrektur
cost [kɒst]**, cost, cost** kosten III 4 (74)
costume [ˈkɒstjuːm] Kostüm, Verkleidung I
°cotton [ˈkɒtn] Baumwolle
could [kəd, kʊd]**: he could ...** er konnte ... II
could [kəd, kʊd]**: we could ...** wir könnten ... II
count [kaʊnt] zählen II
countdown [ˈkaʊntdaʊn] Countdown III 5 (98)
counter [ˈkaʊntə] Spielstein II
country [ˈkʌntri] Land *(auch als Gegensatz zur Stadt)* II • **in the country** auf dem Land II

couple**: a couple of** [ˈkʌpl] ein paar/Paar III 1 (17)
course [kɔːs] Kurs, Lehrgang III 1 (24)
course**: of course** [əv ˈkɔːs] natürlich, selbstverständlich I
court [kɔːt] Platz, Court III 3 (62)
cousin [ˈkʌzn] Cousin, Cousine I
cover [ˈkʌvə] (CD-)Hülle I
cow [kaʊ] Kuh II
crash [kræʃ] abstürzen III 5 (99)
crazy [ˈkreɪzi] verrückt III 4 (85)
crew [kruː] Crew, (Schiffs-)Mannschaft III 4 (75)
cricket [ˈkrɪkɪt] Kricket III 3 (65)
crisps *(pl)* [krɪsps] Kartoffelchips I
°critic [ˈkrɪtɪk] Kritiker/in
crocodile [ˈkrɒkədaɪl] Krokodil II
cross [krɒs] überqueren; (sich) kreuzen II
°crosse [krɒs] Sportgerät für Lacrosse
crowd [kraʊd] (Menschen-)Menge III 1 (17)
crowded [ˈkraʊdɪd] voller Menschen, überfüllt III 1 (24)
cry [kraɪ]
1. schreien I • **cry in pain** vor Schmerzen schreien I
2. weinen III 4 (75)
°culture [ˈkʌltʃə] Kultur
cup [kʌp]
1. Tasse II • **a cup of tea** eine Tasse Tee II
2. Pokal III 3 (65)
cupboard [ˈkʌbəd] Schrank I
cut **(-tt-)** [kʌt]**, cut, cut** schneiden II • **cut sth. off** etwas abschneiden, abtrennen III 3 (69) • **cut sth. out** ausschneiden III 2 (46) • **°Cut!** Schnitt!
cycle [ˈsaɪkl] (mit dem) Rad fahren II
cycle path [ˈsaɪkl pɑːθ] Radweg II

D

dad [dæd] Papa, Vati; Vater I
dance [dɑːns] tanzen I
dance [dɑːns] Tanz I • **dance floor** Tanzfläche III 4 (76)
dancer [ˈdɑːnsə] Tänzer/in II
dancing [ˈdɑːnsɪŋ] Tanzen I
dancing lessons Tanzstunden, Tanzunterricht I
danger [ˈdeɪndʒə] Gefahr I
dangerous [ˈdeɪndʒərəs] gefährlich II
dark [dɑːk] dunkel I
date [deɪt] Datum I
date [deɪt] *(besonders AE)* mit jm. (aus)gehen; sich (regelmäßig) mit jm. treffen III 4 (76)

daughter [ˈdɔːtə] Tochter I
day [deɪ] Tag I • **one day** eines Tages I • **days of the week** Wochentage I • **the day before yesterday** vorgestern II • **°a day out** ein Tagesausflug • **that day** an jenem Tag III 3 (69)
dead [ded] tot I
deaf [def] taub, gehörlos III 5 (99)
deal [diːl]**: make a deal** ein Abkommen/eine Abmachung treffen III 3 (58) • **It's a deal!** Abgemacht! III 3 (58)
dear [dɪə] Schatz, Liebling I
Oh dear! Oje! II
dear [dɪə]**: Dear Jay ...** Lieber Jay, ... I
December [dɪˈsembə] Dezember I
decide (on sth.) [dɪˈsaɪd] sich entscheiden (für etwas), (etwas) beschließen II
°deep [diːp] tief
deer, *pl* **deer** [dɪə] Reh, Hirsch II
defence [dɪˈfens] Verteidigung III 3 (59)
°definition [ˌdefɪˈnɪʃn] Definition
degree [dɪˈɡriː] Grad II
delicious [dɪˈlɪʃəs] köstlich, lecker II
°dentist [ˈdentɪst] Zahnarzt, Zahnärztin
department store [dɪˈpɑːtmənt stɔː] Kaufhaus II
°descent [dɪˈsent] Abstammung
describe sth. (to sb.) [dɪˈskraɪb] (jm.) etwas beschreiben II
description [dɪˈskrɪpʃn] Beschreibung II
design [dɪˈzaɪn] entwickeln, entwerfen I
°designer [dɪˈzaɪnə] Designer/in
desk [desk] Schreibtisch I
destroy [dɪˈstrɔɪ] zerstören III 3 (65)
detail [ˈdiːteɪl] Detail, Einzelheit III 1 (13)
detective [dɪˈtektɪv] Detektiv/in I
°diabetic [daɪəˈbetɪk] Zuckerkranke/r, Diabetiker/in
°diagram [ˈdaɪəɡræm] Diagramm, Schaubild
dial **(-ll-)** [ˈdaɪəl] wählen *(Telefonnummer)* II
°dialogue [ˈdaɪəlɒɡ] Dialog
diary [ˈdaɪəri] Tagebuch; Terminkalender I
dice, *pl* **dice** [daɪs] Würfel II
throw the dice würfeln II
°dictate [dɪkˈteɪt] diktieren
°dictation [dɪkˈteɪʃn] Diktat
dictionary [ˈdɪkʃənri] Wörterbuch, *(alphabetisches)* Wörterverzeichnis I
did [dɪd] *siehe* do • **Did you go?** Bist du gegangen?/Gingst du? I

we didn't go ['dɪdnt] wir sind nicht gegangen/wir gingen nicht I
die (of) (*-ing form:* **dying**) [daɪ] sterben (an) II
difference ['dɪfrəns] Unterschied III 3 (62)
different (from) ['dɪfrənt] verschieden, unterschiedlich; anders (als) I
difficult ['dɪfɪkəlt] schwierig, schwer I
dining room ['daɪnɪŋ ruːm; 'daɪnɪŋ rʊm] Esszimmer I
dinner ['dɪnə] Abendessen, -brot I **have dinner** Abendbrot essen I
°**dinosaur** ['daɪnəsɔː] Dinosaurier
direct [də'rekt] Regie führen III 5 (100/194)
direct speech [də'rekt] direkte Rede III 4 (77)
directions *(pl)* [də'rekʃnz] Wegbeschreibung(en) II
director [də'rektə] Regisseur/in III 5 (100)
dirty ['dɜːti] schmutzig II
disabled [dɪs'eɪbld] (körper)behindert III 3 (70)
disagree (with) [ˌdɪsə'griː] anderer Meinung sein (als), nicht übereinstimmen (mit) II
disappear [ˌdɪsə'pɪə] verschwinden II
disc jockey ['dɪsk dʒɒki] Diskjockey III Intro (10)
disco ['dɪskəʊ] Disko I
discover [dɪ'skʌvə] entdecken; herausfinden II
°**discus** ['dɪskəs] Diskuswerfen
°**discuss** [dɪ'skʌs] besprechen, diskutieren über
discussion [dɪ'skʌʃn] Diskussion II
dish [dɪʃ] Gericht *(Speise)* III 1 (16)
dishes *(pl)* ['dɪʃɪz] Geschirr I • **do the dishes** das Geschirr abwaschen I
dishwasher ['dɪʃwɒʃə] Geschirrspülmaschine I
divide (into) [dɪ'vaɪd] (sich) teilen (in), (sich) aufteilen (in) II
divorced [dɪ'vɔːst] geschieden I
DJ ['diːdʒeɪ] Diskjockey III Intro (10)
DJ ['diːdʒeɪ] (Musik/CDs/Platten) auflegen *(in der Disko)* III Intro (10)
do [duː]**, did, done** tun, machen I **do a gig** einen Auftritt haben, ein Konzert geben III Intro (11) • **do a good job** gute Arbeit leisten II **do an exercise** eine Übung machen II • **do a project** ein Projekt machen, durchführen II • **do sport** Sport treiben I • **do the dishes** das Geschirr abwaschen I • **How am I doing?** Wie komme ich voran? (Wie sind meine Fortschritte?) III 1 (29)
doctor ['dɒktə] Arzt/Ärztin, Doktor I • **at/to the doctor's** beim/zum Arzt III 2 (45)
documentary [ˌdɒkju'mentri] Dokumentarfilm II
dog [dɒg] Hund I
°**dome** [dəʊm] Kuppel
done [dʌn] *siehe* **do**
don't [dəʊnt]**: Don't listen to Dan.** Hör/Hört nicht auf Dan. I • **I don't like ...** Ich mag ... nicht. / Ich mag kein(e) ... I
door [dɔː] Tür I
doorbell ['dɔːbel] Türklingel I
°**doorway** ['dɔːweɪ] Eingang, Türöffnung
dossier ['dɒsieɪ] Mappe, Dossier *(des Sprachenportfolios)* I
double ['dʌbl] zweimal, doppelt, Doppel- I
double bass [ˌdʌbl 'beɪs] Kontrabass III Intro (11)
down [daʊn] hinunter, herunter, nach unten I • **down there** (nach) dort unten II
download [ˌdaʊn'ləʊd] runterladen, downloaden II
downstairs [ˌdaʊn'steəz] unten; nach unten I
dragon ['drægən] Drache III 4 (75)
drama ['drɑːmə] Schauspiel, darstellende Kunst I
drank [dræŋk] *siehe* **drink**
draw [drɔː]**, drew, drawn** zeichnen III 5 (94)
draw [drɔː] Unentschieden III 3 (56/183)
► S.183 A football match
drawing ['drɔːɪŋ] Zeichnung III 5 (94)
drawn [drɔːn] *siehe* **draw**
dream [driːm] Traum I • **dream house** Traumhaus I
dream (of, about) [driːm] träumen (von) III 1 (12) • **dream on** weiterträumen III 1 (12/171)
dress [dres] Kleid I
dressed [drest]**: get dressed** sich anziehen I
drew [druː] *siehe* **draw**
drink [drɪŋk] Getränk I
drink [drɪŋk]**, drank, drunk** trinken I
drive [draɪv]**, drove, driven** *(ein Auto/mit dem Auto)* fahren II
driven ['drɪvn] *siehe* **drive**
driver ['draɪvə] Fahrer/in II
drop (-pp-) [drɒp]
1. fallen lassen I
2. fallen I
drove [drəʊv] *siehe* **drive**
drum [drʌm] Trommel; Schlagzeug III Intro (6) • **drumstick** Trommelstock III 5 (99) • **play the drums** Schlagzeug spielen III Intro (6/169)
drunk [drʌŋk] *siehe* **drink**
dry [draɪ] trocken III 1 (16)
during *(prep)* ['djʊərɪŋ] während III 2 (33)
► S.181 German „während“
dustbin ['dʌstbɪn] Mülltonne II
DVD [ˌdiː viː' diː] DVD I

E

each [iːtʃ] jeder, jede, jedes (einzelne) I • **each other** einander, sich (gegenseitig) III 5 (99)
ear [ɪə] Ohr I
earache ['ɪəreɪk] Ohrenschmerzen II
°**earl** [ɜːl] Graf
early ['ɜːli] früh I
°**earn** [ɜːn] einbringen
earring ['ɪərɪŋ] Ohrring I
east [iːst] Osten; nach Osten; östlich II • **eastbound** ['iːstbaʊnd] Richtung Osten III 1 (14) • **eastern** ['iːstən] östlich, Ost- III Intro (9)
easy ['iːzi] leicht, einfach I
eat [iːt]**, ate, eaten** essen I
eaten ['iːtn] *siehe* **eat**
edit ['edɪt] redigieren III 5 (100)
editor ['edɪtə] Redakteur/in III 5 (94)
e-friend ['iːfrend] Brieffreund/in *(im Internet)* I
°**e.g.** [ˌiː'dʒiː] z.B. (zum Beispiel)
egg [eg] Ei I
either ['aɪðə, 'iːðə]**: not (...) either** auch nicht II
electric [ɪ'lektrɪk] elektrisch, Elektro- III Intro (11)
°**electrician** [ɪˌlek'trɪʃn] Elektriker/in
electricity [ɪˌlek'trɪsəti] Strom, Elektrizität III 1 (27)
electronic [ɪˌlek'trɒnɪk] elektronisch III 2 (32)
elephant ['elɪfənt] Elefant I
elevator ['elɪveɪtə] *(AE)* Fahrstuhl, Aufzug II
else [els]**: anybody/anything else** sonst (noch) jemand/etwas **anywhere else** sonst (noch) irgendwo(hin) • **somebody else** jemand anders • **something else** etwas anderes • **somewhere else** woanders(hin) • **who/what/where/why/... else?** wer/was/wo/warum/... (sonst) noch? III 4 (75/188)
e-mail ['iːmeɪl] E-Mail I
°**emergency call** [ɪ'mɜːdʒənsi ˌkɔːl] Notruf

empty ['empti] leer I
encyclopedia [ɪnˌsaɪklə'piːdiə] Enzyklopädie, Lexikon II
end [end] Ende; Schluss I • **at the end (of)** am Ende (von) I • °**in the end** schließlich, am Ende
°**end** [end] beenden
ending ['endɪŋ] Ende, (Ab-)Schluss *(einer Geschichte, eines Films usw.)* III 1 (28) • **happy ending** Happyend II
enemy ['enəmi] Feind/in II
engineer [ˌendʒɪ'nɪə] Ingenieur/in II
English ['ɪŋglɪʃ] Englisch; englisch I
enjoy [ɪn'dʒɔɪ] genießen I
enough [ɪ'nʌf] genug I
enter sth. ['entə] etwas eingeben, eintragen II
°**entertainment** [ˌentə'teɪnmənt] Unterhaltung, Entertainment
entry ['entri]
1. Eintrag, Eintragung *(im Wörterbuch/Tagebuch)* III 1 (16)
2. Einsendung, Beitrag *(zu einem Wettbewerb)* III 3 (58)
equalize ['iːkwəlaɪz] ausgleichen; das Ausgleichstor erzielen III 3 (67)
equipment [ɪ'kwɪpmənt] Ausrüstung III 2 (47)
°**especially** [ɪ'speʃəli] besonders
essay (about, on) ['eseɪ] Aufsatz (über) I
°**etc. (et cetera)** [et'setərə] usw.
°**ethnic** ['eθnɪk] ethnisch
euro (€) ['jʊərəʊ] Euro I
°**European** [ˌjʊərə'piːən] Europäer/in, europäisch
even ['iːvn]
1. sogar II
2. (sogar) schon III 3 (69)
evening ['iːvnɪŋ] Abend I • **in the evening** abends, am Abend I
on Friday evening freitagabends, am Freitagabend I
event [ɪ'vent] Ereignis II
ever ['evə] je, jemals III 4 (77)
ever? je? / jemals? / schon mal? II
every ['evri] jeder, jede, jedes I
everybody ['evribɒdi] jeder, alle II
everyday *(adj)* ['evrideɪ] Alltags-; alltäglich III 1 (25)
everyone ['evriwʌn] jeder; alle III 4 (75)
everything ['evriθɪŋ] alles I
everywhere ['evriweə] überall I
exact [ɪg'zækt] genau III 1 (13)
example [ɪg'zɑːmpl] Beispiel I
for example zum Beispiel I
°**except** [ɪk'sept] außer, bis auf
exchange [ɪks'tʃeɪndʒ] (Schüler-) Austausch III 3 (57)
exchange [ɪks'tʃeɪndʒ] aus-, umtauschen III 2 (32); *(Geld)* wechseln III 3 (57)
excited [ɪk'saɪtɪd] *(positiv)* aufgeregt, begeistert II
exciting [ɪk'saɪtɪŋ] aufregend, spannend II
Excuse me, ... [ɪk'skjuːz miː] Entschuldigung, ... / Entschuldigen Sie, ... I
exercise ['eksəsaɪz] Übung, Aufgabe I • **do an exercise** eine Übung machen II • **exercise book** ['eksəsaɪz bʊk] Schulheft, Übungsheft I • **prewriting exercise** Übung vor dem Schreiben III 4 (85)
expensive [ɪk'spensɪv] teuer I
°**expert** ['ekspɜːt] Experte, Expertin
explain sth. to sb. [ɪk'spleɪn] jm. etwas erklären, erläutern II
explanation [ˌeksplə'neɪʃn] Erklärung II
explore [ɪk'splɔː] erkunden, erforschen I
explorer [ɪk'splɔːrə] Entdecker/in, Forscher/in II
expression [ɪk'spreʃn] Ausdruck III 4 (89)
extra ['ekstrə] zusätzlich I
eye [aɪ] Auge I • **She couldn't believe her eyes.** Sie traute ihren Augen kaum. III 2 (48)
°**e-zine** ['iːziːn] elektronisches Magazin, elektronische Zeitschrift

F

face [feɪs] Gesicht I
fact [fækt] Tatsache, Fakt III 1 (15)
factory ['fæktri] Fabrik II
fair [feə] fair, gerecht II
fall [fɔːl], **fell, fallen** fallen, stürzen; hinfallen II • **fall down** runterfallen; hinfallen II • **fall off** herunterfallen (von) II
fallen ['fɔːlən] *siehe* **fall**
family ['fæməli] Familie I • **family tree** (Familien-)Stammbaum I
famous (for) ['feɪməs] berühmt (für, wegen) II
fan [fæn] Fan, Anhänger/in III 1 (17)
fantastic [fæn'tæstɪk] fantastisch, toll I
far [fɑː] weit (entfernt) I • **so far** bis jetzt, bis hierher III 5 (94)
faraway ['fɑːrəweɪ] abgelegen III 2 (32)
farm [fɑːm] Bauernhof, Farm II
farmer ['fɑːmə] Bauer/Bäuerin, Landwirt/in; (Fisch-)Züchter/in III 2 (30)
farmhouse ['fɑːmhaʊs] Bauernhaus III 2 (38)
fashion ['fæʃn] Mode II
fast [fɑːst] schnell II
father ['fɑːðə] Vater I
favourite ['feɪvərɪt] Lieblings- I
my favourite colour meine Lieblingsfarbe I
favourite ['feɪvərɪt] Favorit/in; Liebling III 1 (13)
fear (of) ['fɪə] Furcht, Angst (vor) III 4 (85)
February ['februəri] Februar I
fed [fed] *siehe* **feed**
feed [fiːd], **fed, fed** füttern I
feel [fiːl], **felt, felt** fühlen; sich fühlen II; sich anfühlen II
feeling ['fiːlɪŋ] Gefühl III 2 (35)
feet [fiːt] *Plural von „foot"* I
fell [fel] *siehe* **fall**
felt [felt] *siehe* **feel**
felt tip ['felt tɪp] Filzstift I
female ['fiːmeɪl] Weibchen II
°**female** ['fiːmeɪl] weiblich
ferry ['feri] Fähre III 1 (20/174)
festival ['festɪvl] Fest, Festival II
few [fjuː]: **a few** ein paar, einige II
°**fewer** [fjuːə] weniger
fiddle ['fɪdl] *(infml)* Fiedel, Geige III Intro (7) • **play the fiddle** Geige spielen III Intro (7)
field [fiːld] Feld, Acker, Weide II • **in the field** auf dem Feld II
fight (for) [faɪt], **fought, fought** kämpfen (für, um) III 3 (70)
°**file** [faɪl] (Akten-)Ordner, Hefter
file [faɪl]: **background file** *etwa:* Hintergrundinformation II
grammar file *Grammatikanhang* I • **skills file** *Anhang mit Lern- und Arbeitstechniken* I
°**fill in** [ˌfɪl‿'ɪn]
1. einsetzen
2. ausfüllen
film [fɪlm] Film I • **film star** Filmstar I • °**film crew** [kruː] Film-crew, Filmeteam • °**film researcher** [rɪ'sɜːtʃə] Filmrechercheur/in
film [fɪlm] filmen III 2 (45)
final ['faɪnl] Finale, Endspiel III 3 (54) ► S.183 A football match
final ['faɪnl] letzte(r, s); End- III 3 (54/182)
find [faɪnd], **found, found** finden I
find out (about) herausfinden (über) I
fine [faɪn]
1. gut, ausgezeichnet; in Ordnung II
2. *(gesundheitlich)* gut II
I'm/He's fine. Es geht mir/ihm gut. II
finger ['fɪŋgə] Finger I

finish ['fɪnɪʃ] beenden, zu Ende machen; enden I
fire ['faɪə] Feuer, Brand II
fireman ['faɪəmən] Feuerwehrmann II
firewoman ['faɪəˌwʊmən] Feuerwehrfrau II
first [fɜːst]
1. erste(r, s) I
2. zuerst, als Erstes I
be first der/die Erste sein I • **for the first time** zum ersten Mal II
First Nations die Ersten Nationen *(indianische Ureinwohner/innen Kanadas)* III 4 (73)
fish, *pl* **fish/fishes** [fɪʃ] Fisch I
fish [fɪʃ] fischen, angeln III 4 (73/187)
fisherman ['fɪʃəmən], *pl* **fishermen** ['fɪʃəmən] Angler, Fischer III 4 (81)
fit (-tt-) [fɪt] passen I
°**five-part** [ˌfaɪv 'pɑːt] fünfteilige(r, s)
°**flag** [flæg] Fahne
flash [flæʃ] Lichtblitz III 1 (27)
flat [flæt] Wohnung I
flat [flæt] flach, eben II
flavour ['fleɪvə] Geschmack, Geschmacksrichtung II
flea market ['fliː ˌmɑːkɪt] Flohmarkt III 1 (13)
flew [fluː] *siehe* **fly**
flight [flaɪt] Flug II
floor [flɔː] Fußboden I • **dance floor** Tanzfläche III 4 (76)
flow chart ['fləʊ tʃɑːt] Flussdiagramm I
flower ['flaʊə] Blume; Blüte II
flown [fləʊn] *siehe* **fly**
flu [fluː] Grippe II
flute [fluːt] Querflöte III Intro (11)
fly [flaɪ], **flew, flown** fliegen II
fog [fɒg] Nebel II
foggy ['fɒgi] neblig II
°**fold** [fəʊld] falten, zusammenfalten
folk (music) ['fəʊk ˌmjuːzɪk] Folk *(meist englischsprachige, volkstümliche Musik mit Elementen der Rockmusik)* III Intro (7)
folks [fəʊks] *(infml, besonders AE)* Leute III 5 (98)
follow ['fɒləʊ] folgen; verfolgen I
the following ... die folgenden ... III 5 (94)
°**follow-up question** ['fɒləʊ‿ʌp] zweite Frage, Anschlussfrage
food [fuːd] Essen; Lebensmittel; Futter I
foot [fʊt], *pl* **feet** [fiːt] Fuß I • **on foot** zu Fuß III 1 (20)
football ['fʊtbɔːl] Fußball I • **football boots** Fußballschuhe, -stiefel I • **football pitch** Fußballplatz, -feld II • °**Football Association** [əˌsəʊsi'eɪʃn] *(englischer)* Fußballbund
footballer ['fʊtbɔːlə] Fußballspieler/in III 3 (63)
for [fə, fɔː] für I • **for a moment** einen Moment lang II • **for breakfast/lunch/dinner** zum Frühstück/Mittagessen/Abendbrot I
for example zum Beispiel I • **for his birthday** zu seinem Geburtstag III 3 (69) • **for lots of reasons** aus vielen Gründen I • **for miles** meilenweit II • **for the first time** zum ersten Mal II • **for three days** drei Tage (lang) I • **for years** seit Jahren III 1 (17) • **just for fun** nur zum Spaß I • **What for?** [ˌwɒt 'fɔː] Wofür? II • **What's for homework?** Was haben wir als Hausaufgabe auf? I
foreground ['fɔːgraʊnd] Vordergrund II
°**foreign** ['fɒrən] fremd, ausländisch
forest ['fɒrɪst] Wald II
forget (-tt-) [fə'get], **forgot, forgotten** vergessen III 2 (35)
forgot [fə'gɒt] *siehe* **forget**
forgotten [fə'gɒtn] *siehe* **forget**
fork [fɔːk] Gabel III 1 (27)
form [fɔːm]
1. (Schul-)Klasse I • **form teacher** Klassenlehrer/in I
°**2.** Form
°**form** [fɔːm] bilden
fort [fɔːt] Fort III 3 (65)
°**forward** ['fɔːwəd]: **look forward to sth.** sich auf etwas freuen
fought [fɔːt] *siehe* **fight**
foul [faʊl] foulen III 3 (59)
found [faʊnd] *siehe* **find**
°**found** [faʊnd] gründen
fox [fɒks] Fuchs II
free [friː]
1. frei I • **free time** Freizeit, freie Zeit I • **free-time activities** Freizeitaktivitäten II
2. kostenlos I
French [frentʃ] Französisch I
Friday ['fraɪdeɪ, 'fraɪdi] Freitag I
fridge [frɪdʒ] Kühlschrank I
friend [frend] Freund/in I • **make friends (with)** Freunde finden; sich anfreunden (mit) II
friendly ['frendli] freundlich II
frog [frɒg] Frosch II
from [frəm, frɒm]
1. aus I
2. von I
dresses from the 60s Kleider aus den 60ern / aus den 60er Jahren II • **from all over the UK / England** aus dem gesamten Vereinigten Königreich / aus ganz England III Intro (6) • **from all over the world** aus der ganzen Welt II • °**from memory** auswendig • **from Monday to Friday** von Montag bis Freitag III 2 (33) • **from my point of view** aus meiner Sicht; von meinem Standpunkt aus gesehen II
I'm from ... Ich komme/bin aus ... I • **Where are you from?** Wo kommst du her? I
front [frʌnt]: **at the front** vorne, im vorderen Teil III 2 (46) • **in front of** vor *(räumlich)* I • **to the front** nach vorn I • **front door** [ˌfrʌnt 'dɔː] Wohnungstür, Haustür I
front page Titelseite III 5 (99)
fruit [fruːt] Obst, Früchte; Frucht I
fruit salad Obstsalat I
fry [fraɪ] braten III 1 (16)
full [fʊl] voll I
fun [fʌn] Spaß I • **have fun** Spaß haben, sich amüsieren I • **Have fun!** Viel Spaß! I • **just for fun** nur zum Spaß I • **Riding is fun.** Reiten macht Spaß. I
funny ['fʌni] witzig, komisch I
furniture *(no pl)* ['fɜːnɪtʃə] Möbel III 3 (55)
► S.182 Words without a plural
°**fusion** ['fjuːʒn] *aus der Verschmelzung verschiedener Musikrichtungen entstandener Musikstil*
future ['fjuːtʃə] Zukunft I

G

°**Gaelic** ['geɪlɪk, 'gælɪk] Gälisch, gälisch
°**gala** [gɑːlə] Galaveranstaltung
gallery ['gæləri] Galerie III 3 (58)
game [geɪm] Spiel I • **a game of football** ein Fußballspiel II • °**put sb. back in the game** jn. zurück ins Spiel bringen
°**gap** [gæp] Lücke
garage ['gærɑːʒ] Garage II
garden ['gɑːdn] Garten I
gate [geɪt] Flugsteig III 1 (20/174)
gave [geɪv] *siehe* **give**
gear: sports gear *(no pl)* ['spɔːts gɪə] Sportausrüstung, Sportsachen II
general ['genrəli] allgemeine(r, s) III 2 (39)
generally ['dʒenrəl] im Allgemeinen III 1 (13)
geography [dʒi'ɒgrəfi] Geografie, Erdkunde I
German ['dʒɜːmən] Deutsch; deutsch; Deutsche(r) I
Germany ['dʒɜːməni] Deutschland I

get (-tt-) [get], **got, got**
1. bekommen, kriegen II
2. holen, besorgen II
3. gelangen, (hin)kommen I
4. get angry/hot/... wütend/heiß/... werden II
► S.193 German „werden"
5. get off (the train/bus) (aus dem Zug/Bus) aussteigen I • **get on (the train/bus)** (in den Zug/Bus) einsteigen I
6. get up aufstehen I
I don't get it. Das versteh ich nicht. / Das kapier ich nicht. II
get away from sth./sb. von etwas/jm. weggehen, sich entfernen III 1 (28) • **get dressed** sich anziehen I • **get lost** sich verlaufen III 1 (17) • **get ready (for)** sich fertig machen (für), sich vorbereiten (auf) I • **get sth. right** etwas richtig machen III 4 (76) • **get sth. wrong** etwas falsch machen III 4 (76) • **get things ready** Dinge fertig machen, vorbereiten I
What can I get you? Was kann/darf ich euch/Ihnen bringen? II

getting by in English [ˌgetɪŋ 'baɪ] *etwa:* auf Englisch zurechtkommen I
°**gherkin** ['gɜːkɪn] (Essig-)Gurke
gig [gɪg] *(infml)* Gig, Auftritt III Intro (8) • **do a gig** einen Auftritt haben, ein Konzert geben III Intro (8)
giraffe [dʒə'rɑːf] Giraffe II
girl [gɜːl] Mädchen I
girlfriend ['gɜːlfrend] Freundin III 1 (23)
gist [dʒɪst] das Wesentliche III 1 (13)
give [gɪv], **gave, given** geben I
give sth. back etwas zurückgeben I • °**give a talk** einen Vortrag/ein Referat halten
given ['gɪvn] *siehe* **give**
glass [glɑːs] Glas I • **a glass of water** ein Glas Wasser I
glasses *(pl)* ['glɑːsɪz] (eine) Brille I
gloves *(pl)* [glʌvz] Handschuhe II
glue [gluː] (auf-, ein)kleben II
glue [gluː] Klebstoff I • **glue stick** ['gluː stɪk] Klebestift I
go [gəʊ], **went, gone**
1. gehen I; fahren II
2. go hard/bad/deaf/blind/crazy/... hart/schlecht/taub/blind/verrückt/... werden III 5 (99/193)
► S.193 German „werden"
go abroad ins Ausland gehen/fahren II • **go ahead** in Führung gehen III 3 (59) • **go by car/bike/...** mit dem Auto/Rad/... fahren II
go for a walk spazieren gehen, einen Spaziergang machen II • **go home** nach Hause gehen I • **go on 1.** weitergehen; weiterreden III 1 (12/171); **2.** angehen *(Licht)* III 1 (27)
go on a trip einen Ausflug machen II • **go on holiday** in Urlaub fahren II • **go out** weg-, raus-, ausgehen I • **go riding/shopping/swimming** reiten/einkaufen/schwimmen gehen I • **go skiing** Ski laufen/fahren III 3 (62) • **go surfing** wellenreiten gehen, surfen gehen II • **go to** führen nach *(Straße, Weg)* II • **go to bed** ins Bett gehen I • **go to the cinema** ins Kino gehen II • °**go to war with sb.** mit jm. Krieg führen • **go well** gut (ver)laufen, gutgehen II
go with gehören zu, passen zu III Intro (11) • **Let's go.** Auf geht's! *(wörtlich:* Lass uns gehen.) I
What are you going to do? Was wirst du tun? / Was hast du vor zu tun? I

goal [gəʊl] Tor *(im Sport)* III 3 (56)
score a goal ein Tor schießen, einen Treffer erzielen III 3 (56)
goalkeeper ['gəʊlkiːpə] Torwart, Torfrau III 3 (59)
gold [gəʊld] Gold III 3 (70)
gone [gɒn] *siehe* **go** • **be gone** weg sein, nicht da sein II
good [gʊd]
1. gut I • **Good afternoon.** Guten Tag. *(nachmittags)* I • **Good luck (with ...)!** Viel Glück (bei/mit ...)! I
Good morning. Guten Morgen. I
2. brav II
Goodbye. [ˌgʊd'baɪ] Auf Wiedersehen. I • **say goodbye** sich verabschieden I
°**goods train** ['gʊdz treɪn] Güterzug
gossip ['gɒsɪp] schwatzen, klatschen, tratschen III 2 (35)
got [gɒt] *siehe* **get**
got [gɒt]: **I've got ...** Ich habe ... I
I haven't got a chair. Ich habe keinen Stuhl. I
grab (-bb-) [græb] schnappen, packen III 2 (47)
grammar ['græmə] Grammatik I
grammar file *Grammatikanhang* I • **grammar school** Gymnasium III 2 (33)
grandchild ['græntʃaɪld], *pl* **grandchildren** ['-tʃɪldrən] Enkel/in I
granddaughter ['grændɔːtə] Enkelin II
grandfather ['grænfɑːðə] Großvater I
grandma ['grænmɑː] Oma I
grandmother ['grænmʌðə] Großmutter I
grandpa ['grænpɑː] Opa I
grandparents ['grænpeərənts] Großeltern I
grandson ['grænsʌn] Enkel II
granny ['græni] Oma II
great [greɪt] großartig, toll I
great-grandmother/-father [ˌgreɪt 'grænmʌðə], [ˌgreɪt 'grænfɑːðə] Urgroßmutter/-vater III 2 (32)
green [griːn] grün I
°**greens** *(pl)* [griːnz] (grünes) Gemüse
°**greeting** ['griːtɪŋ] Gruß, Begrüßung
grew [gruː] *siehe* **grow**
grey [greɪ] grau II
ground [graʊnd]
1. (Erd-)Boden III 1 (20)
°**2** (Sport-)Platz
group [gruːp] Gruppe I • **group word** Oberbegriff II
grow [grəʊ], **grew, grown** wachsen II • **grow up** erwachsen werden; aufwachsen III 3 (69)
grown [grəʊn] *siehe* **grow**
grumble ['grʌmbl] murren, nörgeln II
°**guard** [gɑːd]: **Changing of the Guard** Wachablösung III 1 (19)
guess [ges] raten, erraten, schätzen II • **Guess what!** [ˌges 'wɒt] Stell dir vor! / Stellt euch vor! II
guest [gest] Gast I
°**guide** [gaɪd] Fremdenführer/in, Reiseleiter/in
°**guide book** ['gaɪd bʊk] Reiseführer
guinea pig ['gɪni pɪg] Meerschweinchen I
guitar [gɪ'tɑː] Gitarre I • **play the guitar** Gitarre spielen I
guy [gaɪ] Typ, Kerl II • **guys** *(pl)* Leute II

H

had [hæd] *siehe* **have**
°**haggis** ['hægɪs] gefüllter Schafsmagen
hair *(no pl)* [heə] Haar, Haare I
► S.182 Words without a plural
hairdresser ['heədresə] Friseur/in III 2 (45) • **at the hairdresser's** beim Friseur III 2 (45/181)
half [hɑːf], *pl* **halves** [hɑːvz]
1. Hälfte III Intro (11)
2. Halbzeit III 3 (67)
half [hɑːf] halbe(r, s) II • **half an hour** eine halbe Stunde II • **half past 11** halb zwölf (11.30 / 23.30) I
°**an hour and a half** eineinhalb/anderthalb Stunden • **half-time** Halbzeit(pause) III 3 (59)

half-pipe ['hɑ:fpaɪp] Halfpipe *(halbierte Röhre für Inlineskater)* III 3 (62/185)
hall [hɔ:l]
1. Flur, Diele I
2. Halle, Saal III 2 (48) • **community hall** Gemeinschaftshalle, -saal III 2 (47) • **sports hall** Sporthalle III 3 (62)
hamburger ['hæmbɜ:gə] Hamburger I
hamster ['hæmstə] Hamster I
hand [hænd] Hand I • °**by hand** von Hand • **second-hand** gebraucht; aus zweiter Hand III 1 (13)
hang out [,hæŋ_'aʊt], **hung, hung** *(infml)* rumhängen, abhängen III 4 (74)
°**hang up** [,hæŋ_'ʌp], **hung, hung** etwas aufhängen
happen (to) ['hæpən] geschehen, passieren (mit) I
happy ['hæpi] glücklich, froh I
Happy birthday. Herzlichen Glückwunsch zum Geburtstag. I - **happy ending** Happyend II
harbour ['hɑ:bə] Hafen III 1 (20)
hard [hɑ:d] hart; schwer, schwierig II • **work hard** hart arbeiten II
hat [hæt] Hut I
hate [heɪt] hassen, gar nicht mögen I
have [həv, hæv], **had, had** haben, besitzen II • **have an argument** eine Auseinandersetzung haben, sich streiten II • **have a baby** ein Baby/Kind bekommen II • **have a bath** baden, ein Bad nehmen II **have a cold** erkältet sein, eine Erkältung haben II • **have a massage** sich massieren lassen II • **have a sauna** in die Sauna gehen II • **have a shower** (sich) duschen I • **have a sore throat** Halsschmerzen haben II • **have a temperature** Fieber haben II **have breakfast** frühstücken I **have dinner** Abendbrot essen I **have ... for breakfast** ... zum Frühstück essen/trinken I • **have fun** Spaß haben, sich amüsieren I **Have fun!** Viel Spaß! I • **have a good time** sich gut amüsieren III 1 (24) • **have to do** tun müssen I
have got: I've got ... [aɪv 'gɒt] Ich habe ... I • **I haven't got a chair.** ['hævnt gɒt] Ich habe keinen Stuhl. I
he [hi:] er I
head [hed] Kopf I • **nod (your head)** (mit dem Kopf) nicken III 4 (85) • **shake your head** den Kopf schütteln III 4 (85) • °**head of state** Staatsoberhaupt
headache ['hedeɪk] Kopfschmerzen II
°**heading** ['hedɪŋ] Überschrift
headline ['hed,laɪn] Schlagzeile III 5 (99)
headphones *(pl)* ['hedfəʊnz] Kopfhörer III 5 (95)
head teacher [,hed 'ti:tʃə] Schulleiter/in III 2 (45)
healthy ['helθi] gesund II
hear [hɪə], **heard, heard** hören I
heard [hɜ:d] *siehe* **hear**
heart [hɑ:t] Herz I
heavy metal [,hevi 'metl] Heavymetal III 5 (100)
hedgehog ['hedʒhɒg] Igel II
held [held] *siehe* **hold**
helicopter ['helɪkɒptə] Hubschrauber, Helikopter II
Hello. [hə'ləʊ] Hallo. / Guten Tag. I
helmet ['helmɪt] Helm III 1 (26)
help [help] helfen I • **Can I help you?** Kann ich Ihnen helfen? / Was kann ich für Sie tun? *(im Geschäft)* I
help [help] Hilfe I
her [hə, hɜ:]
1. ihr, ihre I
2. sie; ihr I
herb [hɜ:b] (Gewürz-)Kraut III 1 (16)
here [hɪə]
1. hier I
2. hierher I
Here you are. Bitte sehr. / Hier bitte. I
hero ['hɪərəʊ], *pl* **heroes** ['hɪərəʊz] Held, Heldin II
hers [hɜ:z] ihrer, ihre, ihrs II
herself [hɜ:'self] sich III 5 (98)
Hey! [heɪ] Hallo! III Intro (8)
Hi! [haɪ] Hallo! I • **Say hi to your parents for me.** Grüß deine Eltern von mir. I
hid [hɪd] *siehe* **hide**
hidden ['hɪdn] *siehe* **hide**
hide [haɪd], **hid, hidden** sich verstecken; (etwas) verstecken I
high [haɪ] hoch III 1 (15)
°**Highlands: the Highlands** ['haɪləndz] das schottische Hochland °**Highland** *(adj)* Hochland-
highlight ['haɪ,laɪt] Höhepunkt III 2 (39)
°**high-tech companies** [,haɪtek 'kʌmpəniz] Hightech-Firmen
hill [hɪl] Hügel II
hilly ['hɪli] hügelig III 2 (38)
him [hɪm] ihn; ihm I
himself [hɪm'self] sich III 5 (98)
hippo ['hɪpəʊ] Flusspferd II
his [hɪz]
1. sein, seine I
2. seiner, seine, seins II
history ['hɪstri] Geschichte I
hit (-tt-) [hɪt], **hit, hit** schlagen III 5 (100)
hobby ['hɒbi] Hobby I
hockey ['hɒki] Hockey I • **hockey pitch** Hockeyplatz, -feld II **hockey shoes** Hockeyschuhe I
hold [həʊld], **held, held** halten II °**hold up** hochhalten • **hold a competition** einen Wettbewerb veranstalten III 3 (58/183)
hole [həʊl] Loch I
holiday(s) ['hɒlədeɪ] Ferien I **be on holiday** in Urlaub sein II **go on holiday** in Urlaub fahren II **holiday home** Ferienhaus, -wohnung III 2 (31)
home [həʊm] Heim, Zuhause I **at home** daheim, zu Hause I **come home** nach Hause kommen I • **get home** nach Hause kommen I • **go home** nach Hause gehen I
°**homeless** ['həʊmləs] obdachlos
homework *(no pl)* ['həʊmwɜ:k] Hausaufgabe(n) I • **do homework** die Hausaufgabe(n) machen I **What's for homework?** Was haben wir als Hausaufgabe auf? I
► S.182 Words without a plural
Hooray! [hu'reɪ] Hurra! II
°**hop on and off** [hɒp] *(an beliebigen Bushaltestellen)* ein- und aussteigen
hope [həʊp] hoffen I • **I hope so.** Ich hoffe es. II
hope [həʊp] Hoffnung III 3 (56)
horrible ['hɒrəbl] scheußlich, grauenhaft II
horror ['hɒrə] Entsetzen, Grauen, Horror III 5 (99)
horse [hɔ:s] Pferd I
hospital ['hɒspɪtl] Krankenhaus II **He's gone to hospital.** Er ist ins Krankenhaus gegangen. III 1 (12/170) • **He's in hospital.** Er ist im Krankenhaus. III 1 (12/170)
► S.170 Places without articles
hostel ['hɒstl] Herberge, Wohnheim III Intro (8) • **youth hostel** Jugendherberge III Intro (8/169)
hot [hɒt] heiß I • **hot chocolate** heiße Schokolade I • **hot-water bottle** Wärmflasche II
hotel [həʊ'tel] Hotel II
hotline ['hɒtlaɪn] Hotline II
hour ['aʊə] Stunde I • **half an hour** eine halbe Stunde II • °**an hour and a half** eineinhalb Stunden,

anderthalb Stunden • **a 24-hour supermarket** ein Supermarkt, der 24 Stunden geöffnet ist III 4 (80/189) **a two-hour operation** eine zweistündige Operation III 4 (80/189)

house [haʊs] Haus I • **at the Shaws' house** im Haus der Shaws / bei den Shaws zu Hause I

how [haʊ] wie I • **How are you?** Wie geht es dir/Ihnen/euch? II **How do you know ...?** Woher weißt/kennst du ...? I • **how many?** wie viele? I • **how much?** wie viel? I • **How much is/are ...?** Was kostet/kosten ...? / Wie viel kostet/kosten ...? I • **How old are you?** Wie alt bist du? I • **How was ...?** Wie war ...? I

huge [hjuːdʒ] riesig, sehr groß III 2 (30)
► S.177 big – large – huge

°**human rights** [ˌhjuːmn 'raɪts] Menschenrechte

hundred ['hʌndrəd] hundert I

hung [hʌŋ] *siehe* **hang**

hungry ['hʌŋgri] hungrig I • **be hungry** Hunger haben, hungrig sein I

hunt [hʌnt] Jagd III 4 (73/187)

hunt [hʌnt] jagen III 4 (73)

hurry ['hʌri] eilen; sich beeilen II • **hurry up** sich beeilen I

hurry ['hʌri]: **be in a hurry** in Eile sein, es eilig haben I

hurt [hɜːt], **hurt, hurt** wehtun; verletzen I

hurt [hɜːt] verletzt II

husband ['hʌzbənd] Ehemann II

hutch [hʌtʃ] (Kaninchen-)Stall I

I

I [aɪ] ich I • **I'm** [aɪm] ich bin I **I'm from ...** Ich komme aus ... / Ich bin aus ... I • **I'm ... years old.** Ich bin ... Jahre alt. I • **I'm sorry.** Entschuldigung. / Tut mir leid. I

ice [aɪs] Eis II

ice cream [ˌaɪs 'kriːm] (Speise-)Eis I

ice hockey ['aɪs hɒki] Eishockey III Intro (11)

ice rink ['aɪs rɪŋk] Schlittschuhbahn II

idea [aɪ'dɪə] Idee, Einfall I

if [ɪf]
1. wenn, falls II
2. ob II

ill [ɪl] krank II

°**imaginary** [ɪ'mædʒɪnəri] imaginär *(nicht wirklich, nur vorgestellt)*

imagine sth. [ɪ'mædʒɪn] sich etwas vorstellen III 2 (32)

imitate ['ɪmɪteɪt] nachmachen III 4 (75)

°**immigration** [ˌɪmɪ'greɪʃn] Immigration, Einwanderung

important [ɪm'pɔːtnt] wichtig II

impossible [ɪm'pɒsəbl] unmöglich II

impressive [ɪm'presɪv] beeindruckend, eindrucksvoll III 2 (39)

improve [ɪm'pruːv] (sich) verbessern III 4 (85)

in [ɪn] in I • **in 2050** im Jahr 2050 II • **in ... Street** in der ...straße I • **in English** auf Englisch I • **in front of** vor *(räumlich)* I • **in here** hier drinnen I • **in next to no time** im Nu III 2 (47) • **in other places** an anderen Orten, anderswo III 1 (13) **in the afternoon** nachmittags, am Nachmittag I • **in the country** auf dem Land II • °**in the end** schließlich, am Ende • **in the evening** abends, am Abend I • **in the field** auf dem Feld II • **in the morning** am Morgen, morgens I **in the photo** auf dem Foto I • **in the picture** auf dem Bild I • **in there** dort drinnen I • **in the sky** am Himmel II • **in the world** auf der Welt II • **in the yard** auf dem Hof II • **in time** [ɪn 'taɪm] rechtzeitig II

infinitive [ɪn'fɪnətɪv] Infinitiv *(Grundform des Verbs)* I

Indian ['ɪndiən]
1. Inder/in I
°**2.** Indianer/in

indirect speech [ˌɪndə'rekt] indirekte Rede III 4 (77)

industrial [ɪn'dʌstriəl] industriell III 3 (65)

industry ['ɪndəstri] Industrie III 3 (65)

information (about/on) *(no pl)* [ˌɪnfə'meɪʃn] Information(en) (über) I
► S.182 Words without a plural

injury ['ɪndʒəri] Verletzung II

inside [ˌɪn'saɪd]
1. innen (drin), drinnen I
2. nach drinnen II
3. inside the car ins Auto (hinein), ins Innere des Autos II

install [ɪn'stɔːl] installieren, einrichten II

installation [ˌɪnstə'leɪʃn] Installation, Einrichtung II

instant message [ˌɪnstənt 'mesɪdʒ] *Nachricht, die man im Internet austauscht (in Echtzeit)* III 2 (32)

instructions *(pl)* [ɪn'strʌkʃnz] (Gebrauchs-)Anweisung(en), Anleitung(en) II

instrument ['ɪnstrəmənt] Instrument III Intro (8)

°**insulin** ['ɪnsjəlɪn] Insulin

interested: **be interested (in)** [ɪntrəstɪd] interessiert sein (an), sich interessieren (für) III 3 (70)

interesting ['ɪntrəstɪŋ] interessant I

international [ˌɪntə'næʃnəl] international II

internet ['ɪntənet] Internet I • **surf the internet** im Internet surfen II

°**interview** ['ɪntəvjuː] Interview

into ['ɪntə, 'ɪntʊ]
1. in ... (hinein) I
2. be into sth. *(infml)* etwas mögen III Intro (7)

introduction (to) [ˌɪntrə'dʌkʃn] Einführung (in) III Intro (6)

°**Inuit** ['ɪnuɪt, 'ɪnjuɪt] Inuit

invent [ɪn'vent] erfinden III 5 (100/194)

inventor [ɪn'ventə] Erfinder/in III 5 (100)

invitation (to) [ˌɪnvɪ'teɪʃn] Einladung (zu) I

invite (to) [ɪn'vaɪt] einladen (zu) I

°**Irish** ['aɪrɪʃ] irisch

irregular [ɪ'regjələ] unregelmäßig III 5 (103)

is [ɪz] ist I

island ['aɪlənd] Insel II

°**issue** ['ɪʃuː] (Streit-)Frage, Thema, Angelegenheit

it [ɪt] er/sie/es I • **It's £1.** Er/Sie/Es kostet 1 Pfund. I

IT [ˌaɪ 'tiː], **information technology** [tek'nɒlədʒi] IT (Informationstechnologie) II

itself [ɪt'self] sich III 5 (98)

°**italics** [ɪ'tælɪks] Kursivschrift

°**italics: in italics** [ɪ'tælɪks] kursiv; in Kursivschrift

its [ɪts] sein/seine; ihr/ihre I

J

jacket ['dʒækɪt] Jacke, Jackett II

January ['dʒænjuəri] Januar I

°**javelin** ['dʒævlɪn] Speerwerfen

jazz [dʒæz] Jazz III Intro (6)

jeans *(pl)* [dʒiːnz] Jeans I

job [dʒɒb] Aufgabe, Job I • **do a good job** gute Arbeit leisten II

join sb./sth. [dʒɔɪn] sich jm. anschließen; bei jm./etwas mitmachen II

join in [ˌdʒɔɪn‿'ɪn] mitmachen III 4 (75)

joke [dʒəʊk] Witz I
joke [dʒəʊk] scherzen, Witze machen II
journey ['dʒɜ:ni] Reise, Fahrt III 2 (39)
judo ['dʒu:dəʊ] Judo I • **do judo** Judo machen I
jug [dʒʌg] Krug I • **a jug of milk** ein Krug Milch I
juice [dʒu:s] Saft I
July [dʒu'laɪ] Juli I
jumblesale ['dʒʌmblseɪl] Wohltätigkeitsbasar I
jump [dʒʌmp] springen II
June [dʒu:n] Juni I
junior ['dʒu:niə] Junioren-, Jugend- I
just [dʒʌst]
1. (einfach) nur, bloß I
2. gerade (eben), soeben II
just then genau in dem Moment; gerade dann II
3. **just like you** genau wie du II
4. einfach III 1 (27)
► S.176 just

K

kangaroo [ˌkæŋgə'ru:] Känguru II
keep [ki:p], **kept, kept** [kept] (be)halten; aufbewahren III 5 (96)
keep sth. warm/cool/open/... etwas warm/kühl/offen/... halten II • **keep in touch** in Verbindung bleiben, Kontakt halten III Intro (11)
keeper ['ki:pə] Torwart, Torfrau III 3 (59)
kept [kept] *siehe* **keep**
key [ki:] Schlüssel I • **key word** Stichwort, Schlüsselwort I
keyboard ['ki:bɔ:d] Keyboard *(elektronisches Tasteninstrument)* III Intro (7)
kid [kɪd] Kind, Jugendliche(r) I
kill [kɪl] töten I
kilogram ['kɪləgræm], **kilo** ['ki:ləʊ] **(kg)** Kilogramm, Kilo III 4 (80)
a kilogram of oranges ein Kilogramm Orangen III 4 (80/189) • **a 150-kilogram bear** ein 150 Kilogramm schwerer Bär III 4 (80/189)
kilometre (km) ['kɪləmi:tə] Kilometer III 2 (43) • **a ten-kilometre walk** eine Zehn-Kilometer-Wanderung III 4 (80/189) • **square kilometre** Quadratkilometer III 4 (72)
°**kilt** [kɪlt] Kilt, Schottenrock
kind of [kaɪnd] Art (von) III Intro (6) • **kind of scary** *(infml)* [kaɪnd əv] irgendwie unheimlich III 1 (26)
king [kɪŋ] König I
kitchen ['kɪtʃɪn] Küche I
kite [kaɪt] Drachen I
knee [ni:] Knie I
knew [nju:] *siehe* **know**
knife [naɪf], *pl* **knives** [naɪvz] Messer III 1 (27)
knock (on) [nɒk] (an)klopfen (an) I
know [nəʊ], **knew, known**
1. wissen I
2. kennen I
How do you know ...? Woher weißt du ...?/Woher kennst du ...? I
know about sth. von etwas wissen; über etwas Bescheid wissen II • **..., you know.** ..., wissen Sie. / ..., weißt du. I • **You know what, Sophie?** Weißt du was, Sophie? I
known [nəʊn] *siehe* **know**

L

°**label** ['leɪbl] beschriften, etikettieren
°**lacrosse** [lə'krɒs] Lacrosse *(Sportart)*
laid [leɪd] *siehe* **lay**
lain [leɪn] *siehe* **lie**
lake [leɪk] (Binnen-)See II
lamp [læmp] Lampe I
land [lænd] landen II
land [lænd] Land III 1 (20) • **on land** auf dem Land III 1 (20)
°**landscape** ['lændskeɪp] Landschaft
lane [leɪn] Gasse, Weg III 1 (13)
language ['læŋgwɪdʒ] Sprache I
large [lɑ:dz] groß III 2 (30/177)
► S.177 big – large – huge
lasagne [lə'zænjə] Lasagne I
last [lɑ:st] letzte(r, s) I • **the last day** der letzte Tag I • **at last** endlich, schließlich I
last-minute: a last-minute shot [ˌlɑ:st 'mɪnɪt] ein Schuss in der letzten Minute III 3 (59)
late [leɪt] spät; zu spät I • **be late** zu spät sein/kommen I • **Sorry, I'm late.** Entschuldigung, dass ich zu spät bin/komme. I
later ['leɪtə] später I
latest ['leɪtɪst] neueste(r, s) III 4 (74)
laugh [lɑ:f] lachen I • **laugh out loud** laut lachen II
laughter ['lɑ:ftə] Gelächter II
lay the table [leɪ], **laid, laid** den Tisch decken I
lay [leɪ] *siehe* **lie**
°**layout** ['leɪaʊt] Layout
°**leaf**, *pl* **leaves** *oder (selten)* **leafs** [li:f] Blatt
°**league** [li:g] Liga
learn [lɜ:n] lernen I • **learn about sth.** etwas über etwas erfahren, etwas über etwas herausfinden II
least: at least [ət 'li:st] zumindest, wenigstens I
leather ['leðə] Leder III 5 (96)
leave [li:v], **left, left**
1. (weg)gehen; abfahren II
2. verlassen II
3. zurücklassen II
left [left] *siehe* **leave** • **be left** übrig sein II
left [left] linke(r, s) I • **look left** nach links schauen I • **on the left** links, auf der linken Seite I • **to the left** nach links III 2 (45) • **turn left** (nach) links abbiegen II
°**the left-hand column** die linke Spalte
leg [leg] Bein I
leisure centre ['leʒə sentə] Freizeitzentrum, -park II
lemonade [ˌlemə'neɪd] Limonade I
lend sb. sth. [lend], **lent, lent** jm. etwas leihen II
lent [lent] *siehe* **lend**
lentil ['lentəl] Linse *(Hülsenfrucht)* III 1 (16)
leotard ['li:ətɑ:d] Gymnastikanzug; Turnanzug III 3 (56)
lesson ['lesn] (Unterrichts-)Stunde I • **lessons** *(pl)* Unterricht I
let [let], **let, let** lassen II • **Let's ...** Lass uns ... / Lasst uns ... I • **Let's go.** Auf geht's! *(wörtlich:* Lass uns gehen.) I • **Let's look at the list.** Sehen wir uns die Liste an. / Lasst uns die Liste ansehen. I • **let sb. do sth.** jm. erlauben, etwas zu tun; zulassen, dass jd. etwas tut III 2 (35)
letter ['letə]
1. Buchstabe I • **capital letter** Großbuchstabe III 5 (104) • **small letter** Kleinbuchstabe III 5 (104/194)
2. **letter (to)** ['letə] Brief (an) II
lettuce ['letɪs] (Kopf-)Salat II
library ['laɪbrəri] Bibliothek, Bücherei I
°**lie** (*-ing form:* **lying**) [laɪ] **(lied, lied)** lügen
°**lie** (*-ing form:* **lying**) [laɪ], **lay, lain** liegen
life [laɪf], *pl* **lives** [laɪvz] Leben I
way of life Lebensart III 4 (73)
lift [lɪft] Fahrstuhl, Aufzug II
light [laɪt] Licht III 1 (28)
like [laɪk]
1. wie I • **just like you** genau wie du II • °**like this** so • **What was the weather like?** Wie war das Wetter? II
2. *(infml)* **als ob** III 1 (17)
like [laɪk] mögen, gernhaben I
like sth. better etwas lieber mögen II • **like sth. very much**

etwas sehr mögen II • **I like swimming/dancing/...** Ich schwimme/tanze/... gern. I • **I'd like ... (= I would like ...)** Ich hätte gern ... / Ich möchte gern ... I • **I'd like to go (= I would like to go)** Ich würde gern gehen / Ich möchte gehen I • **I wouldn't like to go** Ich würde nicht gern gehen / Ich möchte nicht gehen I • **Would you like ...?** Möchtest du ...? / Möchten Sie ...? I

°**likely** ['laɪkli] wahrscheinlich

limit ['lɪmɪt] Begrenzung, Beschränkung III 4 (80) • **speed limit** Geschwindigkeitsbegrenzung, Geschwindigkeitsbeschränkung III 4 (80)

line [laɪn]
1. Zeile II
2. (U-Bahn-)Linie III 1 (14)

link [lɪŋk] verbinden, verknüpfen I

link [lɪŋk] Verbindung III 4 (73/187)

linking word ['lɪŋkɪŋ wɜːd] Bindewort II

lion ['laɪən] Löwe II

list [lɪst] auflisten, aufzählen II

list [lɪst] Liste I

listen (to) ['lɪsn] zuhören; sich etwas anhören I • **listen for sth.** auf etwas horchen, achten III 1 (13)

listener ['lɪsnə] Zuhörer/in II

little ['lɪtl] klein I

live [lɪv] leben, wohnen I

live [laɪv]: **live concert** Livekonzert III 5 (100) • **live music** Livemusik II

lives [laɪvz] *Plural von „life"* I

living room ['lɪvɪŋ ruːm; rʊm] Wohnzimmer I

load [ləʊd] beladen III 3 (58)

local ['ləʊkl] örtlich, Lokal-; am/vom Ort III 4 (75)

location [ləʊ'keɪʃn] (Einsatz-)Ort, Platz III 3 (62/184)

loch [lɒx] (Binnen-)See in Schottland III 2 (43)

lock [lɒk] Schleuse III 1 (13)

°**locomotive** [ləʊkə'məʊtɪv] Lokomotive

lock [lɒk] abschließen, zuschließen I • **lock up** abschließen II

logo ['ləʊgəʊ] Logo, Markenzeichen III 2 (32)

long [lɒŋ] lang I • **a long way (from)** weit entfernt (von) I • **a long time** lange III 1 (13)

look [lʊk]
1. schauen, gucken I
2. **look different/great/old** anders/toll/alt aussehen I • **look after sth./sb.** sich um etwas/jn. kümmern; auf etwas/jn. aufpassen II • **look at** ansehen, anschauen I • **look at sth. closely** etwas genau anschauen III 1 (26) • **look for** suchen II • °**look forward to sth.** sich auf etwas freuen • **look left and right** nach links und rechts schauen I • **look around/round** sich umsehen I • **look up (from)** hochsehen, aufschauen (von) II • **look up words** Wörter nachschlagen III 1 (16)

lose [luːz], **lost, lost** verlieren II

lost [lɒst] *siehe* **lose** • **get lost** sich verlaufen III 1 (17)

lot [lɒt]: **a lot (of), lots of** eine Menge, viel, viele I / II • **He likes her a lot.** Er mag sie sehr. I • **lots more** viel mehr I • **Thanks a lot!** Vielen Dank! I

loud [laʊd] laut I

love [lʌv] lieben, sehr mögen I
love sth. very much etwas sehr lieben II

love [lʌv]
1. Liebe II • **Love ...** Liebe Grüße, ... *(Grußformel am Ende eines Briefes)* I
2. „Liebes", „Liebling" III 2 (33)

lovely ['lʌvli] schön, hübsch, wunderbar II

°**lover** ['lʌvə] Liebende/r

luck [lʌk]: **Good luck (with ...)!** Viel Glück (bei/mit ...)! I

luckily ['lʌkɪli] zum Glück, glücklicherweise II

lucky: **be lucky** ['lʌki] Glück haben III 2 (38)

lunch [lʌntʃ] Mittagessen I • **for lunch** zum Mittagessen III 1 (16)
lunch break Mittagspause I
lunchtime ['lʌntʃtaɪm] Mittagszeit III 1 (17)

lyrics *(pl)* ['lɪrɪks] Liedtext(e) III 4 (75)

M

machine [mə'ʃiːn] Maschine, Gerät II

mad [mæd] verrückt I • **mad about** verrückt nach III Intro (11)

made [meɪd] *siehe* **make**

made: **to be made of sth.** aus etwas (gemacht) sein III 5 (96)

magazine [ˌmægə'ziːn] Zeitschrift, Magazin I

mail sb. [meɪl] jn. anmailen II
mail sb. sth. jm. etwas schicken, senden *(vor allem per E-Mail)* III Intro (11)

main [meɪn] Haupt- III 2 (35)

make [meɪk], **made, made** machen; bauen I • **make a call** ein Telefongespräch führen, telefonieren II
make a deal ein Abkommen/eine Abmachung treffen III 3 (58)
make a mess alles durcheinanderbringen, alles in Unordnung bringen I • °**make comparisons** Vergleiche anstellen, vergleichen
make friends (with) Freunde finden; sich anfreunden (mit) II
°**make notes** (sich) Notizen machen • **make sb. sth.** jn. zu etwas machen III 5 (97)

make-up ['meɪkʌp] Make-up II

male [meɪl] Männchen II

mall [mɔːl, *BE auch* mæl] (großes) Einkaufszentrum III 4 (75)

man [mæn], *pl* **men** [men] Mann I

manager ['mænədʒə] Manager/in III 5 (94)

many ['meni] viele I • **how many?** wie viele? I

map [mæp] Landkarte, Stadtplan II

°**maple** ['meɪpl] Ahorn

March [mɑːtʃ] März I

mark [mɑːk]: **quotation marks** Anführungszeichen, -striche III 5 (105)

mark sth. (up) [ˌmɑːk_'ʌp] etwas markieren, kennzeichnen II

market ['mɑːkɪt] Markt II

marmalade ['mɑːməleɪd] Orangenmarmelade I

married (to) ['mærɪd] verheiratet (mit) I

marry ['mæri] heiraten III 4 (81)

massage ['mæsɑːʒ] Massage II
have a massage sich massieren lassen II

match [mætʃ] Spiel, Wettkampf I

°**match sth. (to sth.)** [mætʃ] etwas zuordnen (zu etwas)

material [mə'tɪəriəl] Material, Stoff II

maths [mæθs] Mathematik I

matter ['mætə]: **What's the matter?** Was ist los? / Was ist denn? II

may [meɪ] dürfen I

May [meɪ] Mai I

maybe ['meɪbi] vielleicht I

me [miː] mir; mich I • **Me too.** Ich auch. I • **more than me** mehr als ich II • **That's me.** Das bin ich. I
Why me? Warum ich? I

meal [miːl] Mahlzeit, Essen III 1 (16)
set meal Menü III 1 (16)

mean [miːn], **meant, meant**
1. bedeuten II
2. meinen, sagen wollen I

meaning ['miːnɪŋ] Bedeutung I

meant [ment] *siehe* **mean**

meat [miːt] Fleisch I

medal ['medl] Medaille III 3 (69)
media *(pl)* ['mi:diə] Medien III 2 (32)
mediation [ˌmi:di'eɪʃn] Vermittlung, Sprachmittlung, Mediation II
medium ['mi:diəm] mittel-, mittlere(r,s); mittelgroß III 1 (16)
meet [mi:t], **met, met**
1. treffen; kennenlernen I
2. sich treffen I
°**memorize** ['meməraɪz] auswendig lernen
°**memory: from memory** ['meməri] auswendig
men [men] *Plural von „man“* I
menu ['menju:] Speisekarte; Menü *(Computer)* III 1 (16)
mess [mes]**: make a mess** alles durcheinanderbringen, alles in Unordnung bringen I
message: instant message [ˌɪnstənt 'mesɪdʒ] *Nachricht, die man im Internet austauscht (in Echtzeit)* III 2 (32)
met [met] *siehe* **meet**
°**method** ['meθəd] Methode, Art und Weise
°**Métis** ['meiti] Métis *(gemischte ethnische Gruppe in Kanada)*
metre ['mi:tə] Meter II
mice [maɪs] *Plural von „mouse“* I
microphone ['maɪkrəfəʊn] Mikrofon III 5 (95)
middle (of) ['mɪdl] Mitte; Mittelteil I
might [maɪt]**: you might need help** du könntest (vielleicht) Hilfe brauchen III 2 (45)
mild [maɪld] mild III 1 (16)
mile [maɪl] Meile *(= ca. 1,6 km)* II
for miles meilenweit II
milk [mɪlk] Milch I
milkshake ['mɪlkʃeɪk] Milchshake I
million ['mɪljən] Million III 2 (43)
mime [maɪm] vorspielen, pantomimisch darstellen II
mind [maɪnd]**: Mind your own business.** Das geht dich nichts an! / Kümmere dich um deine eigenen Angelegenheiten! II • **Never mind.** [ˌnevə 'maɪnd] Kümmere dich nicht drum. / Macht nichts. II
mind map ['maɪnd mæp] Mindmap („Gedankenkarte“, „Wissensnetz“) I
mine [maɪn] meiner, meine, meins II
°**minority** [maɪ'nɒrɪti] Minderheit
mints *(pl)* [mɪnts] Pfefferminzbonbons I
minute ['mɪnɪt] Minute I • **Wait a minute.** Warte mal! / Moment mal! II • **a 30-minute ride** eine 30-minütige Fahrt III 4 (80/189)

mirror ['mɪrə] Spiegel II
Miss White [mɪs] Frau White *(unverheiratet)* I
miss [mɪs]
1. vermissen II
2. verpassen II
Miss a turn. Einmal aussetzen. II
missing ['mɪsɪŋ]**: be missing** fehlen II • °**the missing information/ words** die fehlenden Informationen/Wörter
mistake [mɪ'steɪk] Fehler I
mix [mɪks] mischen, mixen III 2 (32) • °**mix with** sich vermischen (mit) • °**mix up** durcheinanderbringen • °**mixed** gemischt, unterschiedlich
mixture ['mɪkstʃə] Mischung III Intro (9)
mobile (phone) ['məʊbaɪl] Mobiltelefon, Handy I
model ['mɒdl] Modell(-flugzeug, -schiff usw.) I; (Foto-)Modell II
°**modern** ['mɒdn] modern
mole [məʊl] Maulwurf II
mom [mɑ:m] *(AE)* Mutti, Mama; Mutter III 1 (16)
moment ['məʊmənt] Augenblick, Moment I • **at the moment** im Moment, gerade, zurzeit I • **for a moment** einen Moment lang II
Monday ['mʌndeɪ, 'mʌndi] Montag I • **Monday morning** Montagmorgen I
money ['mʌni] Geld I • **Money doesn't grow on trees.** *Redensart:* Geld wächst nicht auf Bäumen; Geld liegt nicht auf der Straße. III 4 (74)
monitor ['mɒnɪtə] Bildschirm, Monitor III 5 (95)
monkey ['mʌŋki] Affe II
monster ['mɒnstə] Monster, Ungeheuer III 2 (43)
month [mʌnθ] Monat I
moon [mu:n] Mond II
more [mɔ:] mehr I • **lots more** viel mehr I • **more boring (than)** langweiliger (als) II • **more quickly (than)** schneller (als) II **more than me** mehr als ich II **no more music** keine Musik mehr I • **not (...) any more** nicht mehr II • **one more** noch ein(e), ein(e) weitere(r, s) I
morning ['mɔ:nɪŋ] Morgen, Vormittag I • **in the morning** morgens, am Morgen I • **Monday morning** Montagmorgen I • **on Friday morning** freitagmorgens, am Freitagmorgen I
mosque [mɒsk] Moschee III 1 (16)

most [məʊst] (der/die/das) meiste ...; am meisten II • **most people** die meisten Leute I • **(the) most boring ...** der/die/das langweiligste ...; am langweiligsten II
motel [məʊ'tel] Motel III 4 (80)
mother ['mʌðə] Mutter I
mountain ['maʊntən] Berg II
mouse [maʊs], *pl* **mice** [maɪs] Maus I
mouth [maʊθ] Mund I
move [mu:v]
1. bewegen; sich bewegen II
Move back one space. Geh ein Feld zurück. II • **Move on one space.** Geh ein Feld vor. II
2. move (to) umziehen (nach, in) II • **move in** einziehen II • **move out** ausziehen II
movement ['mu:vmənt] Bewegung II
MP3 player [ˌempi:'θri: ˌpleɪə] MP3-Spieler I
Mr ... ['mɪstə] Herr ... I
Mrs ... ['mɪsɪz] Frau ... I
Ms ... [mɪz, məz] Frau ... II
much [mʌtʃ] viel I • **how much?** wie viel? I • **How much is/are ...?** Was kostet/kosten ...? / Wie viel kostet/kosten ...? I • **like/love sth. very much** etwas sehr mögen/ sehr lieben II • **Thanks very much!** Danke sehr! / Vielen Dank! II
muesli ['mju:zli] Müsli I
°**multicultural** [ˌmʌlti'kʌltʃərəl] multikulturell
mum [mʌm] Mama, Mutti; Mutter I
°**mummy** [mʌmi] Mumie
murderer ['mɜ:dərə] Mörder/in III 1 (26)
murder ['mɜ:də] (er)morden III 1 (26)
murder ['mɜ:də] Mord III 1 (26)
museum [mju'zi:əm] Museum I
music ['mju:zɪk]
1. Musik I • **Music is for dancing.** *etwa:* Musik ist zum Tanzen da. III 3 (56)
2. Noten III 5 (96) • **I can read music.** Ich kann Noten lesen. III 5 (96/192)
musical ['mju:zɪkl] Musical I
musician [mju:'zɪʃn] Musiker/in III Intro (6)
must [mʌst] müssen I
mustn't do ['mʌsnt] nicht tun dürfen II
my [maɪ] mein/e I • **My name is ...** Ich heiße ... / Mein Name ist ... I
It's my turn. Ich bin dran / an der Reihe. I

myself [maɪ'self] mir/mich III 5 (98)
mystery ['mɪstri] Rätsel, Geheimnis II

N

name [neɪm] Name I • **My name is ...** Ich heiße ... / Mein Name ist ... I • **What's your name?** Wie heißt du? I • **call sb. names** jn. mit Schimpfwörtern hänseln, jm. Schimpfwörter nachrufen III 2 (35)
name [neɪm] nennen; benennen II
nation ['neɪʃn] Nation III 4 (73)
the First Nations die Ersten Nationen *(indianische Ureinwohner/innen Kanadas)* III 4 (73)
national ['næʃnəl] national, National- III Intro (6)
natural ['nætʃrəl] natürlich, Natur- II
°**nature** ['neɪtʃə] Natur
near [nɪə] in der Nähe von, nahe (bei) I
neat [ni:t]
1. gepflegt II • **neat and tidy** schön ordentlich II
2. *(AE, infml)* großartig, toll, klasse III 1 (17)
°**necessary** ['nesəsəri] nötig, notwendig
need [ni:d] brauchen, benötigen I
needn't do ['ni:dnt] nicht tun müssen, nicht zu tun brauchen II
neighbour ['neɪbə] Nachbar/in I
nervous ['nɜ:vəs] nervös, aufgeregt I
°**net** [net] Netz
°**network** ['netwɜ:k] (Wörter-)Netz
never ['nevə] nie, niemals I
Never mind. Kümmere dich nicht drum. / Macht nichts. II
new [nju:] neu I
news *(no pl)* [nju:z] Nachrichten I
► S.182 Words without a plural
newspaper ['nju:speɪpə] Zeitung I
next [nekst]**: be next** der/die Nächste sein I • **the next day** am nächsten Tag I • **the next photo** das nächste Foto I • **What have we got next?** Was haben wir als Nächstes? I
next to [nekst] neben I
nice [naɪs] schön, nett I • **nice and cool/clean/...** schön kühl/sauber/... I • **Nice to meet you.** Nett, dich/euch/Sie kennenzulernen. III Intro (10)
night [naɪt] Nacht, später Abend I
at night nachts, in der Nacht I
on Friday night freitagnachts, Freitagnacht I
nightclub ['naɪtklʌb] Nachtklub III 5 (101)
nil [nɪl] null III 3 (56/183)
► S.183 A football match
no [nəʊ] nein I
no [nəʊ] kein, keine I • **no more music** keine Musik mehr I • **No way!** [ˌnəʊ 'weɪ] Auf keinen Fall! / Kommt nicht in Frage! II; Was du nicht sagst! / Das kann nicht dein Ernst sein! III 4 (77)
no., *pl* **nos.** ['nʌmbə] Nr. III 1 (29)
nobody ['nəʊbədi] niemand II
nod (-dd-) [nɒd] nicken (mit) II
nod (your head) (mit dem Kopf) nicken III 4 (85)
noise [nɔɪz] Geräusch; Lärm I
noisy ['nɔɪzi] laut, lärmend II
no one ['nəʊ wʌn] niemand III 4 (75/188)
north [nɔ:θ] Norden; nach Norden; nördlich II • **northbound** ['nɔ:θbaʊnd] Richtung Norden III 1 (14/172) • **north-east** [ˌnɔ:θ'i:st] Nordosten; nach Nordosten; nordöstlich II • **northern** ['nɔ:ðən] nördlich, Nord- III Intro (9)
north-west [ˌnɔ:θ'west] Nordwesten; nach Nordwesten; nordwestlich II
nose [nəʊz] Nase I
not [nɒt] nicht I • **not (...) any** kein, keine I • **not (...) any more** nicht mehr II • **not (...) anybody** niemand II • **not (...) anything** nichts II • **not (...) anywhere** nirgendwo(hin) II • **not (...) either** auch nicht II • **not (...) yet** noch nicht II
note [nəʊt]
1. Mitteilung, Notiz I • **take notes (on)** sich Notizen machen (über, zu) I • °**make notes** (sich) Notizen machen
2. Ton III 5 (96)
nothing ['nʌθɪŋ] nichts II
°**notice** ['nəʊtɪs] Notiz, Mitteilung
°**novel** ['nɒvəl] Roman
°**novelist** ['nɒvəlɪst] Romanautor/in
November [nəʊ'vembə] November I
now [naʊ] nun, jetzt I • **(and) now for ...** und jetzt ... *(kündigt ein neues Thema an)* III 2 (45) • **now and again** ab und zu, von Zeit zu Zeit III 3 (68)
number ['nʌmbə] Zahl, Ziffer, Nummer I
nut [nʌt] Nuss III 1 (16)

O

o [əʊ] null I
o'clock [ə'klɒk]**: eleven o'clock** elf Uhr I
°**och** [ɒx] ach *(besonders in Schottland und Irland gebräuchlich)*
October [ɒk'təʊbə] Oktober I
°**odd: Which word is the odd one out?** [ˌɒd ˌwʌn 'aʊt] Welches Wort passt/gehört nicht dazu?
of [əv, ɒv] von I • **of the summer holidays** der Sommerferien I • **a kilogram of oranges** ein Kilogramm Orangen III 4 (80/189)
of course [əv 'kɔ:s] natürlich, selbstverständlich I
off [ɒf]**: take 10 c off** 10 Cent abziehen I
°**official** [ə'fɪʃl] offiziell
often ['ɒfn] oft, häufig I
Oh dear! Oje! II
Oh well ... [əʊ 'wel] Na ja ... / Na gut ... I
°**oil** [ɔɪl] Öl
OK [əʊ'keɪ] okay, gut, in Ordnung I
old [əʊld] alt I • **How old are you?** Wie alt bist du? I • **I'm ... years old.** Ich bin ... Jahre alt. I
oldie *(infml)* ['əʊldi] Oldie III 4 (83)
on [ɒn]
1. auf I
2. weiter III 1 (12)
3. *(Radio, Licht usw.)* an, eingeschaltet II • **go on** angehen III 1 (27) • **on 13th June** am 13. Juni I • **on foot** zu Fuß III 1 (20) • **on Friday** am Freitag I • **on Friday afternoon** freitagnachmittags, am Freitagnachmittag I • **on Friday evening** freitagabends, am Freitagabend I • **on Friday morning** freitagmorgens, am Freitagmorgen I • **on Friday night** freitagnachts, Freitagnacht I • **on his street** in seiner Straße III 4 (76) • **on the beach** am Strand II • **on the board** an die Tafel I • **on the left** links, auf der linken Seite I • **on the phone** am Telefon I • **on the plane** im Flugzeug II • **on the radio** im Radio I • **on the right** rechts, auf der rechten Seite I • **on the train** im Zug I • °**on time** pünktlich • **on TV** im Fernsehen I • **What page are we on?** Auf welcher Seite sind wir? I • **be on holiday** in Urlaub sein II • **go on holiday** in Urlaub fahren II
straight on [streɪt‿'ɒn] geradeaus weiter II
► S.171 on („weiter")

°**on and off: hop on and off** [hɒp] *(an beliebigen Bushaltestellen)* ein- und aussteigen
once [wʌns] einmal III 2 (32) • **once/twice a week** (einmal/zweimal) pro Woche III 2 (32)
one ['wʌn] eins, ein, eine I • **one day** eines Tages I • **one more** noch ein/e, ein/e weitere(r, s) I **a new one** ein neuer / eine neue / ein neues II • **my old ones** meine alten II • **one tough girl** *(AE, infml) etwa:* ein wirklich toughes Mädchen III 4 (77)
onion ['ʌnjən] Zwiebel III 1 (16)
online [,ɒn'laɪn] online, Online- III 2 (35)
only ['əʊnli]
1. nur, bloß I
2. erst II
3. **the only guest** der einzige Gast I
onto ['ɒntə, 'ɒntʊ] auf (... hinauf) III 3 (69)
open ['əʊpən]
1. öffnen, aufmachen I
2. sich öffnen I
open ['əʊpən] geöffnet, offen I **open-air concert** [,əʊpən‿'eə ,kɒnsət] Open-Air-Konzert, Konzert im Freien II
opera ['ɒprə] Oper III 5 (97)
opera house ['ɒprə haʊs] Oper, Opernhaus III 5 (97/192)
operation (on) [,ɒpə'reɪʃn] Operation (an) III 3 (70)
opposite ['ɒpəzɪt] gegenüber (von) II
or [ɔ:] oder I
orange ['ɒrɪndʒ] orange(farben) I
orange ['ɒrɪndʒ] Orange, Apfelsine I • **orange juice** ['ɒrɪndʒ dʒu:s] Orangensaft I
order ['ɔ:də] bestellen II
°**order** ['ɔ:də] Reihenfolge • °**word order** Wortstellung
organize ['ɔ:gənaɪz]
1. organisieren, veranstalten III 3 (67)
°2. ordnen
other ['ʌðə] andere(r, s) I • **the others** die anderen I • **the other way round** anders herum II
Ouch! [aʊtʃ] Autsch! I
our ['aʊə] unser, unsere I
ours ['aʊəz] unserer, unsere, unseres II
ourselves [aʊə'selvz] uns III 5 (98)
out [aʊt] heraus, hinaus; draußen II **be out** weg sein, nicht da sein I **out of ...** aus ... (heraus/hinaus) I °**a day out** ein Tagesausflug
outfit ['aʊtfɪt] Outfit *(Kleidung; Ausrüstung)* II
outdoor ['aʊtdɔ:] im Freien, Außen- III 4 (89)
outside [,aʊt'saɪd]
1. draußen I
2. nach draußen II
3. **outside the room** vor dem Zimmer; außerhalb des Zimmers I
over ['əʊvə]
1. über, oberhalb von I • **all over the world** auf der ganzen Welt III Intro (6/169) • **from all over the world** aus der ganzen Welt II **over there** da drüben, dort drüben I • **over to ...** hinüber zu/nach ... II
2. **be over** vorbei sein, zu Ende sein I
own [əʊn]: **our own pool** unser eigenes Schwimmbecken II

P

°**pacifist** ['pæsəfɪst] Pazifist/in
pack [pæk] packen, einpacken II
packet ['pækɪt] Päckchen, Packung, Schachtel I • **a packet of mints** ein Päckchen/eine Packung Pfefferminzbonbons I
paddle ['pædl] paddeln III 4 (75)
paddle ['pædl] Paddel III 4 (75)
pads ['pædz] Knieschützer; Schulterpolster III 3 (62/185)
page [peɪdʒ] (Buch-, Heft-)Seite I **What page are we on?** Auf welcher Seite sind wir? I
paid [peɪd] *siehe* **pay**
pain [peɪn] Schmerz(en) I • **cry in pain** vor Schmerzen schreien I
paint [peɪnt] (an)malen I; anstreichen II
painter ['peɪntə] Maler/in II
painting ['peɪntɪŋ] Gemälde, Bild; Malerei III 3 (58)
pair [peə]: **a pair (of)** ein Paar II
palace ['pæləs] Palast, Schloss III 1 (13)
panic ['pænɪk] in Panik geraten III 1 (13)
paper ['peɪpə] Papier I
paradise ['pærədaɪs] Paradies III 5 (98)
paragraph ['pærəgrɑ:f] Absatz *(in einem Text)* II
Paralympics [,pærə'lɪmpɪks] Paralympische Spiele *(Olympische Spiele für Sportler/innen mit körperlicher Behinderung)* III 3 (70)
paramedic [,pærə'medɪk] Sanitäter/in II
paraphrase ['pærəfreɪz] umschreiben, anders ausdrücken III 3 (57)
parcel ['pɑ:sl] Paket I
parent ['peərənt]: **a single parent** ein(e) Alleinerziehende(r) II
parents ['peərənts] Eltern I °**parents' evening** Elternabend *(in der Schule)*
park [pɑ:k] Park I • **car park** Parkplatz III 2 (38/179)
parliament ['pɑ:ləmənt] Parlament III 1 (13)
parrot ['pærət] Papagei I
part [pɑ:t] Teil I • **take part in sth.** teilnehmen an etwas III 3 (58/183)
partner ['pɑ:tnə] Partner/in I
party ['pɑ:ti] Party I
pass [pɑ:s] (herüber)reichen, weitergeben I • **pass round** herumgeben I
passenger ['pæsɪndʒə] Passagier/in, Fahrgast III 2 (46)
passive ['pæsɪv] Passiv III 3 (58)
past [pɑ:st] Vergangenheit II
past [pɑ:st] vorbei (an), vorüber (an) II • **half past 11** halb zwölf (11.30 / 23.30) I • **quarter past 11** Viertel nach 11 (11.15 / 23.15) I
path [pɑ:θ] Pfad, Weg II • **bridle path** ['braɪdl ,pɑ:θ] Reitweg III 3 (62)
°**patron saint** [,peɪtrən 'seɪnt] Schutzheilige/r
°**pattern** ['pætən] Muster
pay (for) [peɪ], **paid, paid** bezahlen II
PE [,pi:‿'i:], **Physical Education** [,fɪzɪkəl‿edʒu'keɪʃn] Sportunterricht, Turnen I
pen [pen] Kugelschreiber, Füller I
penalty ['penəlti] Strafstoß; Elfmeter *(Fußball)* III 3 (59)
pence (p) *(pl)* [pens] Pence *(Plural von „penny")* I
pencil ['pensl] Bleistift I • **pencil case** ['pensl keɪs] Federmäppchen I • **pencil sharpener** ['pensl ʃɑ:pnə] Bleistiftanspitzer I
penny ['peni] *kleinste britische Münze* I
people ['pi:pl] Menschen, Leute I
per [pɜ:, pə] pro III 4 (80)
per cent (%) [pə'sent] Prozent III 4 (80)
performer: (street) performer [pə'fɔ:mə] Straßenkünstler/in III 1 (17)
person ['pɜ:sn] Person I
personal ['pɜ:sənl] persönlich III 2 (39)
pet [pet] Haustier I • **pet shop** Tierhandlung I

phone [fəʊn] anrufen I
phone [fəʊn] Telefon I • **on the phone** am Telefon I • **phone number** Telefonnummer I • **pick up the phone** den Hörer abnehmen II
photo ['fəʊtəʊ] Foto I • **in the photo** auf dem Foto I • **take photos** Fotos machen, fotografieren I
°**photocopy** ['fəʊtəʊkɒpi] Fotokopie
°**photograph** ['fəʊtəgrɑːf] Fotografie, Foto
photographer [fə'tɒgrəfə] Fotograf/in II
phrase [freɪz] Ausdruck, (Rede-)Wendung II
piano [pi'ænəʊ] Klavier, Piano I
play the piano Klavier spielen I
pick up [ˌpɪk‿'ʌp]: **pick sb. up** jn. abholen III 2 (33) • **pick sth. up** etwas hochheben, aufheben III 5 (99)
pick up the phone den Hörer abnehmen II
picnic ['pɪknɪk] Picknick II
picture ['pɪktʃə] Bild I • **in the picture** auf dem Bild I
pie [paɪ] Obstkuchen; Pastete II
piece [piːs]: **a piece of** ein Stück I
a piece of paper ein Stück Papier I
pink [pɪŋk] pink(farben), rosa I
pipe [paɪp] Pfeife III 5 (96)
pirate ['paɪrət] Pirat, Piratin I
pitch [pɪtʃ]: **football/hockey pitch** Fußball-/Hockeyplatz, -feld II
pity ['pɪti]: **It's a pity (that ...)** Es ist schade, dass ... II
pizza ['piːtsə] Pizza I
place [pleɪs] Ort, Platz I • **take place** stattfinden II • **in other places** an anderen Orten, anderswo III 1 (13)
plan [plæn] Plan I
plan (-nn-) [plæn] planen II
plane [pleɪn] Flugzeug II • **on the plane** im Flugzeug II
planet ['plænɪt] Planet II
°**plantain** ['plæntɪn] Plantainbanane
plate [pleɪt] Teller I • **a plate of chips** ein Teller Pommes frites I
platform ['plætfɔːm] Bahnsteig, Gleis III 1 (20)
play [pleɪ] spielen I • **play a trick on sb.** jm. einen Streich spielen II • **play football** Fußball spielen I • **play the drums** Schlagzeug spielen III Intro (6/169) • **play the fiddle** Geige spielen III Intro (7/169)
play the guitar Gitarre spielen I
play the piano Klavier spielen I
play the violin Geige spielen III Intro (7/169)
play [pleɪ] Theaterstück I
player ['pleɪə] Spieler/in I
°**playlist** ['pleɪlɪst] Playliste
please [pliːz] bitte *(in Fragen und Aufforderungen)* I
plug [plʌg] Stecker III 1 (27)
pm [ˌpiː‿'em]: **7 pm** 7 Uhr abends/19 Uhr I
pocket ['pɒkɪt] Tasche *(an Kleidungsstück)* II • **pocket money** ['pɒkɪt mʌni] Taschengeld II
poem ['pəʊɪm] Gedicht I
°**poet** ['pəʊɪt] Dichter/in
point [pɔɪnt] Punkt II • **11.4 (eleven point four)** 11,4 (elf Komma vier) II
point of view Standpunkt II
from my point of view aus meiner Sicht; von meinem Standpunkt aus gesehen II • **There was no point.** Es hatte keinen Sinn. III 5 (99)
What's the point? Was soll das? III 5 (99/193)
point (at/to sth.) [pɔɪnt] zeigen, deuten (auf etwas) II
police *(pl)* [pə'liːs] Polizei I
police station Polizeiwache, Polizeirevier II
poltergeist ['pəʊltəgaɪst] Poltergeist I
ponytail ['pəʊniteɪl] Pferdeschwanz *(Frisur)* III 2 (34)
pool [puːl] Schwimmbad, Schwimmbecken II
poor [pɔː, pʊə] arm I • **poor Sophie** (die) arme Sophie I
pop (music) [pɒp] Pop(musik) III Intro (6)
popcorn ['pɒpkɔːn] Popcorn II
popular ['pɒpjələ] populär, beliebt III 5 (100)
population [ˌpɒpju'leɪʃn] Bevölkerung, Einwohner(zahl) III 4 (72)
possible ['pɒsəbl] möglich II
post [pəʊst] Post *(Briefe, Päckchen, ...)* III 2 (32)
post office ['pəʊst‿ɒfɪs] Postamt II
postcard ['pəʊstkɑːd] Postkarte II
poster ['pəʊstə] Poster I
postscript ['pəʊstskrɪpt] Postskript III 1 (12)
potato [pə'teɪtəʊ], *pl* **potatoes** Kartoffel I
pound (£) [paʊnd] Pfund *(britische Währung)* I
pound [paʊnd] Pfund *(Gewichtseinheit)*: **a three-pound ball** ein drei Pfund schwerer Ball III 4 (80/189)
practice ['præktɪs] *hier:* Übungsteil I
practise ['præktɪs] üben; trainieren I
precinct ['priːsɪŋkt]: **shopping precinct** Einkaufsviertel, Einkaufsstraße III 2 (38/179)
prefix ['priːfɪks] Präfix III 2 (40)
prepare [prɪ'peə] vorbereiten; sich vorbereiten II • **prepare for** sich vorbereiten auf II
prewriting exercise [ˌpriː'raɪtɪŋ] Übung vor dem Schreiben III 4 (85)
present ['preznt]
1. Gegenwart I
2. Geschenk I
present sth. (to sb.) [prɪ'zent] (jm.) etwas präsentieren, vorstellen I; überreichen III 3 (58)
presentation [ˌprezn'teɪʃn] Präsentation, Vorstellung I
presenter [prɪ'zentə] Moderator/in II
pretty ['prɪti]
1. hübsch I
2. pretty cool/good/... ziemlich cool/gut/... II
price [praɪs] (Kauf-)Preis I
°**pride** [praɪd] Stolz
°**prince** [prɪns] Prinz
print sth. out [ˌprɪnt‿'aʊt] etwas ausdrucken II
prize [praɪz] Preis, Gewinn I
probably ['prɒbəbli] wahrscheinlich II
problem ['prɒbləm] Problem II
produce [prə'djuːs] produzieren, erzeugen, herstellen II
°**profile** ['prəʊfaɪl] Porträt, Beschreibung
programme ['prəʊgræm] Programm I
project (about, on) ['prɒdʒekt] Projekt (über, zu) I • **do a project** ein Projekt machen, durchführen II
promise ['prɒmɪs] versprechen II
°**pronounce** [prə'naʊns] aussprechen
pronunciation [prəˌnʌnsi'eɪʃn] Aussprache I
proof *(no pl)* [pruːf] Beweis(e) II
proud (of sb./sth.) [praʊd] stolz (auf jn./etwas) II
°**province** ['prɒvɪns] Provinz
PS [ˌpiː‿'es] (postscript ['pəʊstskrɪpt]) PS, Postskript *(Nachschrift unter Briefen)* III 1 (12)
pub [pʌb] Kneipe, Lokal II
°**public** ['pʌblɪk] öffentliche(r, s)
°**the public** die Öffentlichkeit
publish ['pʌblɪʃ] veröffentlichen III 5 (94)
pull [pʊl] ziehen I
pullover ['pʊləʊvə] Pullover II
punk [pʌŋk] Punker/in II
purple ['pɜːpl] violett; lila I
purse [pɜːs] Geldbörse II

push [pʊʃ] drücken, schieben, stoßen I
put (-tt-) [pʊt], **put, put** legen, stellen, (etwas wohin) tun I • °**put sb. back in the game** jn. zurück ins Spiel bringen • **put sb. to bed** jn. ins Bett bringen III 5 (102) • **put sth. on** etwas anziehen *(Kleidung)*; etwas aufsetzen *(Hut, Helm)* II °**put sth. together** etwas zusammenstellen
puzzled ['pʌzld] verwirrt II
pyjamas *(pl)* [pə'dʒɑːməz] Schlafanzug II

Q

quarter ['kwɔːtə]: **quarter past 11** Viertel nach 11 (11.15 / 23.15) I **quarter to 12** Viertel vor 12 (11.45 / 23.45) I
quay [kiː] Kai III 2 (46)
queen [kwiːn] Königin III 1 (12)
question ['kwestʃn] Frage I • **ask questions** Fragen stellen I °**question word** Fragewort °**follow-up question** zweite Frage, Anschlussfrage
quick [kwɪk] schnell I
quiet ['kwaɪət] leise, still, ruhig I
quite [kwaɪt] ziemlich; ganz III 1 (13)
quiz [kwɪz], *pl* **quizzes** ['kwɪzɪz] Quiz, Ratespiel I
quotation marks [kwəʊ'teɪʃn ˌmɑːks] Anführungszeichen, -striche III 5 (105)

R

rabbit ['ræbɪt] Kaninchen I
°**race** [reɪs] Rennen
racket ['rækɪt] Schläger *(Badminton, Tennis, Squash)* III 3 (62)
radio ['reɪdiəʊ] Radio I • **on the radio** im Radio I
railway ['reɪlweɪ] Eisenbahn II
rain [reɪn] Regen II
rain [reɪn] regnen II
rainy ['reɪni] regnerisch II • **rainy season** Regenzeit II
ran [ræn] *siehe* **run**
rang [ræŋ] *siehe* **ring**
ranger ['reɪndʒə] Ranger/in, Aufseher/in III 4 (88)
°**rank** [ræŋk] in eine Rangordnung bringen
rap [ræp] Rap(musik) *(rhythmischer Sprechgesang)* I
rapids *(pl)* ['ræpɪdz] Stromschnellen III 4 (88)
rat [ræt] Ratte III 1 (27)
RE [ˌɑːr‿'iː], **Religious Education** [rɪˌlɪdʒəs‿edʒu'keɪʃn] Religion, Religionsunterricht I
reach [riːtʃ] erreichen III 3 (59)
read [riːd], **read, read** lesen I °**read on** weiterlesen • °**read out** vorlesen • °**Read out loud.** Lies laut vor.
reader ['riːdə] Leser/in II
ready ['redi] bereit, fertig I • **get ready (for)** sich fertig machen (für), sich vorbereiten (auf) I • **get things ready** Dinge fertig machen, vorbereiten I
real [rɪəl] echt, wirklich I
real late ['riːəl] *(AE, infml)* wirklich spät, echt spät III 4 (73)
realistic [ˌriːə'lɪstɪk] realistisch, wirklichkeitsnah III 1 (27)
realize ['rɪəlaɪz] erkennen, merken I
really ['rɪəli] wirklich I
reason ['riːzn] Grund, Begründung I • **for lots of reasons** aus vielen Gründen I
receive [rɪ'siːv] erhalten III 3 (58)
record [rɪ'kɔːd] aufnehmen III Intro (11)
recorder [rɪ'kɔːdə] Blockflöte III Intro (11)
recording [rɪ'kɔːdɪŋ] Aufnahme, Aufzeichnung III Intro (11)
recover (from) [rɪ'kʌvə] sich erholen (von) II
recycled [ˌriː'saɪkld] wiederverwertet, wiederverwendet, recycelt II
recycling [ˌriː'saɪklɪŋ] Wiederverwertung, Recycling II
red [red] rot I
°**refer to** [rɪ'fɜː] sich beziehen auf
referee [ˌrefə'riː] Schiedsrichter/in III 3 (67)
regular ['regjələ] regelmäßig III 5 (103)
rehearsal [rɪ'hɜːsl] Probe *(am Theater)* I
rehearse [rɪ'hɜːs] proben *(am Theater)* I
relative ['relətɪv] Verwandte(r) II
relax [rɪ'læks] (sich) entspannen, sich ausruhen II
release [rɪ'liːs] *(CD, Film usw.)* herausbringen, auf den Markt bringen III 5 (97)
remember sth. [rɪ'membə]
1. sich an etwas erinnern I
2. sich etwas merken I
°**Remember ...** Denk dran, ...
°**remind sb. (of/about sth.)** [rɪ'maɪnd] jn. (an etwas) erinnern
°**reopen** [ri'əʊpənɪŋ] wiedereröffnen
repair [rɪ'peə] reparieren, ausbessern III 5 (100)
repeat [rɪ'piːt] wiederholen II
replace sth. (with) [rɪ'pleɪs] etwas ersetzen (durch) III 3 (67)
reply (to) [rɪ'plaɪ] antworten (auf), beantworten; erwidern III 4 (75)
report (on) [rɪ'pɔːt] Bericht, Reportage (über) I
report (to sb.) [rɪ'pɔːt] jm. berichten II
reporter [rɪ'pɔːtə] Reporter/in II
represent [ˌreprɪ'zent] repräsentieren, vertreten III 3 (70)
research *(no pl)* [rɪ'sɜːtʃ, 'riːsɜːtʃ] Recherche, Forschung(en) III 5 (105)
researcher [rɪ'sɜːtʃə, 'riːsɜːtʃə] Rechercheur/in III 2 (33)
°**reserve** [rɪ'zɜːv] Reservat, Schutzgebiet *(in Kanada)*
°**responsible (for)** [rɪ'spɒnsəbl] verantwortlich (für)
rest [rest] Rest II
°**rest** [rest] ruhen
restart [ˌriː'stɑːt] neu starten *(Computer)* II
restaurant ['restrɒnt] Restaurant II
result [rɪ'zʌlt] Ergebnis, Resultat I
revision [rɪ'vɪʒn] Wiederholung *(des Lernstoffs)* I
rhino ['raɪnəʊ] Nashorn II
°**rhyming** ['raɪmɪŋ]: **rhyming pair** Reimpaar • **rhyming words** Reimwörter
rhythm ['rɪðəm] Rhythmus III 4 (76)
rich [rɪtʃ] reich II
ridden ['rɪdn] *siehe* **ride**
riddle ['rɪdl] Rätsel, Scherzfrage III 5 (96)
ride [raɪd], **rode, ridden** reiten I **ride a bike** Rad fahren I
ride [raɪd]: **(bike) ride** (Rad-)Fahrt, (Rad-)Tour II • **(bus) ride** (Bus-)Fahrt II • **take a ride** eine Spritztour/Fahrt machen III 3 (69)
riding ['raɪdɪŋ] Reiten, Reitsport I **go riding** ['raɪdɪŋ] reiten gehen I **riding boots** *(pl)* Reitstiefel III 3 (69) **riding hat** Reitkappe, Reiterhelm III 3 (69)
right [raɪt] richtig I • **all right** [ɔːl 'raɪt] gut, in Ordnung II • **be right** Recht haben I • **get sth. right** etwas richtig machen III 4 (76) **That's right.** Das ist richtig. / Das stimmt. I • **You need a school bag, right?** Du brauchst eine Schultasche, stimmt's? / nicht wahr? I
right [raɪt] rechte(r, s) I • **look right** nach rechts schauen I • **on the right** rechts, auf der rechten Seite I • °**the person on your right**

dein rechter Nachbar / deine rechte Nachbarin • **to the right** nach rechts III 2 (45) • **turn right** (nach) rechts abbiegen II • °**the right-hand column** die rechte Spalte

right [raɪt]**: right behind you** direkt/genau hinter dir II • **right now** jetzt sofort; jetzt gerade I

ring [rɪŋ] Ring II

ring [rɪŋ]**, rang, rung** klingeln, läuten II

ringtone ['rɪŋtəʊn] Klingelton III 2 (32)

river ['rɪvə] Fluss II

road [rəʊd] Straße I • **Park Road** [ˌpɑːk 'rəʊd] Parkstraße I

°**roadie** *(infml)* ['rəʊdi] Roadie *(Helfer einer Band, zuständig für Auf- und Abbau der Anlage)*

rock [rɒk] Fels III 2 (39)

rock (music) [rɒk] Rock(musik) III Intro (6)

rode [rəʊd] *siehe* **ride**

role [rəʊl] Rolle III 2 (33)

roll [rəʊl] Brötchen II

Roman ['rəʊmən] römisch; Römer, Römerin II

roof ['ruːf] Dach II

room [ruːm, rʊm] Raum, Zimmer I

round [raʊnd] rund II

round [raʊnd] um ... (herum); in ... umher II • **the other way round** anders herum II

°**route** [ruːt] Route, Weg

royal ['rɔɪəl] königlich, Königs II

rubber ['rʌbə] Radiergummi I

rubbish ['rʌbɪʃ] (Haus-)Müll, Abfall II • **rubbish collection** ['rʌbɪʃ kəˌlekʃn] Müllabfuhr II

rucksack ['rʌksæk] Rucksack III 2 (34)

rude [ruːd] unhöflich, unverschämt II

rugby ['rʌgbi] Rugby III 3 (69)

rule [ruːl] Regel, Vorschrift III 5 (100)

ruler ['ruːlə] Lineal I

run [rʌn] (Wett-)Lauf II

run (-nn-) [rʌn]**, ran, run** laufen, rennen I • **running shoes** Laufschuhe III 3 (62) • **running track** Laufbahn III 3 (62)

rung [rʌŋ] *siehe* **ring**

runner ['rʌnə] Läufer/in II

°**rush hour** ['rʌʃ aʊə] Hauptverkehrszeit

S

sad [sæd] traurig II

saddle ['sædl] Sattel III 3 (62/185)

safe (from) [seɪf] sicher, in Sicherheit (vor) II

said [sed] *siehe* **say**

°**saint** [seɪnt] Heilige/r • °**patron saint** ['peɪtrən] Schutzheilige/r

salad ['sæləd] Salat *(als Gericht oder Beilage)* I

salmon ['sæmən]**,** *pl* **salmon** Lachs III 2 (30)

same [seɪm]**: the same ...** der-/die-/dasselbe ...; dieselben ... I • **be/look the same** gleich sein/aussehen I

sandwich ['sænwɪtʃ, 'sænwɪdʒ] Sandwich, *(zusammengeklapptes)* belegtes Brot I

sang [sæŋ] *siehe* **sing**

sat [sæt] *siehe* **sit**

°**satellite** ['sætəlaɪt] Satellit

Saturday ['sætədeɪ, 'sætədi] Samstag, Sonnabend I

sauce [sɔːs] Soße III 1 (16)

sauna ['sɔːnə] Sauna II • **have a sauna** in die Sauna gehen II

sausage ['sɒsɪdʒ] (Brat-, Bock-) Würstchen, Wurst I

save [seɪv]
1. retten II
2. sparen II

saw [sɔː] *siehe* **see**

saxophone ['sæksəfəʊn] Saxophon III Intro (11)

say [seɪ]**, said, said** sagen I • **It says here: ...** Hier steht: ... / Es heißt hier: ... II • **say goodbye** sich verabschieden I • **Say hi to your parents for me.** Grüß deine Eltern von mir. I • **say sorry** sich entschuldigen II • **They say ...** Man sagt, ... III 1 (12)

scan (-nn-) [skæn]**: scan a text** einen Text schnell nach bestimmten Wörtern/Informationen absuchen II • °**scan sth. (in)** etwas einscannen

scared [skeəd] verängstigt I • **be scared (of)** Angst haben (vor) I

scary ['skeəri] unheimlich; gruselig I • **kind of scary** *(infml)* irgendwie unheimlich III 1 (26)

scene [siːn] Szene I

scenery ['siːnəri] Landschaft III 2 (31)

school [skuːl] Schule I • **at school** in der Schule I • **from school** aus der Schule III 1 (12/170) • **school bag** Schultasche I • **school subject** Schulfach I

► S.170 Places without articles

science ['saɪəns] Naturwissenschaft I

°**scientist** ['saɪəntɪst] (Natur-)Wissenschaftler/in

score [skɔː] Spielstand; Punktestand III 3 (56) • **final score** Endstand *(beim Sport)* III 3 (56) **What's the score?** Wie steht es? *(beim Sport)* III 3 (56)

► S.183 A football match

score (a goal) [skɔː], [gəʊl] ein Tor schießen, einen Treffer erzielen III 3 (56)

°**Scot** [skɒt] Schotte/Schottin

Scottish ['skɒtɪʃ] schottisch III 2 (43)

°**screen kiss** ['skriːn kɪs] Filmkuss

sea [siː] Meer, (die) See I • **at sea** auf See II

°**search engine** ['sɜːtʃ‿ˌendʒən] Suchmaschine

season ['siːzn] Jahreszeit II • **rainy season** Regenzeit II

second ['sekənd] Sekunde I

second ['sekənd] zweite(r, s) I
second-hand [ˌsekənd 'hænd] gebraucht; aus zweiter Hand III 1 (13)
a second-half goal ein Tor in der zweiten Hälfte/Halbzeit III 3 (59)

section ['sekʃn] Abschnitt, Teil II; (Themen-)Bereich III 5 (94)

see [siː]**, saw, seen**
1. sehen I
2. see sb. jn. besuchen, jn. aufsuchen II
See? Siehst du? I • **See you.** Bis bald. / Tschüs. I

seem (to be/to do) [siːm] (zu sein/tun) scheinen III 1 (17)

seen [siːn] *siehe* **see**

selection (of) [sɪ'lekʃn] Auswahl (an) II

sell [sel]**, sold, sold** verkaufen I

semi-final [ˌsemi'faɪnl] Halbfinale III 3 (54)

send [send]**, sent, sent** senden, schicken II

sent [sent] *siehe* **send**

sentence ['sentəns] Satz I
sentence for sentence Satz um Satz III 3 (65)

September [sep'tembə] September I

series, *pl* **series** ['sɪəriːz] (Sende-) Reihe, Serie II

service ['sɜːvɪs] Dienst (am Kunden), Service II

session ['seʃn]**: training session** Trainingsstunde, -einheit III 3 (54)

set a trap (for sb.) (-tt-) [set]**, set, set** (jm.) eine Falle stellen II

set meal [ˌset 'miːl] Menü III 1 (16/173)

set up (-tt-) [set]**, set, set** aufstellen, aufbauen III 2 (48)

°**settler** ['setlə] Siedler/in

°**sex** [seks] Geschlecht

shadow ['ʃædəʊ] Schatten III 1 (27)

shake your head [ʃeɪk] den Kopf schütteln III 4 (85)

Shall we ...? [ʃæl] Wollen wir ...? / Sollen wir ...? III 2 (34)
shape [ʃeɪp] Form, Gestalt II
share sth. (with sb.) [ʃeə] sich etwas teilen (mit jm.) I
she [ʃi:] sie I
sheep, *pl* **sheep** [ʃi:p] Schaf II
shelf [ʃelf], *pl* **shelves** [ʃelvz] Regal(brett) I
shine [ʃaɪn], **shone, shone** scheinen *(Sonne)* II
°**shiny** ['ʃaɪni] glänzend
ship [ʃɪp] Schiff I
shirt [ʃɜ:t] Hemd I • **football shirt** (Fußball-)Trikot III 3 (56)
shiver ['ʃɪvə] zittern II
shoe [ʃu:] Schuh I
shocked [ʃɒkt] schockiert III 2 (45)
shone [ʃɒn] *siehe* **shine**
shop [ʃɒp] Laden, Geschäft I
shop assistant ['ʃɒp_ə,sɪstənt] Verkäufer/in I
shop (-pp-) [ʃɒp] einkaufen (gehen) I
shopping ['ʃɒpɪŋ] (das) Einkaufen I
go shopping einkaufen gehen I
shopping list Einkaufsliste I
shopping mall (großes) Einkaufszentrum III 4 (75) • **shopping precinct** ['pri:sɪŋkt] Einkaufsviertel, -straße *(autofrei)* III 2 (38/179)
short [ʃɔ:t] kurz I
°**shortbread** ['ʃɔ:tbred] schottischer Butterkeks
shorts *(pl)* [ʃɔ:ts] Shorts, kurze Hose I
shot [ʃɒt] Schuss III 3 (59)
°**shot put** ['ʃɒtpʊt] Kugelstoßen
should [ʃəd, ʃʊd]: **you should ...** du solltest ... / ihr solltet ... I
shoulder ['ʃəʊldə] Schulter I
shout [ʃaʊt] schreien, rufen I
shout at sb. jn. anschreien I
show [ʃəʊ] Show, Vorstellung I
show [ʃəʊ], **showed, shown** zeigen I • **show sb. around** jn. (in der Stadt/im Museum/... herumführen) III 1 (12)
shower ['ʃaʊə] Dusche I • **have a shower** (sich) duschen I
shown [ʃəʊn] *siehe* **show**
shut up [,ʃʌt_'ʌp], **shut, shut** den Mund halten II
shy [ʃaɪ] schüchtern, scheu II
side [saɪd] Seite II
sights *(pl)* [saɪts] Sehenswürdigkeiten II
°**sightseeing** ['saɪtsi:ɪŋ] Besichtigung(en) von Sehenswürdigkeiten
°**sightseeing tour** ['saɪtsi:ɪŋ ,tʊər] Stadtrundfahrt

sign [saɪn] Schild; Zeichen III 1 (26)
sign [saɪn] unterschreiben III 5 (100)
silent letter [,saɪlənt 'letə] „stummer" Buchstabe *(nicht gesprochener Buchstabe)* II
silly ['sɪli] albern, dumm II
since September [sɪns] seit September III 1 (17)
sing [sɪŋ], **sang, sung** singen I
singer ['sɪŋə] Sänger/in II
single ['sɪŋgl] ledig, alleinstehend I
a single parent ein(e) Alleinerziehende(r) II
sink [sɪŋk] Spüle, Spülbecken I
sister ['sɪstə] Schwester I
sit (-tt-) [sɪt], **sat, sat** sitzen; sich setzen I • **sit down** sich hinsetzen II • **sit up** sich aufsetzen II
Sit with me. Setz dich zu mir. / Setzt euch zu mir. I
°**situation** [,sɪtʃu'eɪʃn] Situation
size [saɪz] Größe I
skate [skeɪt] Inliner/Skateboard fahren I
skateboard ['skeɪtbɔ:d] Skateboard I
skates *(pl)* [skeɪts] Inliner I
sketch [sketʃ] Sketch I
ski [ski:] Ski III 3 (62)
ski [ski:] Ski laufen/fahren III 3 (62)
ski slope ['ski: sləʊp] Skipiste III 3 (62)
skiing ['ski:ɪŋ]: **go skiing** Ski laufen/fahren III 3 (62)
skills file ['skɪlz faɪl] Anhang mit Lern- und Arbeitstechniken I
skim a text (-mm-) [skɪm] einen Text überfliegen *(um den Inhalt grob zu erfassen)* III 5 (96)
skirt [skɜ:t] Rock II
sky [skaɪ] Himmel II • **in the sky** am Himmel II
°**skyscraper** ['skaɪskreɪpə] Wolkenkratzer
slave [sleɪv] Sklave, Sklavin II
sledge [sledʒ] Schlitten III 3 (69)
sleep [sli:p], **slept, slept** schlafen I
sleep [sli:p] Schlaf III 4 (73/187)
sleepover ['sli:pəʊvə] Schlafparty III 4 (73)
slept [slept] *siehe* **sleep**
slope: ski slope Skipiste III 3 (62)
slow [sləʊ] langsam II
small [smɔ:l] klein II • **small letters** Kleinbuchstaben III 5 (104)
smell [smel] riechen II
smell [smel] Geruch II
smile [smaɪl] lächeln I • **smile at sb.** jn. anlächeln II
smile Lächeln II
smoothie ['smu:ði] *dickflüssiger Fruchtshake mit Milch, Joghurt oder Eiscreme* II

snack [snæk] Snack, Imbiss II
snake [sneɪk] Schlange I
snow [snəʊ] Schnee II
so [səʊ]
1. also; deshalb, daher I • **So?** Und? / Na und? II • **So what?** [səʊ 'wɒt] Und? / Na und? II
2. so sweet so süß I • **so far** bis jetzt, bis hierher III 5 (94) • **so that** sodass, damit III 4 (85)
3. I hope so. Ich hoffe es. II
I think so. Ich glaube (ja). I
I don't think so. Das finde/glaube ich nicht. I • **Do you really think so?** Meinst du wirklich? / Glaubst du das wirklich? II
► S.182 German „so"
soap [səʊp] Seife I
°**social networking websites** [,səʊʃl 'netwɜ:kɪŋ ,websaɪts] soziale Netzwerkdienste *(Websites, die gegenseitige Vernetzungen unterstützen, z.B. Weblogs und Internet-Communitys)*
sock [sɒk] Socke, Strumpf I
sofa ['səʊfə] Sofa I
soft [sɒft] weich, sanft III 5 (98)
software ['sɒftweə] Software II
sold [səʊld] *siehe* **sell**
sold out [,səʊld_'aʊt]: **be sold out** ausverkauft/vergriffen sein III 5 (97)
some [səm, sʌm] einige, ein paar I
some cheese/juice/money etwas Käse/Saft/Geld I
somebody ['sʌmbədi] jemand I
Find/Ask somebody who ... Finde/Frage jemanden, der ... II
someone ['sʌmwʌn] jemand III 4 (75/188)
something ['sʌmθɪŋ] etwas I
sometimes ['sʌmtaɪmz] manchmal I
somewhere ['sʌmweə] irgendwo(hin) II
son [sʌn] Sohn I
song [sɒŋ] Lied, Song I
soon [su:n] bald I • **as soon as** sobald, sowie II
°**soprano** [sə'prɑ:nəʊ] Sopran, Sopranist/in
sore [sɔ:]: **be sore** wund sein, wehtun II • **have a sore throat** Halsschmerzen haben II
sorry ['sɒri]: **(I'm) sorry.** Entschuldigung. / Tut mir leid. I • **Sorry, I'm late.** Entschuldigung, dass ich zu spät bin/komme. I • **Sorry?** Wie bitte? I • **say sorry** sich entschuldigen II
sort (of) [sɔ:t] Art, Sorte II
soul [səʊl] Soul(musik) III Intro (6)

sound [saʊnd] klingen, sich (gut usw.) anhören I
sound [saʊnd] Laut; Klang I
°**sound assistant** ['saʊnd‿əˌsɪstənt] Tonassistent/in
sound file ['saʊnd faɪl] Tondatei, Soundfile III 1 (12)
soup [su:p] Suppe II
sour ['saʊə] sauer III 1 (16)
°**source** [sɔ:s] Quelle
south [saʊθ] Süden; nach Süden; südlich II • **southbound** ['saʊθbaʊnd] Richtung Süden III 1 (14/172) • **south-east** [ˌsaʊθ'i:st] Südosten; nach Südosten; südöstlich II • **southern** ['sʌðən] südlich, Süd- III Intro (9) • **south-west** [ˌsaʊθ'west] Südwesten; nach Südwesten; südwestlich II
souvenir [ˌsu:və'nɪə] Andenken, Souvenir III 2 (39)
space ['speɪs]
1. Weltraum II
2. **Move back one space.** Geh ein Feld zurück. II • **Move on one space.** Geh ein Feld vor. II
spaghetti [spə'geti] Spaghetti II
speak (to) [spi:k], **spoke, spoken** sprechen (mit), reden (mit) II
special ['speʃl] besondere(r, s) II **Did you do anything special?** Habt ihr irgendetwas Besonderes gemacht? I
°**speech bubble** ['spi:tʃ bʌbl] Sprechblase
speed [spi:d] rasen, schnell fliegen III 2 (47)
speed [spi:d] Geschwindigkeit III 4 (73/187) • **speed limit** Geschwindigkeitsbegrenzung, Geschwindigkeitsbeschränkung III 4 (80)
spell [spel] buchstabieren I
°**spelling** ['spelɪŋ] Schreibung, Schreibweise
spend [spend], **spent, spent: spend money (on)** Geld ausgeben (für) II • **spend time (on)** Zeit verbringen (mit) II
spent [spent] *siehe* **spend**
spice [spaɪs] Gewürz III 1 (16)
spicy ['spaɪsi] würzig, scharf gewürzt III 1 (16)
spoke [spəʊk] *siehe* **speak**
spoken ['spəʊkən] *siehe* **speak**
spoon [spu:n] Löffel III 1 (27)
sport [spɔ:t] Sport; Sportart I **do sport** Sport treiben I
sports gear *(no pl)* ['spɔ:ts gɪə] Sportausrüstung, Sportsachen II
sports hall ['spɔ:ts hɔ:l] Sporthalle III 3 (62)

spot **(-tt-)** [spɒt] entdecken III 3 (62)
spring [sprɪŋ] Frühling I
spy [spaɪ] Spion/in I
square [skweə] Platz *(in der Stadt)* II
square km (sq km) [skweə] Quadratkilometer III 4 (72)
squeeze [skwi:z] drücken; (aus)pressen III 5 (96)
squirrel ['skwɪrəl] Eichhörnchen II
stadium ['steɪdiəm] Stadion III 3 (67)
stage [steɪdʒ] Bühne I
stairs *(pl)* [steəz] Treppe; Treppenstufen I
stamp [stæmp] Briefmarke I
stand [stænd], **stood, stood**
1. stehen; sich (hin)stellen II
2. ertragen, aushalten, ausstehen II • **I can't stand it.** Ich kann es nicht ertragen/aushalten/ausstehen. II
star [stɑ:]
1. Stern II
2. (Film-, Pop-)Star I
start [stɑ:t] starten, anfangen, beginnen (mit) I
state [steɪt] Staat III Intro (10/169) °**head of state** Staatsoberhaupt
°**statement** ['steɪtmənt] Aussage, Aussagesatz
station ['steɪʃn]
1. Bahnhof I • **at the station** am Bahnhof I
2. **(radio/pop) station** (Radio-/Pop-)Sender III 5 (99)
statue ['stætʃu:] Statue II
stay [steɪ] bleiben; wohnen, übernachten II • **stay out** nicht nach Hause kommen, draußenbleiben III 5 (101)
steal [sti:l], **stole, stolen** stehlen II
steel [sti:l] Stahl III Intro (8)
steel drum [ˌsti:l 'drʌm] Steeldrum III Intro (8)
steer [stɪə] lenken, steuern III 4 (76)
step [step] Schritt I • **take steps** Schritte machen/unternehmen III 3 (69)
stereo ['steriəʊ] Stereoanlage III 5 (98)
stew [stju:] Eintopf(gericht) III 2 (47)
°**stewed chicken** [stju:d] geschmortes Hühnchen
°**stick** [stɪk] Stock, Stange
stick (on) [ˌstɪk‿'ɒn], **stuck, stuck** (auf)kleben I
stick: (drum-)stick [stɪk] Trommelstock III 5 (99)
stick out of sth. [stɪk], **stuck, stuck** [stʌk] aus etwas herausragen, herausstehen III 5 (96)

still [stɪl]
1. (immer) noch I
2. trotzdem, dennoch II
stole [stəʊl] *siehe* **steal**
stolen ['stəʊlən] *siehe* **steal**
stomach ['stʌmək] Magen II **stomach ache** Magenschmerzen, Bauchweh II
stone [stəʊn] Stein II
stood [stʊd] *siehe* **stand**
stop (-pp-) [stɒp]
1. aufhören I
2. anhalten I
Stop that! Hör auf damit! / Lass das! I
storm [stɔ:m] Sturm; Gewitter II
stormy ['stɔ:mi] stürmisch II
story ['stɔ:ri] Geschichte, Erzählung I
straight on [streɪt‿'ɒn] geradeaus weiter II
straightaway [ˌstreɪtə'weɪ] sofort, gleich III 4 (76)
strange [streɪndʒ] seltsam, sonderbar I
strawberry ['strɔ:bəri] Erdbeere II
street [stri:t] Straße I • **at 7 Park Street** in der Parkstraße 7 I
street performer [pə'fɔ:mə] Straßenkünstler/in III 1 (17)
stress ['stres] Betonung III 2 (38)
°**stressed** [strest] betont
°**stretch** [stretʃ] sich strecken
strict [strɪkt] streng III 4 (75)
strike [straɪk] Streik III 5 (102) • **be on strike** streiken, sich im Streik befinden III 5 (102/194) • **go on strike** streiken, in den Streik treten III 5 (102/194)
string [strɪŋ] Saite III 5 (101)
strong [strɒŋ] stark II
structure ['strʌktʃə] strukturieren, aufbauen II
structure ['strʌktʃə] Struktur; Gliederung III 2 (39)
stuck [stʌk] *siehe* **stick**
student ['stju:dənt] Schüler/in; Student/in I • **exchange student** Austauschschüler/in III 3 (57)
studio ['stju:diəʊ] Studio I
study ['stʌdi] lernen; studieren III 5 (97)
study skills *(pl)* ['stʌdi skɪlz] Lern- und Arbeitstechniken I
stuff [stʌf] Zeug, Kram I
style [staɪl] Stil III 4 (85)
°**sub-heading** ['sʌb hedɪŋ] Kapitelüberschrift
subject ['sʌbdʒɪkt]
1. Subjekt I
2. Schulfach I

subway ['sʌbweɪ]**: the subway** *(AE)* die U-Bahn II
success [sək'ses] Erfolg III 5 (94)
°**successful** [sək'sesfl] erfolgreich
such [sʌtʃ]**: such a nice person** so ein netter Mensch III 3 (56/182)
such good books so gute Bücher III 3 (56) • **such as** wie zum Beispiel III 2 (39)
▶ S.182 German „so"
suddenly ['sʌdnli] plötzlich, auf einmal I
sugar ['ʃʊgə] Zucker II
°**suggestion** [sə'dʒestʃən] Vorschlag
°**summarize** ['sʌməraɪz] zusammenfassen
summer ['sʌmə] Sommer I
sun [sʌn] Sonne II
Sunday ['sʌndeɪ, 'sʌndi] Sonntag I
sung [sʌŋ] *siehe* **sing**
sunglasses *(pl)* ['sʌnglɑːsɪz] (eine) Sonnenbrille I
sunny ['sʌni] sonnig II
suntan ['sʌnˌtæn]**: have a suntan** sonnengebräunt sein III 1 (24)
supermarket ['suːpəmɑːkɪt] Supermarkt I
support a team [sə'pɔːt] eine Mannschaft unterstützen; Fan einer Mannschaft sein III 3 (56)
supporter [sə'pɔːtə] Anhänger/in, Fan III 3 (56)
suppose [sə'pəʊz] annehmen, vermuten I
sure [ʃʊə, ʃɔː] sicher I
surf the internet [sɜːf] im Internet surfen II
surfboard ['sɜːfbɔːd] Surfbrett II
surfing ['sɜːfɪŋ]**: go surfing** wellenreiten gehen, surfen gehen II
surprise (for/to) [sə'praɪz] Überraschung (für) III 1 (16)
surprise sb. [sə'praɪz] jn. überraschen III 2 (33)
surprised (at sth.) [sə'praɪzd] überrascht (über etwas) III 2 (33)
survey (on) ['sɜːveɪ] Umfrage, Untersuchung (über) II
survival [sə'vaɪvl] Überleben II
survive [sə'vaɪv] überleben II
°**swallow** ['swɒləʊ] (hinunter)schlucken
swam [swæm] *siehe* **swim**
swap (-pp-) [swɒp] tauschen I
sweatshirt ['swetʃɜːt] Sweatshirt I
sweet [swiːt] süß I
sweetheart ['swiːthɑːt] Liebling, Schatz II
sweets *(pl)* Süßigkeiten I
swim (-mm-) [swɪm]**, swam, swum** schwimmen I
swimmer ['swɪmə] Schwimmer/in II
swimming ['swɪmɪŋ] Schwimmen I • **go swimming** schwimmen gehen I
swimming pool ['swɪmɪŋ puːl] Schwimmbad, Schwimmbecken II
swimming trunks [trʌŋks] Badehose III 3 (62/185)
swimsuit ['swɪmsuːt] Badeanzug III 3 (62/185)
swum [swʌm] *siehe* **swim**
syllable ['sɪləbl] Silbe I
°**symbol** ['sɪmbl] Symbol
synagogue ['sɪnəgɒg] Synagoge III 1 (16)

T

table ['teɪbl]
1. Tisch I • **table tennis** ['teɪbl tenɪs] Tischtennis I • **table tennis bat** Tischtennisschläger III 3 (62)
°**2.** Tabelle
take [teɪk]**, took, taken**
1. nehmen I
2. (weg-, hin)bringen I
3. dauern, *(Zeit)* brauchen III 2 (33)
Take another turn. *hier:* Würfel noch einmal. II • **take care of sth./sb.** sich um etwas/jn. kümmern III 1 (28) • **take notes** sich Notizen machen I • **take sth. off** etwas ausziehen *(Kleidung)*; etwas absetzen *(Hut, Helm)* II • **take 10 c off** 10 Cent abziehen I • **take sth. out** etwas herausnehmen I • **take part in sth.** teilnehmen an etwas III Intro (6) • **take photos** Fotos machen, fotografieren I • **take place** stattfinden II • **take a ride** eine Spritztour/Fahrt machen III 3 (69) **take steps** Schritte machen/unternehmen III 3 (69) • °**Take turns.** Wechselt euch ab. • **I'll take it.** (beim Einkaufen) Ich werde es (ihn, sie) nehmen. / Ich nehme es (ihn, sie). I
°**take** *(n)* [teɪk] Einstellung, Take *(beim Filmen)*
takeaway ['teɪkəweɪ] *Restaurant, das auch Essen zum Mitnehmen verkauft; Essen zum Mitnehmen* III 1 (16)
taken ['teɪkən] *siehe* **take**
talent ['tælənt] Talent, Begabung III 3 (70)
talk [tɔːk]**: talk (about)** reden (über), sich unterhalten (über) I
talk (to) reden (mit), sich unterhalten (mit) I
°**talk** [tɔːk] Vortrag, Referat • °**give a talk** einen Vortrag/ein Referat halten
tall [tɔːl]
1. groß *(Person)* III 3 (65)
°**2.** hoch *(Gebäude)*
°**tartan** ['tɑːtn] Schottenstoff *(mit Schottenmuster)*
taught [tɔːt] *siehe* **teach**
taxi ['tæksi] Taxi III 1 (20/174)
tea [tiː] Tee; (auch:) leichte Nachmittags- oder Abendmahlzeit I
teach [tiːtʃ]**, taught, taught** unterrichten, lehren I
teacher ['tiːtʃə] Lehrer/in I • **head teacher** Schulleiter/in III 2 (45)
team [tiːm] Team, Mannschaft I
tear [tɪə] Träne II
tease [tiːz] necken, auf den Arm nehmen III 2 (46)
teaspoon ['tiːspuːn] Teelöffel III 1 (27)
°**technology** [tek'nɒlədʒi] Technologie
teddy bear ['tedi beə] Teddybär III 3 (64)
teen *(besonders AE)* [tiːn] Teenager- III 5 (94)
teenager ['tiːneɪdʒə] Teenager, Jugendliche(r) II
teeth [tiːθ] *Plural von „tooth"* I
telephone ['telɪfəʊn] Telefon I
telephone number Telefonnummer I
television (TV) ['telɪvɪʒn] Fernsehen I
tell (about) [tel]**, told, told** erzählen (von), berichten (über) I • **Tell me your names.** Sagt mir eure Namen. I • **tell sb. the way** jm. den Weg beschreiben II
temperature ['temprətʃə] Temperatur II • **have a temperature** Fieber haben II
tennis ['tenɪs] Tennis I
tense [tens] (grammatische) Zeit, Tempus III 5 (103)
term [tɜːm] Trimester II
terrible ['terəbl] schrecklich, furchtbar I
test [test] Klassenarbeit, Test, Prüfung II
text [tekst] Text I
text message ['tekst ˌmesɪdʒ] SMS II
text sb. [tekst] jm. eine SMS schicken II
°**textile** ['tekstaɪl] Stoff
than [ðæn, ðən] als II • **more than me** mehr als ich II
Thank you. ['θæŋk juː] Danke (schön). I • **Thanks.** [θæŋks] Danke. I • **Thanks a lot!** Vielen

Dank! I • **Thanks very much!** Danke sehr! / Vielen Dank! II

that [ðət, ðæt]
1. das (dort) I
2. jene(r, s) I • **that day** an jenem Tag III 3 (69) • **That's me.** Das bin ich. I • **That's right.** Das ist richtig. / Das stimmt. I • **That's up to you.** Das liegt bei dir. / Das kannst/musst du (selbst) entscheiden. III 5 (94) • **that's why** deshalb, darum I

that [ðət, ðæt] dass I • °**so that** sodass

that [ðət, ðæt] der, die, das; die *(Relativpronomen)* III 3 (55)

°**that much** so sehr, so viel

the [ðə, ði] der, die, das; die I

theatre ['θɪətə] Theater II

their [ðeə] ihr, ihre *(Plural)* I

theirs [ðeəz] ihrer, ihre, ihrs II

them [ðəm, ðem] sie; ihnen I
the two of them die beiden; alle beide II

theme park ['θiːm pɑːk] Themenpark II

themselves [ðəm'selvz] sich III 5 (98)

then [ðen]
1. dann, danach I
2. damals II
Then what? Was dann? II • **just then** genau in dem Moment; gerade dann II

there [ðeə]
1. da, dort I
2. dahin, dorthin I
down there (nach) dort unten II
in there dort drinnen I • **over there** da drüben, dort drüben I
up there dort oben III 1 (12) • **there are** es sind (vorhanden); es gibt I
there's es ist (vorhanden); es gibt I • **there isn't a ...** es ist kein/e ...; es gibt kein/e ... I

thermometer [θə'mɒmɪtə] Thermometer II

these [ðiːz] diese, die (hier) I

they [ðeɪ] sie *(Plural)* I • **They say ...** Man sagt, ... III 1 (12)

thief [θiːf], *pl* **thieves** [θiːvz] Dieb/in II

thing [θɪŋ] Ding, Sache I • **What was the best thing about ...?** Was war das Beste an ...? II

think [θɪŋk], **thought, thought** glauben, meinen, denken I • **Do you really think so?** Meinst du wirklich? / Glaubst du das wirklich? II • **I think so.** Ich glaube (ja). I • **I don't think so.** Das finde/glaube ich nicht. I • **think about** 1. nachdenken über II; 2. denken über, halten von II
think of 1. denken über, halten von II 2. denken an; sich ausdenken II

third [θɜːd] dritte(r, s) I

thirsty ['θɜːsti] durstig I • **be thirsty** Durst haben, durstig sein I

this [ðɪs]
1. dies (hier) I
2. diese(r, s) I
This is Isabel. Hier spricht Isabel. / Hier ist Isabel. *(am Telefon)* II
this morning/afternoon/evening heute Morgen/Nachmittag/Abend I • **this way** hier entlang, in diese Richtung II

those [ðəʊz] die (da), jene (dort) I

thought [θɔːt] *siehe* **think**

thousand ['θaʊznd] tausend I

threw [θruː] *siehe* **throw**

throat Hals, Kehle II • **have a sore throat** [sɔː 'θrəʊt] Halsschmerzen haben II

through [θruː] durch II

throw [θrəʊ], **threw, thrown** werfen I • **throw the dice** würfeln II

thrown [θrəʊn] *siehe* **throw**

Thursday ['θɜːzdeɪ, 'θɜːzdi] Donnerstag I

°**tick** [tɪk] Häkchen

ticket ['tɪkɪt]
1. Eintrittskarte I
2. Fahrkarte III 1 (14)

ticket machine ['tɪkɪt məˌʃiːn] Fahrkartenautomat III 1 (20/174)

tide [taɪd] Gezeiten, Ebbe und Flut II • **the tide is in** es ist Flut II
the tide is out es ist Ebbe II

tidy ['taɪdi] aufräumen I

tidy ['taɪdi] ordentlich, aufgeräumt II

tiger ['taɪgə] Tiger II

tights *(pl)* [taɪts] Strumpfhose III 3 (56)

till [tɪl] bis *(zeitlich)* I

time [taɪm] Zeit; Uhrzeit I • **in time** rechtzeitig II • **What's the time?** Wie spät ist es? I • **a long time** lange III 1 (13)

time(s) [taɪmz] Mal(e); -mal II • **for the first time** zum ersten Mal II

timetable ['taɪmteɪbl] Stundenplan I

°**time zone** ['taɪm zəʊn] Zeitzone

timing ['taɪmɪŋ]: **bad timing** schlechtes Timing III 3 (57)

tip [tɪp] Tipp III 1 (13)

tired ['taɪəd] müde I

title ['taɪtl] Titel, Überschrift I

to [tə, tu]
1. zu, nach I • **an e-mail to** eine E-Mail an I • **to Jenny's** zu Jenny I
to the doctor's zum Arzt III 2 (45/181) • **to the front** nach vorn I • **I've never been to Bath.** Ich bin noch nie in Bath gewesen. II • **write to** schreiben an I
2. **quarter to 12** Viertel vor 12 (11.45 / 23.45) I • **from Monday to Friday** von Montag bis Freitag III 2 (33)
3. **try to do** versuchen, zu tun I
4. um zu I

toast [təʊst] Toast(brot) I

today [tə'deɪ] heute I

toe [təʊ] Zeh I

together [tə'geðə] zusammen I

toilet ['tɔɪlət] Toilette I

told [təʊld] *siehe* **tell**

tomato [tə'mɑːtəʊ], *pl* **tomatoes** Tomate II

tomorrow [tə'mɒrəʊ] morgen I

°**tongue-twister** ['tʌŋtwɪstə] Zungenbrecher

tonight [tə'naɪt] heute Nacht, heute Abend I

too [tuː]: **from Bristol too** auch aus Bristol I • **Me too.** Ich auch. I

too much/big/... [tuː] zu viel/groß/... I

took [tʊk] *siehe* **take**

tooth [tuːθ], *pl* **teeth** [tiːθ] Zahn I

toothache ['tuːθeɪk] Zahnschmerzen II

top [tɒp]
1. Spitze, oberes Ende I • **at the top (of)** oben, am oberen Ende, an der Spitze (von) I
2. Top, Oberteil I

top [tɒp] *(adj)* Spitzen-, oberste(r, s) III 3 (59)

topic ['tɒpɪk] Thema, Themenbereich I • **topic sentence** *Satz, der in das Thema eines Absatzes einführt* II

tortoise ['tɔːtəs] Schildkröte I

°**tossing the caber** [ˌtɒsɪŋ ðə 'keɪbə] Baumstammwerfen

touch [tʌtʃ] berühren, anfassen I

touch [tʌtʃ]: **keep in touch** in Verbindung bleiben, Kontakt halten III Intro (11)

tough [tʌf] tough, selbstsicher, zäh III 4 (77)

tour (of the house) [tʊə] Rundgang, Tour (durch das Haus) I

tourist ['tʊərɪst] Tourist/in II
tourist information Fremdenverkehrsamt II

towards Mr Green [tə'wɔːdz] auf Mr Green zu, in Mr Greens Richtung I

towel ['taʊəl] Handtuch II

tower ['taʊə] Turm I

town [taʊn] Stadt I • **the centre of town** die Mitte der Stadt III 1 (12/70)
in town in der Stadt III 1 (12/170)
into town in die Stadt III 1 (12/170)
► S.170 Places without articles
track [træk] Stück, Titel, Track *(auf einer CD)* III 5 (97)
trade [treɪd] Handel II
traditional [trə'dɪʃənl] traditionell III 4 (73)
traffic ['træfɪk] Verkehr II
°**trail** [treɪl] Lehrpfad, Rundgang
train [treɪn] Zug I • **on the train** im Zug I • °**goods train** Güterzug
train [treɪn] trainieren III 3 (54)
trainers *(pl)* ['treɪnəz] Turnschuhe II
training session ['seʃn] Trainingsstunde, -einheit III 3 (54)
tram [træm] Straßenbahn III 1 (20/174)
translate (from ... into) [træns'leɪt] übersetzen (aus ... in) III 2 (35)
translation [træns'leɪʃn] Übersetzung III 2 (35)
transport *(no pl)* ['trænspɔːt] Transport(wesen) III 1 (20)
trap [træp] Falle II
trap (-pp-) [træp] (mit einer Falle) fangen III 4 (73/187)
travel (-ll-) ['trævl] reisen II
Travelcard ['trævlkɑːd] Tages-/Wochen-/Monatsfahrkarte *(der Londoner Verkehrsbetriebe)* III 1 (14)
°**travel guide** ['trævl gaɪd] Reiseführer (Buch)
tree [triː] Baum I
°**trend** [trend] Trend
trendy ['trendi] modisch, schick III 2 (33)
trick [trɪk]
1. (Zauber-)Kunststück, Trick I
do tricks (Zauber-)Kunststücke machen I
2. Streich II • **play a trick on sb.** jm. einen Streich spielen II
trip [trɪp] Reise; Ausflug I • **go on a trip** einen Ausflug/eine Reise machen II
trombone [trɒm'bəʊn] Posaune III Intro (11)
trouble ['trʌbl] Schwierigkeiten, Ärger II • **be in trouble** in Schwierigkeiten sein; Ärger kriegen II
trousers *(pl)* ['traʊzəz] Hose II
true [truː] wahr II • **come true** wahr werden II
trumpet ['trʌmpɪt] Trompete III Intro (11)
try [traɪ]
1. versuchen I
2. probieren, kosten I
try and do sth. / try to do sth. versuchen, etwas zu tun I • **try sth. on** etwas anprobieren *(Kleidung)* I
tsunami [tsuː'nɑːmi] Tsunami III 5 (100)
T-shirt ['tiːʃɜːt] T-Shirt I
tube [tjuːb]**: the Tube** *(no pl) (BE)* die Londoner U-Bahn III 1 (14)
Tuesday ['tjuːzdeɪ, -di] Dienstag I
tune [tjuːn] Melodie III Intro (8)
tunnel ['tʌnl] Tunnel II
turn [tɜːn]
1. sich umdrehen II • **turn left/right** (nach) links/rechts abbiegen II • **turn to sb.** sich jm. zuwenden; sich an jn. wenden II
2. **turn sth. off/on** etwas aus-/einschalten I • **turn sth. down/up** etwas leiser/lauter stellen III 4 (74)
turn [tɜːn]**: (It's) my turn.** Ich bin dran / an der Reihe. I • **Miss a turn.** Einmal aussetzen. II • **Take another turn.** *hier:* Würfel noch einmal. II • °**Take turns.** Wechselt euch ab.
TV [tiː'viː] Fernsehen I • **on TV** im Fernsehen I • **watch TV** fernsehen I
twice [twaɪs] zweimal III 2 (32)
twin [twɪn]**: twin brother** Zwillingsbruder I • **twins** *(pl)* Zwillinge I • **twin town** Partnerstadt I
°**type** [taɪp] Typ

U

uncle ['ʌŋkl] Onkel I
unclear [ˌʌn'klɪə] unklar, undeutlich II
uncomfortable [ʌn'kʌmftəbl] unbequem II
unconscious [ʌn'kɒnʃəs] bewusstlos II
uncool *(infml)* [ˌʌn'kuːl] uncool III 3 (64)
under ['ʌndə] unter I
underground ['ʌndəgraʊnd]**: the underground** die U-Bahn II
°**underline** [ˌʌndə'laɪn] unterstreichen
°**underneath** [ʌndə'niːθ]
1. unter
2. darunter
understand [ˌʌndə'stænd]**, understood, understood** verstehen, begreifen I
understood [ˌʌndə'stʊd] *siehe* **understand**
unfair [ˌʌn'feə] unfair, ungerecht II
unfriendly [ʌn'frendli] unfreundlich II
unhappy [ʌn'hæpi] unglücklich II
unhealthy [ʌn'helθi] ungesund III 2 (40)
uniform ['juːnɪfɔːm] Uniform I
unimportant [ˌʌnɪm'pɔːtnt] unwichtig III 2 (40)
uninteresting [ʌn'ɪntrəstɪŋ] uninteressant II
unit ['juːnɪt] Kapitel, Lektion I
united: the United Kingdom (UK) [juˌnaɪtɪd 'kɪŋdəm], [ˌjuː 'keɪ] das Vereinigte Königreich *(Großbritannien und Nordirland)* III Intro (6)
the United States (US) [juˌnaɪtɪd 'steɪts], [ˌjuː‿'es] die Vereinigten Staaten (von Amerika) III Intro (10)
unlike [ˌʌn'laɪk] im Gegensatz zu III 4 (76)
unload [ʌn'ləʊd] entladen III 3 (58)
unsafe [ʌn'seɪf] nicht sicher, gefährlich III 2 (40)
unsure [ˌʌn'ʃʊə, ˌʌn'ʃɔː] unsicher II
untidy [ʌn'taɪdi] unordentlich III 2 (40)
until [ən'tɪl] bis III 2 (46)
up [ʌp] hinauf, herauf, nach oben I
up the hill den Hügel hinauf II
up there dort oben III 1 (12)
That's up to you. Das liegt bei dir. / Das kannst/musst du (selbst) entscheiden. III 5 (94)
°**update** [ˌʌp'deɪt] aktualisieren, auf den neuesten Stand bringen
upset (about) [ˌʌp'set] aufgebracht, gekränkt, mitgenommen (wegen) III 2 (35)
upset sb. (-tt-) [ʌp'set]**, upset, upset** jn. ärgern, kränken, aus der Fassung bringen III 2 (35)
upstairs [ˌʌp'steəz] oben; nach oben I
us [əs, ʌs] uns I
use [juːz] benutzen, verwenden I
use [juːs] Gebrauch III 2 (32)
usually ['juːʒuəli] meistens, gewöhnlich, normalerweise I

V

vacation [və'keɪʃn, *AE:* veɪ'keɪʃn] *(AE)* Urlaub, Ferien III 5 (98)
valley ['væli] Tal II • **valley floor** Talboden II
vegetable ['vedʒtəbl] (ein) Gemüse III 1 (16)
very ['veri] sehr I • **like/love sth. very much** etwas sehr mögen / sehr lieben II • **Thanks very much!** Danke sehr! / Vielen Dank! II
victim ['vɪktɪm] Opfer III 1 (26)

video ['vɪdiəʊ] Video III 1 (12)
view (of) [vju:]
1. Aussicht, Blick (auf) II
2. Ansicht, Meinung III 1 (28)
in my view meiner Ansicht nach III 1 (28) • **point of view** [ˌpɔɪnt‿əv 'vju:] Standpunkt II • **from my point of view** aus meiner Sicht; von meinem Standpunkt aus gesehen II
°**Viking** ['vaɪkɪŋ] Wikinger/in
villa ['vɪlə] Ferienhaus; Villa II
village ['vɪlɪdʒ] Dorf I
violin [ˌvaɪə'lɪn] Violine, Geige III Intro (6) • **play the violin** Geige spielen III Intro (7/169)
°**virtual reality (VR)** [ˌvɜ:tʃuəl ri'æləti] virtuelle Realität *(am Rechner o. im Internet künstlich erzeugter Raum)*
visit ['vɪzɪt] besuchen, aufsuchen II
visit ['vɪzɪt] Besuch II
visitor ['vɪzɪtə] Besucher/in, Gast I
vocabulary [və'kæbjələri] Vokabelverzeichnis, Wörterverzeichnis I
voice [vɔɪs] Stimme I
volleyball ['vɒlibɔ:l] Volleyball I
volunteer work [ˌvɒlən'tɪə] Arbeit als Freiwillige(r) III 4 (74)
vote [vəʊt] Stimme; Stimmrecht III 3 (63)
vowel sound ['vaʊəl saʊnd] Vokallaut II

W

wait (for) ['weɪt fɔ:] warten (auf) I
I can't wait to see ... ich kann es kaum erwarten, ... zu sehen I
Wait a minute. Warte mal! / Moment mal! II • **Wait and see!** Wart's ab! III Intro (11)
wake [weɪk], **woke, woken:**
1. wake sb. (up) jn. (auf)wecken III 5 (99/193)
2. wake up aufwachen III 5 (99)
walk [wɔ:k] (zu Fuß) gehen, laufen I; spazieren gehen III 1 (16)
walk on weiterlaufen III 1 (12)
walk around herumlaufen III 1 (17)
walk [wɔ:k] Spaziergang II • **go for a walk** spazieren gehen, einen Spaziergang machen II
wall [wɔ:l] Wand; Mauer II
want [wɒnt] (haben) wollen I
want to do tun wollen I
war [wɔ:] Krieg III 5 (97)
wardrobe ['wɔ:drəʊb] Kleiderschrank I
warm [wɔ:m] warm II
was [wəz, wɒz]**: (I/he/she/it) was** *siehe* **be**
wash [wɒʃ] waschen I • **I wash my hands.** Ich wasche mir die Hände. I
washing machine ['wɒʃɪŋ məˌʃi:n] Waschmaschine II
waste (on) [weɪst] verschwenden, vergeuden (für) III 4 (74)
watch [wɒtʃ] beobachten, sich etwas ansehen; zusehen I
watch TV fernsehen I
watch [wɒtʃ] Armbanduhr I
water ['wɔ:tə] Wasser I
waterfall ['wɔ:təfɔ:l] Wasserfall III 2 (38)
wave [weɪv] winken II
way [weɪ]
1. Weg; Strecke II • **a long way (from)** weit entfernt (von) I • **ask sb. the way** jn. nach dem Weg fragen II • **on the way (to)** auf dem Weg (zu/nach) II • **tell sb. the way** jm. den Weg beschreiben II
What's the best way to get there? Wie komme ich am besten dahin? III 1 (14)
2. Richtung II • **the other way round** anders herum II • **the wrong way** in die falsche Richtung II • **this way** hier entlang, in diese Richtung II • **which way?** in welche Richtung? / wohin? II
3. No way! [ˌnəʊ 'weɪ] Auf keinen Fall! / Kommt nicht in Frage! II; Was du nicht sagst! / Das kann nicht dein Ernst sein! III 4 (77)
4. by the way übrigens, nebenbei (bemerkt) III Intro (7)
°**5.** Weise • **in lots of different ways** auf viele verschiedene Weisen
way of life Lebensart III 4 (73)
we [wi:] wir I
weak [wi:k] schwach II
wear [weə], **wore, worn** tragen, anhaben (Kleidung) I
weather ['weðə] Wetter II
webcam ['webkæm] Webcam, Internetkamera II
website ['websaɪt] Website II
Wednesday ['wenzdeɪ, 'wenzdi] Mittwoch I
°**wee** *(infml)* [wi:] klein *(besonders in Schottland gebräuchlich)*
week [wi:k] Woche I • **days of the week** Wochentage I • **a three-week holiday** ein dreiwöchiger Urlaub III 4 (80/189) • **once a week** einmal pro Woche III 2 (32)
weekend [ˌwi:k'end] Wochenende I
at the weekend am Wochenende I
weigh [weɪ] wiegen III 4 (80)
weird [wɪəd] seltsam III 4 (85)
welcome ['welkəm]
1. Welcome (to Bristol). Willkommen (in Bristol). I
2. You're welcome. Gern geschehen. / Nichts zu danken. I
welcome sb. (to) ['welkəm] jn. begrüßen, willkommen heißen (in) I
They welcome you to ... Sie heißen dich in ... willkommen I
well [wel] *(gesundheitlich)* gut; gesund, wohlauf II
well [wel] gut II • **go well** gut (ver)laufen, gutgehen II • **You looked after them well.** Du hast dich gut um sie gekümmert. II
Oh well ... Na ja ... / Na gut ... I
Well, ... Nun, ... / Also, ... I
°**wellies** *(pl, infml)* ['weli:z] Gummistiefel *(Plural)*
Welsh [welʃ] walisisch; Walisisch II
went [went] *siehe* **go**
were [wə, wɜ:]**: (we/you/they) were** *siehe* **be**
west [west] Westen; nach Westen; westlich II • **westbound** ['westbaʊnd] Richtung Westen III 1 (14/172) • **western** ['westən] westlich, West- III Intro (9)
wet [wet] feucht, nass II
what [wɒt]
1. was I
2. welche(r, s) I
So what? [səʊ 'wɒt] Und? / Na und? II • **Then what?** Was dann? II • **they didn't know what to do** sie wussten nicht, was sie tun sollten; sie wussten nicht, was zu tun war III 2 (45) • **What a bummer!** *(infml)* ['bʌmə] So ein Mist! / Wie schade! III 4 (75) • **What about ...?** **1.** Was ist mit ...? / Und ...? I; **2.** Wie wär's mit ...? I • **What are you talking about?** Wovon redest du? I • **What can I get you?** Was kann/darf ich euch/Ihnen bringen? II
What colour is ...? Welche Farbe hat ...? I • **What for?** [ˌwɒt 'fɔ:] Wofür? II • **What have we got next?** Was haben wir als Nächstes? I • **What kind of car ...?** Was für ein Auto ...? III Intro (6/169)
What page are we on? Auf welcher Seite sind wir? I • **What's for homework?** Was haben wir als Hausaufgabe auf? I • **What's the best way to get there?** Wie komme ich am besten dahin? III 1 (14) • **What's the point?** Was soll das? III 5 (99) • **What's the time?** Wie spät ist es? I • **What's the matter?** Was ist los? / Was ist

denn? II • **What's wrong with you?** Was fehlt dir? II • **What's your name?** Wie heißt du? I **What was the weather like?** Wie war das Wetter? II
wheel [wi:l] Rad III 1 (12) • **big wheel** Riesenrad III 1 (12)
wheelchair ['wi:ltʃeə] Rollstuhl I
when [wen] wann I • **When's your birthday?** Wann hast du Geburtstag? I
when [wen]
1. wenn I
2. als I
where [weə]
1. wo I
2. wohin I
Where are you from? Wo kommst du her? I
which [wɪtʃ] welche(r, s) I • **Which picture ...?** Welches Bild ...? I **which way?** in welche Richtung? / wohin? II
which [wɪtʃ] der, die, das; die *(Relativpronomen)* III 3 (55)
while [waɪl] während III 2 (47)
▶ S.181 German „während"
°**whisky** ['wɪski] Whisky
whisper ['wɪspə] flüstern I
whistle ['wɪsl] pfeifen II
whistle ['wɪsl] Pfiff; (Triller-)Pfeife II
white [waɪt] weiß I
who [hu:]
1. wer I
2. wen / wem II
Who did she talk to? Mit wem hat sie geredet? II
who [hu:] der, die, das; die *(Relativpronomen)* III 3 (55)
whole [həʊl] ganze(r, s), gesamte(r, s) II • **the whole of 2006** das ganze Jahr 2006 II
whose [hu:z] wessen II • **Whose are these?** Wem gehören diese? II
whose [hu:z]: **the man whose statue ...** der Mann, dessen Statue ... II
why [waɪ] warum I • **Why me?** Warum ich? I • **that's why** deshalb, darum I
wide [waɪd] weit, breit III 4 (85)
wife [waɪf], *pl* **wives** [waɪvz] Ehefrau II
wild [waɪld] wild II
will [wɪl]: **you'll be cold (= you will be cold)** du wirst frieren; ihr werdet frieren II • **you'll have travelled** du wirst gereist sein III 5 (98)
win (-nn-) [wɪn], **won, won** gewinnen I
win [wɪn] Sieg III 3 (59)
wind [wɪnd] Wind I
window ['wɪndəʊ] Fenster I
windy ['wɪndi] windig I
winner ['wɪnə] Gewinner/in, Sieger/in II
winter ['wɪntə] Winter I
wish [wɪʃ] sich etwas wünschen III 1 (24) • **You wish!** *etwa:* Das hättest du wohl gern! III 2 (34)
▶ S.174 (to) wish
with [wɪð]
1. mit I
2. bei I
Sit with me. Setz dich zu mir. / Setzt euch zu mir. I
without [wɪ'ðaʊt] ohne I
wives [waɪvz] *pl von „wife"* II
wolf [wʊlf], *pl* **wolves** [wʊlvz] Wolf II
woman ['wʊmən], *pl* **women** ['wɪmɪn] Frau I
won [wʌn] *siehe* **win**
wonder ['wʌndə] sich fragen, gern wissen wollen II
wonderful ['wʌndəfəl] wunderbar II
won't [wəʊnt]: **you won't be cold (= you will not be cold)** du wirst nicht frieren; ihr werdet nicht frieren II
wood [wʊd] Holz II • **woods** *(pl)* Wald, Wälder II
woodpecker ['wʊdpekə] Specht II
woods *(pl)* [wʊdz] Wald, Wälder II
°**wool** [wʊl] Wolle
word [wɜ:d] Wort I • **word building** Wortbildung II • **word field** Wortfeld III 1 (29) • °**word order** Wortstellung
wore [wɔ:] *siehe* **wear**
work [wɜ:k]
1. arbeiten I • **work hard** hart arbeiten II • **work on sth.** an etwas arbeiten I
2. funktionieren III 1 (26)
work [wɜ:k] Arbeit I • **at work** bei der Arbeit / am Arbeitsplatz I • **volunteer work** Arbeit als Freiwillige(r) III 4 (74)
worker ['wɜ:kə] Arbeiter/in II
worksheet ['wɜ:kʃi:t] Arbeitsblatt I
workshop ['wɜ:kʃɒp] Workshop, Lehrgang III Intro (10)
world [wɜ:ld] Welt I • **all over the world** auf der ganzen Welt III Intro (6) • **from all over the world** aus der ganzen Welt II • **in the world** auf der Welt II • **world music** Weltmusik III Intro (6)
worn [wɔ:n] *siehe* **wear**
worried ['wʌrid]: **be worried (about)** beunruhigt, besorgt sein (wegen) I
worry ['wʌri] Sorge, Kummer II
worry (about) ['wʌri] sich Sorgen machen (wegen, um) I • **Don't worry.** Mach dir keine Sorgen. I
worse (than) [wɜ:s] schlechter, schlimmer (als) II
worst [wɜ:st]: **(the) worst** am schlechtesten, schlimmsten; der/die/das schlechteste, schlimmste ... II
would [wəd, wʊd] würde, würdest, würden II • **I'd like ... (= I would like ...)** Ich hätte gern ... / Ich möchte gern ... I • **Would you like ...?** Möchtest du ...? / Möchten Sie ...? I **I'd like to go (= I would like to go)** Ich würde gern gehen / Ich möchte gehen I • **I wouldn't like to go** ich würde nicht gern gehen / ich möchte nicht gehen I
write [raɪt], **wrote, written** schreiben I • **write down** aufschreiben I • **write to** schreiben an I °**write up** ausarbeiten
writer ['raɪtə] Schreiber/in; Schriftsteller/in II
written ['rɪtn] *siehe* **write**
wrong [rɒŋ] falsch, verkehrt I **get sth. wrong** etwas falsch machen III 4 (76) • **the wrong way** in die falsche Richtung II • **What's wrong with you?** Was fehlt dir? II
wrote [rəʊt] *siehe* **write**

Y

yard [jɑ:d] Hof II • **in the yard** auf dem Hof II
yawn [jɔ:n] gähnen II
year [jɪə]
1. Jahr I • **a 70-year-old teacher** ein 70-jähriger Lehrer III 4 (80/189)
2. Jahrgangsstufe I
yellow ['jeləʊ] gelb I
yes [jes] ja I
yesterday ['jestədeɪ, 'jestədi] gestern I • **the day before yesterday** vorgestern II • **yesterday morning/afternoon/evening** gestern Morgen/Nachmittag/Abend I
yet [jet]: **not (...) yet** noch nicht II • **yet?** schon? II
yoga ['jəʊgə] Yoga I
yogurt ['jɒgət] Jogurt III 1 (16)
you [ju:]
1. du; Sie I
2. ihr I
3. dir; dich; euch I
4. man III 1 (12)
How are you? Wie geht es dir/Ihnen/euch? II • **You're welcome.** Gern geschehen. / Nichts zu dan-

ken. I • **you two** ihr zwei I • **You wish!** *etwa:* Das hättest du wohl gerne! III 2 (34)
young [jʌŋ] jung I
your [jɔː]
1. dein/e I
2. Ihr I
3. euer/eure I
yours [jɔːz]
1. deiner, deine, deins II
2. eurer, eure, eures II
yourself [jə'self, jɔː'self] dir/dich III 5 (98) • **about yourself** über dich selbst III 3 (68)
yourselves [jɔː'selvz] euch III 5 (98)
youth [juːθ] Jugend III Intro (6)
youth hostel ['juːθ ˌhɒstəl] Jugendherberge III Intro (8/169)
yummy ['jʌmi] *(infml)* lecker III 1 (17)

Z

zebra ['zebrə] Zebra II
zero ['zɪərəʊ] null I
zone [zəʊn] Zone, Bereich III 1 (14)
zoo [zuː] Zoo, Tierpark I

English sounds (Englische Laute)

Die Lautschrift in den eckigen Klammern zeigt dir, wie ein Wort ausgesprochen wird.
In der folgenden Übersicht findest du alle Lautzeichen.

Vokale (Selbstlaute)

[iː]	green	[ʊ]	book	[ɪə]	here
[i]	happy	[ʌ]	mum	[eə]	where
[ɪ]	in	[ɜː]	T-shirt	[ʊə]	tour
[e]	yes	[ə]	a partner		
[æ]	black	[eɪ]	skate		
[ɑː]	park	[aɪ]	time		
[ɒ]	song	[ɔɪ]	boy		
[ɔː]	morning	[əʊ]	old		
[uː]	blue	[aʊ]	now		

Konsonanten (Mitlaute)

[b]	box	[l]	hello	[ʒ]	television
[p]	play	[r]	red	[tʃ]	teacher
[d]	dad	[w]	we	[dʒ]	Germany
[t]	ten	[j]	you	[θ]	thanks
[g]	good	[f]	full	[ð]	this
[k]	cat	[v]	very	[h]	he
[m]	mum	[s]	sister	[x]	loch
[n]	no	[z]	please		
[ŋ]	sing	[ʃ]	shop		

The English alphabet (Das englische Alphabet)

a	[eɪ]	**h**	[eɪtʃ]	**o**	[əʊ]	**v**	[viː]
b	[biː]	**i**	[aɪ]	**p**	[piː]	**w**	['dʌbljuː]
c	[siː]	**j**	[dʒeɪ]	**q**	[kjuː]	**x**	[eks]
d	[diː]	**k**	[keɪ]	**r**	[ɑː]	**y**	[waɪ]
e	[iː]	**l**	[el]	**s**	[es]	**z**	[zed]
f	[ef]	**m**	[em]	**t**	[tiː]		
g	[dʒiː]	**n**	[en]	**u**	[juː]		

Das **German – English Dictionary** enthält den **Lernwortschatz** der Bände 1 bis 3 von *English G 21*. Es kann dir eine erste Hilfe sein, wenn du vergessen hast, wie etwas auf Englisch heißt.

Wenn du wissen möchtest, wo das englische Wort zum ersten Mal in *English G 21* vorkommt, dann kannst du im **English – German Dictionary** (S. 195–222) nachschlagen.

Im **German – English Dictionary** werden folgende **Abkürzungen** und **Symbole** verwendet:

jm. = jemandem	sb. = somebody	*pl* = *plural* (Mehrzahl)	*BE* = *British English*
jn. = jemanden	sth. = something	*no pl* = *no plural*	*AE* = *American English*

▸ Der Pfeil verweist auf Kästchen im Vocabulary (S. 168–194), in denen du weitere Informationen findest.

A

ab und zu now and again
abbiegen: (nach) links/rechts abbiegen turn left/right [tɜːn]
Abend evening ['iːvnɪŋ]; *(später Abend)* night [naɪt] • am Abend, abends in the evening
Abendbrot, -essen dinner ['dɪnə] **Abendbrot essen** have dinner **zum Abendbrot** for dinner
Abenteuer adventure [əd'ventʃə]
aber but [bət, bʌt]
abfahren *(wegfahren)* leave [liːv]
Abfall rubbish ['rʌbɪʃ]
abgelegen faraway ['fɑːrəweɪ]
Abgemacht! It's a deal! [diːl]
abhängen hang out [ˌhæŋ_'aʊt] *(infml)*
abholen: jn. abholen pick sb. up [ˌpɪk_'ʌp]
Abkommen: ein Abkommen treffen make a deal [diːl]
Abmachung: eine Abmachung treffen make a deal [diːl]
abnehmen: den Hörer abnehmen pick up the phone [ˌpɪk_'ʌp]
Absatz *(in einem Text)* paragraph ['pærəgrɑːf]
abschließen *(Zimmer)* lock up [ˌlɒk_'ʌp]
Abschluss *(einer Geschichte, eines Films usw.)* ending ['endɪŋ]
abschneiden cut off [ˌkʌt_'ɒf]
Abschnitt section ['sekʃn]
absetzen: etwas absetzen *(Hut)* take sth. off [ˌteɪk_'ɒf]
abstürzen crash [kræʃ]
Abtei abbey ['æbi]
abtrennen cut off [ˌkʌt_'ɒf]
abwarten: Wart's ab! Wait and see!
abwaschen: das Geschirr abwaschen do the dishes ['dɪʃɪz]
abziehen: 10 Cent abziehen take 10 c off [ˌteɪk_'ɒf]
achten (auf) *(beim Zuhören)* listen (for) ['lɪsn]
Acker field [fiːld]
addieren (zu) add (to) [æd]
Adresse address [ə'dres]
Affe monkey ['mʌŋki]
akkurat accurate ['ækjərət]
Akrobat/in acrobat ['ækrəbæt]
aktiv active ['æktɪv]
Aktivität activity [æk'tɪvəti]
Akzent accent ['æksənt]
albern silly ['sɪli]
Album album ['ælbəm]
Alkohol alcohol ['ælkəhɒl]
alle *(die ganze Gruppe)* all [ɔːl] **alle beide** the two of them
allein alone [ə'ləʊn]
Alleinerziehende(r) single parent [ˌsɪŋgl 'peərənt]
alleinstehend single ['sɪŋgl]
allergisch (gegen etwas) allergic (to sth.) [ə'lɜːdʒɪk]
alles everything ['evriθɪŋ]; all [ɔːl] **alles, was wir jetzt (noch) tun müssen, ...** all we have to do now ...
allgemeine(r, s) general ['genrəl]
Alltags-; alltäglich everyday *(adj)* ['evrideɪ]
Alphabet alphabet ['ælfəbet]
als 1. *(zeitlich)* when [wen]; *(während)* as [əz, æz]
2. größer/teurer als bigger/more expensive than [ðæn, ðən] • **mehr als** more than • **mehr als ich** more than me
3. als ob like [laɪk] *(infml)*
also *(daher, deshalb)* so [səʊ] **Also, ...** Well, ... [wel]
alt old [əʊld]
Alter age [eɪdʒ] • **im Alter von 16** at (the age of) 16
am 1. am Bahnhof at the station **am Himmel** in the sky • **am oberen Ende (von)** at the top (of) **am Strand** on the beach • **am Telefon** on the phone • **am unteren Ende (von)** at the bottom (of) ['bɒtəm]
2. *(nahe bei)* **am Meer** by the sea
3. *(zeitlich)* **am 13. Juni** on 13th June • **am Morgen/Nachmittag/Abend** in the morning/afternoon/evening • **am Ende (von)** at the end (of) • **am Freitag** on Friday **am Freitagmorgen** on Friday morning • **am nächsten Morgen/Tag** the next morning/day • **am Wochenende** at the weekend
amen amen [ɑː'men]
amüsieren: sich (gut) amüsieren have fun [hæv 'fʌn]; have a good time
an 1. an dem/den Tisch (dort) at that table • **an der Spitze (von)** at the top (of) • **an der/die Tafel** on the board • **schreiben an** write to **an jenem Tag** that day
2. *(nahe bei)* **an der See** by the sea
3. Was war das Beste an ...? What was the best thing about ...?
4. an sein *(Radio, Licht usw.)* be on
Andenken souvenir [ˌsuːvə'nɪə]
andere(r, s) other ['ʌðə] • **die anderen** the others • **ein(e) andere(r, s) ...** another ... [ə'nʌðə] **anderer Meinung sein (als)** disagree (with) [ˌdɪsə'griː]
anders (als) different (from) ['dɪfrənt] **anders herum** the other way round • **etwas anders ausdrücken** paraphrase sth. ['pærəfreɪz]
anders: jemand anders somebody else [els] • **etwas anders** something else
anderswo in other places
Anfang beginning [bɪ'gɪnɪŋ]
anfangen (mit) start [stɑːt]
anfassen touch [tʌtʃ]
anfreunden: sich anfreunden (mit) make friends (with)
anfühlen: sich gut anfühlen feel good [fiːl]
Anführungsstriche, -zeichen quotation marks [kwəʊ'teɪʃn ˌmɑːks]
angehen *(Licht)* go on
Angler fisherman ['fɪʃəmən], *pl* fishermen ['fɪʃəmən]
angreifen attack [ə'tæk]

Angriff attack [ə'tæk]
Angst (vor) fear (of) ['fɪə] • **Angst haben (vor)** be afraid (of) [ə'freɪd]; be scared (of) [skeəd]
anhaben *(Kleidung)* wear [weə]
anhalten stop [stɒp]
Anhänger/in fan [fæn]; supporter [sə'pɔ:tə]
anhören 1. sich etwas anhören listen to sth. ['lɪsn]
2. sich gut anhören sound good [saʊnd]
anklicken: etwas anklicken click on sth. [klɪk]
anklopfen (an) knock (on) [nɒk]
ankommen arrive [ə'raɪv]
Ankündigung announcement [ə'naʊnsmənt]
Ankunft arrival [ə'raɪvl]
anlächeln: jn. anlächeln smile at sb. [smaɪl]
Anleitung(en) *(Gebrauchsanweisung(en))* instructions *(pl)* [ɪn'strʌkʃnz]
anmailen: jn. anmailen mail sb. [meɪl]
anmalen paint [peɪnt]
annehmen *(vermuten)* suppose [sə'pəʊz]
Anorak anorak ['ænəræk]
anprobieren *(Kleidung)* try on [ˌtraɪ_'ɒn]
Anruf call [kɔ:l]; phone call ['fəʊn kɔ:l]
anrufen call [kɔ:l]; phone [fəʊn]
Ansage announcement [ə'naʊnsmənt]
anschauen look at [lʊk] • **etwas genau anschauen** look closely at sth. ['kləʊsli]
anschließen: sich jm. anschließen join sb. [dʒɔɪn]
anschreien: jn. anschreien shout at sb. [ʃaʊt]
Anschrift *(Adresse)* address [ə'dres]
ansehen: sich etwas ansehen look at sth. [lʊk]; watch sth. [wɒtʃ]
Ansicht view [vju:] • **meiner Ansicht nach** in my view
anstreichen paint [peɪnt]
Antwort (auf) answer (to) ['ɑ:nsə]
antworten (auf) answer (to) ['ɑ:nsə]; reply (to) [rɪ'plaɪ]
Anweisung(en) *(Gebrauchsanweisung(en))* instructions *(pl)* [ɪn'strʌkʃnz]
Anzeige *(Inserat)* advert ['ædvɜ:t]
anziehen: etwas anziehen *(Kleidung)* put sth. on [ˌpʊt_'ɒn] • **sich anziehen** get dressed [get 'drest]
Apfel apple ['æpl]
Apfelsine orange ['ɒrɪndʒ]
Apotheke chemist ['kemɪst]
Apotheker: beim Apotheker at the chemist's
Appetit appetite ['æpɪtaɪt]
April April ['eɪprəl]
Arbeit work [wɜ:k] • **bei der Arbeit/am Arbeitsplatz** at work • **gute Arbeit leisten** do a good job
Arbeit als Freiwillige(r) volunteer work [ˌvɒlən'tɪə ˌwɜ:k]
arbeiten (an) work (on) [wɜ:k]
Arbeiter/in worker ['wɜ:kə]
Arbeitsblatt worksheet ['wɜ:kʃi:t]
Arbeits- und Lerntechniken study skills ['stʌdi skɪlz]
Architekt/in architect ['ɑ:kɪtekt]
Ärger *(Schwierigkeiten)* trouble ['trʌbl] • **Ärger kriegen** be in trouble
ärgern: jn. ärgern *(kränken)* upset sb. [ʌp'set]
arm poor [pɔ:, pʊə]
Arm arm [ɑ:m] • **jn. auf den Arm nehmen** *(necken)* tease sb. [ti:z]
Armbanduhr watch [wɒtʃ]
Art *(Sorte)* sort (of) [sɔ:t]; kind (of) [kaɪnd]
Artikel article ['ɑ:tɪkl]
Arzt/Ärztin doctor ['dɒktə] • **beim/zum Arzt** at/to the doctor's
auch: auch aus Bristol from Bristol too [tu:] • **Ich auch.** Me too.
auch nicht not (...) either ['aɪðə, 'i:ðə]
auf on [ɒn]; **auf (... hinauf)** onto ['ɒntə, 'ɒntʊ] • **auf dem Bild/Foto** in the picture/photo • **auf dem Feld** in the field • **auf der ganzen Welt** all over the world • **auf dem Hof** in the yard • **auf dem Land** in the country/land • **auf dem Weg (zu/nach)** on the way (to) • **auf der Welt** in the world • **auf einmal** suddenly ['sʌdnli] • **auf Englisch** in English • **Auf geht's!** Let's go.
auf jn. zu towards sb. [tə'wɔ:dz]
Auf keinen Fall! No way! • **auf See** at sea • **Auf welcher Seite sind wir?** What page are we on?
Auf Wiedersehen. Goodbye. [ˌgʊd'baɪ]
aufbauen *(Ausrüstung)* set up [set]
aufbewahren keep [ki:p]
aufführen *(Szene, Dialog)* act [ækt]
Aufgabe *(im Schulbuch)* exercise ['eksəsaɪz]; *(Job)* job [dʒɒb]
aufgebracht (wegen) upset (about) [ˌʌp'set]
aufgeräumt *(ordentlich)* tidy ['taɪdi]
aufgeregt *(nervös)* nervous ['nɜ:vəs]; *(begeistert)* excited [ɪk'saɪtɪd]
aufheben *(vom Boden)* pick up
aufhören stop [stɒp]
aufkleben stick on [ˌstɪk_'ɒn]
auflegen: *(Musik in der Disko)* **auflegen** DJ ['di:dʒeɪ]
auflisten list [lɪst]
aufmachen open ['əʊpən]
Aufnahme *(Ton, Video)* recording [rɪ'kɔ:dɪŋ]
aufnehmen 1. *(Ton, Video)* record [rɪ'kɔ:d]
2. mit jm. Kontakt aufnehmen contact sb. ['kɒntækt]
aufpassen: auf etwas/jn. aufpassen look after sth./sb. [ˌlʊk_'ɑ:ftə]
aufräumen tidy ['taɪdi]
aufregend exciting [ɪk'saɪtɪŋ]
Aufsatz essay ['eseɪ]
aufschauen (von) look up (from) [ˌlʊk_'ʌp]
aufschreiben write down [ˌraɪt 'daʊn]
Aufseher/in *(im Park)* ranger ['reɪndʒə]
aufsetzen: etwas aufsetzen *(Hut)* put sth. on [ˌpʊt_'ɒn] • **sich aufsetzen** sit up [ˌsɪt_'ʌp]
aufstehen get up [ˌget_'ʌp]
aufstellen *(Ausrüstung)* set up [set]
aufsuchen: jn. aufsuchen see sb. [si:]
auftauchen *(erscheinen)* appear [ə'pɪə]
aufteilen (in); sich aufteilen (in) divide (into) [dɪ'vaɪd]
Auftritt *(Konzert)* gig [gɪg] *(infml)*
einen Auftritt haben do a gig
aufwachen wake up [weɪk]
aufwachsen grow up [grəʊ]
aufwecken: jn. aufwecken wake sb. (up) [weɪk]
aufzählen *(auflisten)* list [lɪst]
Aufzeichnung *(Aufnahme)* recording [rɪ'kɔ:dɪŋ]
Aufzug lift [lɪft] *(BE)*; elevator ['elɪveɪtə] *(AE)*
Auge eye [aɪ] • **Sie traute ihren Augen kaum.** She couldn't believe her eyes. [bɪ'li:v]
Augenblick moment ['məʊmənt]
August August ['ɔ:gəst]
aus: Ich komme/bin aus ... I'm from ... [frəm, frɒm] • **aus ... (heraus/hinaus)** out of ... ['aʊt_əv] • **aus dem gesamten Vereinigten Königreich** from all over the UK • **aus dem Zug/Bus aussteigen** get off the train/bus • **aus der ganzen Welt** from all over the world
aus der Schule from school • **aus etwas (gemacht) sein** to be made of sth. • **aus ganz England** from all over England • **aus meiner Sicht** from my point of view • **aus vielen Gründen** for lots of reasons
Kleider aus den 60ern / aus den

60er Jahren dresses from the 60s ['sɪkstiz] • **aus zweiter Hand** *(gebraucht)* second-hand
ausbessern repair [rɪ'peə]
ausdenken: sich etwas ausdenken think of sth. [θɪŋk]
Ausdruck *((Rede-)Wendung)* phrase [freɪz]; expression [ɪk'spreʃn]
ausdrucken: etwas ausdrucken print sth. out [ˌprɪnt_'aʊt]
Auseinandersetzung argument ['ɑ:gjumənt] • **eine Auseinandersetzung haben** *(sich streiten)* have an argument
Ausflug trip [trɪp] • **einen Ausflug machen** go on a trip
ausgeben: Geld ausgeben (für) spend money (on) [spend]
ausgehen *(weg-, rausgehen)* go out [ˌgəʊ_'aʊt] • **mit jm. ausgehen** *(regelmäßig)* date *(besonders AE)* [deɪt]
ausgezeichnet fine [faɪn]
ausgleichen *(das Ausgleichstor erzielen)* equalize ['i:kwəlaɪz]
aushalten *(ertragen)* stand [stænd] **Ich kann es nicht aushalten.** I can't stand it.
Ausland: im Ausland abroad [ə'brɔ:d] **ins Ausland gehen/fahren** go abroad
ausleihen: sich etwas ausleihen borrow sth. ['bɒrəʊ]
auspressen squeeze [skwi:z]
ausruhen: sich ausruhen relax [rɪ'læks]
Ausrüstung equipment [ɪ'kwɪpmənt]
ausschalten: den Computer ausschalten turn off the computer [ˌtɜ:n_'ɒf]
ausschneiden cut out [ˌkʌt_'aʊt]
aussehen: anders/toll/alt aussehen look different/great/old [lʊk] **gleich aussehen** look the same
Außen- outdoor ['aʊtdɔ:]
außerhalb seines Zimmers outside his room [ˌaʊt'saɪd]
aussetzen: Einmal aussetzen. Miss a turn. [tɜ:n]
Aussicht *(Blick)* view [vju:]
Aussprache pronunciation [prəˌnʌnsi'eɪʃn]
ausstehen *(ertragen)* stand [stænd] **Ich kann es nicht ausstehen.** I can't stand it.
aussteigen (aus dem Zug/Bus) get off (the train/bus) [ˌget_'ɒf]
aussuchen: (sich) etwas aussuchen choose sth. [tʃu:z]
Austausch exchange [ɪks'tʃeɪndʒ]
austauschen exchange [ɪks'tʃeɪndʒ]
Austauschschüler/in exchange student
ausverkauft sein be sold out [səʊld]
Auswahl (an) selection (of) [sɪ'lekʃn]
auswählen choose [tʃu:z]
ausziehen 1. *(aus Wohnung)* move out [ˌmu:v_'aʊt] **2. etwas ausziehen** *(Kleidung)* take sth. off [ˌteɪk_'ɒf]
Auto car [kɑ:]
Autsch! Ouch! [aʊtʃ]

B

Baby baby ['beɪbi] • **ein Baby bekommen** have a baby
Badeanzug swimsuit ['swɪmsu:t]
Badehose swimming trunks *(pl)* [trʌŋks]
baden *(ein Bad nehmen)* have a bath [bɑ:θ]
Badewanne bath [bɑ:θ]
Badezimmer bathroom ['bɑ:θru:m]
Badminton badminton ['bædmɪntən]
Bahnhof station ['steɪʃn] • **am Bahnhof** at the station
Bahnsteig platform ['plætfɔ:m]
bald soon [su:n] • **Bis bald.** See you. ['si: ju:]
Ball *(im Sport; Tanz)* ball [bɔ:l]
Banane banana [bə'nɑ:nə]
Band *(Musikgruppe)* band [bænd]
Banjo banjo ['bændʒəʊ]
Bank *(Sparkasse)* bank [bæŋk]
Bankräuber/in bank robber ['rɒbə]
Bar bar [bɑ:]
Bär bear [beə]
Baseball baseball ['beɪsbɔ:l]
Baseballmütze baseball cap [kæp]
Basketball basketball ['bɑ:skɪtbɔ:l]
Bassgitarre bass; bass guitar [beɪs]
Bauchweh stomach ache ['stʌmək_eɪk]
bauen build [bɪld]
Bauer/Bäuerin farmer ['fɑ:mə]
Bauernhaus farmhouse ['fɑ:mhaʊs]
Bauernhof farm [fɑ:m]
Baum tree [tri:]
beantworten answer ['ɑ:nsə]; reply to [rɪ'plaɪ]
bedeuten mean [mi:n]
Bedeutung meaning ['mi:nɪŋ]
beeilen: sich beeilen hurry ['hʌri]; hurry up [ˌhʌri_'ʌp]
beeindruckend impressive [ɪm'presɪv]
beenden finish ['fɪnɪʃ]
Begabung talent ['tælənt]
begeistert excited [ɪk'saɪtɪd]
Beginn beginning [bɪ'gɪnɪŋ]
beginnen (mit) start [stɑ:t]; begin [bɪ'gɪn]
begreifen understand [ˌʌndə'stænd]
Begrenzung limit ['lɪmɪt]
Begründung reason ['ri:zn]
behalten keep [ki:p]
behindert disabled [dɪs'eɪbld]
bei: bei den Shaws zu Hause at the Shaws' house • **bei der Arbeit** at work • **Englisch bei Mr Kingsley** English with Mr Kingsley • **beim Apotheker/Arzt/Friseur** at the chemist's/doctor's/hairdresser's
beide both [bəʊθ] • **die beiden / alle beide** the two of them
Beifall klatschen cheer [tʃɪə]
Bein leg [leg]
beinahe almost ['ɔ:lməʊst]
Beispiel example [ɪg'zɑ:mpl] • **zum Beispiel** for example • **wie (zum Beispiel)** such as
Beitrag *(Wettbewerbseinsendung)* entry ['entri]
Bekanntgabe announcement [ə'naʊnsmənt]
bekanntgeben announce [ə'naʊns]
bekommen get [get] • **ein Baby bekommen** have a baby
beladen load [ləʊd]
belebt *(Straße; Ort)* busy ['bɪzi]
beliebt popular ['pɒpjələ]
bellen bark [bɑ:k]
benennen name [neɪm]
benötigen need [ni:d]
benutzen use [ju:z]
beobachten watch [wɒtʃ]
bequem comfortable ['kʌmftəbl]
Bereich area ['eəriə]; section ['sekʃn]; zone [zəʊn]
bereit ready ['redi]
bereits already [ɔ:l'redi]
Berg mountain ['maʊntən]
Bericht (über) report (on) [rɪ'pɔ:t]
berichten: jm. etwas berichten tell sb. about sth. [tel]; report sth. to sb. [rɪ'pɔ:t]
berichtigen correct [kə'rekt]
beruhigen: jn. beruhigen calm sb. down [ˌkɑ:m 'daʊn] • **sich beruhigen** calm down
berühmt (für, wegen) famous (for) ['feɪməs] • **berühmte Persönlichkeit** celebrity [sə'lebrəti]
berühren touch [tʌtʃ]
beschäftigt busy ['bɪzi]
Bescheid: über etwas Bescheid wissen know about sth. [nəʊ]
beschließen: (etwas) beschließen decide (on sth.) [dɪ'saɪd]
Beschränkung limit ['lɪmɪt]
beschreiben: (jm.) etwas beschreiben describe sth. (to sb.) [dɪ'skraɪb] **jm. den Weg beschreiben** tell sb. the way

Beschreibung description [dɪ'skrɪpʃn]
besiegen beat [bi:t]
besondere(r, s) special ['speʃl]
besorgen *(holen)* get [get]
besorgt sein (wegen) be worried (about) ['wʌrid]
besser better ['betə]
beste: am besten (the) best [best] **der/die/das beste ...; die besten ...** the best ... • **Was war das Beste an ...?** What was the best thing about ...? • **Wie komme ich am besten dahin?** What's the best way to get there?
bestellen order ['ɔ:də]
Besuch visit ['vɪzɪt]
besuchen: jn. besuchen visit sb. ['vɪzɪt]; see sb. [si:]
Besucher/in visitor ['vɪzɪtə]
Betonung stress ['stres]
Bett bed [bed] • **jn. ins Bett bringen** put sb. to bed
beunruhigt sein (wegen) be worried (about) ['wʌrid]
Beutel bag [bæg]
Bevölkerung population [,pɒpju'leɪʃn]
bevor before [bɪ'fɔ:]
bewegen; sich bewegen move [mu:v]
Bewegung movement ['mu:vmənt]
Beweis(e) proof *(no pl)* [pru:f]
bewölkt cloudy ['klaʊdi]
bewusstlos unconscious [ʌn'kɒnʃəs]
bezahlen: etwas bezahlen pay for sth. [peɪ]
Bezirk *(Stadtteil)* borough ['bʌrə]
Bibliothek library ['laɪbrəri]
Bild picture ['pɪktʃə]; *(Gemälde)* painting ['peɪntɪŋ] • **auf dem Bild** in the picture
Bildschirm monitor ['mɒnɪtə]
billig cheap [tʃi:p]
Bindewort linking word ['lɪŋkɪŋ wɜ:d]
Biografie biography [baɪ'ɒgrəfi]
Biologie biology [baɪ'ɒlədʒi]
bis *(zeitlich)* till [tɪl]; until [ən'tɪl] **Bis bald.** See you. ['si: ju:] • **bis jetzt/hierher** so far • **(spätestens) bis zum Ende des Lieds** by the end of the song • **von Montag bis Freitag** from Monday to Friday
bisschen: ein bisschen a bit [bɪt]
bitte 1. *(in Fragen und Aufforderungen)* please [pli:z]
2. Bitte sehr. / Hier bitte. Here you are.
3. Bitte, gern geschehen. You're welcome. ['welkəm]
4. Wie bitte? Sorry? ['sɒri]
bitten: jn. um etwas bitten ask sb. for sth. [ɑ:sk]
blasen *(wehen)* blow [bləʊ]
blau blue [blu:]
bleiben stay [steɪ] • **in Verbindung bleiben** keep in touch
Bleistift pencil ['pensl]
Bleistiftanspitzer pencil sharpener ['pensl ʃɑ:pnə]
Blick *(Aussicht)* view [vju:]
blind blind [blaɪnd] • **blind werden** go blind
► S.193 German 'werden'
Blockflöte recorder [rɪ'kɔ:də]
bloß just [dʒʌst]; only ['əʊnli]
Blues blues [blu:z]
Blume flower ['flaʊə]
Bluse blouse [blaʊz]
Blut blood [blʌd]
Blüte flower ['flaʊə]
Boden *(Erdboden)* ground [graʊnd]; *(Fußboden)* floor [flɔ:]
Boot boat [bəʊt]
Boss boss [bɒs]
brainstormen *(so viele Ideen wie möglich sammeln)* brainstorm ['breɪnstɔ:m]
Brand fire ['faɪə]
braten fry [fraɪ]
brauchen need [ni:d]; *(Zeit)* take [teɪk] **nicht zu tun brauchen** needn't do ['ni:dnt]
braun brown [braʊn]
brav good [gʊd]
brechen break [breɪk]
breit wide [waɪd]
Brief (an) letter (to) ['letə]
Brieffreund/in *(im Internet)* e-friend ['i:frend]
Briefmarke stamp [stæmp]
Brille: (eine) Brille glasses *(pl)* ['glɑ:sɪz]
bringen: (mit-, her)bringen bring [brɪŋ] • **(weg-, hin)bringen** take [teɪk] • **jn. aus der Fassung bringen** upset sb. [ʌp'set] • **jn. ins Bett bringen** put sb. to bed • **Was kann/darf ich euch/Ihnen bringen?** *(im Restaurant)* What can I get you?
Brite, Britin; britisch British ['brɪtɪʃ]
Broschüre booklet ['bʊklət]
Brot bread *(no pl)* [bred]
Brötchen roll [rəʊl]
Brücke bridge [brɪdʒ]
Bruder brother ['brʌðə]
Buch book [bʊk]
Bücherei library ['laɪbrəri]
Buchstabe letter ['letə]
buchstabieren spell [spel]
Bucht bay [beɪ]
Bühne stage [steɪdʒ]
Burg castle ['kɑ:sl]
Bus bus [bʌs]
Busfahrt bus ride ['bʌs raɪd]
Bushaltestelle bus stop ['bʌs stɒp]
Bus-Monatskarte bus pass ['bʌs pɑ:s]

C

Café café ['kæfeɪ]
Cafeteria cafeteria [,kæfə'tɪəriə]
Cartoon cartoon [kɑ:'tu:n]
CD CD [,si:'di:] • **CD-Spieler** CD player [,si:'di: ,pleɪə]
Cello cello ['tʃeləʊ]
Cent cent (c) [sent]
Champion champion ['tʃæmpiən]
Chance chance [tʃɑ:ns]
Chat *(Unterhaltung)* chat [tʃæt]
Chatroom chat room ['tʃæt ru:m]
chatten chat [tʃæt]
Checkliste checklist ['tʃeklɪst]
Chef/in boss [bɒs]
Chor choir ['kwaɪə]
Clown/in clown [klaʊn]
Cola cola ['kəʊlə]
Comedyshow comedy ['kɒmədi]
Comic-Heft comic ['kɒmɪk]
Computer computer [kəm'pju:tə]
Computerwissenschaft computer science [kəm,pju:tə 'saɪəns]
cool cool [ku:l]
Cornflakes cornflakes ['kɔ:nfleɪks]
Countdown countdown ['kaʊntdaʊn]
Court court [kɔ:t]
Cousin, Cousine cousin ['kʌzn]
Crew crew [kru:]

D

da, dahin *(dort, dorthin)* there [ðeə] **da drüben** over there [,əʊvə 'ðeə]
Dach roof ['ru:f]
daheim at home [ət 'həʊm]
daher *(deshalb)* so [səʊ]; that's why ['ðæts ,waɪ]
damals then [ðen]
damit *(sodass)* so that
danach *(zeitlich)* after that [,ɑ:ftə 'ðæt]
Danke. Thank you. ['θæŋk ju:]; Thanks. • **Danke sehr!** Thanks very much! • **Vielen Dank!** Thanks a lot!
dann then [ðen] • **Was dann?** Then what?
darstellende Kunst drama ['drɑ:mə]
darum so [səʊ]; that's why ['ðæts ,waɪ]
das *(Artikel)* the [ðə, ði]
das *(Relativpronomen)* **1.** *(für Dinge)* which; that
2. *(für Personen)* who; that
das (dort) *(Singular)* that [ðət, ðæt]; *(Plural)* those [ðəʊz] • **Das bin ich.** That's me. • **Das liegt bei dir. / Das kannst/musst du (selbst) entscheiden.** That's up to you.
dass that [ðət, ðæt]

dasselbe the same [seɪm]
Datum date [deɪt]
dauern *(Zeit brauchen)* take [teɪk]
decken: den Tisch decken lay the table [ˌleɪ ðə ˈteɪbl]
dein(e) ... your ... [jɔː]
deiner, deine, deins yours [jɔːz]
denken think [θɪŋk] • **denken an** think of • **Was denkst du über ...?** What do you think about/of ...?
dennoch still [stɪl]
der *(Artikel)* the [ðə, ði]
der *(Relativpronomen)* **1.** *(für Personen)* who; that **2.** *(für Dinge)* which; that
deren *(Relativpronomen)*: **die Frau, deren Statue ...** the woman whose statue ... [huːz]
derselbe the same [seɪm]
deshalb so [səʊ]; that's why [ˈðæts ˌwaɪ]
dessen *(Relativpronomen)*: **der Mann, dessen Statue ...** the man whose statue ... [huːz]
Detail detail [ˈdiːteɪl]
Detektiv/in detective [dɪˈtektɪv]
deuten (auf etwas) *(zeigen)* point (at/to sth.) [pɔɪnt]
deutlich clear [klɪə]
Deutsch; deutsch; Deutsche(r) German [ˈdʒɜːmən]
Deutschland Germany [ˈdʒɜːməni]
Dezember December [dɪˈsembə]
dich you [juː]; *(Reflexivpronomen)* yourself [jəˈself, jɔːˈself]
die *(Artikel)* the [ðə, ði]
die *(Relativpronomen)* **1.** *(für Personen)* who; that **2.** *(für Dinge)* which, that
die (dort) *(Singular)* that [ðət, ðæt]; *(Plural)* those [ðəʊz] • **die (hier)** *(Singular)* this [ðɪs]; *(Plural)* these [ðiːz]
Dieb/in thief [θiːf], *pl* thieves [θiːvz]
Diele hall [hɔːl]
Dienst (am Kunden) *(Service)* service [ˈsɜːvɪs]
Dienstag Tuesday [ˈtjuːzdeɪ, ˈtjuːzdi] (siehe auch unter „Freitag")
dies (hier); diese(r, s) *(Singular)* this [ðɪs]; *(Plural)* these [ðiːz]
dieselbe(n) the same [seɪm]
Ding thing [θɪŋ]
dir you [juː]; *(Reflexivpronomen)* yourself [jəˈself, jɔːˈself]
direkt: direkte Rede direct speech [dəˈrekt] • **direkt hinter dir** right behind you
Diskjockey disc jockey [ˈdɪsk dʒɒki]; DJ [ˈdiːdʒeɪ]
Disko disco [ˈdɪskəʊ]
Diskussion discussion [dɪˈskʌʃn]
Doktor doctor [ˈdɒktə]
Dokumentarfilm documentary [ˌdɒkjuˈmentri]
Dom cathedral [kəˈθiːdrəl]
Donnerstag Thursday [ˈθɜːzdeɪ, ˈθɜːzdi] *(siehe auch unter „Freitag")*
Doppel-, doppelt double [ˈdʌbl]
Dorf village [ˈvɪlɪdʒ]
dort, dorthin there [ðeə] • **dort drinnen** in there • **dort drüben** over there • **dort oben** up there **dort unten** down there
Dossier dossier [ˈdɒsieɪ]
downloaden download [ˌdaʊnˈləʊd]
Drache dragon [ˈdrægən]
Drachen kite [kaɪt]
dran: Ich bin dran. It's my turn. [tɜːn]
draußen outside [ˌaʊtˈsaɪd]; out [aʊt] **nach draußen** outside
draußenbleiben stay out [steɪ‿aʊt]
drei: ein dreiwöchiger Urlaub a three-week holiday
drinnen inside [ˌɪnˈsaɪd] • **dort drinnen** in there [ˌɪn ˈðeə] • **hier drinnen** in here [ˌɪn ˈhɪə] • **nach drinnen** inside
dritte(r, s) third [θɜːd]
Drogerie chemist [ˈkemɪst]
drüben: da/dort drüben over there [ˌəʊvə ˈðeə]
drücken push [pʊʃ]; squeeze [skwiːz]
du you [juː]
dumm *(albern)* silly [ˈsɪli]
dunkel dark [dɑːk]
durch through [θruː]; *(in ... umher)* around [əˈraʊnd] • **durch die Stadt** around the town
durcheinander: alles durcheinanderbringen make a mess [ˌmeɪk‿ə ˈmes]
durchführen: ein Projekt durchführen do a project
Durchsage announcement [əˈnaʊnsmənt]
dürfen can [kən, kæn]; may [meɪ]; be allowed to [əˈlaʊd] • **nicht dürfen** mustn't [ˈmʌsnt]
Durst haben, durstig sein be thirsty [ˈθɜːsti]
Dusche shower [ˈʃaʊə]
duschen; sich duschen have a shower [ˈʃaʊə]
DVD DVD [ˌdiː viːˈ diː]

E

Ebbe und Flut *(Gezeiten)* tide [taɪd] **es ist Ebbe** the tide is out
eben *(flach)* flat [flæt]
echt real [rɪəl] • **echt spät** real late *(AE, infml)*
Ecke corner [ˈkɔːnə] • **Sand Street, Ecke London Road** on the corner of Sand Street and London Road
egal: Geld ist mir egal. I don't care about money. • **Ist doch egal!** Who cares? [ˌhuː ˈkeəz]
Ehefrau wife [waɪf], *pl* wives [waɪvz]
Ehemann husband [ˈhʌzbənd]
Ei egg [eg]
Eichhörnchen squirrel [ˈskwɪrəl]
eigene(r, s): unser eigenes Schwimmbad our own pool [əʊn]
Eile: in Eile sein be in a hurry [ˈhʌri]
eilen *(sich beeilen)* hurry [ˈhʌri]
eilig: es eilig haben be in a hurry [ˈhʌri]
ein(e) a, an [ə, ən]; one [ˈwʌn] **ein(e) andere(r, s) ...** another ... [əˈnʌðə] • **eine Menge** a lot (of) [lɒt]; lots (of) [lɒts] • **ein neuer / eine neue / ein neues** a new one [wʌn] • **ein paar** some [səm, sʌm]; *(einige wenige)* a few [fjuː] • **ein Paar** a pair (of) [peə] • **eines Tages** one day
einander *(sich gegenseitig)* each other
eindrucksvoll impressive [ɪmˈpresɪv]
einfach *(nicht schwierig)* easy [ˈiːzi] **einfach (nur)** just [dʒʌst] ► S.176 just
Einfall *(Idee)* idea [aɪˈdɪə]
Einführung (in) introduction (to) [ˌɪntrəˈdʌkʃn]
eingeben: etwas eingeben *(in den Computer)* enter sth. [ˈentə]
eingeschaltet sein *(Radio, Licht usw.)* be on
einige some [səm, sʌm]; *(einige wenige)* a few [fjuː]
einigen: sich einigen (auf) agree (on) [əˈgriː]
einkaufen: einkaufen gehen go shopping [ˌgəʊ ˈʃɒpɪŋ]
Einkaufen shopping [ˈʃɒpɪŋ]
Einkaufsliste shopping list
Einkaufsstraße, -viertel shopping precinct [ˈpriːsɪŋkt]
Einkaufszentrum (shopping) mall [mɔːl], *BE auch* [mæl]
einladen (zu) invite (to) [ɪnˈvaɪt]
Einladung (zu) invitation (to) [ˌɪnvɪˈteɪʃn]
einmal once [wʌns] • **Einmal aussetzen.** Miss a turn. [tɜːn] • **auf einmal** suddenly [ˈsʌdnli]
einpacken pack [pæk]
eins, ein, eine one [ˈwʌn]
Einsatzort location [ləˈkeɪʃn]
einschalten: den Computer einschalten turn on the computer [ˌtɜːn‿ˈɒn]

einschüchtern bully ['bʊli]
Einsendung *(zu einem Wettbewerb)* entry ['entri]
einsteigen (in den Zug/Bus) get on (the train/bus) [ˌget_'ɒn]
Eintopf(gericht) stew [stjuː]
Eintrag, Eintragung *(im Wörterbuch/ Tagebuch)* entry ['entri]
eintragen: etwas eintragen *(in Formular)* enter sth. ['entə]
eintreffen *(ankommen)* arrive [ə'raɪv]
Eintrittskarte ticket ['tɪkɪt]
Einwohner(zahl) population [ˌpɒpju'leɪʃn]
Einzelheit detail ['diːteɪl]
einziehen *(in Wohnung)* move in [ˌmuːv_'ɪn]
einzig: der einzige Gast the only guest ['əʊnli]
Eis ice [aɪs]; *(Speiseeis)* ice cream [ˌaɪs 'kriːm]
Eisenbahn railway ['reɪlweɪ]
Eishockey ice hockey ['aɪs hɒki]
Elefant elephant ['elɪfənt]
elektrisch electric [ɪ'lektrɪk]
Elektrizität electricity [ɪˌlek'trɪsəti]
Elektro- electric [ɪ'lektrɪk]
elektronisch electronic [ɪˌlek'trɒnɪk]
Elfmeter *(Fußball)* penalty ['penəlti]
Eltern parents ['peərənts]
E-Mail (an) e-mail (to) ['iːmeɪl]
End- final ['faɪnl]
Ende **1.** end [end]; *(einer Geschichte, eines Films usw.)* ending ['endɪŋ]
am Ende (von) at the end (of)
zu Ende machen finish ['fɪnɪʃ]
zu Ende sein be over ['əʊvə]
2. oberes Ende *(Spitze)* top [tɒp]
am oberen Ende (von) at the top (of)
3. unteres Ende bottom ['bɒtəm]
am unteren Ende (von) at the bottom (of) ['bɒtəm]
enden finish ['fɪnɪʃ]
endlich at last [ət 'lɑːst]
Endspiel final ['faɪnl]
Endstand *(beim Sport)* final score [ˌfaɪnl 'skɔː]
► S.183 A football match
Engel angel ['eɪndʒl]
Englisch; englisch English ['ɪŋglɪʃ]
Enkel grandson ['grænsʌn]; grandchild ['græntʃaɪld], *pl* grandchildren ['græntʃɪldrən]
Enkelin granddaughter ['grændɔːtə]; grandchild ['græntʃaɪld], *pl* grandchildren ['græntʃɪldrən]
entdecken discover [dɪ'skʌvə]; spot [spɒt]
Entdecker/in *(Forscher/in)* explorer [ɪk'splɔːrə]
entfernen: sich von etwas/jm. entfernen get away from sth./sb.
entladen unload [ˌʌn'ləʊd]
entlang der Straße / die Straße entlang along the street [ə'lɒŋ]
entleihen: etwas entleihen *(sich etwas ausleihen)* borrow sth. ['bɒrəʊ]
entscheiden: sich entscheiden (für etwas) decide (on sth.) [dɪ'saɪd]
Das kannst/musst du (selbst) entscheiden. That's up to you.
entschuldigen: sich entschuldigen say sorry ['sɒri]
Entschuldigung **1.** *(Tut mir leid)* I'm sorry. ['sɒri] • **Entschuldigung, dass ich zu spät komme.** Sorry, I'm late.
2. Entschuldigung, … / Entschuldigen Sie, … *(Darf ich mal stören?)* Excuse me, … [ɪk'skjuːz miː]
Entsetzen horror ['hɒrə]
entspannen; sich entspannen relax [rɪ'læks]; chill out [ˌtʃɪl_'aʊt] *(infml)*
entwerfen design [dɪ'zaɪn]
entwickeln *(entwerfen)* design [dɪ'zaɪn]
Enzyklopädie encyclopedia [ɪnˌsaɪklə'piːdiə]
er **1.** *(männliche Person)* he [hiː]
2. *(Ding, Tier)* it [ɪt]
Erdbeere strawberry ['strɔːbəri]
Erdboden ground [graʊnd]
Erdkunde geography [dʒi'ɒgrəfi]
Ereignis event [ɪ'vent]
erfahren: etwas über etwas erfahren learn sth. about sth. [lɜːn]
erfinden invent [ɪn'vent]
Erfinder/in inventor [ɪn'ventə]
Erfolg success [sək'ses]
erforschen explore [ɪk'splɔː]
ergänzen add (to) [æd]
Ergebnis result [rɪ'zʌlt]
erhalten receive [rɪ'siːv]
erholen: sich erholen (von) recover (from) [rɪ'kʌvə]
erinnern: sich erinnern (an) remember [rɪ'membə]
erkältet sein have a cold [kəʊld]
Erkältung cold [kəʊld] • **eine Erkältung haben** have a cold
erkennen *(merken)* realize ['rɪəlaɪz]
erklären: jm. etwas erklären explain sth. to sb. [ɪk'spleɪn]
Erklärung explanation [ˌeksplə'neɪʃn]
erkunden explore [ɪk'splɔː]
erlauben allow [ə'laʊ] • **jm. erlauben, etwas zu tun** let sb. do sth.
erläutern: jm. etwas erläutern explain sth. to sb. [ɪk'spleɪn]
ermorden murder ['mɜːdə]
Ernst: Das kann nicht dein Ernst sein! No way! [ˌnəʊ 'weɪ]
erraten guess [ges]
erreichen reach [riːtʃ]
erscheinen appear [ə'pɪə]
ersetzen (durch) replace (with) [rɪ'pleɪs]
erst only ['əʊnli]
erstaunlich amazing [ə'meɪzɪŋ]
erste(r, s) first [fɜːst] • **als Erstes** first • **der erste Tag** the first day
der/die Erste sein be first • **die Ersten Nationen** *(indianische Ureinwohner/innen Kanadas)* the First Nations
ertragen *(aushalten)* stand [stænd]
Ich kann es nicht ertragen. I can't stand it.
erwachsen werden grow up [grəʊ_'ʌp]
Erwachsene(r) adult ['ædʌlt] • **das Leben als Erwachsene/r** adult life
erwarten: ich kann es kaum erwarten, … zu sehen I can't wait to see … [weɪt]
erwidern (auf) reply (to) [rɪ'plaɪ]
erwischen *(fangen)* catch [kætʃ]
erzählen (von) tell (about) [tel]
Erzählung story ['stɔːri]
erzeugen *(produzieren)* produce [prə'djuːs]
erzielen: einen Treffer erzielen score a goal [skɔː], [gəʊl]
es it [ɪt] • **es gibt** *(es ist vorhanden)* there's; *(es sind vorhanden)* there are
essen eat [iːt] • **Abendbrot essen** have dinner • **Toast zum Frühstück essen** have toast for breakfast
Essen food [fuːd]; *(Mahlzeit)* meal [miːl]
Esszimmer dining room ['daɪnɪŋ ruːm]
Etagenbett bunk (bed) [bʌŋk]
etwas something ['sʌmθɪŋ]; *(irgendetwas)* anything ['eniθɪŋ]; *(ein bisschen)* a bit [bɪt] • **etwas Käse/Saft** some cheese/juice [səm, sʌm]
etwas anderes something else [els]
sonst (noch) etwas anything else
euch you [juː]; *(Reflexivpronomen)* yourselves [yɔː'selvz]
euer, eure … your … [jɔː]
eurer, eure, eures yours [jɔːz]
Euro euro ['jʊərəʊ]

F

Fabrik factory ['fæktri]
Fachschule college ['kɒlɪdʒ]
fähig sein, etwas zu tun be able to do sth. ['eɪbl]
Fähre ferry ['feri]

fahren go [gəʊ]; *(ein Auto/mit dem Auto)* drive [draɪv] • **in Urlaub fahren** go on holiday • **mit dem Auto/Zug/Rad/... fahren** go by car/train/bike/... • **Inliner/Skateboard fahren** skate [skeɪt] • **Rad fahren** cycle ['saɪkl]; ride a bike [ˌraɪd ə 'baɪk]
Fahrer/in driver ['draɪvə]
Fahrgast passenger ['pæsɪndʒə]
Fahrkarte ticket ['tɪkɪt]
Fahrkartenautomat ticket machine ['tɪkɪt məˌʃiːn]
Fahrrad bike [baɪk]
Fahrstuhl lift [lɪft] *(BE)*; elevator ['elɪveɪtə] *(AE)*
Fahrt: (Rad-/Bus-)Fahrt (bike/bus) ride [raɪd]; journey ['dʒɜːni]
fair fair [feə]
Fakt fact [fækt]
Fall 1. *(Kriminalfall)* case [keɪs] **2. Auf keinen Fall!** No way! [ˌnəʊ 'weɪ]
Falle trap [træp] • **(jm.) eine Falle stellen** set a trap (for sb.) [set]
fallen fall [fɔːl]; drop [drɒp]
fallen lassen drop [drɒp]
falls if [ɪf]
falsch wrong [rɒŋ] • **etwas falsch machen** get sth. wrong • **in die falsche Richtung** the wrong way
Familie family ['fæməli]
Fan fan [fæn]; supporter [sə'pɔːtə] **Fan einer Mannschaft sein** support a team [sə'pɔːt]
fangen catch [kætʃ]
fantastisch fantastic [fæn'tæstɪk]
Farbe colour ['kʌlə] • **Welche Farbe hat ...?** What colour is ...?
Farm farm [fɑːm]
Fassung: jn. aus der Fassung bringen upset sb. [ʌp'set]
fast almost ['ɔːlməʊst]
Favorit/in favourite ['feɪvərɪt]
Februar February ['februəri]
Federball badminton ['bædmɪntən]
Federballschläger badminton racket ['rækɪt]
Federmäppchen pencil case ['pensl keɪs]
fehlen *(nicht da sein)* be missing ['mɪsɪŋ] • **Was fehlt dir?** *(bei Krankheit)* What's wrong with you?
Fehler mistake [mɪ'steɪk]
Feind/in enemy ['enəmi]
Feld 1. field [fiːld] • **auf dem Feld** in the field **2.** *(bei Brettspielen)* **Geh ein Feld vor.** Move on one space. [speɪs] **Geh ein Feld zurück.** Move back one space.
Fenster window ['wɪndəʊ]
Ferien holidays ['hɒlədeɪz]; vacation *(AE)* [və'keɪʃn, veɪ'keɪʃn] • **Ferien haben/machen** be on holiday
Ferienhaus holiday home; villa
Ferienwohnung holiday home
fern faraway [ˌfɑːrə'weɪ]
fernsehen watch TV [ˌwɒtʃ tiː'viː]
Fernsehen television ['telɪvɪʒn]; TV [tiː'viː] • **im Fernsehen** on TV
fertig *(bereit)* ready ['redi] • **sich fertig machen (für)** *(sich vorbereiten)* get ready (for) • **Dinge fertig machen (für)** *(vorbereiten)* get things ready (for)
Fest, Festival festival ['festɪvl]
feucht wet [wet]
Feuer fire ['faɪə]
Feuerwehrfrau firewoman ['faɪəˌwʊmən]
Feuerwehrmann fireman ['faɪəmən]
Fieber haben have a temperature ['temprətʃə]
Fiedel *(Geige)* fiddle ['fɪdl] *(infml)*
Film film [fɪlm]
filmen film [fɪlm]
Filmstar film star ['fɪlm stɑː]
Filzstift felt tip ['felt tɪp]
Finale final ['faɪnl]
finden *(entdecken)* find [faɪnd] **Freunde finden** make friends
Finger finger ['fɪŋgə]
Firma company ['kʌmpəni]
Fisch fish, *pl* fish [fɪʃ]
Fischer fisherman, *pl* fishermen ['fɪʃəmən, 'fɪʃəmən]
flach *(eben)* flat [flæt]
Flasche bottle ['bɒtl] • **eine Flasche Milch** a bottle of milk
Fleisch meat [miːt]
fliegen fly [flaɪ]
Flohmarkt flea market ['fliː ˌmɑːkɪt]
Flug flight [flaɪt]
Flughafen airport ['eəpɔːt]
Flugsteig gate [geɪt]
Flugzeug plane [pleɪn] • **im Flugzeug** on the plane
Flur hall [hɔːl]
Fluss river ['rɪvə]
Flussdiagramm flow chart ['fləʊ tʃɑːt]
Flusspferd hippo ['hɪpəʊ]
flüstern whisper ['wɪspə]
Flut: Ebbe und Flut *(Gezeiten)* tide [taɪd] • **es ist Flut** the tide is in
folgen follow ['fɒləʊ] • **die folgenden ...** the following ...
Football American football [əˌmerɪkən 'fʊtbɔːl]
Form *(Gestalt)* shape [ʃeɪp]
Forscher/in *(Entdecker/in)* explorer [ɪk'splɔːrə]
Forschung(en) research *(no pl)* [rɪ'sɜːtʃ, 'riːsɜːtʃ]
Fort fort [fɔːt]
fort away [ə'weɪ]
Foto photo ['fəʊtəʊ] • **auf dem Foto** in the photo • **Fotos machen** take photos
Fotoapparat camera ['kæmərə]
Fotograf/in photographer [fə'tɒgrəfə]
fotografieren take photos [teɪk 'fəʊtəʊz]
foulen *(Sport)* foul [faʊl]
Frage question ['kwestʃn] • **Fragen stellen** ask questions • **Kommt nicht in Frage!** No way!
fragen ask [ɑːsk] • **nach etwas fragen** ask about sth. • **jn. nach dem Weg fragen** ask sb. the way
sich fragen wonder ['wʌndə]
Französisch French [frentʃ]
Frau woman ['wʊmən], *pl* women ['wɪmɪn] • **Frau Brown** Mrs Brown ['mɪsɪz]; Ms Brown [mɪz, məz]; *(unverheiratet)* Miss Brown [mɪs]
frei free [friː] • **freie Zeit** free time
im Freien outdoor ['aʊtdɔː]
Freitag Friday ['fraɪdeɪ, 'fraɪdi]
freitagabends, am Freitagabend on Friday evening • **freitagnachts, Freitagnacht** on Friday night
freiwillig: Arbeit als Freiwillige(r) volunteer work [ˌvɒlən'tɪə ˌwɜːk]
Freizeit free time [ˌfriː 'taɪm]
Freizeitaktivitäten free-time activities [ˌfriː taɪm‿æk'tɪvətiz]
Freizeitzentrum, -park leisure centre ['leʒə sentə]
Fremdenverkehrsamt tourist information ['tʊərɪst‿ɪnfəˌmeɪʃn]
Freund friend [frend]; *(Partner)* boyfriend ['bɔɪfrend] • **Freunde finden** make friends
Freundin friend [frend]; *(Partner)* girlfriend ['gɜːlfrend]
freundlich friendly ['frendli]
frieren be cold [kəʊld]
Friseur/in hairdresser ['heədresə] **beim Friseur** at the hairdresser's
froh happy ['hæpi]
Frosch frog [frɒg]
Frucht, Früchte fruit [fruːt]
früh early ['ɜːli]
Frühling spring [sprɪŋ]
Frühstück breakfast ['brekfəst] **zum Frühstück** for breakfast
frühstücken have breakfast
Frühstückspension Bed and Breakfast (B&B) [ˌbed‿ən 'brekfəst]
Fuchs fox [fɒks]
fühlen; sich fühlen feel [fiːl]
führen nach *(Straße, Weg)* go to **ein Telefongespräch führen** make a call ['kɔːl]

Führung: in Führung gehen *(Sport)* go ahead
Füller pen [pen]
funktionieren work [wɜːk]
für for [fə, fɔː] • **Was für ein Auto ...?** What kind of car ...?
Furcht (vor) fear (of) [ˈfɪə]
furchtbar terrible [ˈterəbl]; awful [ˈɔːfl]
Fuß foot [fʊt], *pl* feet [fiːt] • **zu Fuß** on foot
Fußball football [ˈfʊtbɔːl]
Fußballplatz, -feld football pitch [pɪtʃ]
Fußballschuhe, -stiefel football boots [ˈfʊtbɔːl buːts]
Fußballspieler/in footballer [ˈfʊtbɔːlə]
Fußballtrikot football shirt [ʃɜːt]
Fußboden floor [flɔː]
Futter food [fuːd]
füttern feed [fiːd]

G

Gabel fork [fɔːk]
gähnen yawn [jɔːn]
Galerie gallery [ˈgæləri]
ganz quite [kwaɪt] • **Das ist ganz falsch.** This is all wrong.
ganze(r, s) whole [həʊl] • **auf der ganzen Welt** all over the world **aus der ganzen Welt** from all over the world • **das ganze Jahr 2006** the whole of 2006 • **den ganzen Tag (lang)** all day • **die ganze Zeit** all the time
Garage garage [ˈgærɑːʒ]
Garten garden [ˈgɑːdn]
Gasse lane [leɪn]
Gast guest [gest]; *(Besucher/in)* visitor [ˈvɪzɪtə]
Gebäude building [ˈbɪldɪŋ]
geben give [gɪv] • **es gibt** *(es ist vorhanden)* there's; *(es sind vorhanden)* there are • **jm. die Schuld geben (an)** blame sb. (for) [bleɪm]
Gebiet area [ˈeəriə]
geboren sein/werden be born [bɔːn]
Gebrauch use [juːs]
gebraucht *(aus zweiter Hand)* second-hand [ˌsekənd ˈhænd]
gebrochen *(Arm, Bein)* broken [ˈbrəʊkən]
Geburtstag birthday [ˈbɜːθdeɪ] **Herzlichen Glückwunsch zum Geburtstag.** Happy birthday. • **Ich habe im Mai / am 13. Juni Geburtstag.** My birthday is in May / on 13th June. • **Wann hast du Geburtstag?** When's your birthday? • **zu seinem Geburtstag** for his birthday
Gedicht poem [ˈpəʊɪm]
Gefahr danger [ˈdeɪndʒə]
gefährlich dangerous [ˈdeɪndʒərəs]; *(nicht sicher)* unsafe [ʌnˈseɪf]
Gefühl feeling [ˈfiːlɪŋ]
gegen against [əˈgenst] • **gegen sechs Uhr** around six
Gegend area [ˈeəriə]
Gegensatz: im Gegensatz zu unlike [ˌʌnˈlaɪk]
gegenüber (von) opposite [ˈɒpəzɪt]
Gegenwart present [ˈpreznt]
Geheimnis *(Rätsel)* mystery [ˈmɪstri]
gehen 1. go [gəʊ]; *(zu Fuß gehen)* walk [wɔːk]; *(weggehen)* leave [liːv] **Auf geht's!** Let's go. • **einkaufen gehen** go shopping • **Geh ein Feld vor.** Move on one space. [speɪs] **Geh ein Feld zurück.** Move back one space. • **in die Sauna gehen** have a sauna [ˈsɔːnə] • **ins Ausland gehen** go abroad [əˈbrɔːd] • **ins Bett gehen** go to bed • **in Führung gehen** *(Sport)* go ahead • **ins Kino gehen** go to the cinema [ˈsɪnəmə] • **nach Hause gehen** go home • **reiten/schwimmen gehen** go riding/swimming • **spazieren gehen** walk; go for a walk [wɔːk] **2. Es geht mir/ihm gut.** I'm/He's fine. [faɪn] • **Wie geht es dir/Ihnen/euch?** How are you? **3. Es geht um Mr Green.** This is about Mr Green. • **Das geht dich nichts an!** Mind your own business. [ˌmaɪnd jər‿ˌəʊn ˈbɪznəs]
gehören (zu) 1. belong (to) [bɪˈlɒŋ] **Wem gehören diese?** Whose are these? [huːz] **2.** *(passen zu)* go with
gehörlos deaf [def]
Geige violin [ˌvaɪəˈlɪn]; fiddle [ˈfɪdl] *(infml)* • **Geige spielen** play the violin/fiddle
gekränkt (wegen) upset (about) [ˌʌpˈset]
Gelächter laughter [ˈlɑːftə]
gelangen *(hinkommen)* get [get]
gelb yellow [ˈjeləʊ]
Geld money [ˈmʌni] • **Geld ausgeben (für)** spend money (on) [spend]
Geldbörse purse [pɜːs]
Gemälde painting [ˈpeɪntɪŋ]
Gemeindehalle, -saal community hall [kəˌmjuːnəti ˈhɔːl]
Gemeinschaftshalle, -saal community hall [kəˌmjuːnəti ˈhɔːl]
Gemüse: *(ein)* **Gemüse** vegetable [ˈvedʒtəbl]
genannt werden be called [kɔːld]
genau 1. *(Adjektiv)* accurate [ˈækjərət]; exact [ɪgˈzækt] **2.** *(Adverb)* **etwas genau anschauen** look closely at sth. [ˈkləʊsli] **genau hinter dir** right behind you **genau in dem Moment** just then **genau wie du** just like you
genießen enjoy [ɪnˈdʒɔɪ]
genug enough [ɪˈnʌf]
geöffnet open [ˈəʊpən]
Geografie geography [dʒiˈɒgrəfi]
gepflegt neat [niːt]
gerade at the moment; *(soeben)* just [dʒʌst] • **gerade dann** *(genau in dem Moment)* just then • **jetzt gerade** *(in diesem Moment)* right now [raɪt ˈnaʊ]
geradeaus weiter straight on [streɪt‿ˈɒn]
Gerät *(Maschine)* machine [məˈʃiːn]
geraten: in Panik geraten panic [ˈpænɪk]
Geräusch noise [nɔɪz]
gerecht fair [feə]
Gericht *(Speise)* dish [dɪʃ]
gern: Ich hätte gern ... / Ich möchte gern ... I'd like ... (= I would like ...) [laɪk] • **Ich schwimme/tanze/... gern.** I like swimming/dancing/... **Ich würde gern gehen** I'd like to go **Ich würde nicht gern gehen** I wouldn't like to go • **Das hättest du wohl gerne!** You wish! [wɪʃ] **Gern geschehen.** You're welcome. [ˈwelkəm]
gernhaben like [laɪk]
Geruch smell
gesamte(r, s) whole [həʊl] • **aus dem gesamten Vereinigten Königreich** from all over the UK
Geschäft shop [ʃɒp]
geschehen (mit) happen (to) [ˈhæpən]
Geschenk present [ˈpreznt]
Geschichte 1. story [ˈstɔːri] **2.** *(vergangene Zeiten)* history [ˈhɪstri]
geschieden divorced [dɪˈvɔːst]
Geschirr dishes *(pl)* [ˈdɪʃɪz] • **das Geschirr abwaschen** do the dishes
Geschirrspülmaschine dishwasher [ˈdɪʃwɒʃə]
geschlossen closed [kləʊzd]
Geschmack(srichtung) flavour [ˈfleɪvə]
Geschwindigkeit speed [spiːd]
Geschwindigkeitsbegrenzung, -beschränkung speed limit [ˈlɪmɪt]
Gesellschaft company [ˈkʌmpəni]
Gesicht face [feɪs]
Gespräch conversation [ˌkɒnvəˈseɪʃn]
Gestalt *(Form)* shape [ʃeɪp]
gestern yesterday [ˈjestədeɪ, ˈjestədi] **gestern Morgen/Nachmittag/**

Abend yesterday morning/afternoon/evening
gesund healthy ['helθi]
Getränk drink [drɪŋk]
Gewinn prize [praɪz]
gewinnen win [wɪn]
Gewinner/in winner ['wɪnə]
Gewitter storm [stɔ:m]
gewöhnlich usually ['ju:ʒuəli]
Gewürz spice [spaɪs]
Gewürzkraut herb [hɜ:b]
gewürzt: scharf gewürzt spicy ['spaɪsi]
Gezeiten *(Ebbe und Flut)* tide [taɪd]
Gig gig [gɪg] *(infml)*
Giraffe giraffe [dʒə'rɑ:f]
Gitarre guitar [gɪ'tɑ:] • **Gitarre spielen** play the guitar
Glas glass [glɑ:s] • **ein Glas Wasser** a glass of water
glauben think [θɪŋk]; believe [bɪ'li:v] **Das glaube ich nicht. / Ich glaube nicht.** I don't think so. • **Ich glaube (ja).** I think so. • **Glaubst du das wirklich?** Do you really think so?
gleich 1. *(sofort)* straightaway [,streɪtə'weɪ]
2. gleich sein/aussehen be/look the same [seɪm]
Gleis *(Bahnsteig)* platform ['plætfɔ:m]
Gliederung structure ['strʌktʃə]
Gliedsatz clause [klɔ:z]
Glocke bell [bel]
Glück: Glück haben be lucky ['lʌki] • **Viel Glück (bei/mit ...)!** Good luck (with ...)! [gʊd 'lʌk] **zum Glück** *(glücklicherweise)* luckily ['lʌkɪli] • **glücklich** happy ['hæpi]
glücklicherweise luckily ['lʌkɪli]
Glückwunsch: Herzlichen Glückwunsch! Congratulations! [kən,grætʃu'leɪʃnz]; *(zum Geburtstag)* Happy birthday!
Gold gold [gəʊld]
Grad degree [dɪ'gri:]
Grammatik grammar ['græmə]
grau grey [greɪ]
Grauen horror ['hɒrə]
grauenhaft horrible ['hɒrəbl]
Grippe flu [flu:]
groß big [bɪg]; large [lɑ:dʒ]; *(Person)* tall [tɔ:l]; *(riesig)* huge [hju:dʒ]
► S.177 big – large – huge
großartig great [greɪt]; neat *(AE, infml)* [ni:t]
Großbuchstabe capital letter [,kæpɪtl 'letə]
Größe *(Schuhgröße usw.)* size [saɪz]
Großeltern grandparents ['grænpeərənts]
Großmutter grandmother
Großstadt city ['sɪti]
Großvater grandfather
grün green [gri:n]
Grund reason ['ri:zn] • **aus vielen Gründen** for lots of reasons
Gruppe group [gru:p]; *(Musikgruppe)* band [bænd]
gruselig scary ['skeəri]
Gruß: Liebe Grüße, ... *(Briefschluss)* Love ... [lʌv]
Grüß deine Eltern von mir. Say hi to your parents for me.
gucken look [lʊk]
gut good [gʊd]; *(okay)* OK [əʊ'keɪ]; *(in Ordnung)* all right [ɔ:l 'raɪt]; *(gesundheitlich gut, wohlauf)* well [wel]; fine [faɪn] • **gut (ver)laufen** go well • **Du hast dich gut um sie gekümmert.** You looked after them well. [wel] • **Es geht mir/ihm gut.** I'm/He's fine. • **gute Arbeit leisten** do a good job • **Guten Morgen.** Good morning. • **Guten Tag.** Hello.; *(nachmittags)* Good afternoon.
gutgehen *(gut verlaufen)* go well [wel]
Gymnasium grammar school ['græmə ,sku:l]
Gymnastikanzug *(für Frauen und Mädchen)* leotard ['li:ətɑ:d]

H

Haar, Haare hair *(no pl)* [heə]
haben have got ['hæv gɒt]; have [həv, hæv] • **Ich habe keinen Stuhl.** I haven't got a chair. • **Ich habe am 13. Juni/im Mai Geburtstag.** My birthday is on 13th June/in May. **Wann hast du Geburtstag?** When's your birthday? • **haben wollen** want [wɒnt] • **Was haben wir als Hausaufgabe auf?** What's for homework?
Hafen harbour ['hɑ:bə]
Hähnchen chicken ['tʃɪkɪn]
halbe(r, s) half [hɑ:f] • **eine halbe Stunde** half an hour • **halb zwölf** half past 11
Halbfinale semi-final [,semi'faɪnl]
Halbzeit *(Sport)* half, *pl* halves [hɑ:f, hɑ:vz] • **ein Tor in der zweiten Halbzeit** a second-half goal
Halbzeit(pause) half-time
Halfpipe *(halbierte Röhre für Inline-skater)* half-pipe ['hɑ:fpaɪp]
Hälfte half, *pl* halves [hɑ:f, hɑ:vz] **ein Tor in der zweiten Hälfte** a second-half goal
Halle hall [hɔ:l]
Hallo! Hi! [haɪ]; Hello. [hə'ləʊ]; Hey!
Hals throat [θrəʊt]
Halsschmerzen haben have a sore throat [sɔ: 'θrəʊt]
halten 1. hold [həʊld]
2. *(aufbewahren; behalten)* keep [ki:p] • **etwas warm/kühl/offen/... halten** keep sth. warm/cool/open/... • **Kontakt halten** keep in touch [tʌtʃ]
3. den Mund halten shut up [,ʃʌt_'ʌp]
4. Was hältst du von ...? What do you think about/of ...?
Hamburger hamburger ['hæmbɜ:gə]
Hamster hamster ['hæmstə]
Hand hand [hænd] • **aus zweiter Hand** *(gebraucht)* second-hand [,sekənd 'hænd]
Handel trade [treɪd]
Handlung action ['ækʃn]
Handschuhe gloves *(pl)* [glʌvz]
Handtasche bag [bæg]
Handtuch towel ['taʊəl]
Handy mobile (phone) ['məʊbaɪl] *(BE)*; cellphone ['selfəʊn] *(AE)*
hänseln: jn. mit Schimpfwörtern hänseln call sb. names
Happyend happy ending [,hæpi_'endɪŋ]
hart hard [hɑ:d] • **hart arbeiten** work hard • **hart werden** go hard
► S.193 German 'werden'
hassen hate [heɪt]
häufig often ['ɒfn]
Haupt- main [meɪn]
Hauptstadt capital ['kæpɪtl]
Haus house [haʊs] • **im Haus der Shaws / bei den Shaws zu Hause** at the Shaws' house • **nach Hause gehen** go home [həʊm] • **nach Hause kommen** come home; get home • **zu Hause** at home
Hausaufgabe(n) homework *(no pl)* ['həʊmwɜ:k] • **die Hausaufgabe(n) machen** do homework • **Was haben wir als Hausaufgabe auf?** What's for homework?
Hausmeister/in caretaker ['keəteɪkə]
Haustier pet [pet]
Haustür front door [,frʌnt 'dɔ:]
Heim home [həʊm]
heiraten marry ['mæri]
heiß hot [hɒt]
heißen 1. *(genannt werden)* be called [kɔ:ld] • **Ich heiße ...** My name is ... • **Wie heißt du?** What's your name?
2. Sie heißen dich in ... willkommen They welcome you to ... ['welkəm]

Heißluftballon balloon [bə'lu:n]
hektisch busy ['bɪzi]
Held/in hero ['hɪərəʊ], *pl* heroes ['hɪərəʊz]
helfen help [help]
Helikopter helicopter ['helɪkɒptə]
hell *(leuchtend)* bright [braɪt]
Helm helmet ['helmɪt]
Hemd shirt [ʃɜ:t]
herauf up [ʌp]
heraus out [aʊt] • **aus ... heraus** out of ... ['aʊt‿əv]
herausbringen *(CD, Film usw.)* release [rɪ'li:s]
herausfinden find out [ˌfaɪnd‿'aut]; *(entdecken)* discover [dɪ'skʌvə] **etwas über etwas herausfinden** learn sth. about sth. [lɜ:n]
herausnehmen take out [ˌteɪk‿'aut]
herausragen, -stehen (aus) stick out (of) [stɪk]
Herberge hostel ['hɒstl]
herbringen bring [brɪŋ]
Herbst autumn ['ɔ:təm]
Herd cooker ['kʊkə]
hereinkommen come in [ˌkʌm‿'ɪn]
Herr Brown Mr Brown ['mɪstə]
herstellen *(produzieren)* produce [prə'dju:s]
herüber across [ə'krɒs]
herum: anders herum the other way round [raʊnd] • **um ... herum** round, around
herum-: jn. herumführen *(in der Stadt/im Museum/...)* show sb. around • **etwas herumgeben** pass sth. round [raʊnd] • **herumgehen/-laufen** walk around **herumrennen** run around **herumspringen** jump around ► S.175 around
herunter down [daʊn]
herunterfallen (von) fall off [ˌfɔ:l‿'ɒf]
Herz heart [hɑ:t] • **Recycling liegt mir am Herzen.** I care about recycling.
Herzlichen Glückwunsch! Congratulations! [kənˌgrætʃu'leɪʃnz]; *(zum Geburtstag)* Happy birthday!
Herzlichen Glückwunsch zum Geburtstag. Happy birthday. [ˌhæpi 'bɜ:θdeɪ]
heute today [tə'deɪ] • **heute Morgen/Nachmittag/Abend** this morning/afternoon/evening **heute Nacht** tonight [tə'naɪt]
hier here [hɪə] • **Hier bitte.** *(Bitte sehr.)* Here you are. • **hier drinnen** in here [ˌɪn 'hɪə] • **hier entlang** this way ['ðɪs weɪ] • **Hier spricht/ist Isabel.** *(am Telefon)* This is Isabel.
Hier steht: ... / Es heißt hier: ... *(im Text)* It says here: ...
hierher here [hɪə] • **bis hierher** so far
Hilfe help [help]
Himmel sky [skaɪ] • **am Himmel** in the sky
hinauf up [ʌp] • **den Hügel hinauf** up the hill
hinaufklettern (auf) climb [klaɪm] **Klettere auf einen Baum.** Climb a tree.
hinaus out [aʊt] • **aus ... hinaus** out of ... ['aʊt‿əv]
hinein: in ... hinein into ... ['ɪntə, 'ɪntʊ]
hinfallen fall [fɔ:l]; fall down
hinkommen *(gelangen)* get [get]
hinsetzen: sich hinsetzen sit down [ˌsɪt 'daʊn]
hinstellen: sich hinstellen stand (up) [ˌstænd‿'ʌp]
hinten (im Zimmer) at the back (of the room) [bæk]
hinter behind [bɪ'haɪnd] • **im hinteren Teil (des Zimmers)** at the back (of the room) [bæk]
Hintergrund background ['bækgraʊnd]
Hintertür back door
hinüber across [ə'krɒs] • **hinüber zu/nach ...** over to ... ['əʊvə]
hinunter down [daʊn]
hinzufügen (zu) add (to) [æd]
Hirsch deer, *pl* deer [dɪə]
Hobby hobby ['hɒbi], *pl* hobbies
hoch high [haɪ]
hochheben pick up [ˌpɪk‿'ʌp]
Hochschule college ['kɒlɪdʒ]
hochsehen (von) look up (from) [ˌlʊk‿'ʌp]
Hockey hockey ['hɒki]
Hockeyplatz, -feld hockey pitch [pɪtʃ]
Hockeyschuhe hockey shoes ['hɒki ʃu:z]
Hof yard [jɑ:d] • **auf dem Hof** in the yard
hoffen hope [həʊp] • **Ich hoffe es.** I hope so.
Hoffnung hope [həʊp]
Höhepunkt highlight ['haɪlaɪt]
holen *(besorgen)* get [get]
Holz wood [wʊd]
horchen (auf) listen (for)
hören hear [hɪə] • **Na hör mal!** Come on. [ˌkʌm‿'ɒn]
Horror horror ['hɒrə]
Hose trousers *(pl)* ['traʊzəz]
Hotel hotel [həʊ'tel]
Hotline hotline ['hɒtlaɪn]
hübsch pretty ['prɪti]; *(schön; wunderbar)* lovely ['lʌvli]
Hubschrauber helicopter ['helɪkɒptə]
Hügel hill [hɪl]
hügelig hilly ['hɪli]
Huhn chicken ['tʃɪkɪn]
Hülle cover ['kʌvə]
Hund dog [dɒg]
hundert hundred ['hʌndrəd]
Hunger haben, hungrig sein be hungry ['hʌŋgri]
Hurra! Hooray! [hu'reɪ]
Hut hat [hæt]
Hütte cabin ['kæbɪn]

I

ich I [aɪ] • **Ich auch.** Me too. [ˌmi: 'tu:] • **Das bin ich.** That's me. **Warum ich?** Why me?
Idee idea [aɪ'dɪə]
Igel hedgehog ['hedʒhɒg]
ihm him; *(bei Dingen, Tieren)* it
ihn him; *(bei Dingen, Tieren)* it
ihnen them [ðəm, ðem]
Ihnen *(höfliche Anrede)* you [ju:]
ihr *(Plural von „du")* you [ju:]
ihr: Hilf ihr. Help her. [hə, hɜ:]
ihr(e) ... *(besitzanzeigend)* *(zu „she")* her ... [hə, hɜ:]; *(zu „they")* their ... [ðeə]
Ihr(e) ... *(höfliche Anrede)* your ... [jɔ:]
ihrer, ihre, ihrs *(zu „she")* hers [hɜ:z]; *(zu „they")* theirs [ðeəz]
Ihrer, Ihre, Ihrs *(höfliche Anrede)* yours [jɔ:z]
im: im Allgemeinen generally ['dʒenrəli] • **im Ausland** abroad [ə'brɔ:d] • **im Fernsehen** on TV **im Flugzeug** on the plane • **im Haus der Shaws** at the Shaws' house • **im hinteren Teil (des Zimmers)** at the back (of the room) [bæk] • **im Internet surfen** surf the internet • **im Jahr 2050** in 2050 • **im Mai** in May • **im Radio** on the radio • **im Zug** on the train
immer always ['ɔ:lweɪz] • **immer noch** still [stɪl]
in in • **in ... (hinein)** into ... ['ɪntə, 'ɪntʊ] • **in der ...straße** in ... Street **in der Hamiltonstraße 7** at 7 Hamilton Street • **in der Nacht** at night • **in der Nähe von** near **in der Pause** *(zwischen Schulstunden)* at break • **in der Schule** at school • **in der Stadt umher** around the town • **in die falsche Richtung** the wrong way • **in die Sauna gehen** have a sauna • **in die Stadt** into town • **in Eile sein** be in a hurry • **in den Zug/Bus ein-**

steigen get on the train/bus • **ins Bett gehen** go to bed • **ins Kino gehen** go to the cinema • **in Schwierigkeiten sein** be in trouble ['trʌbl] • **in seiner Straße** in/on his street • **in Urlaub fahren** go on holiday • **in Urlaub sein** be on holiday • **in welche Richtung?** which way? • **Ich bin noch nie in Bath gewesen.** I've never been to Bath.
► S.170 Places without articles
indirekt: indirekte Rede indirect speech [ˌɪndə'rekt]
Industrie industry ['ɪndəstri]
industriell industrial [ɪn'dʌstriəl]
Infinitiv infinitive [ɪn'fɪnətɪv]
Informatik computer science [kəm,pju:tə 'saɪəns]
Information(en) (über) information (about/on) *(no pl)* [ˌɪnfə'meɪʃn]
Informationstechnologie (IT) information technology (IT) [tek'nɒlədʒi], [ˌaɪ 'ti:]
Ingenieur/in engineer [ˌendʒɪ'nɪə]
Inliner skates [skeɪts] • **Inliner fahren** skate
innen (drin) inside [ˌɪn'saɪd]
Innenstadt city centre [ˌsɪti 'sentə]
Insel island ['aɪlənd]
Inserat advert ['ædvɜ:t]
Installation installation [ˌɪnstə'leɪʃn]
installieren install [ɪn'stɔ:l]
Instrument instrument ['ɪnstrəmənt]
interessant interesting ['ɪntrəstɪŋ]
interessieren: sich interessieren (für) be interested (in); care (about) [keə]
interessiert (an) interested (in) ['ɪntrəstɪd]
international international [ˌɪntə'næʃnəl]
Internet internet ['ɪntənet] • **im Internet surfen** surf the internet
irgendetwas anything ['eniθɪŋ] **Habt ihr irgendetwas Besonderes gemacht?** Did you do anything special?
irgendjemand anybody ['enibɒdi]; anyone ['eniwʌn]
irgendwelche any ['eni]
irgendwie unheimlich kind of scary [kaɪnd] *(infml)*
irgendwo(hin) somewhere ['sʌmweə]; anywhere ['eniweə]
IT (Informationstechnologie) IT (information technology) [ˌaɪ 'ti:], [tek'nɒlədʒi]

J

ja yes [jes]
Jacke, Jackett jacket ['dʒækɪt]
Jagd hunt [hʌnt]
jagen hunt [hʌnt]
Jahr year [jɪə] • **im Jahr 2050** in 2050 • **Kleider aus den 60er Jahren** dresses from the 60s ['sɪkstiz] • **ein 70-jähriger Lehrer** a 70-year-old teacher
Jahreszeit season ['si:zn]
Jahrgangsstufe year [jɪə]
Jahrhundert century ['sentʃəri]
Januar January ['dʒænjuəri]
Jazz jazz [dʒæz]
je *(jemals)* ever ['evə]
Jeans jeans *(pl)* [dʒi:nz]
jede(r, s) ... *(Begleiter)* **1.** every ... ['evri]
2. (*jeder* einzelne) each ... [i:tʃ]
jeder *(alle)* everybody ['evribɒdi]; everyone ['evriwʌn]
jemals ever ['evə]
jemand somebody ['sʌmbədi]; someone ['sʌmwʌn]; *(irgendjemand)* anybody ['enibɒdi]; anyone ['eniwʌn] **jemand anders** somebody else [els] **sonst jemand** anybody else
jene(r, s) *(Singular)* that [ðət, ðæt]; *(Plural)* those [ðəʊz] • **an jenem Tag** that day
jetzt now [naʊ] • **jetzt gerade, jetzt sofort** right now • **bis jetzt** so far
Job job [dʒɒb]
Jogurt yogurt ['jɒgət]
jubeln cheer [tʃɪə]
Judo judo ['dʒu:dəʊ] • **Judo machen** do judo
Jugend youth [ju:θ]
Jugend- junior ['dʒu:niə]
Jugendherberge youth hostel ['ju:θ ˌhɒstəl]
Jugendliche(r) kid [kɪd]; teenager ['ti:neɪdʒə]
Juli July [dʒu'laɪ]
jung young [jʌŋ]
Junge boy [bɔɪ]
Juni June [dʒu:n]
Junioren- junior ['dʒu:niə]

K

Käfig cage [keɪdʒ]
Kai quay [ki:]
Kalender calendar ['kælɪndə]
kalt cold [kəʊld]
Kamel camel ['kæml]
Kamera camera ['kæmərə]
kämpfen (für, um) fight (for) [faɪt]
Kanal canal [kə'næl]
Känguru kangaroo [ˌkæŋgə'ru:]
Kaninchen rabbit ['ræbɪt]
Kanu canoe [kə'nu:] • **Kanu fahren** canoe
kapieren: Das kapier ich nicht. I don't get it.
Kapitän/in captain ['kæptɪn]
Kappe cap [kæp]
kaputt broken ['brəʊkən] • **kaputt gehen** break [breɪk] • **kaputt machen** break [breɪk]
Karotte carrot ['kærət]
Karriere career [kə'rɪə]
Karte *(Post-, Spielkarte)* card [kɑ:d]
Kartoffel potato [pə'teɪtəʊ], *pl* potatoes
Kartoffelchips crisps *(pl)* [krɪsps]
Käse cheese [tʃi:z]
Kasse *(Theater-, Kinokasse)* box office ['bɒks_ˌɒfɪs]
Kästchen, Kasten box [bɒks]
Kathedrale cathedral [kə'θi:drəl]
Katze cat [kæt]
kaufen buy [baɪ]
Kaufhaus department store [dɪ'pɑ:tmənt stɔ:]
kaum: Sie traute ihren Augen kaum. She couldn't believe her eyes. [bɪ'li:v]
Kehle throat [θrəʊt]
kein(e) no; not a; not (...) any • **Ich habe keinen Stuhl.** I haven't got a chair. • **Ich mag kein(e) ...** I don't like ... • **keine Musik mehr** no more music
Keks biscuit ['bɪskɪt]
kennen know [nəʊ]
kennenlernen meet [mi:t] • **Nett, dich/euch/Sie kennenzulernen.** Nice to meet you.
kennzeichnen mark up [ˌmɑ:k_'ʌp]
Kerl guy [gaɪ]
Keyboard *(elektronisches Tasteninstrument)* keyboard ['ki:bɔ:d]
Kilogramm, Kilo (kg) kilogram, kilo (kg) ['kɪləgræm] • **ein Kilogramm Orangen** a kilogram of oranges **ein 150 Kilogramm schwerer Bär** a 150-kilogram bear
Kilometer kilometre (km) ['kɪləmi:tə] **eine Zehn-Kilometer-Wanderung** a ten-kilometre walk
Kind child [tʃaɪld], *pl* children ['tʃɪldrən]; kid [kɪd]
Kino cinema ['sɪnəmə] • **ins Kino gehen** go to the cinema
Kinokasse box office ['bɒks_ˌɒfɪs]
Kirche church [tʃɜ:tʃ] • **in die Kirche gehen** go to church
► S.170 Places without articles
Kiste box [bɒks]
Klang sound [saʊnd]

klar clear [klɪə]
Klarinette clarinet [ˌklærɪ'net]
Klasse class [klɑ:s]; form [fɔ:m]
klasse great [greɪt]; neat *(AE, infml)* [ni:t]
Klassenarbeit test [test]
Klassenkamerad/in classmate ['klɑ:smeɪt]
Klassenlehrer/in class teacher; form teacher
Klassenzimmer classroom ['klɑ:sru:m]
klassisch *(typisch, zeitlos)* classic [klæsɪk]; *(Musik)* classical ['klæsɪkl]
klatschen 1. Beifall klatschen cheer [tʃɪə]
2. *(tratschen)* gossip ['gɒsɪp]
Klavier piano [pi'ænəʊ] • **Klavier spielen** play the piano
kleben: (auf-, ein)kleben glue [glu:]
Klebestift glue stick ['glu: stɪk]
Klebstoff glue [glu:]
Kleid dress [dres]
Kleiderschrank wardrobe ['wɔ:drəʊb]
Kleidung, Kleidungsstücke clothes *(pl)* [kləʊðz, kləʊz]
klein little ['lɪtl]; small [smɔ:l]
Kleinbuchstabe small letter
Kleinstadt town [taʊn]
klettern climb [klaɪm] • **Klettere auf einen Baum.** Climb a tree.
Klingel bell [bel]
klingeln ring [rɪŋ]
Klingelton ringtone ['rɪŋtəʊn]
klingen sound [saʊnd]
Klinik clinic ['klɪnɪk]
klopfen (an) knock (on) [nɒk]
Klub club [klʌb]
klug clever ['klevə]
knapp: Das war knapp. That was close. [kləʊs]
Kneipe pub [pʌb]
Knie knee [ni:]
Knopf button ['bʌtn]
Koch cook [kʊk]
kochen cook [kʊk]
Köchin cook [kʊk]
Koje *(Etagenbett)* bunk (bed) [bʌŋk]
komisch *(witzig)* funny ['fʌni]
Komma: elf Komma vier (11,4) eleven point four (11.4)
kommen come [kʌm]; *(hinkommen)* get [get] • **Ich komme aus ...** I'm from ... • **Wo kommst du her?** Where are you from? • **nach Hause kommen** come home; get home • **nicht nach Hause kommen** stay out • **zu spät kommen** be late • **Kommt nicht in Frage!** No way! • **Ach komm!** Come on. [ˌkʌm_'ɒn] • **Na los, komm.** Come on. • **Wie komme ich am besten dahin?** What's the best way to get there?
Komödie comedy ['kɒmədi]
König king [kɪŋ]
Königin queen [kwi:n]
königlich, Königs- royal ['rɔɪəl]
können can [kən, kæn]; be able to ['eɪbl]
konnte(n): ich/er konnte ... I/he could ... [kəd, kʊd]
könnte(n): ich/er könnte ... I/he could ... [kəd, kʊd] • **du könntest (vielleicht) Hilfe brauchen** you might need help [maɪt]
Kontakt: Kontakt halten keep in touch [tʌtʃ] • **mit jm. Kontakt aufnehmen** contact sb. ['kɒntækt]
Kontrabass bass, double bass [ˌdʌbl 'beɪs]
kontrollieren *(prüfen)* check [tʃek]
Konzert concert ['kɒnsət] • **ein Konzert geben** do a gig *(infml)*
Open-Air-Konzert, Konzert im Freien open-air concert [ˌəʊpən_'eə ˌkɒnsət]
Kopf head [hed] • **(mit dem Kopf) nicken** nod (your head) [nɒd]
den Kopf schütteln shake your head [ʃeɪk]
Kopfhörer headphones *(pl)* ['hedfəʊnz]
Kopfschmerzen headache ['hedeɪk]
kopieren copy ['kɒpi]
Korb basket ['bɑ:skɪt] • **ein Korb Äpfel** a basket of apples
Körper body ['bɒdi]
körperbehindert disabled [dɪs'eɪbld]
korrekt correct [kə'rekt]
korrigieren correct [kə'rekt]
kosten *(Essen probieren)* try [traɪ]
kosten cost [kɒst] • **Er/Sie/Es kostet 1 Pfund.** It's £1. • **Sie kosten 35 Pence.** They are 35 p. • **Wie viel kostet/kosten ...?** How much is/ are ...?
kostenlos free [fri:]
köstlich delicious [dɪ'lɪʃəs]
Kostüm *(Verkleidung)* costume ['kɒstju:m]
Kram stuff [stʌf]
krank ill [ɪl]
kränken: jn. kränken *(aus der Fassung bringen)* upset sb. [ʌp'set]
Krankenhaus hospital ['hɒspɪtl] • **Er ist im Krankenhaus.** He's in hospital. • **Er ist ins Krankenhaus gegangen.** He's gone to hospital.
► S 170 Places without articles
Krankenwagen ambulance ['æmbjələns]
Kraut herb [hɜ:b]
Kreis circle ['sɜ:kl]
kreuzen; sich kreuzen cross [krɒs]
Kricket cricket ['krɪkɪt]
Krieg war [wɔ:]
kriegen get [get]
Krokodil crocodile ['krɒkədaɪl]
Krug jug [dʒʌg] • **ein Krug Orangensaft** a jug of orange juice
Küche kitchen ['kɪtʃɪn]
Kuchen cake [keɪk]
Kugelschreiber pen [pen]
Kuh cow [kaʊ]
kühl cool [ku:l]
Kühlschrank fridge [frɪdʒ]
Kummer worry ['wʌri]
kümmern: sich um etwas/jn. kümmern look after sth./sb. [ˌlʊk_'ɑ:ftə]; care about sth./sb. [keə]; take care of sth./sb. • **Kümmer dich nicht drum.** Never mind. [ˌnevə 'maɪnd] • **Kümmere dich um deine eigenen Angelegenheiten!** Mind your own business. [ˌmaɪnd jər_ˌəʊn 'bɪznəs]
Kunst art [ɑ:t]
Kunst-, künstlich artificial [ˌɑ:tɪ'fɪʃl]
Kurs course [kɔ:s]
kurz short [ʃɔ:t] • **kurze Hose** shorts *(pl)* [ʃɔ:ts]
Küste coast [kəʊst]

L

lächeln smile [smaɪl]
Lächeln smile [smaɪl]
lachen laugh [lɑ:f] • **laut lachen** laugh out loud
Lachs salmon *pl* salmon ['sæmən]
Laden *(Geschäft)* shop [ʃɒp]
Lage: in der Lage sein, etwas zu tun be able to do sth. ['eɪbl]
Lampe lamp [læmp]
Land *(auch als Gegensatz zur Stadt)* country ['kʌntri]; *(Grund und Boden)* land [lænd] • **auf dem Land** *(im Gegensatz zur Stadt)* in the country; *(nicht auf dem Wasser)* on land
landen land [lænd]
Landkarte map [mæp]
Landschaft scenery ['si:nəri]
Landwirt/in farmer ['fɑ:mə]
lang long [lɒŋ] • **drei Tage lang** for three days • **einen Moment lang** for a moment • **lange** a long time
langsam slow [sləʊ]
langweilig boring ['bɔ:rɪŋ]
Lärm noise [nɔɪz]
lärmend noisy ['nɔɪzi]
Lasagne lasagne [lə'zænjə]
lassen let [let] • **Lass uns ... / Lasst uns ...** Let's ... • **Lass das!** Stop that!

Lauf run [rʌn]
Laufbahn *(Sport)* running track [træk]
laufen run [rʌn] • **gut laufen** *(gutgehen)* go well
Läufer/in runner ['rʌnə]
Laufschuhe running shoes
laut loud [laʊd]; *(lärmend)* noisy ['nɔɪzi] • **laut lachen** laugh out loud
Laut sound [saʊnd]
läuten ring [rɪŋ]
leben live [lɪv]
Leben life [laɪf], *pl* lives [laɪvz] • **am Leben sein** be alive [ə'laɪv] • **das Leben als Erwachsene/r** adult life
Lebensart way of life
Lebensmittel food [fu:d]
lecker delicious [dɪ'lɪʃəs]; yummy ['jʌmi] *(infml)*
Leder leather ['leðə]
ledig single ['sɪŋgl]
leer empty ['empti]
legen *(hin-, ablegen)* put [pʊt]
lehren teach [ti:tʃ]
Lehrer/in teacher ['ti:tʃə]
Lehrgang course [kɔ:s]; workshop ['wɜ:kʃɒp]
leicht *(nicht schwierig)* easy ['i:zi]
Leichtathletik athletics [æθ'letɪks]
leid: Tut mir leid. I'm sorry. ['sɒri]
leider I'm afraid [ə'freɪd]
leihen: jm. etwas leihen lend sb. sth. [lend] • **sich etwas leihen** borrow sth. ['bɒrəʊ]
leise quiet ['kwaɪət]
Lektion *(im Schulbuch)* unit ['ju:nɪt]
lenken steer [stɪə]
lernen learn [lɜ:n]; study ['stʌdi]
Lern- und Arbeitstechniken study skills ['stʌdi skɪlz]
lesen read [ri:d]
Leser/in reader ['ri:də]
letzte(r, s) last [lɑ:st]; final ['faɪnl]
ein Schuss in der letzten Minute a last-minute shot [,lɑ:st 'mɪnɪt]
► S.183 A football match
leuchtend bright [braɪt]
Leute people ['pi:pl]; guys [gaɪz]; folks [fəʊks] *(infml, besonders AE)*
Lexikon encyclopedia [ɪn,saɪklə'pi:diə]
Licht light [laɪt]
Lichtblitz flash [flæʃ]
Liebe love [lʌv]
Liebe Grüße, ... *(Briefschluss)* Love ... [lʌv]
lieben love [lʌv] • **etwas sehr lieben** love sth. very much
lieber: etwas lieber mögen like sth. better
Lieber Jay, ... Dear Jay ... [dɪə]
Liebling dear [dɪə]; love [lʌv]; sweetheart ['swi:thɑ:t]; *(Favorit/in)* favourite ['feɪvərɪt]
Lieblings-: meine Lieblingsfarbe my favourite colour ['feɪvərɪt]
Lied song [sɒŋ]
Liedtext(e) lyrics *(pl)* ['lɪrɪks]
liegen: Das liegt bei dir. That's up to you. • **Recycling liegt mir am Herzen.** I care about recycling.
lila purple ['pɜ:pl]
Limonade lemonade [,lemə'neɪd]
Lineal ruler ['ru:lə]
Linie *(U-Bahn)* line [laɪn]
linke(r, s) left [left] • **links, auf der linken Seite** on the left • **(nach) links abbiegen** turn left • **nach links** to the left • **nach links schauen** look left
Linse *(Hülsenfrucht)* lentil ['lentəl]
Liste list [lɪst]
Livekonzert live concert [laɪv]
Livemusik live music [laɪv]
Loch hole [həʊl]
Löffel spoon [spu:n]
Logo logo ['ləʊgəʊ]
Lokal *(Kneipe)* pub [pʌb]
lokal local ['ləʊkl]
Löwe lion ['laɪən]
Luft air [eə]
Luftballon balloon [bə'lu:n]

M

machen do [du:]; make [meɪk] • **die Hausaufgabe(n) machen** do homework • **einen Ausflug machen** go on a trip • **einen Spaziergang machen** go for a walk
eine Spritzfahrt/-tour machen take a ride • **eine Übung machen** do an exercise • **etwas falsch/ richtig machen** get sth. wrong/ right • **Ferien machen** be on holiday • **Fotos machen** take photos • **jm. Vorwürfe machen (wegen)** blame sb. (for) [bleɪm]
jn. zu etwas machen make sb. sth. • **Judo machen** do judo
Macht nichts. Never mind. [,nevə 'maɪnd] • **sich Notizen machen** take notes • **Schritte machen** take steps • **sich Sorgen machen (wegen, um)** worry (about) ['wʌri]
(Zauber-)Kunststücke machen do tricks • **Reiten macht Spaß.** Riding is fun.
Mädchen girl [gɜ:l]
Magazin *(Zeitschrift)* magazine [,mægə'zi:n]
Magen stomach ['stʌmək]
Magenschmerzen stomach ache ['stʌmək_eɪk]
Mahlzeit meal [mi:l]
Mai May [meɪ]
Make-up make-up ['meɪkʌp]
Mal(e); -mal time(s) [taɪmz] • **zum ersten Mal** for the first time
malen paint [peɪnt]
Maler/in painter ['peɪntə]
Malerei painting ['peɪntɪŋ]
Mama mum [mʌm]; mom *(AE)* [mɑ:m]
man you [ju:] • **Man sagt, ...** They say ...
Manager/in manager ['mænədʒə]
manchmal sometimes ['sʌmtaɪmz]
Mann man [mæn], *pl* men [men] • **Mann!** boy! *(AE, infml)*
Männchen male [meɪl]
Mannschaft team [ti:m]; crew [kru:]
Mappe *(des Sprachenportfolios)* dossier ['dɒsieɪ]
Markenzeichen logo ['ləʊgəʊ]
markieren mark up [,mɑ:k_'ʌp]
Markt market ['mɑ:kɪt] • **auf den Markt bringen** *(CD, Film usw.)* release [rɪ'li:s]
Marmelade *(Orangenmarmelade)* marmalade ['mɑ:məleɪd]
März March [mɑ:tʃ]
Maschine machine [mə'ʃi:n]
Massage massage ['mæsɑ:ʒ]
massieren: sich massieren lassen have a massage ['mæsɑ:ʒ]
Material material [mə'tɪəriəl]
Mathematik maths [mæθs]
Mauer wall [wɔ:l]
Maulwurf mole [məʊl]
Maus mouse [maʊs], *pl* mice [maɪs]
Medaille medal ['medl]
Mediation *(Sprachmittlung)* mediation [,mi:di'eɪʃn]
Medien media *(pl)* ['mi:diə]
Meer sea [si:]
Meerschweinchen guinea pig ['gɪni pɪg]
mehr more [mɔ:] • **mehr als** more than • **mehr als ich** more than me • **nicht mehr** not (...) any more • **viel mehr** lots more
keine Musik mehr no more music
Meile *(= ca. 1,6 km)* mile [maɪl]
meilenweit for miles [maɪlz]
mein(e) ... my ... [maɪ] • **meine neuen** my new ones [wʌnz]
meinen *(glauben, denken)* think [θɪŋk]; *(sagen wollen)* mean [mi:n]
Meinst du wirklich? Do you really think so?
meiner, meine, meins mine [maɪn]
Meinung view [vju:] • **anderer Meinung sein (als)** disagree (with) [,dɪsə'gri:]

meist: (der/die/das) meiste ...; am meisten most [məʊst] • **die meisten Leute** most people
meistens usually ['ju:ʒuəli]
Meister/in *(Champion)* champion ['tʃæmpiən]
Meisterschaft championship ['tʃæmpiənʃɪp]
Melodie tune [tju:n]
Menge 1. *(Menschenmenge)* crowd [kraʊd]
2. eine Menge *(viel, viele)* a lot (of) [lɒt]; lots (of)
Mensch! boy! *(AE, infml)*
Menschen people ['pi:pl] • **voller Menschen** crowded ['kraʊdɪd]
Menschenmenge crowd [kraʊd]
Menü 1. *(Restaurant)* set meal [ˌset 'mi:l]
2. *(Computer)* menu ['menju:]
merken 1. *(erkennen)* realize ['rɪəlaɪz]
2. sich etwas merken remember sth. [rɪ'membə]
Messer knife, *pl* knives [naɪf]
Meter metre ['mi:tə]
mich me [mi:]; *(Reflexivpronomen)* myself [maɪ'self]
Mikrofon microphone ['maɪkrəfəʊn]
Milch milk [mɪlk]
Milchshake milkshake ['mɪlkʃeɪk]
mild mild [maɪld]
Million million ['mɪljən]
Mindmap mind map ['maɪnd mæp]
Minute minute ['mɪnɪt] • **ein Schuss in der letzten Minute** a last-minute shot • **eine 30-minütige Fahrt** a 30-minute ride
mir me [mi:]; *(Reflexivpronomen)* myself [maɪ'self]
mischen mix [mɪks]
Mischung mixture ['mɪkstʃə]
Mist: So ein Mist! What a bummer! ['bʌmə] *(infml)*
mit with [wɪð] • **mit dem Auto/ Zug/Rad/... fahren** go by car/ train/bike/... • **mit 16** at (the age of) 16 • **Mit wem hat sie geredet?** Who did she talk to?
mitbringen bring [brɪŋ]
mitgenommen (wegen) upset (about) [ˌʌp'set]
mitmachen join in [dʒɔɪn] • **bei etwas/jm. mitmachen** join sth./sb. [dʒɔɪn]; take part in sth.
Mitschüler/in classmate ['klɑ:smeɪt]
Mittagessen lunch [lʌntʃ] • **zum Mittagessen** for lunch
Mittagspause lunch break ['lʌntʃ breɪk]
Mittagszeit lunchtime ['lʌntʃtaɪm]
Mitte centre ['sentə]; middle ['mɪdl]
die Mitte der Stadt the centre of town
► S.170 Places without articles
Mitteilung *(Notiz)* note [nəʊt]
Mittel- central ['sentrəl]
mittelgroß, mittel- medium ['mi:diəm]
Mittwoch Wednesday ['wenzdeɪ, 'wenzdi] *(siehe auch unter „Freitag")*
mixen mix [mɪks]
Möbel furniture *(no pl)* ['fɜ:nɪtʃə]
► S.182 Words without a plural
Möbelstück piece of furniture [ˌpi:s_əv 'fɜ:nɪtʃə]
Mobiltelefon mobile phone [ˌməʊbaɪl 'fəʊn]; mobile ['məʊbaɪl] *(BE)*, cell-phone ['selfəʊn] *(AE)*
möchte: Ich möchte gern ... (haben) I'd like ... (= I would like ...) [laɪk]
Ich möchte gehen I'd like to go
Ich möchte nicht gehen I wouldn't like to go • **Möchtest du / Möchten Sie ...?** Would you like ...?
Mode fashion ['fæʃn]
Modell*(-auto, -schiff; Fotomodell)* model ['mɒdl]
Moderator/in presenter [prɪ'zentə]
modisch trendy ['trendi]
mögen like [laɪk]; *(sehr mögen)* love [lʌv]; be into sth. *(infml)* • **etwas lieber mögen** like sth. better
etwas sehr mögen like sth. very much
möglich possible ['pɒsəbl]
Möhre carrot ['kærət]
Moment moment ['məʊmənt]
einen Moment lang for a moment
im Moment at the moment
genau in dem Moment just then
Moment mal! Wait a minute. ['mɪnɪt]
Monat month [mʌnθ]
Monatsfahrkarte *(der Londoner Verkehrsbetriebe)* Travelcard ['trævlkɑ:d]
Mond moon [mu:n]
Monitor monitor ['mɒnɪtə]
Monster monster ['mɒnstə]
Montag Monday ['mʌndeɪ, 'mʌndi] *(siehe auch unter „Freitag")*
Mord murder ['mɜ:də]
morden murder ['mɜ:də]
Mörder/in murderer ['mɜ:dərə]
morgen tomorrow [tə'mɒrəʊ]
Morgen morning ['mɔ:nɪŋ] • **am Morgen, morgens** in the morning
Moschee mosque [mɒsk]
Motel motel [məʊ'tel]
MP3-Spieler MP3 player [ˌempi:'θri: ˌpleɪə]
müde tired ['taɪəd]
Müll rubbish ['rʌbɪʃ]
Müllabfuhr rubbish collection ['rʌbɪʃ kəˌlekʃn]
Mülltonne bin [bɪn]; dustbin ['dʌstbɪn]
Mund mouth [maʊθ] • **den Mund halten** shut up [ˌʃʌt_'ʌp]
murren grumble ['grʌmbl]
Museum museum [mju'zi:əm]
Musical musical ['mju:zɪkl]
Musik music ['mju:zɪk]
Musiker/in musician [mju:'zɪʃn]
Müsli muesli ['mju:zli]
müssen have to; must [mʌst]
nicht müssen needn't ['ni:dnt]
Mutter mother ['mʌðə]
Mutti mum [mʌm]; mom *(AE)* [mɑ:m]
Mütze cap [kæp]

N

Na ja ... / Na gut ... Oh well ... [əʊ 'wel]
Na und? So? [səʊ]; So what? [səʊ 'wɒt]; Who cares? [ˌhu: 'keəz]
nach 1. *(örtlich)* to [tə, tu] • **nach draußen** outside • **nach drinnen** inside • **nach Hause gehen** go home • **nach Hause kommen** come home; get home • **nach oben** up; *(im Haus)* upstairs [ˌʌp'steəz] • **nach unten** down; *(im Haus)* downstairs [ˌdaʊn'steəz]
nach vorn to the front [frʌnt]
2. *(zeitlich)* after • **Viertel nach 11** quarter past 11 [pɑ:st]
3. nach etwas fragen ask about sth. [ə'baʊt] • **jn. nach dem Weg fragen** ask sb. the way
Nachbar/in neighbour ['neɪbə]
nachdem after ['ɑ:ftə]
nachdenken über think about [θɪŋk]
nachmachen imitate ['ɪmɪteɪt]
Nachmittag afternoon [ˌɑ:ftə'nu:n]
am Nachmittag, nachmittags in the afternoon
Nachrichten news *(no pl)* [nju:z]
nachrufen: jm. Schimpfwörter nachrufen call sb. names
nächste(r, s): am nächsten Tag the next day [nekst] • **der Nächste sein** be next • **Was haben wir als Nächstes?** What have we got next?
Nacht night [naɪt] • **heute Nacht** tonight [tə'naɪt] • **in der Nacht, nachts** at night
Nachtklub nightclub ['naɪtklʌb]
nahe (bei, an) near [nɪə]; close (to) [kləʊs]
Nähe: in der Nähe von near [nɪə]
Name name [neɪm]
Nase nose [nəʊz]

Nashorn rhino ['raɪnəʊ]
nass wet [wet]
Nation nation ['neɪʃn] • **die Ersten Nationen** *(indianische Ureinwohner/innen Kanadas)* the First Nations
national national ['næʃnəl]
natürlich *(selbstverständlich)* of course [əv 'kɔːs]
natürlich, Natur- natural ['nætʃrəl]
Naturwissenschaft science ['saɪəns]
Nebel fog [fɒg]
neben next to [nekst]
nebenbei (bemerkt) by the way
neblig foggy ['fɒgi]
necken tease [tiːz]
nehmen take [teɪk] • **Ich nehme es.** *(beim Einkaufen)* I'll take it. • **auf den Arm nehmen** *(necken)* tease [tiːz] • **wichtig nehmen** care (about) [keə]
nein no [nəʊ]
nennen *(rufen, bezeichnen)* call [kɔːl]; *(benennen)* name [neɪm]
nervös nervous ['nɜːvəs]
nett nice [naɪs] • **Nett, dich/euch/Sie kennenzulernen.** Nice to meet you.
neu new [njuː] • **neu starten** *(Computer)* restart [ˌriː'stɑːt]
neueste(r, s) latest ['leɪtɪst]
nicht not [nɒt] • **auch nicht** not (...) either ['aɪðə, 'iːðə] • **nicht mehr** not (...) any more • **Das glaube ich nicht. / Ich glaube nicht.** I don't think so. • **Du brauchst ein ..., nicht wahr?** You need a ..., right? **noch nicht** not (...) yet [jet]
nichts nothing ['nʌθɪŋ]; not (...) anything ['eniθɪŋ] • **Macht nichts.** Never mind. [ˌnevə 'maɪnd] • **Nichts zu danken.** You're welcome. ['welkəm]
nicken: (mit dem Kopf) nicken nod your head [nɒd]
nie, niemals never ['nevə]
niemand nobody ['nəʊbədi]; no one ['nəʊ wʌn]; not (...) anybody ['enibɒdi]; not (...) anyone
nirgendwo(hin) not (...) anywhere ['eniweə]
noch: noch ein(e) ... another ... [ə'nʌðə]; one more ... [mɔː] • **noch einmal** again [ə'gen] • **noch nicht** not (...) yet [jet] • **noch 70 Meter** another 70 metres • **(immer) noch** still [stɪl] • **wer/was/wo/... noch** who/what/where/... else [els]
Nord- northern ['nɔːðən]
Norden north [nɔːθ] • **nach Norden** north • **Richtung Norden** northbound ['nɔːθbaʊnd]
nördlich north [nɔːθ]; northern ['nɔːðən]
Nordosten north-east [ˌnɔːθ'iːst] **nach Nordosten** north-east
nordöstlich north-east [ˌnɔːθ'iːst]
Nordwest north-west [ˌnɔːθ'west] **nach Nordwesten** north-west
nordwestlich north-west [ˌnɔːθ'west]
nörgeln grumble ['grʌmbl]
normalerweise usually ['juːʒuəli]
Noten music ['mjuːzɪk] • **Noten lesen** read music
Notiz note [nəʊt] • **sich Notizen machen** take notes
November November [nəʊ'vembə]
Nr. No. ['nʌmbə], *pl* Nos.
Nu: im Nu in next to no time
null o [əʊ]; zero ['zɪərəʊ]; *(beim Sport)* **nil** [nɪl]
► S.183 A football match
Nummer number ['nʌmbə]
nun now [naʊ] • **Nun, ...** Well, ... [wel]
nur only ['əʊnli]; just [dʒʌst] • **nur zum Spaß** just for fun
Nuss nut [nʌt]

O

ob if [ɪf]
oben *(an der Spitze)* at the top (of) [tɒp]; *(im Haus)* upstairs [ˌʌp'steəz] **dort oben** up there • **nach oben** up; *(im Haus)* upstairs
Oberbegriff group word ['gruːp wɜːd]
oberhalb von over ['əʊvə]; above [ə'bʌv]
oberste(r, s) top [tɒp]
Oberteil top [tɒp]
Obst fruit [fruːt]
Obstkuchen pie [paɪ]
Obstsalat fruit salad ['fruːt ˌsæləd]
obwohl although [ɔːl'ðəʊ]
oder or [ɔː]
öffnen open ['əʊpən]
oft often ['ɒfn]
ohne without [wɪ'ðaʊt]
Ohr ear [ɪə]
Ohrenschmerzen earache ['ɪəreɪk]
Ohrring earring ['ɪərɪŋ]
Oje! Oh dear! [əʊ 'dɪə]
okay OK [əʊ'keɪ]
Oktober October [ɒk'təʊbə]
Oldie oldie ['əʊldi] *(infml)*
Oma grandma ['grænmɑː]; granny ['græni]
Onkel uncle ['ʌŋkl]
online, Online- online [ˌɒn'laɪn]
Opa grandpa ['grænpɑː]
Open-Air-Konzert open-air concert [ˌəʊpən‿'eə ˌkɒnsət]
Oper, Opernhaus opera (house) ['ɒprə haʊs]
Operation (an) operation (on) [ˌɒpə'reɪʃn]
Opfer victim ['vɪktɪm]
Orange orange ['ɒrɪndʒ]
orange(farben) orange ['ɒrɪndʒ]
Orangenmarmelade marmalade ['mɑːməleɪd]
Orangensaft orange juice ['ɒrɪndʒ dʒuːs]
ordentlich tidy ['taɪdi]
Ordnung: in Ordnung all right [ɔːl 'raɪt]; fine [faɪn]
organisieren organize ['ɔːgənaɪz]
Ort place [pleɪs]; location [lə'keɪʃn] **am/vom Ort** local ['ləʊkl] • **an anderen Orten** in other places
örtlich local ['ləʊkl]
Ost- eastern ['iːstən]
Osten east [iːst] • **nach Osten** east **Richtung Osten** eastbound ['iːstbaʊnd]
östlich east [iːst]; eastern ['iːstən]
Outfit *(Kleidung; Ausrüstung)* outfit ['aʊtfɪt]

P

paar: ein paar some [səm, sʌm]; a couple (of) ['kʌpl]; *(einige wenige)* a few [fjuː]
Paar: ein Paar a pair (of) [peə]; a couple (of) ['kʌpl]
Päckchen packet ['pækɪt] • **ein Päckchen Pfefferminzbonbons** a packet of mints
packen **1.** *(Koffer, Auto)* pack [pæk] **2.** *(greifen, schnappen)* grab [græb]
Packung packet ['pækɪt] • **eine Packung Pfefferminzbonbons** a packet of mints
Paddel paddle ['pædl]
paddeln canoe [kə'nuː]; paddle ['pædl]
Paket parcel ['pɑːsl]
Palast palace ['pæləs]
Panik: in Panik geraten panic ['pænɪk]
pantomimisch darstellen mime [maɪm]
Papa dad [dæd]
Papagei parrot ['pærət]
Papier paper ['peɪpə]
Paradies paradise ['pærədaɪs]
Paralympische Spiele Paralympics [ˌ∞pærə'lɪmpɪks]
Park park [pɑːk]
Parkplatz *(für viele Autos)* car park
Parlament parliament ['pɑːləmənt]
Partner/in partner ['pɑːtnə]
Partnerstadt twin town [ˌtwɪn 'taʊn]

Party party ['pɑ:ti]
Passagier/in passenger ['pæsɪndʒə]
passen fit [fɪt] • **passen zu** go with
passieren (mit) happen (to) ['hæpən]
Passiv passive ['pæsɪv]
Pastete pie [paɪ]
Pause break [breɪk] • **in der Pause** *(zwischen Schulstunden)* at break
Pence pence (p) [pens]
Person person ['pɜ:sn]
persönlich personal ['pɜ:sənl]
Persönlichkeit: berühmte Persönlichkeit celebrity [sə'lebrəti]
Pfad path [pɑ:θ]
Pfefferminzbonbons mints [mɪnts]
Pfeife 1. *(zum Rauchen; Orgelpfeife)* pipe [paɪp]
2. *(Trillerpfeife)* whistle ['wɪsl]
pfeifen whistle ['wɪsl]
Pferd horse [hɔ:s]
Pferdeschwanz *(Frisur)* ponytail ['pəʊniteɪl]
Pfiff whistle ['wɪsl]
Pfund 1. *(britische Währung)* pound (£) [paʊnd] • **Es kostet 1 Pfund.** It's £1.
2. *(Gewichtseinheit)* pound [paʊnd] **ein drei Pfund schwerer Ball** a three-pound ball
Piano piano [pi'ænəʊ]
Picknick picnic ['pɪknɪk]
piepsen bleep [bli:p]
Piepton bleep [bli:p]
pink(farben) pink [pɪŋk]
Pirat/in pirate ['paɪrət]
Pizza pizza ['pi:tsə]
Plan plan [plæn]
planen plan [plæn]
Planet planet ['plænɪt]
Platz *(Ort, Stelle)* place [pleɪs]; *(in der Stadt, quadratisch)* square [skweə]; *(in der Stadt, rund)* circus ['sɜ:kəs]; *(im Sport)* court [kɔ:t]; *(Einsatzort)* location [ləʊ'keɪʃn]
Plätzchen biscuit ['bɪskɪt]
plaudern chat [tʃæt]
plötzlich suddenly ['sʌdnli]
Pokal cup [kʌp]
Polizei police *(pl)* [pə'li:s]
Polizeiwache, Polizeirevier police station [pə'li:s steɪʃn]
Poltergeist poltergeist ['pəʊltəgaɪst]
Pommes frites chips *(pl)* [tʃɪps]
Popcorn popcorn ['pɒpkɔ:n]
Pop(musik) pop (music) [pɒp]
Popsender pop station ['steɪʃn]
populär popular ['pɒpjələ]
Posaune trombone [trɒm'bəʊn]
Post *(Briefe, Päckchen, ...)* post [pəʊst]
Postamt post office ['pəʊst_ɒfɪs]
Poster poster ['pəʊstə]
Postkarte postcard ['pəʊstkɑ:d]
Postskript *(Nachschrift unter Briefen)* postscript ['pəʊstskrɪpt]
Präfix prefix ['pri:fɪks]
Präsentation presentation [,prezn'teɪʃn]
präsentieren: (jm.) etwas präsentieren present sth. (to sb.) [prɪ'zent]
Preis *(Kaufpreis)* price [praɪs]; *(Gewinn)* prize [praɪz]
pressen squeeze [skwi:z]
pro per [pɜ:, pə] • **einmal/zweimal pro Woche** once/twice a week
Probe *(Theater)* rehearsal [rɪ'hɜ:sl]
proben *(Theater)* rehearse [rɪ'hɜ:s]
probieren try [traɪ]
Problem problem ['prɒbləm]
produzieren produce [prə'dju:s]
Programm programme ['prəʊgræm]
Projekt (über, zu) project (on, about) ['prɒdʒekt] • **ein Projekt machen, durchführen** do a project
Prominente(r) celebrity [sə'lebrəti]
Prozent per cent (%) [pə'sent]
prüfen *(überprüfen)* check [tʃek]
Prüfung *(Test, Klassenarbeit)* test [test]
PS *(Nachschrift unter Briefen)* PS ['pi:_'es]
Pullover pullover ['pʊləʊvə]
Punker/in punk [pʌŋk]
Punkt *(bei Test, Quiz)* point [pɔɪnt]
Punktestand score [skɔ:]
► S.183 A football match
pusten blow [bləʊ]
putzen clean [kli:n] • **sich die Zähne putzen** clean your teeth
Putzfrau, -mann cleaner ['kli:nə]

Q

Quadratkilometer square kilometre (sq km) [skweə]
Querflöte flute [flu:t]
Quiz quiz [kwɪz], *pl* quizzes ['kwɪzɪz]

R

Rad 1. wheel ['wi:l]
2. *(Fahrrad)* bike [baɪk] • **Rad fahren** cycle ['saɪkl]; ride a bike [,raɪd ə 'baɪk]
Radfahrt bike ride ['baɪk raɪd]
Radiergummi rubber ['rʌbə]
Radio radio ['reɪdiəʊ] • **im Radio** on the radio
Radiosender radio station ['steɪʃn]
Radtour bike tour ['baɪk tʊə]
Radweg cycle path ['saɪkl pɑ:θ]
Ranger/in ranger ['reɪndʒə]
Rap rap [ræp]
rasen speed [spi:d]
raten guess [ges]
Ratespiel quiz [kwɪz], *pl* quizzes ['kwɪzɪz]
Rätsel *(Geheimnis)* mystery ['mɪstri]; *(Spiel)* riddle ['rɪdl]
Ratte rat [ræt]
Raum room [ru:m]
realistisch realistic [,ri:ə'lɪstɪk]
Rechercheur/in researcher [rɪ'sɜ:tʃə, 'ri:sɜ:tʃə]
Recht haben be right [raɪt]
rechte(r, s) right [raɪt] • **rechts, auf der rechten Seite** on the right **(nach) rechts abbiegen** turn right **nach rechts** to the right • **nach rechts schauen** look right
rechtzeitig in time [ɪn 'taɪm]
recycelt recycled [,ri:'saɪkld]
Recycling recycling [,ri:'saɪklɪŋ]
Redakteur/in editor ['edɪtə]
Rede: direkte Rede direct speech [də'rekt] • **indirekte Rede** indirect speech [,ɪndə'rekt]
reden (mit, über) talk (to, about) [tɔ:k]; speak (to, about) [spi:k] **Wovon redest du?** What are you talking about?
redigieren edit ['edɪt]
Regal(brett) shelf [ʃelf], *pl* shelves [ʃelvz]
Regel *(Vorschrift)* rule [ru:l]
regelmäßig regular ['regjələ]
Regen rain [reɪn]
Regenzeit rainy season ['reɪni ,si:zn]
Regie führen direct [də'rekt]
Regisseur/in director [də'rektə]
regnen rain [reɪn]
regnerisch rainy ['reɪni]
Reh deer, *pl* deer [dɪə]
reich rich [rɪtʃ]
reichen *(weitergeben)* pass [pɑ:s]
Reihe: 1. Du bist an der Reihe. It's your turn. [tɜ:n]
2. *(Sendereihe, Serie)* series, *pl* series ['sɪəri:z]
Reise trip [trɪp]; journey ['dʒɜ:ni] **eine Reise machen** go on a trip
reisen travel ['trævl]
reiten ride [raɪd] • **reiten gehen** go riding
Reiterhelm, -kappe riding hat [hæt]
Reitstiefel riding boots *(pl)* [bu:ts]
Reitweg bridle path ['braɪdl pɑ:θ]
relaxen chill out [,tʃɪl_'aʊt] *(infml)*
Religion *(Religionsunterricht)* RE [,ɑ:r_'i:], Religious Education [rɪ,lɪdʒəs_edʒu'keɪʃn]
rennen run [rʌn]
reparieren repair [rɪ'peə]
Reportage (über) report (on) [rɪ'pɔ:t]

Reporter/in reporter [rɪ'pɔ:tə]
repräsentieren represent [ˌreprɪ'zent]
Rest rest [rest]
Restaurant restaurant ['restrɒnt]; *(Imbissstube, Café)* café ['kæfeɪ]
Resultat result [rɪ'zʌlt]
retten save [seɪv]
Rhythmus rhythm ['rɪðəm]
richtig right [raɪt]; *(korrekt)* correct [kə'rekt] • **etwas richtig machen** get sth. right
Richtung way [weɪ] • **in diese Richtung** this way • **in die falsche Richtung** the wrong way • **in welche Richtung?** which way? **Richtung Norden** northbound ['nɔ:θbaʊnd] • **Richtung Osten** eastbound ['i:stbaʊnd] • **Richtung Süden** southbound ['saʊθbaʊnd] **Richtung Westen** westbound ['westbaʊnd]
riechen smell [smel]
Riesenrad big wheel
riesig huge [hju:dʒ]
► S.177 big – large – huge
Ring ring [rɪŋ]
Rock skirt [skɜ:t]
Rock(musik) rock (music) [rɒk]
Rolle role [rəʊl]
Rollstuhl wheelchair ['wi:ltʃeə]
Römer, Römerin; römisch Roman ['rəʊmən]
rosa pink [pɪŋk]
rot red [red]
Rucksack rucksack ['rʌksæk]
Ruf call [kɔ:l]
rufen call [kɔ:l]; shout [ʃaʊt] • **die Polizei rufen** call the police
Rugby rugby ['rʌgbi]
ruhig quiet ['kwaɪət]
rumhängen hang out [ˌhæŋ_'aʊt] *(infml)*
rund round [raʊnd]
Rundgang (durch das Haus) tour (of the house) [tʊə]
runterladen download [ˌdaʊn'ləʊd]

S

Saal hall [hɔ:l]
Sache thing [θɪŋ]
Saft juice [dʒu:s]
sagen say [seɪ] • **Man sagt, ...** They say ... • **Sagt mir eure Namen.** Tell me your names. [tel] • **Was du nicht sagst!** No way! [ˌnəʊ 'weɪ]
Saite string [strɪŋ]
Salat 1. *(Kopfsalat)* lettuce ['letɪs] **2.** *(Gericht, Beilage)* salad ['sæləd]
sammeln collect [kə'lekt]
Sammler/in collector [kə'lektə]
Samstag Saturday ['sætədeɪ, 'sætədi] *(siehe auch unter „Freitag“)*
Sandwich sandwich ['sænwɪtʃ]
sanft soft [sɒft]
Sänger/in singer ['sɪŋə]
Sanitäter/in paramedic [ˌpærə'medɪk]
Sattel saddle ['sædl]
Satz sentence ['sentəns]; *(Teil-, Gliedsatz)* clause [klɔ:z] • **Satz um Satz** sentence for sentence
sauber clean [kli:n] • **sauber machen** clean
sauer sour ['saʊə]
Säule column ['kɒləm]
Sauna sauna ['sɔ:nə] • **in die Sauna gehen** have a sauna
Saxophon saxophone ['sæksəfəʊn]
Schachtel packet ['pækɪt]
schade: Es ist schade, dass ... It's a pity (that ...) ['pɪti] • **Wie schade!** What a bummer! ['bʌmə] *(infml)*
Schaf sheep, *pl* sheep [ʃi:p]
Schale bowl [bəʊl] • **eine Schale Cornflakes** a bowl of cornflakes
scharf: scharf gewürzt spicy ['spaɪsi]
Schatten *(einer Person, eines Gegenstands)* shadow ['ʃædəʊ]
Schatz dear [dɪə]; sweetheart ['swi:thɑ:t]
schätzen *(erraten)* guess [ges]
schauen look [lʊk]
Schauspiel drama ['drɑ:mə]
Schauspieler/in actor ['æktə]
scheinen *(Sonne)* shine [ʃaɪn]
scheinen: zu sein/tun scheinen seem to be/to do [si:m]
scherzen joke [dʒəʊk]
Scherzfrage riddle ['rɪdl]
scheu shy [ʃaɪ]
scheußlich horrible ['hɒrəbl]
schick trendy ['trendi]
schicken (an) send (to) [send]; *(vor allem per E-Mail)* mail (to) • **jm. eine SMS schicken** text sb. [tekst]
schieben push [pʊʃ]
Schiedsrichter/in referee [ˌrefə'ri:]
schießen: ein Tor schießen score a goal [skɔ:]
Schiff boat [bəʊt]; ship [ʃɪp]
Schiffsmannschaft crew [kru:]
Schild sign [saɪn]
Schildkröte tortoise ['tɔ:təs]
Schimpfwort: jn. mit Schimpfwörtern hänseln, jm. Schimpfwörter nachrufen call sb. names
Schinkenspeck bacon ['beɪkən]
Schlaf sleep [sli:p]
Schlafanzug pyjamas *(pl)* [pə'dʒɑ:məz]
schlafen sleep [sli:p]; *(nicht wach sein)* be asleep [ə'sli:p]
Schlafparty sleepover ['sli:pəʊvə]
Schlafzimmer bedroom ['bedru:m]
schlagen beat [bi:t]; hit [hɪt]
Schläger *(Badminton, Tennis, Squash)* racket ['rækɪt]
Schlagzeile headline ['hedˌlaɪn]
Schlagzeug drums [drʌmz] **Schlagzeug spielen** play the drums
Schlange snake [sneɪk]
schlau clever ['klevə]
schlecht bad [bæd] • **schlechter** worse [wɜ:s] • **am schlechtesten; der/die/das schlechteste** (the) worst [wɜ:st] • **schlecht werden** go bad • **schlechtes Timing** bad timing ['taɪmɪŋ]
► S.193 German 'werden'
Schleuse lock [lɒk]
schließen *(zumachen)* close [kləʊz]
schließlich at last [ət 'lɑ:st]
schlimm bad [bæd] • **schlimmer** worse [wɜ:s] • **am schlimmsten; der/die/das schlimmste** (the) worst [wɜ:st]
Schlitten sledge [sledʒ]
Schlittschuhbahn ice rink ['aɪs rɪŋk]
Schloss castle ['kɑ:sl]; palace ['pæləs]
Schluss *(einer Geschichte, eines Films usw.)* ending ['endɪŋ]
Schlüssel key [ki:]
Schlüsselwort key word ['ki: wɜ:d]
Schmerz(en) pain [peɪn] • **schreien vor Schmerzen** cry in pain [kraɪ]
schmutzig dirty ['dɜ:ti]
schnappen *(greifen)* grab [græb]
Schnee snow [snəʊ]
schneiden cut [kʌt]
schnell quick [kwɪk]; fast [fɑ:st]
schockiert shocked [ʃɒkt]
Schokolade chocolate ['tʃɒklət]
schon already [ɔ:l'redi] • **schon?** yet? [jet] • **schon mal?** ever? ['evə] **(vorher) schon mal** before [bɪ'fɔ:] **sogar schon** even ['i:vn]
schön beautiful ['bju:tɪfl]; *(nett)* nice [naɪs]; *(hübsch; wunderbar)* lovely ['lʌvli] • **schön kühl/sauber/...** nice and cool/clean/... • **schön ordentlich** neat and tidy
Schönheit beauty ['bju:ti]
schottisch Scottish ['skɒtɪʃ]
Schrank cupboard ['kʌbəd]; *(Kleiderschrank)* wardrobe ['wɔ:drəʊb]
schrecklich terrible ['terəbl]; awful ['ɔ:fl]
schreiben (an) write (to) [raɪt]
Schreiber/in writer ['raɪtə]
Schreibtisch desk [desk]
schreien shout [ʃaʊt]; cry [kraɪ] **schreien vor Schmerzen** cry in pain
Schriftsteller/in writer ['raɪtə]

Schritt step [step] • **Schritte machen/unternehmen** take steps
schüchtern shy [ʃaɪ]
Schuh shoe [ʃu:]
Schuld: jm. die Schuld geben (an) blame sb. (for) [bleɪm]
Schule school [sku:l] • **aus der Schule** from school • **in der Schule** at school
► S.170 Places without articles
Schüler/in student ['stju:dənt]
Schüleraustausch exchange [ɪks'tʃeɪndʒ]
Schulfach (school) subject ['sʌbdʒɪkt]
Schulheft exercise book ['eksəsaɪz bʊk]
Schulklasse class [klɑ:s]; form [fɔ:m]
Schulleiter/in head teacher [ˌhed 'ti:tʃə]
Schultasche school bag ['sku:l bæg]
Schulter shoulder ['ʃəʊldə]
Schulterpolster *(beim American Football)* pad [pæd]
Schultyrann bully ['bʊli]
Schuss shot [ʃɒt]
Schüssel bowl [bəʊl]
schütteln: den Kopf schütteln shake your head [ʃeɪk]
Schützer *(Knieschützer usw. für Inlineskater)* pad [pæd]
schwach weak [wi:k]
schwarz black [blæk]
schwatzen *(klatschen, tratschen)* gossip ['gɒsɪp]
schwer *(schwierig)* difficult ['dɪfɪkəlt]; hard [hɑ:d]
Schwester sister ['sɪstə]
schwierig difficult ['dɪfɪkəlt]; hard [hɑ:d]
Schwierigkeiten trouble ['trʌbl] **in Schwierigkeiten sein** be in trouble
Schwimmbad, -becken swimming pool ['swɪmɪŋ pu:l]
schwimmen swim [swɪm] schwimmen gehen go swimming
Schwimmer/in swimmer ['swɪmə]
See **1.** lake [leɪk]; *(in Schottland)* loch [lɒx]
2. *(die See, das Meer)* sea [si:] • **auf See** at sea
sehen see [si:] • **Siehst du?** See?
Sehenswürdigkeiten sights *(pl)* [saɪts]
sehr very ['veri] • **Danke sehr!** Thanks very much! • **Er mag sie sehr.** He likes her a lot. [ə 'lɒt] **etwas sehr mögen/sehr lieben** like/love sth. very much
Seife soap [səʊp]
sein *(Verb)* be [bi:]
sein(e) ... *(besitzanzeigend) (zu „he")* his ...; *(zu „it")* its ...
seiner, seine, seins his [hɪz]
seit **1.** *(mit Zeitpunkt)* since [sɪns] **since September** seit September
2. *(mit Zeitraum)* for [fɔ:] • **seit Jahren** for years
Seite **1.** side [saɪd] • **auf der linken Seite** on the left • **auf der rechten Seite** on the right
2. *(Buch-, Heftseite)* page [peɪdʒ] **Auf welcher Seite sind wir?** What page are we on?
Sekunde second ['sekənd]
Selbstbedienungsrestaurant *(Cafeteria)* cafeteria [ˌkæfə'tɪəriə]
selbstsicher tough [tʌf]
selbstverständlich of course [əv 'kɔ:s]
seltsam strange [streɪndʒ]; weird [wɪəd]
senden (an) send (to) [send]; *(vor allem per E-Mail)* mail (to) [meɪl]
Sender *(Radio)* station
Sendereihe series, *pl* series ['sɪəri:z]
September September [sep'tembə]
Serie *(Sendereihe)* series, *pl* series ['sɪəri:z]
Service *(Dienst am Kunden)* service ['sɜ:vɪs]
Sessel armchair ['ɑ:mtʃeə]
setzen: sich setzen sit [sɪt] • **Setz dich / Setzt euch zu mir.** Sit with me. • **sich mit jm. in Verbindung setzen** contact sb. ['kɒntækt]
Shorts shorts *(pl)* [ʃɔ:ts]
Show show [ʃəʊ]
sich **1.** *(Reflexivpronomen)* herself [hɜ:'self]; himself [hɪm'self]; itself [ɪt'self]; themselves [ðəm'selvz]
2. sich (gegenseitig) *(einander)* each other [ˌi:tʃ_'ʌðə]
sicher **1.** *(in Sicherheit)* safe (from) [seɪf] • **nicht sicher** unsafe [ʌn'seɪf]
2. sicher sein *(nicht zweifeln)* be sure [ʃʊə, ʃɔ:]
Sicherheit: in Sicherheit (vor) safe (from) [seɪf]
Sicht: aus meiner Sicht from my point of view [ˌpɔɪnt_əv 'vju:]
sie **1.** *(weibliche Person)* she [ʃi:] **Frag sie.** Ask her. [hə, hɜ:]
2. *(Ding, Tier)* it [ɪt]
3. *(Plural)* they [ðeɪ] • **Frag sie.** Ask them. [ðəm, ðem]
4. Sie *(höfliche Anrede)* you [ju:]
Sieg win [wɪn]
Sieger/in winner ['wɪnə]
Silbe syllable ['sɪləbl]
singen sing [sɪŋ]
Sinn: Es hatte keinen Sinn. There was no point. [pɔɪnt]
sitzen sit [sɪt]
Skateboard skateboard ['skeɪtbɔ:d] **Skateboard fahren** skate [skeɪt]
Sketch sketch [sketʃ]
Ski ski [ski] • **Ski laufen/fahren** ski; go skiing
Skipiste ski slope ['ski: sləʊp]
Sklave, Sklavin slave [sleɪv]
SMS text message ['tekst ˌmesɪdʒ] **jm. eine SMS schicken** text sb. [tekst]
Snack snack [snæk]
so **1. so groß/aufregend wie** as big/exciting as
2. so süß so sweet [səʊ] • **so ein netter Mensch** such a nice person [sʌtʃ] • **so gute Bücher** such good books
► S.182 German 'so'
sobald as soon as [əz 'su:n_əz]
Socke sock [sɒk]
sodass so that
soeben just [dʒʌst]
Sofa sofa ['səʊfə]
sofort straightaway [ˌstreɪtə'weɪ]
Software software ['sɒftweə]
sogar even ['i:vn]
Sohn son [sʌn]
sollen: Sollen wir ...? Shall we ...? [ʃæl] • **Was soll das?** What's the point? [pɔɪnt]
sollte(n): ich/er sollte ... I/he should [ʃəd, ʃʊd] • **sie wussten nicht, was sie tun sollten** they didn't know what to do
Sommer summer ['sʌmə]
sonderbar strange [streɪndʒ]
Song song [sɒŋ]
Sonnabend Saturday ['sætədeɪ, 'sætədi] *(siehe auch unter „Freitag")*
Sonne sun [sʌn]
Sonnenbrille: (eine) Sonnenbrille sunglasses *(pl)* ['sʌnglɑ:sɪz]
sonnengebräunt sein have a suntan ['sʌnˌtæn]
sonnig sunny ['sʌni]
Sonntag Sunday ['sʌndeɪ, 'sʌndi] *(siehe auch unter „Freitag")*
sonst: sonst (noch) jemand/etwas/irgendwo anybody/anything/anywhere else [els]
Sorge worry ['wʌri] • **sich Sorgen machen (wegen, um)** worry (about) • **Mach dir keine Sorgen.** Don't worry.
Sorte sort (of) [sɔ:t]
Soße sauce [sɔ:s]
Soul(musik) soul [səʊl]
Souvenir souvenir [ˌsu:və'nɪə]
sowie *(sobald)* as soon as [əz 'su:n_əz]
sowieso anyway ['eniweɪ]

Spaghetti spaghetti [spəˈgeti]
spannend exciting [ɪkˈsaɪtɪŋ]
sparen save [seɪv]
Spaß fun [fʌn] • **Spaß haben** have fun • **nur zum Spaß** just for fun **Reiten macht Spaß.** Riding is fun. **Viel Spaß!** Have fun!
spät late [leɪt] • **Wie spät ist es?** What's the time? • **zu spät sein/ kommen** be late
später later [ˈleɪtə]
spazieren gehen go for a walk [wɔːk]; walk [wɔːk]
Spaziergang walk [wɔːk] • **einen Spaziergang machen** go for a walk
Specht woodpecker [ˈwʊdpekə]
Speisekarte menu [ˈmenjuː]
Spiegel mirror [ˈmɪrə]
Spiel game [geɪm]; *(Wettkampf)* match [mætʃ]
spielen play [pleɪ]; *(Szene, Dialog)* act [ækt] • **Fußball spielen** play football • **Gitarre/Klavier/Geige/ Schlagzeug spielen** play the guitar/the piano/the violin/the drums • **jm. einen Streich spielen** play a trick on sb.
Spieler/in player [ˈpleɪə]
Spielstand *(Punktestand)* score [skɔː]
▶ S.183 A football match
Spielstein *(für Brettspiele)* counter [ˈkaʊntə]
Spion/in spy [spaɪ]
Spitze *(oberes Ende)* top [tɒp] • **an der Spitze (von)** at the top (of)
Spitzen- top [tɒp]
Sport; Sportart sport [spɔːt] • **Sport treiben** do sport
Sportausrüstung, Sportsachen sports gear *(no pl)* [ˈspɔːts gɪə]
Sporthalle sports hall [ˈspɔːts hɔːl]
Sportunterricht PE [ˌpiː‿ˈiː], Physical Education [ˌfɪzɪkəl‿edʒuˈkeɪʃn]
Sprache language [ˈlæŋgwɪdʒ]
Sprachmittlung *(Mediation)* mediation [ˌmiːdiˈeɪʃn]
sprechen (mit) speak (to) [spiːk] **Hier spricht Isabel.** *(am Telefon)* This is Isabel.
springen jump [dʒʌmp]
Spritztour: eine Spritztour machen take a ride [raɪd]
Spülbecken, Spüle sink [sɪŋk]
Staat state [ˈsteɪt]
Stadion stadium [ˈsteɪdiəm]
Stadt *(Großstadt)* city [ˈsɪti]; *(Kleinstadt)* town [taʊn] • **die Mitte der Stadt** the centre of town • **in der Stadt** in town
▶ S.170 Places without articles

Stadtplan map [mæp]
Stadtzentrum city centre [ˌsɪti ˈsentə]
Stahl steel [stiːl]
Stall *(für Kaninchen)* hutch [hʌtʃ]
Stammbaum family tree [ˈfæməli triː]
Standpunkt point of view [ˌpɔɪnt‿əv ˈvjuː] • **von meinem Standpunkt aus gesehen** from my point of view
Star *(Film-, Popstar)* star [stɑː]
stark strong [strɒŋ]
starten start [stɑːt] • **neu starten** *(Computer)* restart [ˌriːˈstɑːt]
stattfinden take place [ˌteɪk ˈpleɪs]
Statue statue [ˈstætʃuː]
Stecker plug [plʌg]
Steeldrum steel drum [ˌstiːl ˈdrʌm]
stehen stand [stænd] • **Hier steht: ...** *(im Text)* It says here: ... • **Wie steht es?** *(beim Sport)* What's the score?
▶ S.183 A football match
stehlen steal [stiːl]
Steigerung comparison [kəmˈpærɪsn]
Stein stone [stəʊn]
stellen *(hin-, abstellen)* put [pʊt] **etwas leiser/lauter stellen** turn sth. down/up • **Fragen stellen** ask questions • **(jm.) eine Falle stellen** set a trap (for sb.) [set] **sich (hin)stellen** stand [stænd] **Stell dir vor! / Stellt euch vor!** Guess what! [ˌges ˈwɒt]
sterben (an) die (of) [daɪ]
Stereoanlage stereo [ˈsteriəʊ]
Stern star [stɑː]
steuern steer [stɪə]
Stichwort *(Schlüsselwort)* key word [ˈkiː wɜːd]
Stiefel boot [buːt]
Stil style [staɪl]
still quiet [ˈkwaɪət]
Stimme voice [vɔɪs]; *(bei Abstimmungen)* vote [vəʊt]
stimmen: Das stimmt. That's right. [raɪt] • **Du brauchst ein Lineal, stimmt's?** You need a ruler, right?
Stimmrecht vote [vəʊt]
Stoff *(Material)* material [məˈtɪəriəl]
stolz (auf jn./etwas) proud (of sb./ sth.) [praʊd]
stoßen push [pʊʃ]
Strafstoß penalty [ˈpenəlti]
Strand beach [biːtʃ] • **am Strand** on the beach
Straße road [rəʊd]; street [striːt] • **in seiner Straße** in/on his street
Straßenbahn tram [træm]
Straßenkünstler/in (street) performer [pəˈfɔːmə]
Strecke way [weɪ]
Streich trick [trɪk] • **jm. einen Streich spielen** play a trick on sb.

Streik strike [straɪk]
streiken 1. *(sich im Streik befinden)* be on strike [straɪk] **2.** *(in den Streik treten)* go on strike
Streit argument [ˈɑːgjumənt]
streiten: sich streiten argue [ˈɑːgjuː]; have an argument [ˈɑːgjumənt]
streng strict [strɪkt]
Strom electricity [ɪˌlekˈtrɪsəti]
Stromschnellen rapids *(pl)* [ˈræpɪdz]
Struktur structure [ˈstrʌktʃə]
strukturieren structure [ˈstrʌktʃə]
Strumpf sock [sɒk]
Strumpfhose tights *(pl)* [taɪts]
Stück piece [piːs]; *(auf einer CD)* track [træk] • **ein Stück Papier** a piece of paper
Student/in student [ˈstjuːdənt]
studieren study [ˈstʌdi]
Studio studio [ˈstjuːdiəʊ]
Stuhl chair [tʃeə]
stumm: „stummer" Buchstabe *(nicht gesprochener Buchstabe)* silent letter [ˌsaɪlənt ˈletə]
Stunde hour [ˈaʊə]; *(Schulstunde)* lesson [ˈlesn] • **eine halbe Stunde** half an hour [hɑːf] • **ein Supermarkt, der 24 Stunden geöffnet ist** a 24-hour supermarket • **eine zweistündige Operation** a two-hour operation [ˌɒpəˈreɪʃn]
Stundenplan timetable [ˈtaɪmteɪbl]
Sturm storm [stɔːm]
stürmisch stormy [ˈstɔːmi]
stürzen *(hinfallen)* fall [fɔːl]
Subjekt subject [ˈsʌbdʒɪkt]
suchen look for [ˈlʊk fɔː]
Süd- southern [ˈsʌðən]
Süden south [saʊθ] • **nach Süden** south • **Richtung Süden** southbound [ˈsaʊθbaʊnd]
südlich south [saʊθ]; southern [ˈsʌðən]
Südosten south-east [ˌsaʊθˈiːst] **nach Südosten** south-east
südöstlich south-east [ˌsaʊθˈiːst]
Südwesten south-west [ˌsaʊθˈwest] **nach Südwesten** south-west
südwestlich south-west [ˌsaʊθˈwest]
Supermarkt supermarket [ˈsuːpəmɑːkɪt]
Suppe soup [suːp]
Surfbrett surfboard [ˈsɜːfbɔːd]
surfen gehen go surfing [ˈsɜːfɪŋ] **im Internet surfen** surf the internet [sɜːf]
süß sweet [swiːt]
Süßigkeiten sweets *(pl)* [swiːts]
Sweatshirt sweatshirt [ˈswetʃɜːt]
Synagoge synagogue [ˈsɪnəgɒg]
Szene scene [siːn]

T

Tafel *(Wandtafel)* board [bɔːd] • **an der/die Tafel** on the board
Tag day [deɪ] • **an jenem Tag** that day • **drei Tage (lang)** for three days • **eines Tages** one day
Guten Tag. Hello.; *(nachmittags)* Good afternoon. [gʊd_ɑːftəˈnuːn]
Tagebuch diary [ˈdaɪəri]
Tagesfahrkarte *(der Londoner Verkehrsbetriebe)* Travelcard [ˈtrævlkɑːd]
Tal valley [ˈvæli]
Talboden valley floor [ˌvæli ˈflɔː]
Talent talent [ˈtælənt]
Talkshow chat show [ˈtʃæt ʃəʊ]
Tante aunt [ɑːnt]; auntie [ˈɑːnti]
Tanz dance [dɑːns]
tanzen dance [dɑːns]
Tänzer/in dancer [ˈdɑːnsə]
Tanzfläche dance floor [ˈdɑːns flɔː]
Tanzstunden, Tanzunterricht dancing lessons [ˈdɑːnsɪŋ ˌlesnz]
Tasche *(Tragetasche, Beutel)* bag [bæg]; *(Hosentasche, Jackentasche)* pocket [ˈpɒkɪt]
Taschengeld pocket money [ˈpɒkɪt mʌni]
Tasse cup [kʌp] • **eine Tasse Tee** a cup of tea
Tat action [ˈækʃn]
Tätigkeit activity [ækˈtɪvəti]
Tatsache fact [fækt]
taub deaf [def] • **taub werden** go deaf
► S.193 German 'werden'
tausend thousand [ˈθaʊznd]
Taxi taxi [ˈtæksi]
Team team [tiːm]
Teddybär teddy bear [ˈtedi beə]
Tee tea [tiː]
Teelöffel teaspoon [ˈtiːspuːn]
Teenager teenager [ˈtiːneɪdʒə]
Teenager- teen [tiːn] *(besonders AE)*
Teil part [pɑːt]; *(eines Textes)* section [ˈsekʃn]
teilen: (sich) teilen (in) divide (into) [dɪˈvaɪd] • **sich etwas teilen (mit jm.)** share sth. (with sb.) [ʃeə]
teilnehmen an etwas take part in sth.
Teilsatz clause [klɔːz]
Telefon (tele)phone [ˈtelɪfəʊn] • **am Telefon** on the phone
Telefongespräch: ein Telefongespräch führen make a call [kɔːl]
Telefonnummer (tele)phone number [ˈtelɪfəʊn ˌnʌmbə]
Teller plate [pleɪt] • **ein Teller Pommes frites** a plate of chips
Temperatur temperature [ˈtemprətʃə]
Tempus *(grammatische Zeit)* tense [tens]
Tennis tennis [ˈtenɪs]
Termin appointment [əˈpɔɪntmənt]
Terminkalender diary [ˈdaɪəri]
Test test [test]
teuer expensive [ɪkˈspensɪv]
Text text [tekst]
Theater theatre [ˈθɪətə]
Theaterkasse box office [ˈbɒks ˌɒfɪs]
Theaterstück play [pleɪ]
Thema, Themenbereich topic [ˈtɒpɪk]; section [ˈsekʃn]
Themenpark theme park [ˈθiːm pɑːk]
Thermometer thermometer [θəˈmɒmɪtə]
Tier animal [ˈænɪml]; *(Haustier)* pet [pet]
Tierhandlung pet shop [ˈpet ʃɒp]
Tierpark zoo [zuː]
Tiger tiger [ˈtaɪgə]
Timing: schlechtes Timing bad timing [ˈtaɪmɪŋ]
Tipp tip [tɪp]
Tisch table [ˈteɪbl]
Tischtennis table tennis [ˈteɪbl tenɪs]
Tischtennisschläger table tennis bat [bæt]
Titel title [ˈtaɪtl]; *(auf einer CD)* track [træk]
Titelseite front page [ˌfrʌnt ˈpeɪdʒ]
Toast(brot) toast [təʊst]
Tochter daughter [ˈdɔːtə]
Toilette toilet [ˈtɔɪlət]
toll fantastic [fænˈtæstɪk]; great [greɪt]; neat [niːt] *(AE, infml)*
Tomate tomato [təˈmɑːtəʊ], *pl* tomatoes
Ton note [nəʊt]
Tondatei sound file [ˈsaʊnd faɪl]
Top *(Oberteil)* top [tɒp]
Tor *(im Sport)* goal [gəʊl] • **ein Tor schießen** score a goal
Torte cake [keɪk]
Torwart, Torfrau (goal)keeper [ˈkiːpə]
tot dead [ded]
töten kill [kɪl]
tough tough [tʌf]
Tour: (Rad-)Tour (bike) tour [tʊə]
Tour durch das Haus *(Rundgang)* tour of the house
Tourist/in tourist [ˈtʊərɪst]
Track *(auf einer CD)* track [træk]
traditionell traditional [trəˈdɪʃənl]
tragen *(Kleidung)* wear [weə]
Trainer/in coach [kəʊtʃ]
trainieren practise [ˈpræktɪs]; train [treɪn]
Trainingseinheit, -stunde training session [ˈseʃn]
Träne tear [tɪə]
Transport(wesen) transport *(no pl)* [ˈtrænspɔːt]
tratschen gossip [ˈgɒsɪp]
trauen: Sie traute ihren Augen kaum. She couldn't believe her eyes. [bɪˈliːv]
Traum dream [driːm]
träumen (von) dream (of, about) [driːm]
Traumhaus dream house
traurig sad [sæd]
treffen; sich treffen meet [miːt]
ein Abkommen / eine Abmachung treffen make a deal [diːl] • **sich (regelmäßig) mit jm. treffen** date (sb.) [deɪt] *(besonders AE)*
Treffer: einen Treffer erzielen score a goal [skɔː], [gəʊl]
Treppe(nstufen) stairs *(pl)* [steəz]
Trick *(Zauberkunststück)* trick [trɪk]
Trikot shirt [ʃɜːt]
Trimester term [tɜːm]
trinken drink [drɪŋk] • **Milch zum Frühstück trinken** have milk for breakfast
trocken dry [draɪ]
Trommel drum [drʌm]
Trommelstock drumstick [ˈdrʌmstɪk]
Trompete trumpet [ˈtrʌmpɪt]
trotzdem anyway [ˈeniweɪ]; still [stɪl]
Tschüs. Bye. [baɪ]; See you. [ˈsiː juː]
T-Shirt T-shirt [ˈtiːʃɜːt]
Tsunami tsunami [tsuːˈnɑːmi]
tun do [duː] • **Tue, was ich tue.** Do what I do. • **tun müssen** have to do • **tun wollen** want to do [wɒnt]
Tut mir leid. I'm sorry. [ˈsɒri]
Tunnel tunnel [ˈtʌnl]
Tür door [dɔː]
Türklingel doorbell [ˈdɔːbel]
Turm tower [ˈtaʊə]
Turnanzug *(für Frauen und Mädchen)* leotard [ˈliːətɑːd]
Turnen *(Sportunterricht)* PE [ˌpiː_ˈiː], Physical Education [ˌfɪzɪkəl_edʒuˈkeɪʃn]
Turnschuhe trainers *(pl)* [ˈtreɪnəz]
Tut mir leid. I'm sorry. [ˈsɒri]
Tüte bag [bæg]
Typ *(Kerl)* guy [gaɪ]
Tyrann bully [ˈbʊli]
tyrannisieren bully [ˈbʊli]

U

U-Bahn: die U-Bahn the underground [ˈʌndəgraʊnd] *(BE)*; the subway [ˈsʌbweɪ] *(AE)*; *(in London)* the Tube *(no pl)* [tjuːb]
U-Bahn-Linie line [laɪn]
üben practise [ˈpræktɪs]

über **1.** about [ə'baʊt] • **über dich selbst** about yourself
2. *(räumlich)* over ['əʊvə]; *(quer über)* across [ə'krɒs]; *(oberhalb von)* above [ə'bʌv]
3. *(mehr als)* over

überall everywhere ['evriweə]

übereinstimmen: nicht übereinstimmen (mit) disagree (with) [ˌdɪsə'griː]

überfliegen: einen Text überfliegen *(um den Inhalt grob zu erfassen)* skim a text [skɪm]

überfüllt crowded ['kraʊdɪd]

überleben survive [sə'vaɪv]

Überleben survival [sə'vaɪvl]

übernachten *(über Nacht bleiben)* stay [steɪ]

überprüfen check [tʃek]

überqueren cross [krɒs]

überraschen surprise [sə'praɪz]

überrascht (über etwas) surprised (at sth.) [sə'praɪzd]

Überraschung (für) surprise (for/to) [sə'praɪz]

Überschrift title ['taɪtl]

überreichen present [prɪ'zent]

übersetzen (aus ... in) translate (from ... into) [træns'leɪt]

Übersetzung translation [træns'leɪʃn]

übrig sein be left [left]

übrigens by the way

Übung *(Schulbuch)* exercise ['eksəsaɪz] • **eine Übung machen** do an exercise

Übungsheft exercise book ['eksəsaɪz bʊk]

Uhr **1.** *(Armbanduhr)* watch [wɒtʃ]; *(Wand-, Stand-, Turmuhr)* clock [klɒk]
2. elf Uhr eleven o'clock • **7 Uhr morgens/vormittags** 7 am [ˌeɪ‿'em] • **7 Uhr nachmittags/abends** 7 pm [ˌpiː‿'em] • **um 8 Uhr 45** at 8.45

Uhrzeit time [taɪm]

um **1.** *(örtlich)* **um ... (herum)** round [raʊnd]; around [ə'raʊnd] • **um den See (herum)** around the lake
2. *(zeitlich)* **um 8.45** at 8.45 **um sechs Uhr herum** around six
3. Es geht um Mr Green. This is about Mr Green.
4. um zu to

umdrehen: sich umdrehen turn [tɜːn]

Umfrage (über) survey (on) ['sɜːveɪ]

umher: in ... umher round [raʊnd]; around [ə'raʊnd] • **in der Stadt umher** around the town

umher-: umhergehen walk around **umherrennen** run around • **umherspringen** jump around
► S.175 around

umschreiben *(anders ausdrücken)* paraphrase ['pærəfreɪz]

umsehen: sich umsehen look round/around [ˌlʊk 'raʊnd]

umsteigen change [tʃeɪndʒ]

umtauschen exchange [ɪks'tʃeɪndʒ]

umziehen (nach, in) *(die Wohnung wechseln)* move (to) [muːv]

unbequem uncomfortable [ʌn'kʌmftəbl]

uncool uncool [ˌʌn'kuːl] *(infml)*

und and [ənd, ænd] • **Und? / Na und?** So? [səʊ]; So what? [səʊ 'wɒt]! Who cares? [ˌhuː 'keəz]

undeutlich *(unklar)* unclear [ˌʌn'klɪə]

Unentschieden draw [drɔː] • **2:2 unentschieden** 2 all
► S.183 A football match

unfair unfair [ˌʌn'feə]

Unfall accident ['æksɪdənt]

unfreundlich unfriendly [ʌn'frendli]

ungefähr about [ə'baʊt]

Ungeheuer monster ['mɒnstə]

ungerecht unfair [ˌʌn'feə]

ungesund unhealthy [ʌn'helθi]

unglaublich amazing [ə'meɪzɪŋ]

unglücklich unhappy [ʌn'hæpi]

unheimlich scary ['skeəri]

unhöflich rude [ruːd]

Uniform uniform ['juːnɪfɔːm]

uninteressant uninteresting [ʌn'ɪntrəstɪŋ]

unklar unclear [ˌʌn'klɪə]

unmöglich impossible [ɪm'pɒsəbl]

unordentlich untidy [ʌn'taɪdi]

Unordnung: alles in Unordnung bringen make a mess [ˌmeɪk‿ə 'mes]

unregelmäßig irregular [ɪ'regjələ]

uns us [əs, ʌs]; *(Reflexivpronomen)* ourselves [aʊə'selvz]

unser(e) ... our ... ['aʊə] • **unser eigenes Schwimmbad** our own pool [əʊn]

unserer, unsere, unseres ours ['aʊəz]

unsicher unsure [ˌʌn'ʃʊə, ˌʌn'ʃɔː]

unten *(im Haus)* downstairs [ˌdaʊn'steəz] • **am unteren Ende (von)** at the bottom (of) ['bɒtəm] **dort unten** down there • **nach unten** down [daʊn]; *(im Haus)* downstairs

unter under ['ʌndə]; below [bɪ'ləʊ]

untere(r, s): am unteren Ende (von) at the bottom (of) ['bɒtəm]

unterhalb (von) below [bɪ'ləʊ]

unterhalten: sich unterhalten (mit, über) talk (to, about) [tɔːk]

Unterhaltung *(Gespräch)* conversation [ˌkɒnvə'seɪʃn]

Unterricht lessons *(pl)* ['lesnz]

unterrichten teach [tiːtʃ]

Unterschied difference ['dɪfrəns]

unterschiedlich different ['dɪfrənt]

unterschreiben sign [saɪn]

unterstützen: eine Mannschaft unterstützen support a team [sə'pɔːt]

Untersuchung (über) *(Umfrage)* survey (on) ['sɜːveɪ]

unverschämt rude [ruːd]

unwichtig unimportant [ˌʌnɪm'pɔːtnt]

Urgroßmutter great-grandmother [ˌgreɪt 'grænmʌðə]

Urgroßvater great-grandfather [ˌgreɪt 'grænfɑːðə]

Urlaub holiday ['hɒlədeɪ]; vacation [və'keɪʃn, veɪ'keɪʃn] *(AE)* • **in Urlaub fahren** go on holiday • **in Urlaub sein** be on holiday

V

Vater father ['fɑːðə]

Vati dad [dæd]

Verabredung appointment [ə'pɔɪntmənt]

verabschieden: sich verabschieden say goodbye [ˌseɪ gʊd'baɪ]

verängstigt scared [skeəd]

veranstalten organize ['ɔːgənaɪz] **einen Wettbewerb veranstalten** hold a competition [ˌkɒmpə'tɪʃn]

verbessern **1.** *(besser machen)* improve [ɪm'pruːv]
2. *(korrigieren)* correct [kə'rekt]

verbinden *(einander zuordnen)* link [lɪŋk]

Verbindung link [lɪŋk] • **in Verbindung bleiben** keep in touch [tʌtʃ] **sich mit jm. in Verbindung setzen** contact sb. ['kɒntækt]

verbringen: Zeit verbringen (mit etwas) spend time (on sth.) [spend]

Verein club [klʌb]

vereinigt: das Vereinigte Königreich *(Großbritannien und Nordirland)* the United Kingdom [juˌnaɪtɪd 'kɪŋdəm], the UK [ˌjuː 'keɪ] • **die Vereinigten Staaten (von Amerika)** the United States (of America) [juˌnaɪtɪd 'steɪts], the US [ˌjuː‿'es]

verfolgen follow ['fɒləʊ]

Vergangenheit past [pɑːst]

vergessen forget [fə'get]

vergeuden (für) waste (on) [weɪst]

Vergleich comparison [kəm'pærɪsn]

vergleichen compare [kəm'peə]

vergriffen sein be sold out [ˌsəʊld‿'aʊt]

verheiratet (mit) married (to) ['mærɪd]

verkaufen sell [sel]
Verkäufer/in shop assistant ['ʃɒp_əˌsɪstənt]
Verkehr traffic ['træfɪk]
verkehrsreich busy ['bɪzi]
verkehrt *(falsch)* wrong [rɒŋ]
Verkleidung *(Kostüm)* costume ['kɒstjuːm]
verknüpfen *(einander zuordnen)* link [lɪŋk]
verlassen leave [liːv]
verlaufen: sich verlaufen get lost [lɒst]
verletzen hurt [hɜːt]
verletzt hurt [hɜːt]
Verletzung injury ['ɪndʒəri]
verlieren lose [luːz]
vermissen miss [mɪs]
Vermittlung *(Sprachmittlung, Mediation)* mediation [ˌmiːdi'eɪʃn]
vermuten suppose [sə'pəʊz]
veröffentlichen publish ['pʌblɪʃ]
verpassen miss [mɪs]
verrückt mad [mæd]; crazy ['kreɪzi] **verrückt nach** mad about [mæd] **verrückt werden** go crazy
► S.193 German 'werden'
verschieden different ['dɪfrənt]
verschwenden (für) waste (on) [weɪst]
verschwinden disappear [ˌdɪsə'pɪə]
versprechen promise ['prɒmɪs]
verstecken; sich verstecken hide [haɪd]
verstehen understand [ˌʌndə'stænd] **Das versteh ich nicht.** I don't get it.
versuchen try [traɪ] • **versuchen zu tun** try and do / try to do
Verteidigung defence [dɪ'fens]
vertreten *(repräsentieren)* represent [ˌreprɪ'zent]
Verwandte(r) relative ['relətɪv]
verwenden use [juːz]
verwirrt puzzled ['pʌzld]
Video video ['vɪdiəʊ]
viel a lot (of) [lɒt]; lots (of) [lɒts]; much [mʌtʃ] • **viele** a lot (of); lots (of); many ['meni] • **Viel Glück (bei/mit ...)!** Good luck (with ...)! **viel mehr** lots more • **Viel Spaß!** Have fun! • **wie viel?** how much? **wie viele?** how many? • **Vielen Dank!** Thanks a lot!
vielleicht maybe ['meɪbi] • **du könntest vielleicht Hilfe brauchen** you might need help [maɪt]
Viertel: Viertel nach 11 quarter past 11 ['kwɔːtə] • **Viertel vor 12** quarter to 12
Villa villa ['vɪlə]
violett purple ['pɜːpl]
Violine violin [ˌvaɪə'lɪn]; fiddle ['fɪdl] *(infml)*
Vogel bird [bɜːd]
Vokabelverzeichnis vocabulary [və'kæbjələri]
Vokallaut vowel sound ['vaʊəl saʊnd]
voll full [fʊl] • **voller Menschen** crowded ['kraʊdɪd]
Volleyball volleyball ['vɒlibɔːl]
von of [əv, ɒv]; from [frəm, frɒm] **ein Aufsatz von ...** an essay by ... [baɪ] • **von Montag bis Freitag** from Monday to Friday
vor 1. *(räumlich)* in front of [ɪn 'frʌnt_əv] 2. *(zeitlich)* **vor dem Abendessen** before dinner [bɪ'fɔː] • **vor einer Minute** a minute ago [ə'gəʊ] **Viertel vor 12** quarter to 12
vorankommen: Wie komme ich voran? How am I doing?
vorbei (an) *(vorüber)* past [pɑːst]
vorbei sein be over ['əʊvə]
vorbereiten prepare [prɪ'peə] • **sich vorbereiten (auf)** prepare (for); get ready (for) ['redi] • **Dinge vorbereiten** get things ready
vordere(r, s): im vorderen Teil at the front [frʌnt]
Vordergrund foreground ['fɔːgraʊnd]
vorgestern the day before yesterday
Vormittag morning ['mɔːnɪŋ]
vorne at the front [frʌnt]
Vorschrift rule [ruːl]
vorsichtig careful ['keəfl]
vorspielen *(pantomimisch darstellen)* mime [maɪm]
vorstellen 1. **(jm.) etwas vorstellen** *(präsentieren)* present sth. (to sb.) [prɪ'zent] 2. **sich etwas vorstellen** imagine sth. [ɪ'mædʒɪn] • **Stell dir vor! / Stellt euch vor!** Guess what! [ˌges 'wɒt]
Vorstellung *(Präsentation)* presentation [ˌpreznˈteɪʃn]; *(Show)* show [ʃəʊ]
vorüber (an) *(vorbei)* past [pɑːst]
Vorwurf: jm. Vorwürfe machen (wegen) blame sb. (for) [bleɪm]

W

wachsen grow [grəʊ]
wählen *(auswählen)* choose [tʃuːz]; *(Telefonnummer)* dial ['daɪəl]
wahr true [truː] • **wahr werden** come true
während 1. **während des Spiels** during the game ['djʊərɪŋ] 2. **während wir spielten** while we were playing [waɪl]
► S.181 German 'während'
wahrscheinlich probably ['prɒbəbli]
Wald forest ['fɒrɪst]; woods *(pl)* [wʊdz]
walisisch; Walisisch Welsh [welʃ]
Wand wall [wɔːl]
wann when [wen]
warm warm [wɔːm]
Wärmflasche hot-water bottle [ˌhɒt 'wɔːtə bɒtl]
warten (auf) wait (for) [weɪt] **Warte mal!** Wait a minute. ['mɪnɪt]
warum why [waɪ] • **Warum ich?** Why me?
was what [wɒt] • **Was dann?** Then what? • **Was fehlt dir?** *(bei Krankheit)* What's wrong with you? **Was für ein Auto ...?** What kind of car ...? • **Was haben wir als Hausaufgabe auf?** What's for homework? • **Was haben wir als Nächstes?** What have we got next? • **Was ist los? / Was ist denn?** What's the matter? ['mætə] **Was ist mit ...?** What about ...? **Was kann/darf ich euch/Ihnen bringen?** What can I get you? **Was kostet/kosten ...?** How much is/are ...? • **Was war das Beste an ...?** What was the best thing about ...? • **alles, was wir jetzt (noch) tun müssen, ...** all we have to do now ...
waschen wash [wɒʃ] • **Ich wasche mir das Gesicht.** I wash my face.
Waschmaschine washing machine ['wɒʃɪŋ məˌʃiːn]
Wasser water ['wɔːtə]
Wasserfall waterfall ['wɔːtəfɔːl]
Webcam webcam ['webkæm]
Website website ['websaɪt]
Wechselgeld change [tʃeɪndʒ]
wechseln *(Geld)* exchange [ɪks'tʃeɪndʒ]
wecken: jn. wecken wake sb. (up) [weɪk]
Wecker alarm clock [ə'lɑːm klɒk]
weg away [ə'weɪ] • **weg sein** *(nicht da sein)* be gone [gɒn]; *(aus dem Haus sein)* be out [aʊt]
Weg way [weɪ]; *(Pfad)* path [pɑːθ]; *(Gasse)* lane • **auf dem Weg (zu/nach)** on the way (to) • **jm. den Weg beschreiben** tell sb. the way • **jn. nach dem Weg fragen** ask sb. the way
Wegbeschreibung(en) directions *(pl)* [də'rekʃnz]

weggehen leave [liːv]; *(raus-, ausgehen)* go out; get away
wehen blow [bləʊ]
wehtun hurt [hɜːt]; be sore [sɔː]
Weibchen female ['fiːmeɪl]
weich soft [sɒft]
Weide field [fiːld]
weil because [bɪ'kɒz]
weinen cry [kraɪ]
weiß white [waɪt]
weit **1.** *(breit)* wide [waɪd]
2. weit (entfernt) far [fɑː]; a long way
weiter **geradeaus weiter** straight on [streɪt_'ɒn]
weitere(r, s): ein(e) weitere(r, s) one more [mɔː] • **weitere 70 Meter** another 70 metres [ə'nʌðə]
weiter-: weitergeben pass [pɑːs]
weitergehen continue [kən'tɪnjuː]; go on[,gəʊ_'ɒn] • **weiterlaufen** walk on [,wɔːk_'ɒn] • **weitermachen** continue; go on • **weiterreden** continue; go on • **weiterträumen** dream on [,driːm_'ɒn]
► S.171 on („weiter")
welche(r, s) which [wɪtʃ] • **Auf welcher Seite sind wir?** What page are we on? [wɒt] • **Welche Farbe hat ...?** What colour is ...?
wellenreiten gehen go surfing ['sɜːfɪŋ]
Wellensittich budgie ['bʌdʒi]
Welt world [wɜːld] • **auf der Welt** in the world • **auf der ganzen Welt** all over the world • **aus der ganzen Welt** from all over the world
Weltmusik world music
Weltraum space ['speɪs]
wem? who? [huː] • **Mit wem hat sie geredet?** Who did she talk to? **Wem gehören diese?** Whose are these? [huːz]
wen? who? [huː]
wenden: sich an jn. wenden turn to sb. [tɜːn]
wenigstens at least [ət 'liːst]
wenn **1.** *(zeitlich)* when [wen]
2. *(falls)* if [ɪf]
wer who [huː]
Werbespot advert ['ædvɜːt]
werden become [bɪ'kʌm] • **geboren werden** be born [bɔːn] • **wütend/heiß/... werden** get angry/hot/... **wahr werden** come true • **hart/schlecht/taub/blind/verrückt/... werden** go hard/bad/deaf/blind/crazy/... • **du wirst frieren; ihr werdet frieren** you'll be cold (= you will be cold) [wɪl] • **du wirst nicht frieren; ihr werdet nicht frieren** you won't be cold (= you will not be cold) [wəʊnt] • **du wirst gereist sein** you'll have travelled
► S.193 German 'werden'
werfen throw [θrəʊ]
wesentlich: das Wesentliche gist [dʒɪst]
wessen? whose? [huːz]
West- western ['westən]
Westen west [west] • **nach Westen** west • **Richtung Westen** westbound ['westbaʊnd]
westlich west [west]; western ['westən]
Wettbewerb competition [,kɒmpə'tɪʃn] • **einen Wettbewerb veranstalten** hold a competition
wetten bet (-tt-) [bet]
Wetter weather ['weðə]
wichtig important [ɪm'pɔːtnt]
wichtig nehmen care about [keə]
wie **1.** *(Fragewort)* how [haʊ] • **Wie bitte?** Sorry? ['sɒri] • **Wie geht es dir/Ihnen/euch?** How are you? [,haʊ_'ɑː jʊ] • **Wie heißt du?** What's your name? • **Wie spät ist es?** What's the time? • **wie viel?** how much? • **wie viele?** how many? **Wie war ...?** How was ...? • **Wie war das Wetter?** What was the weather like? **Wie wär's mit ...?** What about ...?
2. as • **so groß/aufregend wie** as big/exciting as
3. wie ein Filmstar like a film star [laɪk] • **genau wie du** just like you **wie (zum Beispiel)** such as [,sʌtʃ_'æz]
wieder again [ə'gen]
wiederholen repeat [rɪ'piːt]
Wiederholung *(des Lernstoffs)* revision [rɪ'vɪʒn]
Wiedersehen: Auf Wiedersehen. Goodbye. [,gʊd'baɪ]
wiederverwendet/-verwertet recycled [,riː'saɪkld]
Wiederverwertung recycling [,riː'saɪklɪŋ]
wiegen weigh [weɪ]
wild wild [waɪld]
willkommen: Willkommen (in ...). Welcome (to ...). ['welkəm] • **Sie heißen dich in ... willkommen** They welcome you to ...
Wind wind [wɪnd]
windig windy ['wɪndi]
Windjacke anorak ['ænəræk]
winken wave [weɪv]
Winter winter ['wɪntə]
wir we [wiː]
wirklich **1.** *(Adverb: tatsächlich)* really ['rɪəli]; real ['riːəl] *(AE, infml)* **Meinst du wirklich?/Glaubst du das wirklich?** Do you really think so?
2. *(Adjektiv: echt)* real [rɪəl]
wirklichkeitsnah realistic [,riːə'lɪstɪk]
wissen know [nəʊ] • **sie wussten nicht, was sie tun sollten** they didn't know what to do • **von etwas wissen; über etwas Bescheid wissen** know about sth.
..., wissen Sie. / ..., weißt du. ..., you know. • **Weißt du was, Sophie?** You know what, Sophie? **Woher weißt du ...?** How do you know ...?
wissen wollen wonder ['wʌndə]
Witz joke [dʒəʊk] • **Witze machen** joke
witzig funny ['fʌni]
wo where [weə] • **Wo kommst du her?** Where are you from?
woanders somewhere else [els]
Woche week [wiːk] • **ein dreiwöchiger Urlaub** a three-week holiday • **einmal/zweimal pro Woche** once/twice a week
Wochenende weekend [,wiːk'end] **am Wochenende** at the weekend
Wochenfahrkarte *(der Londoner Verkehrsbetriebe)* Travelcard ['trævlkɑːd]
Wochentage days of the week
Wofür? What for? [,wɒt 'fɔː]
Woher weißt du ...? How do you know ...? [nəʊ]
wohin where [weə]; *(in welche Richtung)* which way
Wohlfahrtsorganisation charity ['tʃærəti]
Wohltätigkeitsbasar jumble sale ['dʒʌmbl seɪl]
wohnen live [lɪv]
Wohnheim hostel ['hɒstl]
Wohnung flat [flæt]
Wohnungstür front door [,frʌnt 'dɔː]
Wohnwagen caravan ['kærəvæn]
Wohnzimmer living room ['lɪvɪŋ ruːm]
Wolf wolf, *pl* wolves [wʊlf, wʊlvz]
Wolke cloud [klaʊd]
wollen *(haben wollen)* want [wɒnt] **tun wollen** want to do • **Wollen wir ...?** Shall we ...? [ʃæl]
Workshop workshop ['wɜːkʃɒp]
Wort word [wɜːd]
Wortbildung word building ['wɜːd ,bɪldɪŋ]
Wörterbuch dictionary ['dɪkʃənri]
Wörterverzeichnis vocabulary [və'kæbjələri]; *(alphabetisches)* dictionary ['dɪkʃənri]

Wortfeld word field
Wovon redest du? What are you talking about?
wund sein be sore [sɔ:]
wunderbar wonderful ['wʌndəfəl]; *(schön, hübsch)* lovely ['lʌvli]
wünschen: sich etwas wünschen wish sth. [wɪʃ]
► S.174 (to) wish
würde(n): ich/er würde ... I/he would ... [wəd, wʊd]
Würfel dice, *pl* dice [daɪs]
würfeln throw the dice [ˌθrəʊ ðə 'daɪs] **Würfel noch einmal.** Take another turn. [tɜ:n]
Wurst, Würstchen sausage ['sɒsɪdʒ]
würzig spicy ['spaɪsi]
wütend sein (über etwas/auf jn.) be angry (about sth./with sb.) ['æŋgri]

Y

Yoga yoga ['jəʊgə]

Z

zäh tough [tʌf]
Zahl number ['nʌmbə]
zählen count [kaʊnt]
Zahn tooth [tu:θ], *pl* teeth [ti:θ] **sich die Zähne putzen** clean one's teeth
Zahnschmerzen toothache ['tu:θeɪk]
zanken: sich zanken argue ['ɑ:gju:]
Zauberkunststück trick [trɪk] • **Zauberkunststücke machen** do tricks
Zebra zebra ['zebrə]
Zeh toe [təʊ]
Zeichen sign [saɪn]
zeichnen draw [drɔ:]
Zeichnung drawing ['drɔ:ɪŋ]
zeigen show [ʃəʊ] • **auf etwas zeigen** point at/to sth. [pɔɪnt]
Zeile line [laɪn]
Zeit time [taɪm]; *(grammatische Zeit)* tense [tens] • **von Zeit zu Zeit** now and again • **Zeit verbringen (mit)** spend time (on) [spend]
Zeitschrift magazine [ˌmægə'zi:n]
Zeitung newspaper ['nju:speɪpə]
zelten camp [kæmp]
Zeltplatz campground ['kæmpgraʊnd] *(AE)*; campsite ['kæmpsaɪt] *(BE)*
Zentimeter centimetre (cm) ['sentɪmi:tə]
Zentral- central ['sentrəl]
Zentrum centre ['sentə]
zerbrechen break [breɪk]
zerbrochen broken ['brəʊkən]
zerstören destroy [dɪ'strɔɪ]
Zeug *(Kram)* stuff [stʌf]
ziehen pull [pʊl]
Ziel aim [eɪm]
ziemlich gut quite good [kwaɪt]; pretty good ['prɪti]
Ziffer number ['nʌmbə]
Zimmer room [ru:m]
zittern shiver ['ʃɪvə]
Zone zone [zəʊn]
Zoo zoo [zu:]
zu 1. *(örtlich)* to [tə, tu] • **zum Arzt** to the doctor's • **zu Jenny** to Jenny's • **zu Hause** at home
Setz dich zu mir. Sit with me.
2. zum Beispiel for example [ɪg'zɑ:mpl] • **zum Frühstück/Mittagessen/Abendbrot** for breakfast/lunch/dinner • **zu seinem Geburtstag** for his birthday
3. zu viel too much [tu:] • **zu spät sein/kommen** be late
4. versuchen zu tun try and do / try to do
5. um zu to
zubereiten *(kochen)* cook [kʊk]
Zucker sugar ['ʃʊgə]
zuerst first [fɜ:st]
Zug train [treɪn] • **im Zug** on the train
Zuhause home [həʊm]
zuhören listen (to) ['lɪsn]
Zuhörer/in listener ['lɪsnə]
zulassen *(erlauben)* allow [ə'laʊ]
zulassen, dass jd. etwas tut let sb. do sth.
zumachen close [kləʊz]
zumindest at least [ət 'li:st]
zurück (nach) back (to) [bæk]
zurückgeben give back [ˌgɪv 'bæk]
zurücklassen leave [li:v]
zurzeit at the moment ['məʊmənt]
zusammen together [tə'geðə]
zusätzlich extra ['ekstrə]
zusehen watch [wɒtʃ]
zustimmen: jm. zustimmen agree with sb. [ə'gri:]
zuwenden: sich jm. zuwenden turn to sb. [tɜ:n]
zweimal twice [twaɪs]
zweite(r, s) second ['sekənd] • **aus zweiter Hand** second-hand
Zwiebel onion ['ʌnjən]
Zwillinge twins *(pl)* [twɪnz]
Zwillingsbruder twin brother ['twɪn ˌbrʌðə]
zwischen between [bɪ'twi:n]

Infinitive	Simple past form	Past participle	
(to) **be**	**was/were**	**been**	sein
(to) **beat**	**beat**	**beaten**	schlagen; besiegen
(to) **become**	**became**	**become**	werden
(to) **begin**	**began**	**begun**	beginnen, anfangen (mit)
(to) **blow**	**blew**	**blown**	wehen, blasen, pusten
(to) **bring**	**brought**	**brought**	(mit-, her)bringen
(to) **break**	**broke**	**broken**	zerbrechen, kaputt machen
(to) **build**	**built**	**built**	bauen
(to) **buy**	**bought**	**bought**	kaufen
(to) **catch**	**caught**	**caught**	fangen; erwischen
(to) **choose** [uː]	**chose** [əʊ]	**chosen** [əʊ]	(aus)wählen; (sich) aussuchen
(to) **come**	**came**	**come**	kommen
(to) **cut**	**cut**	**cut**	schneiden
(to) **do**	**did**	**done** [ʌ]	tun, machen
(to) **draw**	**drew**	**drawn**	zeichnen
(to) **drink**	**drank**	**drunk**	trinken
(to) **drive** [aɪ]	**drove**	**driven** [ɪ]	*(ein Auto)* fahren
(to) **eat**	**ate** [et, eɪt]	**eaten**	essen
(to) **fall**	**fell**	**fallen**	(hin)fallen, stürzen
(to) **feed**	**fed**	**fed**	füttern
(to) **feel**	**felt**	**felt**	(sich) fühlen; sich anfühlen
(to) **fight**	**fought**	**fought**	kämpfen
(to) **find**	**found**	**found**	finden
(to) **fly**	**flew**	**flown**	fliegen
(to) **forget**	**forgot**	**forgotten**	vergessen
(to) **get**	**got**	**got**	bekommen; holen; werden; (hin)kommen
(to) **give**	**gave**	**given**	geben
(to) **go**	**went**	**gone** [ɒ]	gehen, fahren
(to) **grow**	**grew**	**grown**	wachsen; anbauen, anpflanzen
(to) **hang out** *(infml)*	**hung out**	**hung out**	rumhängen, abhängen
(to) **have (have got)**	**had**	**had**	haben, besitzen
(to) **hear** [ɪə]	**heard** [ɜː]	**heard** [ɜː]	hören
(to) **hide** [aɪ]	**hid** [ɪ]	**hidden** [ɪ]	(sich) verstecken
(to) **hit**	**hit**	**hit**	schlagen
(to) **hold**	**held**	**held**	halten
(to) **hurt**	**hurt**	**hurt**	wehtun; verletzen
(to) **keep**	**kept**	**kept**	(be)halten; aufbewahren
(to) **know** [nəʊ]	**knew** [njuː]	**known** [nəʊn]	wissen; kennen
(to) **lay** the table	**laid**	**laid**	den Tisch decken
(to) **leave**	**left**	**left**	(weg)gehen; abfahren; verlassen; zurücklassen
(to) **lend**	**lent**	**lent**	leihen

Infinitive	Simple past form	Past participle	
(to) **let**	**let**	**let**	lassen
(to) **lose** [uː]	**lost** [ɒ]	**lost** [ɒ]	verlieren
(to) **make**	**made**	**made**	machen; bauen; bilden
(to) **mean** [iː]	**meant** [e]	**meant** [e]	bedeuten; meinen
(to) **meet**	**met**	**met**	(sich) treffen
(to) **pay**	**paid**	**paid**	bezahlen
(to) **put**	**put**	**put**	legen, stellen, *(wohin)* tun
(to) **read** [iː]	**read** [e]	**read** [e]	lesen
(to) **ride** [aɪ]	**rode**	**ridden** [ɪ]	reiten; *(Rad)* fahren
(to) **ring**	**rang**	**rung**	klingeln, läuten
(to) **run**	**ran**	**run**	rennen, laufen
(to) **say** [eɪ]	**said** [e]	**said** [e]	sagen
(to) **see**	**saw**	**seen**	sehen; besuchen, aufsuchen
(to) **sell**	**sold**	**sold**	verkaufen
(to) **send**	**sent**	**sent**	schicken, senden
(to) **set** a trap	**set**	**set**	eine Falle stellen
(to) **shake**	**shook**	**shaken**	schütteln
(to) **shine**	**shone** [ɒ]	**shone** [ɒ]	scheinen *(Sonne)*
(to) **show**	**showed**	**shown**	zeigen
(to) **shut up**	**shut**	**shut**	den Mund halten
(to) **sing**	**sang**	**sung**	singen
(to) **sit**	**sat**	**sat**	sitzen; sich setzen
(to) **sleep**	**slept**	**slept**	schlafen
(to) **speak**	**spoke**	**spoken**	sprechen
(to) **spend**	**spent**	**spent**	*(Zeit)* verbringen; *(Geld)* ausgeben
(to) **stand**	**stood**	**stood**	stehen; sich (hin)stellen
(to) **steal**	**stole**	**stolen**	stehlen
(to) **stick**	**stuck**	**stuck**	herausragen, herausstehen; (auf)kleben
(to) **swim**	**swam**	**swum**	schwimmen
(to) **take**	**took**	**taken**	nehmen; (weg-, hin)bringen; dauern, *(Zeit)* brauchen
(to) **teach**	**taught**	**taught**	unterrichten, lehren
(to) **tell**	**told**	**told**	erzählen, berichten
(to) **think**	**thought**	**thought**	denken, glauben, meinen
(to) **throw**	**threw**	**thrown**	werfen
(to) **understand**	**understood**	**understood**	verstehen
(to) **upset**	**upset**	**upset**	ärgern, kränken, aus der Fassung bringen
(to) **wake** up	**woke**	**woken**	aufwachen; wecken
(to) **wear** [eə]	**wore** [ɔː]	**worn** [ɔː]	tragen *(Kleidung)*
(to) **win**	**won** [ʌ]	**won** [ʌ]	gewinnen
(to) **write**	**wrote**	**written**	schreiben

First names (Vornamen)
Adrian ['eɪdriən]
Alan ['ælən]
Alexander [ˌælɪg'zɑ:ndə]
Alice ['ælɪs]
Alicia [ə'lɪsiə]
Alison ['ælɪsn]
Alistair ['ælɪstə]
Ann [æn]
Ashley ['æʃli]
Asif [æ'si:f]
Avril ['ævrɪl]
Barry ['bæri]
Benjamin ['bendʒəmɪn]
Bill [bɪl]
Billy ['bɪli]
Bobby ['bɒbi]
Brendan ['brendn]
Bryan ['braɪən]
Cecilia [sə'si:liə]
Chad [tʃæd]
Charlene [ʃɑ:'li:n]
Charlie ['tʃɑ:li]
Cho [tʃəʊ]
Chris [krɪs]
Christopher ['krɪstəfə]
Cindy ['sɪndi]
Claire [kleə]
Craig [kreɪg]
Dave [deɪv]
David ['deɪvɪd]
Dawn [dɔ:n]
Deirdre ['dɪədri]
Dermot ['dɜ:mət]
Don [dɒn]
Drugh [dru:]
Elizabeth [ɪ'lɪzəbəθ]
Elvis ['elvɪs]
Emily ['eməli]
Emmeline ['eməli:n]
Eric ['erɪk]
Fiona [fi'əʊnə]
Fred [fred]
Frederick ['fredərɪk]
Frideric ['fridərɪk]
Gary ['gæri]
George [dʒɔ:dʒ]
Giles [dʒaɪlz]
Gordon ['gɔ:dn]
Graham ['greɪəm]
Harry ['hæri]
Hassan [hə'sɑ:n]
Jacqueline ['dʒækəlɪn]
Jake [dʒeɪk]
James [dʒeɪmz]
Jaz [dʒæz]
Jenny ['dʒeni]
Jessica ['dʒesɪkə]
Jill [dʒɪl]
Joan [dʒəʊn]
John [dʒɒn]
Johnny ['dʒɒni]
Jordan ['dʒɔ:dn]
Judi ['dʒu:di]
Julia ['dʒu:liə]
Katie ['keɪti]
Katrina [kə'tri:nə]
Kaz [kæz]
Keith [ki:θ]
Kelly ['keli]
Kirsty ['kɜ:sti]
Latisha [lə'tɪʃə]
Lauren ['lɒrən]
Leo ['li:əʊ]
Les [lez]
Linda ['lɪndə]
Lisa ['li:sə, 'li:zə]
Madonna [mə'dɒnə]
Maggie ['mægi]
Margaret ['mɑ:grət]
Mark [mɑ:k]
Matthew ['mæθju:]
Michael ['maɪkəl]
Mick [mɪk]
Mika ['mi:kə]
Minnie ['mɪni]
Mitsu ['mɪtsu:]
Myra ['maɪrə]
Natalie ['nætəli]
Nathan ['neɪθən]
Norman ['nɔ:mən]
Owen ['əʊɪn]
Pandora [ˌpæn'dɔ:rə]
Patricia [pə'trɪʃə]
Paul [pɔ:l]
Pete [pi:t]
Peter ['pi:tə]
Petunia [pə'tju:niə]
Phil [fɪl]
Pia ['piə]
Ray [reɪ]
Robbie ['rɒbi]
Robert ['rɒbət]
Roger ['rɒdʒə]
Sam [sæm]
Samantha [sə'mænθə]
Sandra ['sɑ:ndrə]
Sean [ʃɔ:n]
Shakira [ʃə'kɪərə]
Shania [ʃə'naɪə]
Shaz [ʃæz]
Sheena ['ʃi:nə]
Stanley ['stænli]
Sting [stɪŋ]
Sue [su:]
Tim [tɪm]
Walter ['wɔ:ltə]
Wayne [weɪn]
William ['wɪljəm]
Winston ['wɪnstən]

Family names (Familiennamen)
Adams ['ædəmz]
Atwood ['ætwʊd]
Azad [ə'zɑ:d]
Banting ['bæntɪŋ]
Barfield ['bɑ:fi:ld]
Barrymore ['bæriˌmɔ:]
Bell [bel]
Bond [bɒnd]
Braithwaite ['breɪθweɪt]
Britten ['brɪtn]
Burns [bɜ:nz]
Byrd [bɜ:d]
Cabot ['kæbət]
Calder [kɔ:ldə]
Cartwright ['kɑ:traɪt]
Chang [tʃæŋ]
Chetham [tʃi:təm]
Clapton ['klæptn]
Cohn [kəʊn]
Connery ['kɒnəri]
Cookson ['kʊksn]
Cooper ['ku:pə]
Davies ['deɪvɪs]
Dench [dentʃ]
Devlin ['devlɪn]
Fagan ['feɪgən]
Fender ['fendə]
Fleming ['flemɪŋ]
Fossington-Gore [ˌfɒsɪŋten'gɔ:]
Foster ['fɒstə]
Gilmour ['gɪlmɔ:]
Gordon ['gɔ:dn]
Handel ['hændl]
Hooley ['hu:li]
Hucknall ['hʌknəl]
Jones ['dʒəʊnz]
Kent [kent]
Kirk [kɜ:k]
Knopfler ['nopflə]
Kroeger ['krəʊgə]
Kowalski [kə'wɒlski]
Lavigne [læ'vi:n]
Leung ['li:əŋ]
Livingston ['lɪvɪŋstən]
Lowry ['laʊri]
Marks [mɑ:ks]
McCartney [mə'kɑ:tni]
McFadden [mək'fædn]
McGough [mə'gɒf]
McKay [mə'kaɪ]
McLean [mə'kleɪn]
Mole [məʊl]
Nagora ['nægərɑ:]
Neeposh ['ni:pɒʃ]
Neilson [ni:lsən]
O'Keefe [əʊ'ki:f]
Owen ['əʊɪn]
Pankhurst ['pæŋkhɜ:st]
Paul [pɔ:l]
Peters ['pi:təz]
Peterson ['pi:təsən]
Potter ['pɒtə]
Poulson [pu:lsən]
Presley ['prezli]
Raleigh ['rɔ:li]
Richards ['rɪtʃədz]
Rooney ['ru:ni]
Rowling ['rəʊlɪŋ]
Shakespeare ['ʃeɪkspɪə]
Simmons ['sɪmnz]
Simon ['saɪmən]
Smith [smɪθ]
Stephenson ['sti:vənsən]
Sutherland ['sʌðələnd]
Swann [swɒn]
Townshend ['taʊnzend]
Turing ['tju:rɪŋ]
Twain [tweɪn]
Wain [weɪn]
Waites [weits]
Williams ['wɪliəmz]
Wilson ['wɪlsn]
Wordsworth ['wɜ:dzwəθ]
Wren [ren]
Wright [raɪt]
Wynne-Jones [ˌwɪn 'dʒəʊnz]

Place names (Ortsnamen)
Aberdeen [ˌæbə'di:n]
Albert Street ['ælbət stri:t]
Aldgate East [ˌɔ:ldgeɪt‿'i:st]
Algonquin [æl'gɒŋkwɪn]
the **Arctic Circle** [ˌɑ:ktɪk 'sɜ:kl]
the **Atlantic** [ət'læntɪk]
Bakerloo [ˌbeɪkə'lu:]
Banglatown ['bæŋlətaʊn]
Bath [bɑ:θ]
Beirut [beɪ'ru:t]
Ben Nevis [ˌben 'nevɪs]
Berlin [bɜ:'lɪn]
Bethlehem ['beθləhem]
Birmingham ['bɜ:mɪŋəm]
the **Black Forest** [ˌblæk 'fɒrɪst]
Schwarzwald
Bloomsbury ['blu:mzbəri]
Bond Street ['bɒnd stri:t]
Brick Lane [ˌbrɪk 'leɪn]
Bristol ['brɪstl]
the **British Empire** [ˌbrɪtɪʃ‿'empaɪə]
the **British Museum** [ˌbrɪtɪʃ mju:'ziəm]
Brodgar ['brɒdgɑ:]
Buckingham Palace [ˌbʌkɪŋəm 'pæləs]
Cairo ['kaɪrəʊ]
Camden Lock [ˌkæmdən 'lɒk]
Cape Breton [ˌkeɪp 'bretɒn]
the **Caribbean** [kærə'biən]
Karibik
Castlefield ['kɑslfi:ld]
Charing Cross [ˌtʃærɪŋ 'krɒs]
Chelsea ['tʃelsi]
Covent Garden [ˌkɒvənt 'gɑ:dn]
Docklands ['dɒkləndz]
Dundee [dʌn'di:]
Ealing ['i:lɪŋ]
Earls Court [ˌɜ:lz 'kɔ:t]
the **East End** [ˌi:st 'end]
Edinburgh ['edɪnbərə]
Everton ['evətən]
Flotta ['flɒtə]
Fort Augustus [ˌfɔ:t ɔ:'gʌstəs]
Glasgow ['glæzgəʊ, 'glɑ:zgəʊ]
the **Globe Theatre** [ˌgləʊb 'θɪətə]

Greenwich ['grenɪtʃ]
Helmsdale ['helmzdeɪl]
the **Houses of Parliament** [ˌhaʊzɪz_əv 'pɑ:ləmənt]
Houton ['hu:tn]
Hoy [hɔɪ]
Hyde Park [ˌhaɪd 'pɑ:k]
Inuvik [ɪ'nu:vɪk]
Inverness [ˌɪnvə'nes]
Kensington ['kenzɪŋtən]
Kirkwall ['kɜ:kwɔ:l]
Knightsbridge ['naɪtsbrɪdʒ]
Kutaisi [ˌkʊtə'i:si]
Lancashire ['læŋkəʃə]
Laventille [ˌlævən'ti:l]
Leicester Square [ˌlestə 'skweə]
Loch Morar [ˌlɒx 'mɔ:rə]
Loch Ness [lɒx 'nes]
London ['lʌndən]
the **London Eye** [ˌlʌndn 'aɪ]
Lowestoft ['ləʊstɒft]
Lyness ['laines]
Mainland ['meɪnlənd]
Majorca [mə'jɔ:kə]
Manchester ['mæntʃestə]
Mancunium [mæn'kju:niəm]
Maple Ridge [ˌmeɪpl 'rɪdʒ]
Marble Arch [ˌmɑ:bl 'ɑ:tʃ]
Melbourne ['melbən]
the **Millennium Bridge** [mɪ'leniəm ˌbrɪdʒ]
Missinaibi Lake [ˌmɪsɪ'neɪbi 'leɪk]
Moaness ['məʊnes]
Montreal [ˌmɒntri'ɔ:l]
the **Natural History Museum** [ˌnætʃrəl 'hɪstri]
Nelson's Column [ˌnelsnz 'kɒləm]
Nemaska [nə'mæskə]
New York [ˌnju: 'jɔ:k]
Newfoundland ['nju:fəndlənd]
the **North Sea** [ˌnɔ:θ 'si:]
North Bay [ˌnɔ:θ 'beɪ]
Nunavut ['nu:nəvu:t]
Old Trafford [əʊld 'træfəd]
Ontario [ɒn'teəriəʊ]
Orkney ['ɔ:kni]
the **Orkney Islands** ['ɔ:kni_ˌaɪləndz]
Ottowa ['ɒtəwə]
Oxford Circus [ˌɒksfəd 'sɜ:kəs]
the **Pacific** [pə'sɪfɪk]
Palma ['pɑ:mə]
Paris ['pærɪs]
Perth [pɜ:θ]
Piccadilly [ˌpɪkə'dɪli]
Piccadilly Circus [ˌpɪkədɪli 'sɜ:kəs]
Port of Spain [ˌpɔ:t_əv 'speɪn]
Princes Street ['prɪnsəz stri:t]
Québec [kwɪ'bek, kebek]
Queensway ['kwi:nzweɪ]
Rackwick ['rækwɪk]
Reading ['redɪŋ]
Redcliffe ['redklɪf]
Regent Street ['ri:dʒənt stri:t]
Richmond ['rɪtʃmənd]
the **River Clyde** [ˌrɪvə 'klaɪd]
the **River Thames** [ˌrɪvə 'temz]
Rochdale ['rɒtʃdeɪl]
the **Royal Mile** [ˌrɔɪəl 'maɪl]
Russell Square [ˌrʌsl 'skweə]
Salford ['sɔ:lfəd]
Salford Quays [ˌsɔ:lfəd 'ki:z]
San Francisco [ˌsæn frən'sɪskəʊ]
Sandwich ['sænwitʃ, 'sænwidʒ]
the **Science Museum** ['saɪəns]
Soho ['səʊˌhəʊ]
the **South Bank** [ˌsaʊθ 'bæŋk]
South Kensington [ˌsaʊθ 'kenzɪŋtn]
Southampton Street [saʊ'θæmptən ˌstri:t]
St Pancras [sənt 'pænkrəs]
St Paul's Cathedral [sənt ˌpɔ:lz kə'θi:drəl]
Staffordshire ['stæfədʃə]
Stamford Bridge [ˌstæmfəd 'brɪdʒ]
Stenness [sten'nes]
Stirling ['stɜ:lɪŋ]
the **Strand** [strænd]
Stromness ['strɒmnes]
Swiss Cottage [ˌswɪs 'kɒtɪdʒ]
the **Tate Modern** [ˌteɪt 'mɒdən]
Toronto [tə'rɒntəʊ]
Tower Bridge [ˌtaʊə 'brɪdʒ]
Tower Hamlets [ˌtaʊə 'hæmləts]
Tower Hill [ˌtaʊə 'hɪl]
the **Tower of London** [ˌtaʊər_əv 'lʌndn]
Trafalgar Square [trəˌfælgə 'skweə]
Trinidad ['trɪnɪdæd]
the **Trocadero** [ˌtrɒkə'dɪərəʊ]
Troy [trɔɪ]
Turin [ˌtjʊə'rɪn]
Uranus ['jʊərənəs]
Vancouver [væn'ku:və]
Vermont [və'mɒnt]
Victoria Embankment [vɪkˌtɔriə_em'bæŋkmənt]
Victoria Station [vɪkˌtɔ:riə 'steɪʃn]
Vienna [vi'enə]
Virginia [və'dʒɪniə]
Waterloo [ˌwɔ:tə'lu:]
the **West End** [ˌwest 'end]
Westminster ['westmɪnstə]
Westminster Abbey [ˌwestmɪnstər_'æbi]
Westminster Bridge [ˌwestmɪnstə 'brɪdʒ]
Whitechapel ['waɪtˌtʃæpl]
Wimbledon ['wɪmbldən]
Winnipeg ['wɪnɪpeg]

Other names (Andere Namen)

10CC [ˌten si: 'si:]
Barnsey ['bɑ:nzi]
The Beatles ['bi:tlz]
Belle & Sebastian [bel_ənd sə'bæstɪən]
Big Ben [ˌbɪg 'ben]
Biscuits ['bɪskɪts]
Celtic F.C. ['seltɪk]
Celtic Nomads [ˌkeltɪk 'nəʊmædz]
Cottonopolis [ˌkɒtən'ɒpəlɪs]
the **District Line** ['dɪstrɪkt ˌlaɪn]
Dumbo ['dʌmbəʊ]
the **Eiffel Tower** [ˌaɪfl 'taʊə]
Fishface ['fɪʃfeɪs]
Franz Ferdinand [ˌfrænts 'fɜ:dɪnənd]
Funland ['fʌnlænd]
Global Deejays [ˌgləʊbl 'di:dʒeɪz]
Harbourfront ['hɑ:bəfrʌnt]
Hollies ['hɒli:z]
Jack the Ripper [ˌdʒæk ðə 'rɪpə]
Joy Division ['jɔɪ ˌdɪvɪʒən]
the **Jubilee Line** ['dʒu:bɪli: ˌlaɪn]
The Lovin' Spoonful [ˌlʌvɪn 'spu:nfʊl]
Morcheeba [mɔ:'tʃi:bə]
Nessie [nesi]
Nickelback ['nɪklbæk]
Oasis [əʊ'eɪsɪs]
Rangers F.C. ['reɪndʒəz]
Rocket ['rɒkɪt]
Simply Red [ˌsɪmpli 'red]
Spree [spri:]
Stratocaster ['strætəkɑ:stə]
Take That [ˌteɪk 'ðæt]
Titanic [taɪ'tænɪk]
Travis ['trævɪs]
Wet Wet Wet [ˌwet ˌwet 'wet]

Country/Continent	Adjective	Person	People
Africa ['æfrɪkə] *Afrika*	African ['æfrɪkən]	an African	the Africans
America [ə'merɪkə] *Amerika*	American [ə'merɪkən]	an American	the Americans
Asia ['eɪʃə, 'eɪʒə] *Asien*	Asian ['eɪʃn, 'eɪʒn]	an Asian	the Asians
Australia [ɒ'streɪliə] *Australien*	Australian [ɒ'streɪliən]	an Australian	the Australians
Austria ['ɒstriə] *Österreich*	Austrian ['ɒstriən]	an Austrian	the Austrians
Bangladesh [ˌbæŋglə'deʃ] *Bangladesch*	Bangladeshi [ˌbæŋglə'deʃi]	a Bangladeshi	the Bangladeshis
Belgium ['beldʒəm] *Belgien*	Belgian ['beldʒən]	a Belgian	the Belgians
Brazil [brə'zɪl] *Brasilien*	Brazilian [brə'zɪliən]	a Brazilian	the Brazilians
Canada ['kænədə] *Kanada*	Canadian [kə'neɪdiən]	a Canadian	the Canadians
Chile ['tʃɪli] *Chile*	Chilean ['tʃɪliən]	a Chilean	the Chileans
China ['tʃaɪnə] *China*	Chinese [ˌtʃaɪ'ni:z]	a Chinese	the Chinese
Colombia [kə'lɒmbiə] *Kolumbien*	Colombian [kə'lɒmbiən]	a Colombian	the Colombians
Croatia [krəʊ'eɪʃə] *Kroatien*	Croatian [krəʊ'eɪʃn]	a Croatian	the Croatians
Cuba ['kju:bə] *Kuba*	Cuban [kju:bən]	a Cuban	the Cubans
the Czech Republic [ˌtʃek rɪ'pʌblɪk] *Tschechien, die Tschechische Republik*	Czech [tʃek]	a Czech	the Czechs
Denmark ['denmɑ:k] *Dänemark*	Danish ['deɪnɪʃ]	a Dane [deɪn]	the Danes
England ['ɪŋglənd] *England*	English ['ɪŋglɪʃ]	an Englishman/-woman	the English
Europe ['jʊərəp] *Europa*	European [ˌjʊərə'pi:ən]	a European	the Europeans
Finland ['fɪnlənd] *Finnland*	Finnish ['fɪnɪʃ]	a Finn [fɪn]	the Finns
France [frɑ:ns] *Frankreich*	French [frentʃ]	a Frenchman/-woman	the French
Germany ['dʒɜ:məni] *Deutschland*	German ['dʒɜ:mən]	a German	the Germans
Ghana ['gɑ:nə] *Ghana*	Ghanaian [gɑ:'nəɪən]	a Ghanaian	the Ghanaians
(Great) Britain ['brɪtn] *Großbritannien*	British ['brɪtɪʃ]	a Briton ['brɪtn]	the British
Greece [gri:s] *Griechenland*	Greek [gri:k]	a Greek	the Greeks
Holland ['hɒlənd] *Holland die Niederlande*	Dutch [dʌtʃ]	a Dutchman/-woman	the Dutch
Hungary ['hʌŋgəri] *Ungarn*	Hungarian [hʌŋ'geəriən]	a Hungarian	the Hungarians
India ['ɪndiə] *Indien*	Indian ['ɪndiən]	an Indian	the Indians
Iran [ɪ'rɑ:n, ɪ'ræn] *Iran*	Iranian [ɪ'reɪniən]	a Iranian	the Iranians
Ireland ['aɪələnd] *Irland*	Irish ['aɪrɪʃ]	an Irishman/-woman	the Irish
Israel ['ɪzreɪl] *Israel*	Israeli [ɪz'reɪli]	an Israeli	the Israelis
Italy ['ɪtəli] *Italien*	Italian [ɪ'tæliən]	an Italian	the Italians
Jamaica [dʒə'meɪkə] *Jamaika*	Jamaican [dʒə'meɪkən]	a Jamaican	the Jamaicans
Japan [dʒə'pæn] *Japan*	Japanese [ˌdʒæpə'ni:z]	a Japanese	the Japanese
Lebanon ['lebənən] *Libanon*	Lebanese [ˌlebə'ni:z]	a Lebanese	the Lebanese
Luxembourg ['lʌksəmbɜ:g] *Luxemburg*	Luxembourg	a Luxembourger ['lʌksəmbɜ:gə]	the Luxembourgers
Nepal [nə'pɔ:l] *Nepal*	Nepalese [ˌnepə'li:z]	a Nepalese	the Nepalese
the Netherlands ['neðələndz] *die Niederlande, Holland*	Dutch [dʌtʃ]	a Dutchman/-woman	the Dutch
New Zealand [ˌnju: 'zi:lənd] *Neuseeland*	New Zealand [ˌnju: 'zi:lənd]	a New Zealander	the New Zealanders
Norway ['nɔ:weɪ] *Norwegen*	Norwegian [nɔ:'wi:dʒən]	a Norwegian	the Norwegians
Pakistan [ˌpækɪ'stæn, ˌpɑ:kɪ-, -'stɑ:n] *Pakistan*	Pakistani [ˌpækɪ'stæni, ˌpɑ:kɪ-, -'stɑ:ni]	a Pakistani	the Pakistanis
Poland ['pəʊlənd] *Polen*	Polish ['pəʊlɪʃ]	a Pole [pəʊl]	the Poles
Portugal ['pɔ:tʃʊgl] *Portugal*	Portuguese [ˌpɔ:tʃu'gi:z]	a Portuguese	the Portuguese
Puerto Rico [ˌpwɜ:təʊ 'ri:kəʊ]	Puerto Rican [ˌpwɜ:təʊ 'ri:kən]	a Puerto Rican	the Puerto Ricans
Russia ['rʌʃə] *Russland*	Russian ['rʌʃn]	a Russian	the Russians
Scotland ['skɒtlənd] *Schottland*	Scottish ['skɒtɪʃ]	a Scotsman/-woman, a Scot	the Scots
Slovakia [sləʊ'vækiə] *die Slowakei*	Slovak ['sləʊvæk]	a Slovak	the Slovaks
Slovenia [sləʊ'vi:niə] *Slowenien*	Slovenian [sləʊ'vi:niən], Slovene ['sləʊvi:n]	a Slovene, a Slovenian	the Slovenes, the Slovenians
Spain [speɪn] *Spanien*	Spanish ['spænɪʃ]	a Spaniard ['spænɪəd]	the Spaniards
Sri Lanka [ˌsri 'læŋkə] *Sri Lanka*	Sri Lankan [ˌsri 'læŋkən]	a Sri Lankan	the Sri Lankans
Sweden ['swi:dn] *Schweden*	Swedish ['swi:dɪʃ]	a Swede [swi:d]	the Swedes
Switzerland ['swɪtsələnd] *die Schweiz*	Swiss [swɪs]	a Swiss	the Swiss
Taiwan [taɪ'wɒn, taɪ'wɑ:n] *Taiwan*	Taiwanese [ˌtaɪwə'ni:z]	a Taiwanese	the Taiwanese
Thailand ['taɪlænd]	Thai [taɪ]	a Thai	the Thais

Country/Continent	Adjective	Person	People
Trinidad ['trɪnɪdæd]	Trinidadian [ˌtrɪnɪ'dædiən]	a Trinidadian	the Trinidadians
Turkey ['tɜːki] *die Türkei*	Turkish ['tɜːkɪʃ]	a Turk [tɜːk]	the Turks
the United Kingdom (the UK) [juˌnaɪtɪd 'kɪŋdəm, ˌjuː'keɪ] *das Vereinigte Königreich (Großbritannien und Nordirland)*	British ['brɪtɪʃ]	a Briton ['brɪtn]	the British
the United States of America (the USA) [juˌnaɪtɪd ˌsteɪts‿əv‿ə'merɪkə, ˌjuː‿es‿'eɪ] *die Vereinigten Staaten von Amerika*	American [ə'merɪkən]	an American	the Americans
Wales [weɪlz] *Wales*	Welsh [welʃ]	a Welshman/-woman	the Welsh

Classroom English

Was *du* im Klassenzimmer sagen kannst	What *you* can say in the classroom

Du brauchst Hilfe / You need help

Können Sie mir bitte helfen?	**Can you help me, please?**
Auf welcher Seite sind wir, bitte?	**What page are we on, please?**
Was heißt ... auf Englisch/Deutsch?	**What's ... in English/German?**
Wie spricht man das erste Wort in Zeile 2 aus?	**How do you say the first word in line 2?**
Können Sie bitte ... buchstabieren?	**Can you spell ..., please?**
Können Sie es bitte an die Tafel schreiben?	**Can you write it on the board, please?**
Kann ich es auf Deutsch sagen?	**Can I say it in German?**
Können Sie/Kannst du bitte lauter sprechen?	**Can you speak louder, please?**
Können Sie/Kannst du das bitte noch mal sagen?	**Can you say that again, please?**

Über Texte und Themen sprechen / Talking about texts and topics

Ich finde die Geschichte ...	**I think the story is ...**
schön/interessant/langweilig/schrecklich/....	**nice/interesting/boring/terrible/...**
Es war lustig/gruselig/langweilig/..., als ...	**It was funny/scary/boring/... when ...**
Ich fand es gut/nicht gut, als ...	**I liked it/didn't like it when ...**
Ich finde, Tom hat recht/nicht recht, weil ...	**I think Tom is right/wrong because ...**
Ich bin mir nicht sicher. Vielleicht ...	**I'm not sure. Maybe ...**
Was meinst du?	**What do you think?**
Ich stimme ... zu/nicht zu, weil ...	**I agree/disagree (with ...) because ...**

Hausaufgaben und Übungen / Homework and exercises

Tut mir leid, ich habe mein Schulheft nicht dabei, Herr ...	**Sorry, I haven't got my exercise book, Mr ...**
Ich habe meine Hausaufgaben vergessen, Frau ...	**I've forgotten my homework, Mrs/Ms/Miss ...**
Ich kann Nummer 3 nicht lösen.	**I can't do number 3.**
Entschuldigung, ich bin noch nicht fertig.	**Sorry, I haven't finished yet.**
Ich habe ... Ist das auch richtig?	**I've got ... Is that right too?**
Tut mir leid, das weiß ich nicht.	**Sorry, I don't know.**
Was haben wir (als Hausaufgabe) auf?	**What's for homework?**

Bei der Partnerarbeit / Work with a partner

Kann ich mit Julian arbeiten?	**Can I work with Julian?**
Wer ist dran? - Du bist dran.	**Whose turn is it? - It's your turn.**
Ich finde, wir sollten/könnten ...	**I think we should/could ...**
Was machen wir zuerst?	**What are we going to do first?**

What your teacher says / Was dein/e Lehrer/in sagt

Open your books at page 24, please.	Schlagt bitte Seite 24 auf.
Look at the picture/line 8/... on page 24.	Seht euch das Bild/Zeile 8/... auf Seite 24 an.
Copy/Complete the chart/network/...	Übertragt/Vervollständigt die Tabelle/das Wörternetz/...
Correct the mistakes.	Verbessert die Fehler.
Take notes.	Macht euch Notizen.
Do exercise 3 for homework, please.	Macht bitte Übung 3 als Hausaufgabe.
Have you finished?	Seid ihr fertig? / Bist du fertig?
Switch off your mobile phones.	Schaltet eure Handys aus.
Walk around the class and ask other students.	Geht durch die Klasse und fragt andere Schüler/innen.
Discuss ... with ...	Diskutiere/Diskutiert ... mit ...
Give a presentation about ...	Halte/Haltet einen Vortrag über ...
Report to the class.	Berichte/Berichtet der Klasse.

Illustrationen

Roland Beier, Berlin (S. 18; 20 (M); S. 23; S. 29; S. 41–43; S. 49; S. 52; S. 62–71; S. 81–83; S. 89–95; S. 106–111; S. 133–145 oben; S. 146–193); **Carlos Borrell**, Berlin (vordere u. hintere Umschlaginnenseite; S. 25; S. 30; S. 78); **Graham-Cameron Illustrations**, UK: **Fliss Cary** (S. 21; S. 26–28; S. 34; S. 45–47; S. 56; S. 75–76; S. 85–87; S. 102; S. 112); **John Rabou** (S. 50; S. 53); **Linda Rogers Associates**, London: **Gary Rees** (S. 115); **Michael Teßmer**, Hamburg (S. 119); **Korinna Wilkes**, Berlin (S. 97)

Bildquellen

action press, Hamburg (S. 37 (u. 141) Franz Ferdinand: ALL ACTION DIGITAL, Katie Leung: Everett Collection, Inc.; S. 55 trainers: ALTERPHOTOS; S. 104: 2Vista); **Alamy**, Abingdon (Inhaltsverz. bear: ImageState/Rosemary Calvert; S. 6 oben Mitte (u. 54): The Photolibrary Wales, unten Mitte: Photofusion Picture Library/Vehbi Koca, unten re.: Paul Doyle; S. 12 Bild 1: Peter Barritt, Bild 2: Ernst Wrba, Bild 3: Caroline Cortizo; S. 13 Bild 4: Mike Booth, Bild 5: Alan Copson City Pictures; S. 15 Bild B: Richard Cooke, Bild C: Kevin Allen; S. 17: Jon Arnold Images; S. 18 Mitte: PCL/picturescolourlibrary; S. 19 Mitte re.: Kathy deWitt; S. 20 oben (M): Brand X Pictures/ Burke/Triolo Productions, unten li.: imagestopshop, unten Mitte: Trevor Smith, unten re.: Stan Kujawa; S. 30 Bild A: Neil McAllister, Bild B (M): Doug Houghton, sheep and lamb (M): Suzy Bennett; S. 31 Bild C: Doug Houghton, Bild F: Graham Uney, sheep: orkneypics; S. 36 shortbread: Ingram Publishing (Superstock Limited); S. 37 oil rig: Malcolm Fife; S. 39 oben: Doug Blane (www.DougBlane.com), unten: Worldwide Picture Library/Hugh Webster; S. 40 Bild 7: orkneypics; S. 59 oben (u. 123 unten): artpartner-images.com; S. 61 oben li.: Phil Portus, oben re.: Mary Evans Picture Library, unten li.: All Star Picture Library; S. 70 unten li. u. re. (M): George S de Blonsky; S. 73 fishing: Keith Douglas, Mitte: Alaska Stock LLC; S. 74 Mitte re.: RubberBall, unten li.: Vstock, unten re.: david sanger photography/davidsanger.com; S. 78 unten: Robert McGouey; S. 79 Margaret Atwood: Jeff Morgan Hay on Wye; S. 84: UrbanEye; S. 86 unten: Arco Images; S. 94 hat: Bill Brooks; S. 96 oben re. u. unten li.: Lebrecht Music and Arts Photo Library/Chris Stock/ Lebrecht; S. 117 li.: Alex Segre; S. 130 unten: Hugh Threlfall; S. 138: vario images GmbH & Co.KG/Stefan Kiefer; S. 142: The Print Collector); **Avenue Images**, Hamburg (S. 15 Bild A: Index Stock/David Ball); **Bildmaschine.de**, Berlin (S. 98 Bild 5: Peter Engelke); **John Birdsall Social Issues Photolibrary**, Nottingham (Inhaltsverz. kids; S. 7–11; S. 15 Bild E (u. 137) (M)); S. 35; S. 40 Katrina; S. 54 (u. 64) Anna Beckmann; S. 56 oben re. u. li.; S. 57; S. 72 Mitte li.; S. 74 oben re.; S. 83; S. 94–95 schoolbook kids); **Britain on View**, London (S. 15 Bild E (u. 137) (M): Nigel Hicks; S. 18 unten re.: www.britainonview.com; S. 19 Mitte li.: Pawel Libera; S. 31 Bild E: Joe Cornish); **Blickwinkel**, Witten (S. 31 bird: H. J. Igelmund); **Bulls Pressedienst GmbH**, Frankfurt/Main (S. 117 re.: Pressnet); **Cartoonbank.com**, Yonkers (S. 32 re.: Peter Steiner. Published in the New Yorker 7/5/1993); **CartoonStock Ltd.**, Somerset (S. 88: Karsten Schley; S. 96 unten re.: Ralph Hagen); **Corbis**, Düsseldorf (Inhaltsverz. Tower Bridge (u. 15 Bild D): Angelo Hornak; S. 6 oben li. (u. 54): Jeremy Horner; S. 18 oben: Toby Melville/Reuters; S. 19 oben: Bill Varie; S. 56 unten li. u. re.: Kevin Dodge; S. 73 unten: Graham Bell; S. 75: Annie Griffiths Belt; S. 79 lacrosse: Aristide Economopoulos/Star Ledger; S. 91: David Muench; S. 92: James Marshall); **Corel Library** (Inhaltsverz. Old Man of Hoy; S. 22); **defd Deutscher Fotodienst**, Hamburg (S. 108 Shrek); **Barbara Derkow Disselbeck**, Köln (S. 40 Bild 1); **Gareth Evans**, Berlin (S. 32 li.; S. 40 Bild 3, 4 u. 8; S. 65); **fabfoodpix.com**, London (S. 36 haggis); **Fotolia**, Berlin: (S. 122 Mitte re.: Roger Asbury); **Fotosearch**, Waukesha (S. 69 unten re.: Brand X Pictures); **GB eye Ltd**, Sheffield (S. 55 poster: © 2006 MUML Crest & Imagery © MU Ltd.); **Getty Images**, München (S. 36 Mitte: Rubberball Productions; S. 59 unten: AFP/Johannes Eisele; S. 60 oben li.: Man Utd via Getty Images/Matthew Peters, Mitte li.: Michael Steele; Mitte re., unten re.: Paul Gilham; S. 63 Bild 2: Evan Agostini, Bild 5: Time & Life Pictures/Life Magazine; S. 97: WireImage/John Stanton; S. 98 Bild 3: AFP/Tim Sloan; S. 108 Franz Ferdinand: Dave Hogan; S. 123 oben: Man Utd via Getty Images: John Peters, Mitte: Phil Cole); **Harbourfront Centre**, Toronto (S. 94 logo); **Dick Hemingway Photographs**, Toronto (S. 79 commuters: Photographers Direct/Dick Hemingway); **Home Office**, London (S. 118: “ru alone when u meet online m8s in real life?” Home Office. © Crown copyright material is reproduced with the permission of the Controller of HMSO and Queen’s Printer for Scotland); **IPNstock.com**, New York (S. 74 oben li: Jim Powell); **Keystone**, Hamburg (S. 36 unten li.: Topham Picturepoint); **laif**, Köln (S. 38 li. (M): Hemispheres); **LOOK-foto**, München (S. 93: Thomas Peter Widmann; S. 122 unten: Ingolf Pompe); **The Lowry**, Salford Quays (S. 58 oben, Mitte: Going to the Match, 1953 © The Lowry Estate, unten: One Love: The Football Art Prize used by permission of The Lowry, Salford Quays and Umbro UK); **mauritius images**, Mittenwald (S. 73 oben: Pixtal); **OCS Group Marketing**, Lancashire (S. 69 oben); **PA Photos**, Nottingham (S. 70 oben); **Photofusion**, London (S. 19 unten: Bipinchandra); **Picture Alliance**, Frankfurt/Main (Inhaltsverz. (u. 60 oben re.) Old Trafford: dpa-Sportreport; S. 37 John Logie Baird: 91020/KPA/WHA, bacteria: dpa-Report/ZB/Jan-Peter Kasper, sheep: dpa-Fotoreport/PA, Sean Connery: Picture Press/CAMERA PRESS/Bob Penn, Prince Charles Edward Stuart: KPA/HIP/The British Library/90100; S. 61 unten re.: Photoshot; S. 63 Bild 1: dpa-Report/epa Lambert, Bild 4: Photoshot/Band Photo, Bild 6: dpa/dpaweb/Daniel Karmann, Bild 7: KPA/HIP/MuseumofLondon/90100; S. 66 oben: ZB-Fotoreport, unten: dpa/ZB/Wolfgang Thieme; S. 79 ice hockey: dpa/Landov Katie Mcmahon; S. 98 Bild 1: KPA/ CBI/90078/Sven Hoogerhuis; S. 108 Kate Moss: dpa/Pa Topshop, Rock am Ring: SCHROEWIG/Jens Koch, Nelly Furtado: dpa/ Roland Weihrauch, Alexander Kapranos: dpa/Harald Tittel; S. 117 Mitte: dpa-Fotoreport/epa pa); **Picture Press**, Hamburg (S. 6 oben re. (u. 54): Maruan Bahrour; S. 95 li.: Frank P. Wartenberg); **Marion Schönenberger**, Berlin (S. 54–55; S. 107; S. 130 oben; S. 131); **Scottish Tartans World Register**, Crieff (S. 36 oben); **Nick Sharratt** (S. 120–121: illustrations taken from Cliffhanger by Jacqueline Wilson. Reprinted by permission of David Higham Associates Limited, London); **Shutterstock**, New York (S. 18 unten li.: Robyn Mackenzie; S. 38 cow (M):

Norma Cornes; S. 40 Bild 5: Lebedinski Vladislav, Bild 6: Katharyna Ulriksen; S. 55 screen: Andrew Barker; S. 64 camera (M): Christoph Weihs, couple (M): Konstantin Sutyagin; S. 72 oben: Gordon Snell, unten: Martine Oger, Mitte re.: mypokcik, Canadian flag: Sasha Daves, German flag: Kurt de Bruyn; S. 74 Mitte li.: Eduardo Jose; S. 86 oben: Andre Nantel; S. 94 basketball: Vincent Giordano, CD (u. 96): Andresr, film: Olga Langerova; S. 98 Bild 2 suitcase: Danny Smythe, rucksack: Rafa Irusta, Bild 4: Cecilia Lim H M; S. 100 li.: Andrea Leone, re.: M.E. Mulder; S. 110: Doug Stacey; S. 122 oben: Clarence s lewis, Mitte li.: David Romero Corral; S. 128 oben: puchan, unten: Hannamariah; S. 129 li.: szefei); **Friedrich Stark**, Dortmund (S. 78 oben); **Stills-Online**, Hamburg (S. 69 unten li.); **Stuck on Scotland Holidays**, Scotland (S. 38 re.); **Charles Tait Photographic Limited**, Orkney (S. 31 Bild G u. S. 44: www.charles-tait.co.uk); **TopFoto**, Edenbridge (S. 33: Doug Houghton); **Transport for London**, London (S. 14); **ullstein bild**, Berlin (S. 6 unten li. (u. 54): Wöstmann; S. 31 Bild D: Still Pictures; S. 63 Bild 3: KPA; S. 79 Frederick Banting: Roger Viollet; S. 82: ddp); **Visum Foto GmbH**, Hamburg (S. 129 re.: Thomas Lerch); **WILDLIFE**, Hamburg (S. 31 salmon: J. Mallwitz); **Webb Aviation**, Bramhall (S. 60 unten li.: © www.webbaviation.co.uk)

Titelbild

Alamy, Abingdon (London Eye (M): Ian MacPherson); **Corbis**, Düsseldorf (bus (M): Royalty-Free); **IFA-Bilderteam**, Ottobrunn (Union Jack: Jon Arnold Images)

Textquellen

S. 34: *Billy doesn't like school really* by Paul Cookson taken from "The Works – Poems chosen by Paul Cookson". Macmillan Children's Books, London 2000. © Paul Cookson; S. 116–117: *Class Four-D's trip to the British Museum* adapted from "The Secret Diary of Adrian Mole Aged 13 3/4". © Sue Townsend. Permission granted by Curtis Brown Ltd.; S. 119: *The lost girl* adapted from "The Mermaid Bride and other Orkney Folk Tales" told by Tom Muir. The Orcadian Limited (Kirkwall Press), Orkney. © 1998 Tom Muir and Bryce Wilson; S. 120–121: *Tim goes abseiling* adapted from "Cliffhanger" by Jacqueline Wilson, published by Corgi Yearling. Reprinted by permission of the Random House Group Ltd.; S. 124–127: *Dawn*. Text copyright © 1994 by Tim Wynne-Jones from "The Book of Changes". First published in Canada by Groundwood Bookds Ltd. Adapted from the original and reprinted by permission of the publisher; S. 128: *Wilderness* by Joan Poulson from "The Works 2", chosen by Brian Moses and Pie Corbett. Macmillan Children's Books. Macmillan Publisher's Limited. London, 2002. © Joan Poulson, *Shell* by Myra Cohn Livingston from "The Works 2", chosen by Brian Moses and Pie Corbett. Macmillan Children's Books, Macmillan Publisher's Limited. London, 2002 (from "Worlds I know and other poems by Myra Cohn Livingston", McElderry Books/Arthenum. © 1986 Myra Cohn Livingston. Used by permission of Marian Reiner; S. 129: *Where?* by Dave Calder from The Ring of Words, edited by Roger McGough, Faber & Faber Limited. London, 1998. © Dave Calder, *Storm*: by Roger McGough from "The Works 3", chosen by Paul Cookson, Macmillan Children's Books, Macmillan Publishers Limited. London, 2004. © Roger McGough; S. 130–132: *Fans* from "Forty Short Plays" by Ann Cartwright. Reprinted by permission of Harcourt Education, Oxford; S. 135–136: Auszüge von S. 311 and S. 725 aus "English G 2000 Wörterbuch – Das Wörterbuch zum Lehrwerk". Herausgegeben von der Langenscheidt-Redaktion Wörterbücher und der Cornelsen-Redaktion Englisch. © 2002 Cornelsen Verlag GmbH & Co. OHG, Berlin und Langenscheidt KG, Berlin und München

Liedquellen

S. 82: *If everyone cared* M+T: Kroeger, Chad / Kroeger, Michael / Peake, Ryan / Adair, Daniel © 2005 by Warner-Tamerlane Publishing Corp., Arm your Dillo Publishing Inc., Black Diesel Music, Inc., ZeroG Music Inc. and Daniel Adair SVL: Neue Welt Musikverlag GmbH & Co. KG; S. 113: *You'll never walk alone* by Oscar Hammerstein. © Williamson Music Inc. D/A/CH/ osteuropäische Länder: EMI Music Publishing (Germany GmbH), Hamburg, *We are the champions* by Freddie Mercury. Words and Music by Freddie Mercury. © 1977 Queen Music Ltd Reproduced by permission of International Music Publications Ltd (a trading name of Faber Music Ltd) All rights reserved